Rudyard Kipling

EAST AND WEST:

A Biography of
Rudyard Kipling

Thomas N. Cross, M.D.

To the memory of my father

CONTENTS

ILLUSTRATIONS

ACKNOWLEDGMENTS

I am most grateful to Mr. Walter S. Rosenberry III and the Charles H. Weyerhaeuser Foundation for support during a sabbatical year.

I wish to extend my thanks to the following libraries and individuals: The University Library at the University of Michigan, Donald Riggs; the Clements Library at the University of Michigan, John H. Dann; the Michigan Historical Collections, Bentley Library, Francis Blouin; the Houghton Library, Harvard University, Richard Wendorf Bond; the Beinecke Rare Book and Manuscript Library, Yale University, Ralph W. Franklin and Herman W. Liebert; the Berg Collection of the New York Public Library, Timothy S. Healy and Francis Mattson; the Firestone Library, Princeton University, Donald Koepp; the Library of Congress, James H. Billington. I also want to extend my appreciation to the personnel at the Prince of Wales Hospital, Hamilton, Bermuda.

I have been greatly helped by letters from, and conversations with, the following members of the Kipling Society: Lisa A. F. Lewis, the late Roger Lancelyn Green, George H. Webb, Professor Enamul Karim, and the late Charles E. Carrington, whose *Life of Rudyard Kipling* is indispensable for any biographer. I also want to thank Francis H. Lewis of Beaver College; Mary K. Moorehead, of the class of 1894 at that college; Edmund Wilson; S. J. Perelman; Caroline Foster of Morristown, New

Jersey; Dr. William G. Niederland; Dr. George Pollock; Dr. Phyllis Greenacre; Mr. and Mrs. F. Cabot Holbrook of Brattleboro, Vermont; Mrs. Elia Long; Professors Donald L. Hill, Carlton Wells, Gerald S. Brown, all of the University of Michigan, Professor Thomas Pinney, of Pomona College, and Professor David H. Stewart, of the University of Texas A. & M. I particularly want to extend my thanks for conversations with Sir Angus Wilson, whose biography *The Strange Ride of Rudyard Kipling* has been so helpful.

I want to extend my gratitude to the following institutions for their permission to use their photographs: the portrait of Rudyard Kipling: (the National Portrait Gallery); the photographs of Kipling's parents, and of Kipling as a child: (the National Trust/Bateman's); the drawings by Kipling illustrating "Baa Baa, Black Sheep": (the Berg Collection); the photograph of Lorne Lodge: (Mr. R. Lancelyn Green); the picture of Wolcott Balestier: (the Houghton Library); the photograph of Kipling at Naulakha: (the Library of Congress); the picture of Kipling and Carrie: (the Associated Press). I have been unable to find the present owners of the painting "The Vampire," which evoked the line "A rag and a bone and a hank of hair," for permission to reproduce it.

The dust jacket drawing is by Victoria L. Kurnat.

I am greatly indebted to two new sources of information. Dr. and Mrs. William Beebe knew the Kiplings and have given me numerous accounts of them late in their lives. Mr. and Mrs. Stowe C. Phelps, Jr., allowed me to look at the papers of his mother, whose maiden name was Edith Catlin. She and her sister were friends of the Kiplings for decades.

I especially want to thank Gwendolyn Day, for her dedicated work on the word processor, and Christina Postema for her excellent copy editing.

Lastly, I want to pay tribute to generations of secretaries, too numerous to list, who have struggled to decipher my handwriting, and to a brother and sister who made many helpful suggestions. And most of all, I want to thank my wife, whose reading of the manuscript caught many of my more horrendous errors.

PREFACE

Since the dawn of civilization man has been fascinated by the creative individual, the person who, in a mysterious way, has the capacity to produce something new that moves others. Perhaps the earliest cave men admired and feared the one among them who could carve ivory or make a painting.

For ninety years or more psychoanalysts have attempted to shed some light on creativity, usually with little success. In recent decades the most important papers seem to me to be those of Kris, Eissler, Greenacre and especially Niederland,[1] whose work summarizes that of the others in what he has termed the Loss-Restoration Principle. His hypothesis is, first, that the artist or writer suffered confusing and puzzling losses in childhood, such as the death of a parent, and second, that one of these losses often was some disturbance in body image, the way in which the child saw his or her body—some deformity, some real or imagined defect. To compensate for these losses the child turns to an innate ability to create imagery. With this talent new things, new people, new visions can be created; creations enable the child to cope with confusion and depair, and may even outlive the creator and achieve immortality, defeating the forces of loss and death.

If Niederland's Loss-Restoration Principle is sound, we should find many incidents of confusing losses, sometimes involving physical disabilities, in the lives of creative individuals; and there have been findings to indicate that indeed these have occurred. Pollock[2] studied the lives of 1,200 successful writers and found that more than half of them had experienced parental death in childhood. Studies of writers show that the trauma suffered in childhood often appears as the central theme in their works. Edgar Allen Poe, for example, when a child witnessed his mother's demise under particularly harrowing circumstances. Poe was horrified—and fascinated—by death throughout his life; his writings revolve around the idea of loss, through death, of the loved one.

Rudyard Kipling's life also illustrates the Loss-Restoration Principle and provides us with a partial understanding of his creativity. The outstanding event in his childhood was a terrible disruption. His blissful early years in India suddenly came to an end when, at the age of five, he was taken by his parents to England and then deserted (to use his word), in the home of strangers, where he was repeatedly beaten. Later his eyesight began to fail. He stumbled a lot and walked into furniture. He was accused of "showing off" and punished for this as well. These wrenching experiences, however, were accompanied by early signs of an amazing creativity. Even as a child he showed remarkable abilities in writing. At school, then as a journalist, and finally as a writer he leaped to the very pinnacle of success.

I have attempted two things in this book; first of all, to write an accurate, objective biography of Rudyard Kipling. Also, at the same time I want to point out how his being brought up by a native nurse, then abandoned with a white family in England, and finally having problems with his vision, left him with two unconscious preoccupations: Is my mother Indian or white? And secondly, am I going blind? These two themes are apparent both in what he wrote and how he led his life. By using his remarkable gifts as a writer Kipling found answers to these questions stemming from the losses he suffered in childhood.

INTRODUCTORY
QUOTATIONS

"[Kipling] is a relic of Victorian times, and is antediluvian on the subject of women. . . . The more you consider the women in those stories, the more you see he knew nothing about them. . . . He must have had a nasty knock about the time he wrote 'The Light That Failed.' In all the stories written about that period he is shying away from women."

> Gilbert Frankau, "The Female of the Species," KJ No. 17, 1931, p. 5. Includes next quotation.

"At school Kipling was referred to as a great authority when the question of women was raised. One cannot judge from his work. His pen is one thing, his personality another. . . . He is not a man of action, though his pen writes action, and that is the difficulty to people who think they see Kipling in his books. . . . He does not reveal his personality at all in 'A woman is only a woman, but a good cigar is a smoke.'"

> G. C. Beresford.

"And actually, the whole work of Kipling's life [was] shot through with hatred."

> Edmund Wilson, *The Wound and the Bow*, Houghton Mifflin Co., Cambridge, 1941, p. 111.

"I frequently wonder if psycho-analysts are correct in their claim that early influences can poison or seriously overshadow later life. According to their gloomy theories my brother should have grown up morbid, misanthropic, narrow-minded, self-centered, shunning the world and bearing all men a burning grudge . . . . Whereas, of course, he was just the opposite."

> "Trix" Kipling Fleming, "My Brother, Rudyard Kipling," KJ No. 84, 1947, p. 3.

I.

"BOUGHT INTO INDIA"

In Bombay, at the very end of the year 1865, a child was born to English parents. Surely, in spite of all the soaring hopes and fantasies we have about our children, neither parent dreamed that this infant would become the most popular writer of his time, the first Englishman awarded the Nobel Prize, a man whose works would never fade, never be forgotten.

Later in life, Rudyard Kipling described himself as a Yorkshire-man, and his father's side of the family certainly came from there. His grandfather Joseph, born in 1805, was described as "ever of studious habits and a thoughtful disposition."[1] Early in his life he decided to enter the Methodist ministry and in 1831 left home for his first position. In the 1830s he married a Frances Lockwood. "Never was a couple more fitly mated. To the dreamy disposition of the student was joined that of shrewd common sense and practical ability." This was a combination that was to appear in their son's and grandson's marriages. Their oldest son, John Lockwood Kipling (Rudyard Kipling's father), was born in 1837; it was a family custom to alternate the names "Joseph" and "John" at the christening of the oldest son of each generation. Lockwood Kipling (as I will call him to avoid confusion) grew up in a strict household. He was sent to a "dreary Methodist school"[2] a month before his eighth

1

birthday. He himself said he was a "timorous child," and that going to school at such an age was upsetting, it was "much too early." As we shall see, leaving home and mother at an early age was a pivotal experience in the life of his son, Rudyard Kipling. In 1851, when he was thirteen, Lockwood Kipling was taken to London to see the Great Exhibition at Hyde Park. Even as a child he had shown remarkable abilities in a wide variety of artistic pursuits, and this trip to the Great Exhibition was a turning point in his life. Fired with enthusiasm, he resolved to become an artist and went about this with strong natural talents and an un-quenchable enthusiasm.

He was small, only five feet three inches in height. He had bushy eyebrows and a large, dark beard. A quiet, gentle, tolerant person, he never had a critical word for anyone. He had the broadest of interests and was skilled at drawing, painting, sculpture, and writing. Rudyard described his father as "a humorous, tolerant, and expert fellow craftsman."[3] When, at the height of his fame, Rudyard Kipling was asked the inevitable question: "Are you really *the* Mr. Kipling?" his reply reveals something of his relationship with Lockwood—and was also an expert putdown for the inquirer: "My father is not here. I am only his son."[4]

Reading letters that Lockwood Kipling wrote in those days, one gets the picture of a pleasant, delightful person. The letters bubble with vitality, occasionally have gentle jokes and puns, and are often illustrated with little sketches. Soon after his father's death in 1862—Lockwood was then twenty-five—he made friends with Frederic Macdonald, a young Methodist minister, and met his sister Alice, who was to be Rudyard Kipling's mother. She was the second oldest in a family of seven children. A rather small and slender person, she had a pale com-plexion, dark brown hair, and gray eyes with black lashes.

> In those eyes lay the chief fascination of her face, so expressive were they that they seemed to deepen or pale in color according to passing emotion. The Irish blood which is pretty certainly in our family seemed to take effect in Alice; she had the ready wit and power of repartee, the sentiment, and I may say the unexpectedness which one associates with that race. It was impossible to predict how she would act at any given point.[5]

Frederic Macdonald thought his sister Alice and Lockwood were a perfect match.

2

The perfect mental companionship of Mr. and Mrs. Kipling had for a foundation common ideals, with striking differences of temperament and qualities. My sister had the nimblest mind and the quickest wits I have ever known. She saw things in a moment, and did not so much reason as pounce upon her conclusions. . . . When she was at her ease and the subject was to her mind she was very brilliant, and her felicities of speech and illuminating epigrams were a delight to us all. She did not, as a rule, care for argument; intuition took its place, often to our amusement, sometimes to our satisfaction. Her wit was for the most part humorous and genial, but on occasion it was a weapon of whose keenness of point there could be no doubt, and foolish or mischievous people were made to feel it.

In the spring of 1863 Alice and Lockwood became engaged during a picnic at Rudyard Lake.

According to Alice it was after the meal that they walked in a field where they saw a dejected old horse. John looked at it pityingly and said: "Thrust out past service from the devil's stud." To which the reply came at once from Alice: "He must be wicked to deserve such pain." John turned to her at delight at her knowing the lines from Browning's "Men and Women" . . . "It was done in that moment," Alice recalled.[6]

In those days of the strictest control of behavior, she was thought of as a daring and unconventional person. One night she went out to a party and did not come back at the expected hour. She returned, very late, finding her father preparing to set out in search of her. She lightly said that a young man she had met at the party had offered to take her home, and the night was so fine that they had taken a long, roundabout walk through London on their way back. He reproved her for this sternly, which sent her off to bed in tears.

Another example of her startling behavior occurred when she was helping to pack in one of their frequent moves from one place to another. She came across an envelope on which was written in fading letters, "A lock of Mr. Wesley's hair" (John Wesley, founder of the Methodist church). Opening the envelope, she took the precious relic out, and to everyone's horror she said, "See! A hair of the dog that bit us!," and threw it on the fire.

Two family stories illustrate her quick wit. Years later Rudyard Kipling described his returning after a long absence to his parents' home in India. The family's small terrier promptly remembered him and jumped and wriggled and nuzzled him all evening. "None of us thought that she would remember and I own that I had quite forgotten [her]; but she belied us all—dear little beast. In a moment of expansiveness I said egotistically: "I shall think better of myself hence-forward." "Hear him!, said the Mother. "Anyone but a man would have said he would think better of the dog."[7]

On another occasion the Kiplings were in the midst of moving to the hills at the beginning of the hot season, and things were all about in different piles ready to be packed. A guest in the house looked about the pleasant bungalow and said, "I say, Mrs. Kipling, your house is simply A-1." Immediately Alice Kipling replied, with a wave of her hand, replied, "Ah, but you should have seen it B-4."[8]

Kipling's parents came from very different sorts of families. On the Kipling side the relatives were few in number, and they tended to go their various ways and not keep in touch with each other. Of one aunt and uncle of his there are now no records whatsoever. During most of Rudyard Kipling's life, the only one he knew was his Aunt Hannah, and he saw little enough of her. And besides their lack of family cohesiveness the Kiplings were not brilliant. They produced no outstanding accomplishments.

The Macdonalds were just the opposite. Kipling had six aunts and uncles and many cousins. Of his four aunts, three of them married husbands or had sons who achieved international fame. His Aunt Georgiana married a famous painter, as did his Aunt Agnes. His Aunt Louisa married the wealthy Alfred Baldwin, and their son, Stanley, was Prime Minister twice in the 1920s and 1930s. With such an absence of Kipling relatives, and such outstanding individuals on every hand from the Macdonalds, Kipling's background must have seemed a little odd and one-sided to him.

Lockwood Kipling had a position as one of three new art teachers at a school in Bombay.* Soon after their marriage in March of 1865 he and Alice set sail, arriving at the beginning of the hot season. India seemed incredibly distant: it took weeks to get there, and even weeks for

---

*In what appears to be an unconscious act of admiration many biographers have stated that he went to India as principal of the school, not merely as one of three teachers hired.

John Lockwood Kipling, Alice Kipling, Rudyard Kipling—Ruddy at the age of five.

a telegram to reach someone there. The Macdonald parents regarded their daughter's departure with the penniless art teacher with some misgivings.

The huge, sprawling subcontinent, walled off from the rest of the world by the Himalayas, at that time had 200 million inhabitants (about a fifth of the present population). The gigantic country lay as if recuperating from the Mutiny, which had taken place only eight years before. With peace returned, the old status quo was resumed; the British, finding themselves in a country with an elaborate caste system, logically established themselves as a super-caste on top of the whole heap. The Mutiny had been put down, the control of the East India Company had been abolished, the rule of India had been transferred to the Crown, and all was well with the world.

Bombay was situated in an area rich in resources. With an excellent harbor and a large textile industry, it was rapidly becoming the main seaport for all of western India. The Kiplings moved into the large, prosperous city, the most European in all India, and set to work establishing themselves.

Lockwood Kipling's job was not to bring English art to India, but rather to encourage the revival of all aspects of native Indian art. His interest, versatility, and powers of keen observation all combined to make him a success. Alice Kipling, as usual, made her mark with her nimble mind and charming personality.

Any newcomer to Bombay soon learned the central importance of the seasons. India, like China, was always at the mercy of the weather. Two years after the Kiplings' arrival, crop failures due to drought and scorching heat caused one-quarter of the population of Orissa province to starve to death. Bombay, at sea-level, had two seasons; the "cool season" from November to April, and the "hot season" from May to October. The cool season was tolerable enough, but the hot, with its breathless nights and seemingly endless spells of temperatures in the nineties and hundreds, was a nightmare. As the Kiplings were to find out, whether a woman gave birth in July or in January could literally be a matter of life or death. These seasons were fixed periods around which every Indian and Englishman had to adjust his life. For the English, cool "hill stations" were established, where one went, if at all possible, at the worst of the hot season.

Alice Kipling had become pregnant soon after her marriage, but before their departure for India. At the end of 1865, on December 30th, Ruddy, to use his childhood nickname, a wanted child, was born. Alice Kipling had a long and dangerous labor; it was only relieved, the servants said, by one of them ransoming the infant's life by sacrificing a kid to Kali, the Hindu goddess of death and evil. In later life, this ancient ritual had a deep meaning for Kipling. It centered on the idea, of course, that a new life coming into the world had to be balanced by one leaving it. Of more significance were the powerful feelings we all have about blood. The spell would not work if the animal was merely hit on the head or poisoned; it had to be slaughtered. He used the ritual in two of his better pieces, "Without Benefit of Clergy," and "Mowgli's Brothers." Knowing that his birth had been accompanied by this primitive rite made him feel that by this sacrifice he had been "bought into India," that India was home, India was in his blood.

In keeping with the family custom of alternating "John" and "Joseph" in successive generations, he was given his grandfather's name Joseph, and the middle name Rudyard after the lake in Staffordshire where his parents had become engaged.

The Kiplings had several servants, as was the custom, and particularly important to the infant was his *ayah*, or nurse, and Meeta, a Hindu boy who was his "bearer" and general companion. The earliest record we have of young Ruddy was when he was six months old. His mother wrote, "He notices everything he sees, and when he is not sitting up in his *ayah's* arms he turns round to follow things with his eyes very comically."[9] In keeping with the times, he seldom saw his mother and father, who were not important people to him. He was constantly catered to by his *ayah* and Meeta. Like some prince in a magical kingdom, his every wish was indulged. If he wanted to go somewhere to eat something or have a story told to him or acted out in front of him, it was done. It was an idyllic world with, however, an awareness of frightening things outside that world—death and mutilation. The Kiplings' house was near the Towers of Silence, where the Parsees exposed their dead to be devoured by vultures. "I did not understand my Mother's distress when she found 'a child's hand' in our garden, and said I was not to ask questions about it. I wanted to see that child's hand. But my *ayah* told me."[10] Here the child's frightened and fascinated questions about life

7

and death are rebuffed by his mother, but he gets the answer from the person most important to him: "my *ayah* told me."

In his autobiography he describes how

> Meeta unconsciously saved me from any night terrors or dread of the dark. Our *ayah*, with a servant's curious mixture of deep affection and shallow device, had told me that a stuffed leopard's head on the nursery wall was there to see that I went to sleep. But Meeta spoke of it scornfully as "the head of an animal," and so I took it off my mind as a fetish, good or bad, for it was only some unspecified "animal."

Being the adored favorite of these two servants gave Ruddy a sense of strength and even grandiosity. "If a man has been his mother's undisputed darling, he retains throughout life the triumphant feeling, the confidence in success, which not seldom brings actual success along with it."[11] As an adult, Kipling, although modest and quiet, was secure, self-confident and energetic, like so many of the heroes in his books—Kim, Mowgli, and George Cottar.

Alice Kipling was much affected by the terrible heat of Bombay. After Ruddy's difficult delivery, it was thought wisest to have her go to England for the birth of her second child, who was expected in June of 1868. She left for England in February, taking Ruddy with her but having to leave her husband behind. At the time of the trip Ruddy was only two years and two months old. Adults do not ordinarily remember events before the age of three. Ruddy, however, recalled every detail of the train ride to Alexandria (the Suez Canal opened the next year). He describes the memory: "There was a train across the desert and a halt in it, and a small girl wrapped in a shawl on the seat opposite me whose face stands out still."[12] Arriving in England, Mrs. Kipling stayed with her sister, Ruddy's Aunt Georgiana, who had married Sir Edward Burne Jones, the painter. Ruddy was taken to the town of Bewdley to be looked after by his mother's parents. For a two-year-old, his powers of observation and speech were amazing. He roamed about the house, quickly sorting out the location and relative importance of the various rooms, and then protested that his grandparents had " gone and tooken the best rooms for themselves!"[13] Spoiled by his loving *ayah* back in India, he was uninhibited and aggressive; his behavior was not at all that expected of an English child at the time. He became a real trial to his grandparents.

One day he stamped along the Bewdley street, shouting, "Out of the way, out of the way, there's an angry Ruddy coming!" Later, soon after Alice and the children returned to India, her father died, and her relatives were quick to blame this on Ruddy's misbehavior. Kipling himself remembers the visit as being in a "dark land, and a darker room full of cold, in one wall of which a white woman made naked fire, and I cried aloud with dread, for I had never before seen a grate."[14]

Notice that the thing that frightens him is the fire lit by a *white* woman: in England, the servant would obviously be nothing else but white. This seems an expression of his yearning to be back with his familiar native *ayah* who, although of Portuguese descent, was very dark, almost black, in contrast to this white woman in this frightening land.

In June Mrs. Kipling was delivered of a daughter, after an even longer labor and more complications than she had experienced with Ruddy's birth. The child was named Alice after her mother, but was always known as "Trix."

Ruddy was then two and one-half years old. There is no direct record of his feelings about his younger sister's birth. Since he remembers the trip with such distaste and fear, however, it may be that he did not welcome the arrival of the infant that caused the trip in the first place. The "small girl wrapped in a shawl on the seat opposite me whose face stands out still" may well represent the newborn sister. And one can wonder if Ruddy knew that the birth presented a medical problem, and a serious one. It seems likely that an extraordinarily observant child, like Ruddy, sensed something of what was going on.

They went back to India in the fall, just in time for the cool season, and the reunited family resumed life in the bungalow at the School of Art. Kipling tells of his earliest memory:

> My first impression is of daybreak, light and colour and golden and purple fruits at the level of my shoulder. This would be the memory of the early morning walks to the Bombay fruit market with my *ayah* and later with my sister in her perambulator, and of our returns with our purchases piled high in the bows. of it. Our *ayah* was a Portuguese Roman Catholic who would pray—I beside her—at a wayside Cross. Meeta, my Hindu bearer, would sometimes go into little Hindu temples where, being below the age of caste, I held his hand and looked at the dimly-seen, friendly Gods.
> Our evening walks were by the sea in the shadow of palm-groves

which, I think, were called the Mahim woods. When the wind blew the great nuts would tumble, and we fled—my *ayah*, and my sister in her perambulater—to the safety of the open. I have always felt the menacing darkness of tropical eventides . . .

He resumed his Eden-like existence with his loving *ayah* and Meeta, now shared with his sister. They told the children stories and sang them Indian nursery songs that Kipling could remember when he was seventy. Both children spoke Hindustani as their primary tongue, and in the evening, after being dressed up, they were taken to their parents "with the caution 'Speak English now to Papa and Mama.' So one spoke 'English' haltingly translated out of the vernacular idiom that one thought and dreamed in."

These years were marred by the death of Alice Kipling's second son in the hot season of 1870. The infant only lived long enough to be christened John, and was then buried in a Bombay cemetery. We may assume that this had a significant impact on Ruddy, then four and one-half. In later years, upon his return to India, he wrote a poem about it. But in general, he looked back on those early Indian years as a period of absolute bliss. He roamed the house and grounds, content and happy, curious about everything he saw. A friend of the family, Pestonjee Bomonjee, remembered that at the age of five little Ruddy never forgot a name or a face. Little wonder that in Kipling's autobiography he begins the first chapter with a saying of the Jesuits, "Give me the first six years of a child's life and you can have the rest."

He saw little of his parents, but his *ayah* and Meeta more than filled their places. He only remembered his mother singing " wonderful songs at a black piano." But the memory is significant. She used to sing the hymn "Son of my Soul, Thou Saviour Dear." He thought she was saying, "Sonny my Soul. . . ."[15]

There was nothing unusual in the Kipling parents having almost no part in their children's upbringing. In those days the beloved English nanny who took care of the children from birth onward was quite the common thing. The important difference here is that the *ayah* and Meeta were of a different racial and cultural background, and spoke a different language, *his* language, Hindustani.

His mother remembered an incident when he was walking away from her with his hand in that of a Hindu, and called back to her in

Hindustani, "Goodbye, this is my brother."[16] With this background, one can see how Ruddy felt that he had two mothers, one Indian and one white.

These blissful years stopped abruptly when his parents again took him to England—and left him there. It was then customary for all Anglo-Indian* parents to take their children back to England when they were about six or seven, since it was believed children could not stand the hot seasons, and to leave them in England for their education. Like everything else, Ruddy found out about this not from his parents, but from his *ayah* and Meeta. In his account of it, (fictional, but surely drawn from his memories), his *ayah* says he "'is going away. In another week there will be no Punch-*baba* to pull my hair anymore.' She sighed softly, for the boy of the household was very dear to her heart."[17] Punch (Ruddy) asks if they will be going, as usual, "up the Ghauts to Nassick" (the cool hill station), but Meeta replies that they will not. "Down to the sea where the cocoanuts are thrown, and across the sea in a big ship." Note that Meeta says he will leave from the Mahim woods, which Kipling had described before as the frightening place where "the great nuts would tumble" and his *ayah* would rush him and his sister to safety.

In an account written many years later, Kipling described parents—thinking of his own—sadly making preparations for the separation from their children.

> "We are only one case among hundreds," said Papa bitterly. . . . They were standing over the cots in the nursery late at night, and I think Mama was crying softly. After Papa had gone away she knelt down by the side of Judy's cot. The *ayah* saw her and put up a prayer that the *memsahib* might never find the love of her children taken away from her and given to a stranger.

---

*"Anglo-Indian" meant any English man, woman, or child residing in India.

II

THE HOUSE OF
DESOLATION

Leaving Bombay in April 1871, the Kiplings in due time arrived in England and stayed with various relatives throughout the summer and fall. In all these months, when Trix became three and Ruddy five and one-half, neither the Kiplings nor any of their relatives told either of the children what was going to happen to them. It was a secret, never discussed, that they were not going to return to India with their parents, but would be staying behind in England. Worse than that, they would not be staying with any of the various relatives they had seen, but with complete strangers!

Generations of biographers have asked how the parents could do such a thing, when Mrs. Kipling had, in England, four sisters and a brother. Three of the sisters were married and had children about the age of Ruddy and Trix. As a family they were close-knit and caring about one another. Ruddy's Aunt "Aggie" Poynter, his Aunt "Louie" Baldwin, above all his Aunt "Georgie" Burne Jones whom Kipling repeatedly described as "the beloved aunt" — why weren't the children left with one of them? Perhaps the aunts remembered what problems Ruddy had caused when the Kiplings had been in England three years before. A friend of Alice Kipling's said she never thought of leaving the children with her own family, since it led to difficulties and complica-

Lorne Lodge ("The House of Desolation") as Kipling drew it in 1888, and as it appears in a recent photograph.

tions. Pride may have entered the picture. The Kiplings were not well off. Perhaps they preferred to pay for the children's staying somewhere, rather than feeling obligated to relatives who were better off financially.

In December the Kiplings went to Southsea, where they sought out a Mr. and Mrs. Holloway who lived there with their son Harry, aged about eleven. Mr. Holloway was a retired Merchant Marine officer; they took in children whose parents were overseas or away for a period of time. The Kiplings had obtained no references or information, and merely picked the Holloways' name from a newspaper advertisement. Neither child was to see the parents for more than five years. Moreover, the children were given no preparation for, or explanation of, this shattering event; and, to top it all, the Kiplings didn't even say good-bye. When their children's attention was distracted, they simply disappeared. Years later, Alice Kipling said she had been advised to do this to spare the children the pain of saying good-bye. Whatever her reason, the parents' vanishing only added to an experience that obviously scarred both son and daughter for life.

These were terrible things, but worse ones followed. The Kiplings had chanced upon an unfortunate family in Lorne Lodge, as this place was called—Kipling in later life referred to it as the House of Desolation. Mr. Holloway was a kind old man, but he was ailing and died three years later. His wife, a character straight out of Dickens, was a punitive, narrow-minded woman of extreme religiosity. The Kipling children may have been told to call them "Uncle Harry" and "Auntie Rosa," courtesy titles customary at the time.

Back in India, the children had stayed with a "sitter" when their parents were away for a few days, and they imagined that, similarly, they would return soon. But that first morning "The black haired boy met them with the information that Papa and Mama had gone to Bombay, and they [the two children] were to stay at Lorne Lodge 'forever.' Auntie Rosa, tearfully appealed to for a contradiction, said that Harry had spoken the truth. . . ."[1]

Trix, in her later years, described their feelings:

> We had had no preparation or explanation; it was like a double death or rather, like an avalanche that had swept away everything happy and familiar. . . . We felt that we had been deserted, almost as much as on a doorstep, and what was the reason? Of course, Auntie used to say it was

because we were so tiresome, and she had taken us in out of pity, but in a desperate moment Ruddy appealed to Uncle Harry and he said it was only Auntie's fun, and Papa had left us to be taken care of, because India was too hot for little people. But we knew better than that, because we had been to Nassick, so what was the real reason? . . . . They had gone happily back to our own lovely home, and had not taken us with them. There was no getting out of that, as we often said.

Harry, who had all a crow's quickness in finding a wound to pick at, discovered our trouble and teased us unmercifully . . . he assured us we had been taken in out of charity and must do exactly as he told us. . . . We were just like workhouse brats, that none of our toys really belonged to us.[2]

Kipling described the feelings of an abandoned child:

When a mature man discovers that he has been deserted by Providence, deprived of his God, and cast, without help, comfort, or sympathy, upon a world which is new and strange to him, his despair, which may find expression in evil-living, the writing of his experiences, or the more satisfactory diversion of suicide, is generally supposed to be impressive. A child, under exactly similar conditions as far as its knowledge goes, cannot very well curse God and die. It howls until its nose is red, its eyes are sore, and its head aches.[3]

We can now understand that the children were subjected to conditions that could end in soul murder, as Shengold so clearly states.[4] This is the confrontation of a helpless individual by an all-powerful figure who deprives him of any individuality, any rights, any love from others; and if he objects, twists it around so that the objection is seen as a fault, a flaw in the captive, who is then made to feel guilty. In this century the technique is seen in the "brainwashing" employed in military and political arenas. The individual is isolated, helpless, and allowed no contact with those who love him. He is tripped up in conflicting statements, even ridiculous ones, that further his helplessness and need to surrender, to identify with the aggressor—the "doublethink" of Orwell's *1984*. If all this is done with religious or moral motivation—that is, the victim is told it is really being done for his own good—it becomes that much more powerful a weapon. And if brainwashing is sometimes difficult with an adult, it is of course much easier with a child. All these elements of brainwashing were now inflicted on Ruddy, for Mrs. Holloway and Harry began to catch him at "lies" and then beat him. Kipling describes this in his autobiography:

Kipling's drawings, from the manuscript of "Baa Baa, Black Sheep," of "Auntirosa," "Uncleharri," and their son, "a boy of twelve, black-haired and oily in appearance." "Uncleharri" is drawn as small and subdued beside his formidable wife.

If you cross-examine a child of seven or eight on his day's doings (specially when he wants to go to sleep) he will contradict himself very satisfactorily. If each contradiction be set down as a lie and retold at breakfast, life is not easy. I have known a certain amount of bullying, but this was calculated torture—religious as well as scientific. Yet it made me give attention to the lies I soon found it necessary to tell: and this, I presume, is the foundation of literary effort. [He describes another occasion when he was "put through the third degree," always followed by] punishments and humiliation—above all humiliation. That alternation was quite regular. I can but admire the infernal laborious ingenuity of it all. *Exempli gratia.* Coming out of the church once I smiled. The Devil-Boy demanded why. I said I didn't know, which was child's truth. He replied that I *must* know. People didn't laugh for nothing. Heaven knows what explanation I put forward; but it was duly reported to the woman as a "lie." Result, afternoon upstairs with the Collect to learn. I learned most of the Collects that way and a great deal of the Bible. The son after three or four years went into a Bank and was generally too tired on his return to torture me, unless things had gone wrong with him. I learned to know what was coming from his step into the house.[5]

All of this punishment was done in the name of God, utilizing one of the most powerful tools of the brainwashing technique.

It was an establishment run with the full vigour of the Evangelical as revealed to the Woman. I had never heard of Hell, so I was introduced to it in all its terrors. . . . Myself I was regularly beaten. The Woman had an only son of twelve or thirteen as religious as she. I was a real joy for him, for when his mother had finished with me for the day he (we slept in the same room) took me on and roasted the other side.

In "Baa Baa, Black Sheep," he described how Punch (his choice of the names "Punch" and "Judy" for himself and his sister of course reflects the violence and beatings of the puppet shows) is confronted with:

. . . an abstraction called God, the intimate friend and ally of Auntie Rosa . . . . Afterwards he learned to know the Lord as the only thing in the world more awful than Auntie Rosa—as a Creature that stood in the background and counted the strokes of the cane.[6]*

---

*Several biographers have pointed out that Mrs. Holloway probably wasn't the evil monster that Kipling and Trix made her out to be. They have discovered, for example, that an aunt, or an uncle, or both, visited Lorne Lodge at least once a year, and all were apparently satisfied with Mrs. Holloway, feeling she was a pleasant and capable person. The biographers' conclusion that she was not the horror Kipling described is probably correct, but it is also irrelevant. Let us suppose that she was much kinder and less punitive than he allows. It makes no difference; what counts is how he experienced her and all those years in her house. What he had been through gnawed at him, partly

These attacks failed in one respect; they did not completely isolate him. Uncle Harry supported Ruddy and remonstrated with his wife over the beatings, but apparently he could not stand up to the Woman, as Kipling always referred to Mrs. Holloway in his autobiography. Then, too, he was old and ailing, and died in 1874 when Ruddy was almost nine. But he still had an ally, his sister, Trix. Mrs. Holloway attempted to separate them emotionally, treating Trix as a favorite and never beating her, and telling her that she (Trix) was always right and Ruddy was always wrong. Fortunately, she failed. Besides his ties to Trix, Ruddy had another bond to loved ones—relatives—that he believed saved him.

> But, for a month each year I possessed a paradise which I verily believe saved me. Each December I stayed with my Aunt Georgie, my mother's sister, wife of Sir Edward Burne Jones, at "The Grange," North End Road. At first I must have been escorted there, but later I went alone, and arriving at the house would reach up to the open-work iron bell-pull on the wonderful gate that let me into all felicity. When I had a house of my own, and The Grange was emptied of meaning, I begged for and was given that bell-pull for my entrance, in the hope that other children might also feel happy when they rang it.
>
> At The Grange I had love and affection as much as the greediest, and I was not very greedy, could desire. There were most wonderful smells of paints and turpentine whiffing down from the big studio on the first floor where my Uncle worked; there was the society of my two cousins, and a sloping mulberry tree which we used to climb for our plots and conferences . . . . There was an incessant come and go of young people and grown-ups all willing to play with us—except an elderly person called "Browning," who took no proper interest in the skirmishes. . . . Best of all, immeasurably, was the beloved Aunt herself reading us *The Pirate* or *The Arabian Nights* of evenings, when one lay out on the big sofas sucking toffee, and calling our cousins "Ho, Son," or "Daughter of my Uncle" or "O True Believer."
>
> . . . It was a jumble of delights and emotions culminating in being allowed to blow the big organ in the studio for the beloved Aunt. . . . Then it was hard to keep the little lead weight on its string below the chalk mark, and if the organ ran out in squeals the beloved Aunt would be sorry. Never, *never* angry!

because of other problems, like the contrast between his Indian life and his English life, between his *ayah* and Mrs. Holloway; the problems of his parents disappearing without explanation, and his near-blindness. He felt he had been deserted, imprisoned, and abused. The fact that an impartial observer wouldn't think these experiences so terrible is immaterial. He found them terrible.

Again, "Uncleharri" seems bent and castrated (without a penis) beside "Auntirosa."

. . . But on a certain day—one tried to fend off the thought of it—the delicious dream would end, and one would return to the House of Desolation, and for the next two or three mornings there cry on waking up. Hence more punishments and cross-examinations.

Often and often afterwards, the beloved Aunt would ask me why I had never told anyone how I was being treated. Children tell little more than animals, for what comes to them they accept as eternally established. Also, badly-treated children have a clear notion of what they are likely to get if they betray the secrets of a prison-house before they are clear of it.[7]

It is easy to see a relationship between the sufferings that Ruddy underwent and certain aspects of his personality years later as an adult—his fear of women and worship of men, the feeling that he had two mothers, one Indian and one white, and his preoccupation with pain and violence, to mention only three. While these are worth pointing out, I think it is even more interesting to consider not what psychopathology can be found, but how he overcame these things that happened to him, what sort of strengths did it take to survive such abuse? Is there anything here that casts light on his enormous powers of creativity? For it is for these that he is remembered, not because, for instance, he wrote a lot about violence.

First of all, he had those first five years and four months of blissful existence in India. Remembering that past—which Trix could not—gave him hope for the future. He constantly told Trix about the years past in India, often using Hindustani words and phrases to throw off the eavesdropping Mrs. Holloway and her son. He fought courageously to keep Trix close to him, and resisted the efforts to split them apart and thus isolate him completely. Another important weapon was his quick mind, curious about everything. In India he had been so wrapped up in the native world of his *ayah* and Meeta that he could neither read nor write when he began living at the Holloways' (it is striking that his parents seemingly ignored these deficiencies). But when he learned to read he found that books offered a world of freedom. Books were, he said,

a means to everything that would make me happy. So I read all that came within my reach. As soon as my pleasure in this was known, deprivation from reading was added to my punishments. I then read by stealth and the more earnestly.

20

Drawings showing Black Sheep, "Auntirosa," Harry and Judy. At the
top right, "If you're old enough to do that" she said—her temper was
always worse after dinner—"you're old enough to be beaten."

Black Sheep's response to the card being stitched to his back.

I bring this up now because when he learned to read, he also began to write. He was only ten when he wrote this poem, one of his earliest known, about the sinking of a ship called *The Carolina*.*

> Aurora rose in a cloudless sky
> And looked on all so beamingly
> Portsmouth's dark walls stood out so bright
> Amid the flood of beaming light
> A vessel from the harbour came
> The Carolina was her name
> With stun'-sails set and royals too
> Over the billows she lightly flew
> Three hundred souls bonds for London town
> Each one doomed alas! to drown
> For o'er the deck deaths dark shape hung
> Loud and wierd were the songs he sung.
> The sun had set there came clouds and rain
> The Ship was never seen again
> She had sunk on a rock then gone down
> With three hundred souls bound for London town
> She had sunk like lead with no canvas rent
> And never a spar or catline bent
> The waves sighed mid the masts of the wreck
> And fishes darted athwart the deck
> Down down she lies full fifty fathoms down
> Does the Carolina bound for London town.[8]

What an extraordinary poem for a ten-year-old to write! It is human nature to feel a sense of satisfaction, of accomplishment, after producing something new, something that satisfies an awareness of value. There is a realization "*I* did that," an important step in seeing one's worth, one's own uniqueness. Ruddy's remarkable creativity gave him a world into which he could escape from the House of Desolation.

Being able to write meant he could send letters to his parents in India, but this was no help, for his letters were often censored or even dictated by Mrs. Holloway.

But his reading and writing, so vital in preserving some positive feelings about himself, were now taken from him. He began to suffer from severe myopia. Things began to look indistinct ten feet away, then five feet away, and finally right in front of him. In one of his accounts

---

*The spelling and punctuation are reproduced as they appear in the original poem.

of this, he describes how flapping curtains looked like ghosts and coats on pegs became monsters. We may assume that he complained about his symptoms; if so, his complaints were ignored.

> My eyes went wrong, and I could not well see to read. For which reason I read the more and in bad lights. My work at the terrible little day school where I had been sent suffered in consequence, and my monthly reports showed it. The loss of "reading time" was the worst of my "home" punishments for bad school-work.[9]

His problem amounted to near-blindness, and left his eyes permanently damaged. His visual problem steadily became worse until his release from the House of Desolation, when he was given eyeglasses. Before he left he received the most extreme and humiliating punishment that Mrs. Holloway ever inflicted on him.

> One report was so bad that I threw it away and said that I had never received it. But this is a hard world for the amateur liar. My web of deceit was swiftly exposed—the son spared time after banking hours to help in the auto-da-fe—and I was well beaten and sent to school through the streets of Southsea with the placard "Liar" between my shoulders.[10]

What he describes as "some sort of nervous breakdown" followed, in which he "imagined I saw shadows and things that were not there, and they worried me more than the Woman." When a doctor sent down by his Aunt Georgiana reported that he was half-blind, "This, too, was supposed to be 'showing-off' [he quotes Mrs. Holloway] and I was segregated from my sister, another punishment, as a sort of moral leper."

A few months before his death, more than sixty years later, Trix told him of being near Southsea once and deciding to go and see if the House of Desolation was still there. A feeling of revulsion swept over her and she turned back: "I dared not face it."[11] Kipling said he had the same experienced the same horror. "I think," she continues, "we both dreaded a kind of spiritual imprisonment that would affect our dreams. . . . I asked him whether he knew if the house still stood. 'I don't know, but if so, I should like to burn it down and plough the place with salt.'"

What effect did his eye trouble and the beatings and humiliation he suffered have on him?

Children who become ill, or are afflicted with some physical handicap, experience anxiety. The anxiety is greater when the illness is internal and mysterious—like diabetes or impaired vision—and less when it is external and understandable—as in the case of a cut from a piece of glass or the loss of a fingernail in a slammed door. The feeling of intactness, of having a whole and healthy body, is an important part of a child's development. Failure to achieve this sense of well-being leaves the child thinking he is somehow to blame for the problem; he feels "sick" and "bad" whereas other children are "well" and "good." This was particularly emphasized in Ruddy's case by his being punished for his near-blindness—he was accused of "showing-off" and separated from his sister as a "moral leper." (Note that in this description of himself he connects sin with a physical illness. The two always went together in his mind.) The blindness wasn't just something an unkind fate visited on him, it was another of Mrs. Holloway's punishments, and a further humiliation at the hands of a woman. It left him with a strong feeling, "There's something wrong with my body," with all the attendant confusion and self-doubt.

Being beaten is an upsetting experience for a child who, as he grows up, should experience enough security, encouragement, and support to emerge into maturity with self-confidence and assertiveness. Beatings have just the opposite effect; an adult, bigger and stronger than the child, overwhelms him and inflicts pain on him. He feels he is being told, "You are worthless. I do not care about you, the only thing that's important is that you submit and do as I say." The child feels helpless, humiliated, and angry. If beatings are frequent, they can interfere with the child's development. He may be unable to feel healthy self-esteem and to act assertively, and may have urges to abuse others as he was abused. Being beaten was particularly hard for Ruddy because of all that was associated with the punishment—his moving from India to England and then being abandoned without explanation at the Holloways'.

In evaluating a situation of this sort it is important to find out how much anger the child is able to express. If the humiliation and control were extreme, the child may give in, embrace the ideas of the torturer, and submit to "soul murder."[12] Here the oppressor is seen as wholly right, the victim wrong. He can never feel good about himself or his body, and can never love another human being. Down this path may lie homosexuality and sado-masochism. Ruddy, however, felt plenty of anger. This is amply documented in all accounts of his years there; in his illustration for "Baa Baa, Black Sheep," for example, he says, using the words from the story, "If you make me do that . . . I shall burn this house down and perhaps I'll kill you. I don't know whether I can kill you—you're so bony—but I'll *try*."[13] It is exceedingly fortunate, and a tribute to his courage when a child, that he was able to feel hatred for Mrs. Holloway, could fight her off, and not be totally driven to submission. Probably it was Trix's presence, an "Asian" ally so to speak, with whom he could share memories of India, that saved him and his masculinity, as Shengold described so well in his paper on Kipling's childhood. But, as can be seen in much of what he wrote and in his behavior throughout life, it left him with a deep backlog of smoldering anger, quick to flare up at any provocation. This was his heritage from a confusing childhood, vain attempts to answer such questions as "What is going on?" "How could my parents do this to me?" and "What is the matter with my body?"

His near-blindness brought his mother from India. In his autobiography, he states, "I do not remember that I had any warning."[14] "Warning" seems an odd word. He could have said that he had no notice, he wasn't told, he didn't know she was coming, but why *warning*? This implies notice of a danger, of something evil. I think it represents his confusion—what kind of a mother have I? On the first night that they were together, when she went up to kiss him goodnight Kipling says, "I flung up an arm to guard off the cuff that I had been trained to expect." Alice Kipling took both children out of the House of Desolation, where they had been for more than five years. They both experienced it as a rescue, a release from some prison. Most of the manuscript of "Baa Baa, Black Sheep" is written in Kipling's usual tiny, neat handwriting, but on the last page, when the mother comes and takes the two children out, the words and letters become large, flowing, and exuberant. One does not have to be a graphologist to see the enormous relief expressed here.

She took them to a small farmhouse near Epping Forest. There they both "ran wild" for months, and, as Kipling puts it, "I was not encouraged to refer to my guilty past." (Note the word "guilty"—what had happened was a punishment, not just a terrible time of unhappiness.) He remembers he felt "completely happy . . . except for my spectacles." These were exceedingly unusual on a child in those days, and caused constant comment, always a reminder of Mrs. Holloway. It was a wild and wonderful time; his mother only "drew the line at my returning to meals red-booted from assisting at the slaughter of swine," another indication of his underlying anger at what he had gone through.

After spending spring, summer, and fall at Epping Forest, Ruddy went off to a boarding school. Mrs. Kipling, with a shocking lack of judgment, returned Trix to the care of Mrs. Holloway. Ruddy had the soul-saving experience of his first five years in India to get him through the next five; it is not surprising that Trix, a critical two and a half years younger, in later life suffered from chronic, severe mental illness.

Kipling later made two statements about the effects of those five terrible years on his capacity to feel hatred and love. Both confirmed that his childhood experiences at Lorne Lodge affected him throughout his life. In his autobiography, he wrote of his torment and humiliation, "In the long run these things, and many more of the like, drained me of any capacity for real, personal hate for the rest of my days." "I hated her so much," he is saying, "I could never hate anyone else ever after."

If we accept this statement—a difficult thing to do—it still leaves room for hatred of such things as groups, concepts, and political parties; it is only "personal hate" that is disclaimed. But, as can be shown, Kipling was perfectly capable of personal hatred. He denied it, he attempted to conceal it, and above all he kept it hidden from the glare of publicity, but it was there.

He continues: "So close must any life-filling passion lie to its opposite. Who having known the Diamond will concern himself with glass?" Here he says, as I understand it, "My being drained of hatred left me all the more able to love. Who, having experienced love, would ever want to hate?"

This idea is easier to accept. A person who has been tormented may well resolve never to inflict similar cruelties on anyone else, and may emerge an unusually loving person as a result. Kipling, all his life, was the soul of kindness to children. Over and over again the story is told of worshipping adults who gathered at his home to see the great Rudyard Kipling. They waited and waited; no Rudyard Kipling. Eventually their host was found upstairs, or out in the garden, or gathering mushrooms, happily playing with the children. It was not that he was ill at ease with adults and preferred the company of children. Indeed, he was a delightful person, full of ideas and enthusiasm, and able to make friends easily. His confusing childhood did not deprive him of his ability to love, as happened with his sister. He was able to laugh—to roar with laughter—but one always gets the feeling that suspicion and hostility lay close behind.

As for Mrs. Kipling's inexplicable decision to return Trix to Mrs. Holloway's, Trix recalled, in later years, that Mrs. Holloway urged her to beg her mother to "leave [her] with dear Auntie for always."[15] "Then you shall live with me as my own little girl," she quotes Mrs. Holloway further, "and if you are very good and obedient, perhaps when you *grow up* you will be dear Harry's sweet little wife." Trix replied that "nothing would induce [her] to stay on in Southsea if Ruddy were not there." "You would soon find you would have to if you were left with me," Auntie would say, and in the light of the night-light her snapping eyes and large teeth made her look like Red Riding Hood's wolf. . . ."

If her favorite saw Mrs. Holloway as such a frightening, violent woman, Ruddy, "The Black Sheep," must have had an even more fearful impression. His feelings toward women, for the rest of his life, were marked by a deep fear, often connected with the idea of blindness. This can be seen in the last two sentences of "Baa Baa, Black Sheep" where Punch tells Judy:

> "There! 'Told you so. . . . It's all different now, and we are just as much Mother's as if she had never gone." [But Kipling adds:] "Not altogether, O Punch, for when young lips have drunk deep of the bitter waters of Hate, Suspicion, and Despair, all the Love in the world will not wholly take away that knowledge; though it may turn darkened eyes for a while to the light, and teach Faith where no Faith was."[16]

III

WESTWARD HO!

After Kipling's mother took her children out of Lorne Lodge in April 1877 they had a free and wild spring, summer, and fall with her.

Approaching the age of twelve, Kipling was now old enough to be sent to boarding school, and in January he went off to a new school on Bideford Bay in North Devon.

His parents had planned for some time to send Kipling there, since the headmaster, Cormell Price, was an old friend of theirs and was already "Uncle Crom" to Kipling. Cormell Price had taught at Haileybury, one of the new private schools that were springing up at the time, following the influence of Thomas Arnold at Rugby. A group of Army officers started another school, the United Services College, at Westward Ho!, a tiny village named after Charles Kingsley's novel. They got Price from Haileybury as the headmaster and the school was only five years old when Kipling went there.

It was a bleak little school on a bleak and empty shore. The founders had merely bought a row of twelve small houses and connected them with a covered walk on the outside and a long hall, piercing the walls of the houses, on the inside. The entire emphasis was on thrift and simplicity; the officers, on slim salaries, wanted to provide their sons with a cheap education, one that would get them past the new Army

Entrance Examination so that they, in turn, could obtain commissions and serve, in most cases, in the Army. The living was Spartan. "Even by the standards of those days," wrote Kipling years later, "it was primitive in its appointments, and our food would now raise a mutiny in Dartmoor."[1] No matter; after the House of Desolation anything was an improvement. A classmate has left us a detailed picture of Kipling at that time:

> Into the small boy's house at Westward Ho! in the grey, chill January days of 1878 there fluttered a cheery, capering, podgy, little fellow, as precocious as ever he could be. Or, rather, a broad smile appeared with a small boy behind it, carrying it about and pointing it in all directions. On persistent inquiry the name of the smile turned out to be 'Kipling'—only that and nothing more, a modest name, almost diminutive, for such a broad smile and such a podgy person. Over the smile there was, strangely enough, a pair of spectacles. . . .
>
> Kipling was rather short for his age of twelve years, but he took it out in extra width. He was not noticeably muscular or sinewy, and was accordingly ineffectual at fisticuffs, for which, in any case, his exceedingly short sight unfitted him. He preferred to side-track physical violence by his tact and friendliness, and by not quarreling with any boy unless he had allies. He was always noticeable for his caution and his habit of 'getting there' by diplomatic methods.
>
> The modeling of his head was peculiar. His skull appeared of moderate size in relation to his rather large face; his forehead retreated sharply from a heavy browline—in fact, so sharp was the set-back from the massive eyebrow ridges that he appeared almost 'cave-boy.' His lower jaw was massive, protruding and strong; the chin had a deep central cleft or dimple that at once attracted attention. Owing to its width, his face appeared rather Mongolian, and, bar the specs, he looked rather more formidable than he was. His complexion was dark rather than pale; the darkish hair was always close-cropped.
>
> His mouth was wide, with very well-shaped lips that suggested song—a promise that actuality denied. His hands and fingers were small. The short neck was set on rather round shoulders. He had a very slight stoop and a slightly round back that would be unpleasing to a sergeant-major. The curve in the shoulder region and an apparently small head close to the shoulders earned him the nickname of 'The Beetle.'*[2]

---

*Although "Beetle" was the name Kipling used for himself in *Stalky & Co.*, the book based on his school years, he was actually much more commonly called "Gigs" or "Gigger" from "Giglamps," his eyeglasses. Kipling was the only boy in school with glasses.

Relatively little is known about his first two years in school and a great deal about the last two. This is because he was miserable during the first period and then happy thereafter. The school, as was the custom in England at the time, emphasized discipline with harsh punishments for offenders. Caning of pupils by masters was common, and the younger boys were constantly bullied by the older ones. He may have been, as described, energetic, smiling and precocious, but most of the time he was desperately unhappy. As in the House of Desolation, again he was being bullied or beaten almost every day. Naturally, he and all his biographers have tended to forget, and to minimize the importance of, those first two years. He felt lonely, deserted, and again was being beaten by people older and bigger than he was. Another classmate in his reminiscences described how he continually suffered from "blows and kicks."[3] He continues, "I must have been perpetually black and blue . . . [The experience was] likely to injure permanently a not very robust temperament." Trix tells how, "for the first month or so he wrote to us, twice or thrice daily (and my mother cried bitterly over the letters) that he could neither eat nor sleep."[4] Mrs. Kipling wrote the headmaster:

> It is the roughness of the lads he seems to feel most . . . he is lonely and down—I was his chum, you know, and he hasn't found another yet.
> This lad has a great deal that is feminine in his nature, and a little sympathy from any quarter will reconcile him to his changed life more than anything.[5]

She was concerned and trying to be helpful. But consider how headstrong and thoughtless she was being. To tell the head of a school that your son is inclined to be "feminine" — particularly a hundred years ago—is likely permanently to taint the headmaster's feelings about the boy in his care. And if the word "feminine" were leaked out, think what a teasing that would produce from all the other students! Alice Kipling was charming, she was witty, and no one could have been a more entertaining dinner guest. But she was also outspoken and impetuous. By nature she was not tender, warm, nor motherly. She seems often to have been thoughtless about her children's feelings. This made her seem to Kipling all the more of a contrast with the *ayah* of his childhood.

A classmate, G. C. Beresford, gives an interesting account about Kipling's choice of a name. The boys avoided telling their first names, since this could lead to diminutives and mocking associations in certain cases. Kipling's actual first name, Joseph, says Beresford, would have led to ridicule—"Joe the joker" or "poor old Joe"—so he "showed his skill in quiet maneuver by deftly changing the undesirable Joseph into non-committal John."[6]

He had to pick a new name for himself, any name at all. Perhaps he would have preferred one beginning with a "J," since the other boys might have known his initials. He chose, not Jack nor Jim, but John, the name of his brother who had died when Kipling was four and a half and who lay buried in far-away India. Kipling had two mothers, his biological mother and his *ayah*, his emotional mother. As a result he felt he was half Indian, that a part of him would be in India forever, that only there would he feel at home. He felt a bond with his brother very much like the bond between two identical twins who share appearance. Just as twins do, Kipling felt he was not one person but two; in his case, one Indian and one white. In this splitting of his image of himself part was his Indian self (his brother John) and part his white self (the boy at school in England, Joseph). Throughout his life there are many examples of the resulting racial confusion, as if Kipling is asking himself, "Am I white? Am I Indian? Am I a mixture?" I think these feelings entered into his choice of the name John.

A respite from the bullying at school, and a joyful time he always remembered, came in the summer of 1878, toward the end of his first year at school. Lockwood Kipling, who had not seen his son for more than six years, came home from India to work at the Indian exhibition at the Paris Exposition of that year. He took Kipling, then twelve and one-half, to Paris with him. One might imagine that the lonely boy would have clung to his father and stayed with him all day, but not Kipling. He wanted to be alone. From his harsh experiences he had developed a strong sense of independence. He was friendly and witty—his father later wrote Cormell Price that he was "delightfully amiable and companionable"[7]—but was cautious about trusting anyone. His busy father gave him some money every day for meals, a free pass to the Exposition, and left him to his own devices. Kipling wrote of that time:

> Imagine the delight of a child let loose among all the wonders of all the world as they emerged from packing-cases, free to enter every unfinished building that was being raised round an edifice called the Trocadero, and to

pass at all times through gates in wooden barricades behind which workmen
put up kiosques and pavilions, or set out plants and trees![8]

He found himself curiously drawn to a painting that depicted the
burial of Manon Lescaut. Not until twelve years later did he understand
why.

He made friends with an English boy and the two of them got
involved in all sorts of lively mischief. When not at the Exposition, he
roamed about Paris, learning a smattering of French, and, as usual,
seeming to see everything and forget nothing. It was the beginning of
warm feelings for France that lasted the rest of his life. All too soon the
vacation ended and he had to return to Westward Ho!

His school years are best described in the *Stalky & Co.* stories. For
instance, in "The Moral Reformers," Kipling describes how he and two
friends, Beresford and Dunsterville ("McTurk" and "Stalky" in the stories) find that two senior boys, Campbell and Sefton, have been bullying
a younger boy, Clewer. By a trick, they tie the two older boys up in a
crouched, doubled-up position with ankles and wrists tied, and a stick
thrust under the knees and over the elbows, and proceed to torture them.
They administer a variety of torments. Before each one they ask: "Did
you give Clewer Head-knuckles?"[9] and when Campbell and Sefton finally admit it, "Knuckled they were. Head-knuckling is no trifle; 'Molly'
Fairburn of the old days could not have done better." Then they are
asked, "Did you give Clewer Brush-Drill?" and after endless repetition
"—no boy can stand the torture of one unvarying query, which is the
essence of bullying—" they admit it, and "Brush-Drill was dealt out for
the space of five minutes by Stalky's watch. . . . No brush is employed
in Brush-Drill." The same ritual is used with "the Key—which has no
Key at all," and "the Corkscrew—this has nothing to do with cork-
screws" and always "Between each new torture came the pitiless, dazing
rain of questions." Beetle (Kipling) then beats the tied-up Sefton, who
had called him a "blind beast." "Blind, am I," said Beetle, "and a
beast?". . . "*I* think I can see. Can't I see, Sefton?" He then forces his
victim to make a series of admissions, wrung out by pain, about his eyes:
how lovely they are, their color and how well he can see. When Stalky
remonstrates with Beetle over his cruelty, he replies, "I've had it done to
me."

Obviously, Kipling here gives expression to his experiences at Lorne Lodge. There he was tormented, questioned endlessly, and punished for no reason. This left him with a barely-concealed anger that periodically erupted, volcano-like, for the rest of his life. More importantly, he sought solutions to his bewildering experiences at the House of Desolation. Why did they do these things to me? And especially, Did it cause my blindness? In this story, he finds a simple answer, the first one any child discovers: the answer to torment is to catch the tormentor and pay him back in his own kind—"an eye for an eye, and a tooth for a tooth."

A child who is forced to submit to the kind of humiliation that Kipling experienced may suffer a partial collapse of his personality, submitting to the tortures and eroticizing them. He then derives latent or overt sexual pleasure from inflicting pain, or having it inflicted on himself. These feelings were largely absent in Kipling. But in "The Moral Reformers" and numberless others stories, there is a fascination with torture (as in the almost-affectionate nicknames for the different torments—the Key, the Corkscrew) and a connection between it and blindness that reveals an understandable element of sadism in his personality.

During Kipling's years at school, he changed from a boy to a man, from an "amiable . . . little chap"[10] to an adult, with goals for his life, a strong sense of responsibility, and a mature sexual orientation. He seems to have had a quiet awareness of his future powers as a writer. He looked much older than his age; in pictures with classmates, Kipling is instantly recognizable, looking like a miniature adult in the midst of a group of boys (although his eyeglasses, the only ones in the group, may contribute to this impression). Taking advantage of his appearance, he cultivated a superior, know-it-all attitude that impressed the others.

However, during the first year and one-half or two years at school Kipling was, to use his own words, miserable and lonely. He was haunted by a cruel master, the Reverend J. C. Campbell*, of whom Dunsterville later wrote, "I can never recall his face without an expres-

---

*Note that Kipling used the same name for one of the tortured bullies in "The Moral Reformers."

sion of ferocity on it, nor his hand without a cane in it."[11] Campbell's constant accusation "Don't prevaricate!" must have reminded Kipling of Lorne Lodge, where Mrs. Holloway and her son were constantly catching him in innocent remarks that they termed "lies" for which he was beaten and forced to read the Bible.

During Kipling's second year, to everyone's delight, Campbell left for another school. He gave an emotional farewell sermon in which he admitted his cruelties, asked for forgiveness, and finally even wept in the pulpit. His congregation of little souls was touched, some even to the point of tears themselves—with the notable exception of Kipling. After the service, gathered around the church door, the boys were in agreement that old Campbell ought to be forgiven: "We'll let him depart with no ill feelings." Kipling brought them all to their senses, and quickly changed their point of view, with one growled sentence: "Two years' bullying is not paid for with half-an-hour's blubbering in a pulpit."[12]

Punishment at the school, if not administered with a cane, often consisted of being made to write a single line one hundred times. Someone came up with the idea of tying two pens together with thread, so that two lines could be written at the same time, thereby reducing the task to fifty repetitions. Since the handwriting in every two lines was identical, however, the masters quickly caught on to this trick and it had to be abandoned. Kipling set his mind to this and came up with a wide penholder, with the nibs set so far apart that there was a blank line left between the two written ones. Now only every other line was identical, and the blank space could occasionally be written in by itself, making deception much easier. What is striking is that although Kipling came up with the idea, he was of no use in the actual making of the gadget—an inability at mechanical skills that was to appear on other occasions.

When he was fourteen, Kipling joined Beresford and Dunsterville in Number Five Study, years later to be the scene of most of the *Stalky & Co.* stories. They made a notable trio; the acid-tongued Beresford ("McTurk"), the worldly Kipling ("Beetle"), and their ingenious leader, Dunsterville ("Stalky"). It was to the Dunsterville that the other two turned for guidance; he had been at the school the longest and possessed a flair for games and trickery that was unequaled. He would guiltily slip into an examination room and begin writing, glancing surreptitiously at a bit of paper concealed in one hand; the master in charge would triumphantly pounce on this bit of flagrant cheating, and the paper would then be found to be blank. Kipling, who always enjoyed jokes and mischief, thought the world of Dunsterville. He was Kipling's first object of hero worship, the first of a long line.

At the school, he was most influenced by three masters: H. A. Evans, a kind, tolerant man who directed the school theatrical productions; F. W. Haslam, from whom he learned "to loathe Horace for two years; to forget him for twenty, and then to love him for the rest of my days and through many sleepless nights."[13] The last of the three, William Crofts, who taught English, had the greatest impact on Kipling. Crofts, large and powerful, had been an outstanding rower. He was hot-tempered, sarcastic, and with a gift for invective that Kipling quickly learned to copy. English classes frequently would be reduced to verbal battles between Kipling, objecting to Crofts' belief that all great poetry had ended with Milton and Tennyson, and Crofts, who would comment acidly on Kipling's admiration for Browning and Rossetti, for Walt Whitman and Mark Twain. For the young Kipling was always interested in contemporary American writers, and was to remain so for the rest of his life. He had read Emerson's *Poems* when only eleven, in Epping Forest, and followed this with Edgar Allen Poe and Bret Harte. Besides reading them all, he copied their style, to the open disgust of Mr. Crofts, who ridiculed Kipling's interest in these young poets who, he assured everyone, would be quickly forgotten. The other boys in class would watch open-mouthed, for the level of intellectual discussion between the two was high. Crofts would rage at Kipling, heaping sarcasm and derision on him, to which Kipling would innocently reply by pointing out inconsistencies in Crofts' argument, buttressed by extensive quotations—all of them memorized—from the writer under discussion. Now there would be a point for Crofts, now one for Kipling. Crofts' attacks were so bitter that some of the boys—in that harsh environment—felt he was really being cruel to Kipling; but the schoolboy was not hurt. He could take it, and dish it out as well. He sensed that Crofts was damping down some of his boyish enthusiasm in contemporary writers by insisting that he study the classics first, and it was to Crofts that he wrote letters, in later years, from India.

Besides these impressive, fiery interchanges with Crofts, the other boys remembered Kipling as being pleasant, animated, and popular.

36

They couldn't get over the number of books he read, and the speed with which he consumed them. He would prop his glasses up on his fore-head—being nearsighted, he didn't need them for reading—and would sweep over a page in twenty seconds, and then flip on to the next. He must be fooling them; they tested him by demanding that he recount the contents of the just-turned page. They could hardly believe it when he did so, accurately. And he was reading Dryden, Marlowe, and Donne, when they were content with juvenile adventure stories. Words abso-lutely fascinated him, and he was forever looking up their meanings. In later life, when asked the usual "desert island" question, Kipling said the books he wanted were a dictionary—and the Bible, that he had learned under Mrs. Holloway in the House of Desolation.

During Kipling's last two years the headmaster revived the school newspaper and made him the editor. As might be expected, he plunged into the job energetically, writing most of it himself, correcting the proofs, and then watching every step of its printing at a small local press. Reading what he wrote, one is struck with his ability; and yet, perhaps, it is no more outstanding than what one would expect of the best writer among 150 boys. Cormell Price also gave Kipling the free use of his own personal library. Here was a real feast for a boy starving for literature.

Although Kipling was generally accepted as a future literary man, and his real ability was recognized, he had a striking deficiency noted by the other boys.[14] He found it hard to tell a story. His forte was the incisive remark, the one-liner (as in the case of the Reverend Campbell); he had a keen awareness of individuals and issues, and could describe them remarkably well. But he was no good at spinning out a story; many of the other boys could do this better than he. This difficulty was to be evident in his writing for the rest of his career.

The school gave Kipling a sense of belonging—really, of being in a family—an orderliness, in contrast to the chaos from which he had come. This relief from the confusion of years past cannot be overem-phasized. The school gave him a definite framework of existence. There were rules to be obeyed (although Kipling's stories about the school are mostly about *breaking* rules, the boys set very careful limits on their misdemeanors). There were conventions to be observed, rituals to be followed, and a definite social hierarchy into which he successfully fit-ted. There were studies to be completed and academic successes to be won. A definite philosophy was in the air: a man should find his place in the world and give it his best effort. There was no acceptance of laziness or excuses.

He was popular with his classmates, noted for his vivacity and humor, but an important handicap prevented him from fully feeling he "belonged" with the others. He had a pronounced lack of coordination. It made him completely inept athletically. When Dunsterville first met him, he wrote his family that Kipling was "as clumsy as a bull in a china shop."[15] In Beresford's reminiscences, he described his swimming: "He went forward in a rather jerky manner by fits and starts, owing to a certain want of deftness in his makeup, or a dissociation of body and brain."[16]*

In talking about Kipling's failure at sports, generations of writers have ascribed it to his poor vision; indeed, Kipling does so himself in his autobiography: "swimming in the big open sea baths . . . was the one accomplishment that brought me any credit. I played footer (Rugby Union), but here again my sight hampered me."[18] (Note how important it was to him; no other physical "accomplishment" brought him any "credit.") Kipling's poor eyesight became a convenient excuse used by a succession of biographers; but it would not have affected his swimming in the way Beresford describes, nor other activities to be mentioned later. The two conditions—his sight and bad coordination—were connected, but not in a cause-and-effect manner. They were both physical deficiencies, leading to a feeling of impairment that was of great importance to Kipling. It is a theme that he returns to again and again throughout his life, in his actions as well as in what he wrote.

In other ways he felt he was the "odd man out." The other boys were almost all the sons of Army officers, going to school to pass the

---

*The only opposing view of his coordination came from Mrs. Bambridge, his daughter, who wrote, "Deftness and certainty of movement were characteristics of his. The way he handled things, lit a cigarette, made a gesture or movement, was compact [sic] of neatness and energy. He never fumbled, and his gestures were always expressive. Up to the time of his death at seventy his slim and upright figure moved surely and lightly."[17] Any statement of Mrs. Bambridge's regarding an imperfection of her father must be questioned. Her view of herself seems to have been wholly derived from being Rudyard Kipling's daughter, and she vehemently attacked any criticism, no matter how mild, of her father. Her opinion in this case is so radically opposed to all others that I cannot accept it; in fact, her denial constitutes further evidence of Kipling's uncoordination.

examination for Army commissions, and they all shared in the antici-
pation of lives in the Army, with Army talk, Army customs, and Army
marriages for the rest of their days. All this was wholly unlike Kipling's
world. He always felt he was in some way different, that he was outside
some inner circle that admitted others but excluded him. This idea did
not begin in school, however; it was racial in origin, coming from the
feeling he was half Indian.

Kipling's world was one of literature and the arts. He had a secret
bond with Cormell Price, who on vacations became "Uncle Crom," the
old friend of his parents. When the boys walked to the nearby town of
Bideford, they used to admire, in a store window, a gory painting by
Poynter of the Israelites, under the lashes of the cruel Egyptians, building
the pyramids. Kipling never revealed to the others that Edward Poynter
was his uncle. They had no idea that when away from the school he spent
time with various Macdonald cousins, whose parents were at the forefront
of artistic circles, where all the talk was of painters, their various tech-
niques, their use of different media, their new and exciting ideas.

In 1880, when he was fourteen, he joined his mother who came to
England for a brief visit; she also helped nurse him through a minor
illness. They were joined by Trix, up from Mrs. Holloway's. The house
was overflowing, so Kipling was sent to his Uncle Frederic Macdonald's, whose children never forgot the wild time they had after Kipling
came to stay. One family story a cousin told illustrates his high spirits:
Kipling came in one day in a fury; lay down and beat his fists on the
floor in anger. "Why, Ruddy! What's the matter?" "The porter at the
station boxed my ears." "But what made him box your ears?" "Oh, I
expect I cheeked him." His expression changed, he got up smiling and
went toward the door with a purposeful look. "Where are you going,
Ruddy?" "Back to the station to cheek that porter again."[19]

In spite of these childish highjinks—expressing a boyish side of his
nature that he retained throughout his life—Kipling was physically far
ahead of his classmates; he went through puberty at a very early age.
When he arrived at school, just twelve, he had a distinct pubescent
mustache, as can be seen in contemporary sketches.[20] Later, when he
was ill and a mustard plaster had to be applied to his chest, it had to be
shaved first. This was a very early change and especially then, at a time
when boys and girls matured later than nowadays. And at fourteen and

a half, when he went down to Mrs. Holloway's to take Trix to visit relatives over a vacation, he fell in love. This was no teenage crush, felt from afar, intense but brief. He fell deeply in love and remained so for six or seven years.

The girl was Violet Garrard, always known as "Flo." She was a year or two older than he, a paying occupant of Lorne Lodge just as Kipling had been, and as Trix perhaps still was. (Information is lacking on when Trix left Mrs. Holloway's.) He fell head-over-heels in love with her, wrote her constantly, saw her as often as possible, and begged that they be engaged when he left for India a year and four months later.

So far as I know, no photograph of her exists—not remarkable, more than a hundred years later. There are some unrevealing drawings that show her from a distance, which Kipling drew in her sketchbook, now in the Berg Collection. Contemporaries describe her as pale-faced, slender, dark-haired, and lovely, but also as a cold and distant. She was entirely wrapped up in her art studies. Brought up in a variety of places like Lorne Lodge, and by a variety of people, she appears, not surprisingly, to have been incapable of love. Certainly, there is not a shred of evidence that she ever encouraged Kipling in the slightest. On the contrary, his love-poems to her, "Sundry Phansies," also in the Berg Collection, are all highly romanticized, pre-Raphaelite variations of the "Why-won't-you-return-my-love?" theme.

Flo is transparently portrayed as Maisie, Dick's companion in *The Light That Failed*, a cold, selfish, demanding person whom he keeps pursuing, although she never shows the slightest interest in him. It is certainly significant that Kipling's first love was a girl who, like himself and his sister, was a product of the House of Desolation at Southsea. Was it merely coincidence that the place where he had suffered so much became the place where he first felt intense love for a girl? It is possible, but hardly likely; and on further examination, other things make it seem even less so. Two possibilities immediately come to mind. First, that Kipling unconsciously identifed Flo with his sister. She was a girl at Mrs. Holloway's house, as Trix had been; it should be remembered that in *The Light That Failed*, Dick and Maisie, in cruel Mrs. Jennett's house, are unrelated. They fall in love and exchange kisses. As a Kipling scholar, J. M. S. Tomkins, put it:

Dick Heldar . . . is an answer to [Kipling's] question: "What might have become of me if I had been left in the house for years, without parents or relations, and if the other child there had not been my sister?" What becomes of Dick is that his strong and unexercised affections fasten on Maisie, his partner in hardship. . . .[21]

She wrote this *before* she knew of Flo's existence and of Kipling's love for her. Her statement immediately, if unwittingly, suggests the probable intensity of Kipling's feelings toward his own sister, "his partner in hardship." One remembers that Punch and Judy, the brother and sister in "Baa Baa, Black Sheep," also exchange kisses.

A second possibility about Kipling's falling in love with Flo Garrard is that she was connected in his mind with Mrs. Holloway. At first glance, this would seem contradictory; he loved Flo and he hated "Auntie Rosa." One can be certain, however, that when a boy is beaten by a woman over a period of years, the experience becomes eroticized for him. Women he came to care for in later years would be unconsciously chosen; they would have, to some degree, the same qualities "Auntie Rosa" had. His relationship to them would have some of the same elements of helplessness, submission, and pain, besides normal feelings of love and tenderness. A man with this unconscious need falls in love with women not in spite of some feelings of hatred, but *because* of them.

Kipling's relationship with Flo certainly fits this view. He adored her, worshipped the ground she walked on, and obediently would do anything she asked; while she, petty and selfish, gave him no encouragement. The cooler she was, the more ardently he pursued her; one almost gets the impression that if she had suddenly changed her mind and become interested, he would have broken it off. There was something of Mrs. Holloway in Flo, as there was in other women in his later life. What is most striking about this is not the element of psychopathology that can be seen, the passivity previously mentioned, but rather the way in which Kipling was somehow able to fight this off, to transcend it, and to be truly capable of loving a woman.

Kipling's marks at graduation were good if not outstanding. His parents, always pinched for money, could not consider his going on to college. In any event, Kipling, bursting with energy, in some ways precocious and in some ways boyish, may well have preferred the idea of plunging into journalism rather than continuing his education. His classmates, having triumphantly passed the long-awaited Army examination, went streaming off to various military posts. Again, he was the odd man out, planning to sail for India in September 1882 so as to arrive at the end of the hot season. Strings had been pulled, that supremely Victorian custom, and a job awaited him at Lahore, on a provincial newspaper, the *Civil and Military Gazette*. He was to be the assistant editor.

Angus Wilson's interesting discovery of letters written by Kipling during this time to a Mrs. Perry reveals the intensity of his feelings for Flo and his mixed emotions about leaving England. To his school friends he said that he wanted to stay in England; a strong and unrevealed reason was, of course, so that he could be with Flo. Little did they know how much truth lay behind his joke that he would cable his father, "I have married a wife and therefore I cannot come."[22] But to Mrs. Perry, whom he addressed as "Dearest Mater,"[23] he wrote of being anxious to leave England. Probably, as was to happen repeatedly during his life, he felt a marked confusion of feelings. He wanted to be home; but where was home—England or India?

IV

"KUPPELEEN SAHIB" I

In September 1882 Kipling left for India on the P. & O. steamer *Brindisi*. He was lonely and depressed. As he gazed through the gray rain at the fading shore, he presumably thought longingly of his friends, and, most of all, of Flo Garrard. England was home for him; he was leaving his close friends, his relatives with whom he had had such good times, and the girl he loved, to go to faraway India. He was returning to parents whom he really didn't know.

He had left India when he was five, and lived in the torture chamber of Lorne Lodge for the next five years, during which time he never saw either of his parents. From twelve to sixteen, he had been in school, years when he had seen his mother only rarely, and his father only once. Three months short of seventeen, he was in the confusing situation of going to stay with parents who were strangers to him. But, a few days out, his boyish nature asserted itself. If he was only sixteen, he looked as if he were in his twenties. Again, he took advantage of his mature appearance, fooling the other passengers with a very know-it-all look and tales of journalistic experience.

The ship arrived in India, and as he himself describes it, "I found myself at Bombay where I was born, moving among sights and smells that made me deliver in the vernacular sentences whose meaning I knew not."[1] He was speaking Hindustani, the language he "thought and dreamed in" before he learned English.

After arriving at Bombay, he had a three-day train trip north to Lahore, where his parents had lived for seven years, his father now being principal of the Art School there. In later years, Trix wrote of him, "Funnily enough, just at the time when most boys cast off home life, Ruddy returned to it like a duck to its pond."[2] In light of what we have seen, it was not at all odd that Kipling greatly enjoyed being part of a family. He wasn't returning to it—he had never had it—but had yearned for it, and now could finally enjoy it. But when he arrived at the railroad station in Lahore, there was no blissful reunion, no rush to a loving embrace (such a nice Victorian picture!) despite what many biographers have described. He really scarcely knew his parents, and developing feelings for them was going to take some time. He kept on writing Mrs. Perry, continuing to address her as "Dearest Mater," and now signing the letters "your own graceless boy."[3] He had to get to know his parents gradually, and in the back of his mind was the old question, never answered, "How could they have done it to me?"

But when some months had passed, and particularly after Trix came from England to make the family complete, they melted into a warm and loving foursome, a truly happy family. Kipling's wish to stay in England disappeared; he says, of this time, "My English years fell away, nor ever, I think, came back in full strength."[4] He is saying, "My strongest bond was with India." It was there that his deepest roots lay. It was the only place that would ever really be "home" for him. In later years he lived in London, then in Vermont, which he approached with eagerness but some reservations, then in the English countryside, then in South Africa (always ruined by the shattering of so many dreams), and finally for good, back in England, where he loudly and persistently sang the praises of Sussex—so loudly and persistently, in fact, that one begins to doubt the truth of his feelings. It was India, India, India that was really home—the India where the safety of his birth had been insured by the native's sacrifice of a kid to Kali. Kipling always felt he had been "bought into India" and that it was his only true home—and so, not being Indian, he could never quite feel at home there or anywhere else.

He immediately started working on the *Civil and Military Gazette*.

His superior, Stephen Wheeler—representing the other half of the two Europeans on the paper's staff—had briefly interviewed him back in London.

The *Gazette* had been founded ten years before by two prominent local men, James Walker and William Rattigan; the first had made his fortune in railroads and transportation, and the second by becoming perhaps the most successful lawyer in Lahore. They were both friends of Kipling's parents, and it was through them, primarily Walker, that Kipling secured his job. But it would be pleasing, as Angus Wilson puts it, if there was evidence that Kipling knew Rattigan, and his life story, well. For Wilson found that Rattigan, who ultimately rose to be a member of the Governor General's Legislative Council, was the son of an illiterate Irish private in Her Majesty's Indian Army, who had had to "make his mark" when he enlisted. His son, Kipling's benefactor, managed to get an education in India, and then attended King's College in London, and after this became a lawyer. This story might have provided the seed of Kipling's greatest book, *Kim*, the life of an Irish boy, Kimball O'Hara.

In Lahore Kipling began what he later called his "seven years' hard," referring to a judge's sentencing a criminal to seven years of hard labor. His life was indeed hard. For four of those seven years he worked under Stephen Wheeler, a stern taskmaster who saw the bubbling Kipling as a frivolous young fellow who must be taught to keep his nose to the grindstone. One wonders if Wheeler may not have recognized, and envied, a superior talent, all the more so since soon after Kipling arrived, Wheeler was injured in a carriage accident and Kipling was left with the responsibility for editing the paper. He handled the 170 natives—who set the type, ran the presses, and did all the manual labor involved in getting the paper out—and proved entirely capable of the task. However that may be, Wheeler sternly discouraged Kipling's stories and handed him endless copying and proofreading of the most routine sort. Characteristically, Kipling worked ten to fifteen hours a day, turning out enormous amounts of work, without a murmur of complaint.

During the hot season all the white population of Lahore that could fled to the coolness of the hills. At these times there would be only sixty to seventy whites in the entire city of 200,000— junior people like Kipling, carrying the increased load while their superiors were up at Simla.

As the hot season of 1883 arrived, his parents were so concerned about Kipling's work, his health (both he and his mother were particularly oppressed by the heat), and his unceasing yearning for Flo Garrard that they decided Alice Kipling would stay down at Lahore, while Lockwood went up to the hills alone. She saw her son through part of his first hot season, and then, in July, she set off for England to bring Trix back to join the family. Kipling had a vacation in Simla in July and then, in August, at the worst of the heat, returned to Lahore. His father, after a stay in the cool hills, was busy for two months planning an art exhibition in Calcutta, so Kipling was left alone.

It was a situation that is—in spite of what he wrote about it—hard for us, in our air-conditioned, sanitized life, to imagine. Even the most rudimentary knowledge of health was lacking; it was not known, for instance, that mosquitoes transmitted malaria. Kipling was set down in a city where there were 3,000 Asiatics for each European. And the heat! It went to the hundreds during the day and only fell to the nineties at night. The other whites spent their free hours at the Club or in their stifling bungalows; but Kipling, restless, too tired and tense to sleep, and also by inclination, roamed the sleeping city.

He would let fate decide where he went. "I set my walking-stick on end in the middle of the garden, and waited to see how it would fall. It pointed directly down the moonlit road that leads to the City of Dreadful Night."[5] A hare "ran across a disused . . . burial-ground . . . ." [where lay exposed] "jawless skulls and rough-butted shank-bones" [and] "on either side of the road lay corpses disposed on beds in fantastic attitudes. Some shrouded all in white with bound-up mouths; some naked and black as ebony in the strong light; and one—that lay face upwards with dropped jaw, far away from the others—silvery white and ashen grey . . . [a] leper asleep. They lie—some face downwards, arms folded, in the dust; some with clasped hands flung up above their heads; some curled up dog-wise; some thrown like limp gunny-bags over the side of the grain-carts; and some bowed with their brows on their knees in the full glare of the Moon."

He decided to climb to the top of the great Mosque of Wazir Khan. ". . . [A] deeply-sleeping janitor lies across the threshold . . . a rat dashes out of his turban at the sound of approaching footsteps . . . Doré might have drawn it! Zola could describe it—this spectacle of sleeping thousands in the moonlight and in the shadow of the Moon." "I drop off into an uneasy doze, conscious that three o'clock has struck, and that there is a slight, a very slight, coolness in the atmosphere. Several weeks of darkness pass after this. I watch for the first light of the dawn before making my way homeward." [But as he leaves], "'Will the Sahib, out of his kindness, make room?' What is it? Something borne on men's shoulders comes by the half-light, and I stand back. A woman's corpse going down to the burning-ghat, and a bystander says, 'She died at midnight from the heat.' So the city was of Death as well as Night, after all."

Kipling roamed the city during the day even more than he did at night. The average Englishman simply ignored the natives or treated them with condescension; Kipling went everywhere, including the most squalid sections of the city that his companions would have scrupulously avoided. And, as always, his eyes and ears were open to everything. He was earning a reputation for knowing an amazing amount about a wide variety of things. "Of the various races of India, whom the ordinary Englishman lumps together as 'natives,' Kipling knew the quaintest details respecting habits, language and distinctive ways of thought. One long-limbed Pathan, indescribably filthy . . . Mahbub Ali, I think, was his name . . . regarded Kipling as a man apart from all other 'Sahibs'."[6] Periodically "Mahbub Ali . . . used to turn up travel-stained, dirtier and more majestic than ever, for a confidential colloquy with 'Kuppeleen Sahib,' his 'friend.'"

In spite of Stephen Wheeler's discouraging attitude, he began to write more and more, first sending homesick letters to Mr. Crofts and to Stalky; but then, as some of his work began to appear in the *Gazette*, he began to feel more at home and to write the poems and short stories that were to make him famous.

He began every day with a jog on his pony, Joe. He tried hard to see if practice would prevail over his extreme clumsiness, so that he could become an adequate horseman; but "horse and rider sometimes returned separately"[7] from these canters. With his mother still in England fetching Trix, and his father in Calcutta, Kipling ended 1883 in hard-working loneliness. He was too busy to become involved in social activities, and perhaps too shy. He joined a local civilian outfit, the 1st Punjab Volunteers, but never appeared at drill. Here, too, his marked lack of coordination prevented any participation. And his loneliness was made all the worse by his continued love for Flo Garrard, unresponsive in faraway England.

Then, in January of 1884, his father having come back from Calcutta, his mother returned from England with Trix, and the family was finally together.

They were four people who were close, loving, and open with each other. Kipling states, "I do not remember the smallest friction in any detail of our lives. Our cup was filled to the brim. Not only were we happy, but we knew it."[8] Trix confirms this memory: "I have never laughed so much, before or since."[9] They used to have "Shakespeare evenings," when all conversation had to consist of quotations from the Bard. She learned to distrust her brilliant brother, who could come up with an authentic-sounding quotation he had just made up. They were indeed a striking family; the father, quiet, knowledgeable, and industrious; the mother, quick, witty, and perceptive; his sister, now attractive, intuitive, and with an almost frightening ability to memorize literature; and Kipling himself, a short, stocky, quick figure, full of energy and enthusiasm, with an intense curiosity about anything new. "The Family Square," his mother called it, naming it after a standard British military formation that was proudly considered impregnable at the time.

But we must question this rather pat picture of an all-loving foursome. What sort of a relationship did Kipling and his sister have with their parents?

In his autobiography Kipling writes:

> For consider!—I had returned to a father and mother of whom I had seen but little since my sixth year. I might have found my mother "the sort of woman *I* didn't care for," as in one terrible case that I know: and my father intolerable. But the mother proved more delightful than all my imaginings or memories. My father was not only a mine of knowledge and help, but a humorous, tolerant, and expert fellow-craftsman. I had my own room in the house; my servant, handed over to me by my father's servant, whose son he was, with all the solemnity of a marriage-contract; my own horse, cart, and groom; my own office-hours and direct responsibilities; and—oh joy!—my own office-box, just like my father's, which he took daily to the Lahore Museum and School of Art.[10]

Note the length and enthusiasm of his description of his father, and of things having to do with him, compared with what he says about his mother. She is dismissed in two laudatory lines. His father, in contrast, is seen as a kindred soul, someone with the same interest and goals, someone he could admire and want to be like for the rest of his life. What were his feelings about his mother? If he turned to his father with such relief, mightn't it be because his father, calm and easy-going, offered some protection from a waspish mother, with a biting tongue? And then mightn't it be that his parents were the real villains, his mother so hostile and critical, his father so timid and helpless around her, rather than the Holloways? The House of Desolation was terrible, but his parents had put him and his sister in there, hadn't they?

I think it can be demonstrated that Kipling's fear of women, and his connecting them with blindness, did not come from his relationship with his mother. He always wondered how she could have done such a thing as to leave him at the House of Desolation, and he never found an answer. But, during all those years at the Holloways', his parents were hazy figures from childhood. He had been brought up by his *ayah* and Meeta. The only ongoing contact he had with his parents was the letters they exchanged, and Mrs. Holloway often dictated his answers. Enduring daily torment from her, and having only dim memories of his distant parents, the beatings and punishments naturally loomed largest in his mind. Mrs. Holloway was the key figure in his love-fear feelings toward women, a conflict that was firmly in place long before he returned to India as a teenager and began to find out what kind of people his parents were. Mrs. Holloway influenced in his on-again, off-again relationship with Flo Garrard—which was to be the model for how he got along with subsequent women—and he fell in love with Flo while he was still in England.

Accepting the idea that Mrs. Holloway was the central person in his conflicts, mightn't his mother have added to them? What was her relationship with her children?

To understand this we must turn back and see something of her background and personality. She was the eldest of five sisters, daughters of a hard-working Methodist minister whom she seldom saw. Of the girls, she was the outspoken, unconventional one. Once they were all talking with a young man about what a person might be driven to eat in an emergency. He claimed that he would have no problem, emergency or no emergency, with eating a mouse. Alice—and only she would have done such a thing—challenged this, caught a mouse and baked it in a bit of pastry, and then invited him to lunch to eat it. When he failed to appear she crowed that she had called his bluff. All this was done amicably, however, and the young man remained a friend.

Alice was competitive and liked challenges. She was repeatedly engaged but then backed out, seeming to enjoy the ripples she stirred up with this sort of headstrong behavior. But for someone who seems to have been so sure of herself she had a curious touchiness about her age and appearance. Few pictures of her exist, since she hated being photographed, perhaps because her sister Agnes, the most attractive—and most tactless—one of the five once hurt her feelings by saying that Alice's face never came out right in a picture. Alice kept her age a deep secret and greatly disliked anyone knowing that she was older than her husband. She felt so strongly about this that for years she reminded everyone that her date of birth was not to appear on her tombstone.

As the marriageable years approached for the five sisters a question, a critical one in Victorian times, arose: which sister was going to take care of their parents? It was a rock-solid custom a hundred years ago that one of the daughters in every family took on this task, and with it gave up all thoughts of marriage herself (at least until her parents died).

Apparently Alice felt there was some pressure on her to be the one to do this, and although she was as dutiful as the next person she shrank from such a fate. She then met Lockwood Kipling. She saw going to India as an adventure and an escape from a life that might become dull and tiresome. (The care of the parents ended up as her sister Edith's responsibility; she was the only daughter who never married.)

After a long engagement she married Lockwood in a quick and simple ceremony, going through it all with such a dead-pan expression on her face that her sisters commented on it. They were upset at her going to faraway India; Alice seemed only impatient to be off, and she and Lockwood left three weeks later on April 12, 1865. If Alice had seen India as a delightful and exciting place to live, it turned out to be just the opposite. Arriving at the beginning of the hot season in early pregnancy, she became so ill that her life was in serious danger. Among other things, she could not eat the highly spiced Indian food. She would have been more than glad to cook the meals herself but all preparation was done in a separate building, the servants' quarters, and custom forbade even the strong-minded Alice from entering the place. She hated India with a passion for the next twenty-eight years although, always competitive, she usually took care to conceal her unhappiness from her sisters back in England and instead emphasized the success of her husband and, later, of her son. She was always one to make the best of things. She saw herself, quite accurately, as someone who was good at influencing others and set herself the goal of furthering her husband's career. In this she was eminently successful.

Every biographer recounts examples of her dazzling wit. There is no doubt that if she had a quick wit it was occasionally a cruel one. A young girl who had recently arrived in India was described by Alice as "nearly as big as her mother and crouching and stooping in such a ridiculous manner that presently I imagine she will go on all fours."[11] Another young woman was considered "very plain till her cousin Mrs. Lambert's daughter came—and by her transcending ugliness made Miss Black seem almost beautiful."

But this sort of harshness would have had little effect on Kipling. He was a tough one, and was not touchy about disapproval. His father urged Kipling's cousin Margaret Burne-Jones to write him and openly express her criticisms: "No need to fear hurting him." And lastly, Kipling was shielded from his mother's sharp tongue by the gender-linked roles of that time. Men earned the livings, women ran the households, and each sphere was almost entirely prevented from interfering with the other. If Alice had been nasty to Kipling about his writing, he could have simply ignored her and retired behind the conventional view that he was doing "man's work" (applauded by everyone else) that she "didn't understand." (Note that the two examples of her unkindness, and almost all others that I have seen, are directed at women.)

During his years in India, and afterward, Kipling openly expressed his love for his mother. In one letter he said he wanted to find a wife who would be "as sweet and perfect and almost as old as my Mother." In another he declared, "Love is a scarce commodity and I hold the best is a Mother's." Although these were partly conventional statements of filial devotion, nothing has come down to us to suggest he was "protesting too much," that these loving declarations were masking a deeper hostility. When he wrote about his fear of women it was connected with the idea of blindness, and therefore derived from his years with Mrs. Holloway;

it was not linked to desertion, helplessness, or verbal attacks, which would reasonably be seen as coming from feelings about his mother.

But if she was not a problem for him, she certainly was for his sister Trix. The gender-linked roles just mentioned, which gave Kipling some protection from his mother, put Trix squarely under her thumb, and Alice was very intrusive in her daughter's life. When Trix later developed into a very attractive young woman, Alice felt jealous and made special efforts, with her sparkling conversation, to push Trix aside and to keep herself at the center of attention. In 1884 Kipling wrote a poem about their competition; one verse is as follows:

> The young men come, the young men go,
> Each pink and white and neat,
> She's older than their mothers, but
> They grovel at her feet.
> They walk beside her rickshaw-wheels—None ever walk by mine;
> And that's because I am seventeen
> And she is forty-nine.[12]

If Kipling had been afraid of his mother, he would never have written a poem like this, knowing her extreme sensitivity about her age. It would seem we can accept as accurate the accounts of the happy "family square" that Kipling and Trix have given us—at least during the first half of those years in India.

A description of the culture in which Kipling lived is necessary if we are to understand his feelings toward those about him, toward the "Home English" when he returned there, and, later, toward America and Americans.

An Anglo-Indian community was not just a group of British subjects cast into exile. On the contrary, it had a strong sense of integrity and a high esprit de corps. It was a small, elite group, chosen by competitive examination, strictly separated from the natives. Being sent to India in those days was not viewed with dismay, but rather was considered a high honor. Finally, it was a homogeneous group, for it consisted very largely of civil and military officials and their families. There were no rich, no poor, no tradesmen, no farmers, no city folk, no country folk. This is not to say that they regarded everyone as equal; these middle-class Englishmen and women of course divided themselves up into a hierarchy, largely based on the levels of attainment of the men, as people did everyhere. For all, however, there was a strong sense of pride in past military and administrative accomplishments—and a suspicion that these were not appreciated by high officials far away in England, many of whom had never set foot in India.

The governing of India was carried out by the Viceroy and his Council. The country was divided into fifteen provinces, each with a governor and council. In turn, each province was divided into districts, and the district officer, in direct contact with the natives, administered justice and enforced the laws. For many years after the Queen's Rule began in 1858 these district officers held almost absolute power. They were like little kings, each in his little kingdom. Around the time Kipling returned to India, however, there was a steady swing of authority toward the central government. The Viceroy and the provincial councils began investigating district officers and instituting reforms and changes. The ultimate goal was the education of the Indians toward self-government. The district officers bitterly complained that their former close relationship with the natives was being lost, and that they were merely doing paperwork and carrying out orders from above—orders that, issued without down-to-earth knowledge of Indian life, made no sense.

Socially, during these first years, the Kiplings were at the level of the district officer. (In later years, their social status changed drastically, rising so that they were at the level of the Viceroy and his staff.) As might be expected, they, like almost all Anglo-Indians, vehemently took the side of the district officer in this administrative battle. Kipling was furious at attacks by the Home English on these officers, such as one by Francis Adams, who snorted that a typical military man in India had "the courage of a mastiff and the brains of a rabbit."[13] He wrote many stories about Strickland, a police officer who could so disguise himself, and speak the dialect so well, that he could mix with the natives unrecognized. But this only got him disapproval from those above him. "His crowning achievement was spending eleven days as a *faquir* or priest . . . and there picking up the threads of the great Nagiban murder case. But people said, justly enough, 'Why on earth can't Strickland sit in his office . . . and keep quiet, instead of showing up the incapacity of his seniors?' So the Nagiban murder case did him no good departmentally. . . ."[14] In story after story, Kipling portrayed the local official's wisdom, his all-important knowledge of native life, as contrasted with the vacuous proclamations of the high administrators. At another point Kipling describes the district officers "who live in patriarchal fashion among the People, respecting and respected, knowing their ways and their wants; believing (soundest of all beliefs) that too much progress is bad, and compassing with their heads and their hands real, concrete and undeniable Things. As distinguished from the speech which dies and the paperwork which perishes."[15]

Here Kipling shows what was to be a lifelong contempt for administrators and policy-makers, and an infinite preference for those who produce immediate, tangible results. A similarity can be seen between this inclination and his creative work. All his life he preferred to write short stories and brief poems. Over and over again he said he could not stand back and see the beginning, middle, and end of a larger work. This lack of an "overview" might be a partial explanation for his political position. I emphasize *partial*, for, to repeat, nearly every other Anglo-Indian agreed with him.

Kipling wrote many stories portraying Indians as being *inherently* ignorant—not just uneducated—and unreliable, and felt that any talk of self-government was mere nonsense. In "New Brooms," to take just one example, he tells of Ram Buksh, an average village Indian, who dies; his body, incorrectly disposed of, begins an epidemic of typhus followed by smallpox. The district officer arrives and begins to handle the situation with his usual efficiency. But now the Government of India, proclaiming that "The Liberty of the Subject is sacred,"[16] orders the officer out so that local sanitation can be taken over by "Boards of Control and Supervision—Fund Boards—all sorts of Boards." The district officer protests that to let the average Indian work out his own welfare is merely to let him kill himself.

What is important to note here is not the offensive belief in white supremacy, but that Kipling, for all his chanting the popular beliefs, felt deep within himself a certain conflict about them. He was all for technological improvements, like sanitation and transportation, while savagely opposed to any attempt at changing Indian culture and beliefs. The other Anglo-Indians had not been "bought into India" as he had, and did not have the unconscious idea that they were half Asiatic. At the very deepest level, Kipling could identify with Indians in a way that they could not. Later on in his life, Kipling exhibited interesting contradictory beliefs, again reflecting his confusion about his origin and his identity.

One way in which he achieved some measure of a feeling of "belonging" was to become a Freemason. It was the only organization in an India split into a multitude of castes that allowed entrance to persons of all religions and levels of society. It was obviously important to Kipling that "Here I met Muslims, Hindus, Sikhs, members of the Araya and Brahmo Samaj, and a Jew tyler, who was priest and butcher to his little community in the city. So yet another world opened to me which I needed."[17]

Three things about Freemasonry attracted him; it was multi-racial; it required no physical exertion that would display his lack of coordination; and last, it excluded women—for the know-it-all Kipling was still extremely inhibited. And just as we could almost predict that he would become a Mason, we could also foresee that he would never become completely involved, study Freemasonry, rise in the ranks. All his life he enjoyed exchanging secret codes and phrases with other Masons—particularly with an American novelist, Edward Lucas White—but to become really involved in any fraternal organization requires revealing things about one's self, and this he could not do—not was unwilling to do, but *could not* do. His early life had left him with a confused sense of identity; his beliefs, philosophy, goals in life, relationships with others, were often muddled, obscure, and sometimes contradictory. Behavior that has been accurately described as an "obsession with privacy" partly came from this confusion. It arose from his struggles to achieve a secure sense of himself, a problem that originated in his childhood. With this insecurity, he avoided introspection, and revealing anything personal that could be pounced on and used against him—the sort of attack that Mrs. Holloway had carried out.

In the spring of 1885, Kipling had a chance to go on an adventuresome hiking trip up the Himalaya-Tibet road, climbing in the foothills to a height of nine thousand feet. Indulging a sort of adolescent curiosity, he went on the trip with a young couple on their delayed honeymoon! We don't know if the choice was his or theirs. But we can be sure that normal strong sexual feelings were aroused in him. In a brief diary, now in the Houghton Library, that he kept at very irregular intervals for a few months, he described the mission-station at Kotgarh, feeling that the attractiveness of the voluptuous hill-women would more than compensate for the isolation of the mission. He wrote, "Very pretty females. Small wonder that the padre has a charge of fornication preferred against him by non-converts. Should like to be padre in these parts."[18]

In May he left his companions and returned to civilization, having to control the quarrelsome bearers all by himself. He always remembered taking on this frightening responsibility and succeeding at it.

Toward the end of May, in the hot season, Kipling was again hard at work in Lahore, living with his mother and sister. Lockwood Kipling returned to Simla, and Alice and Trix went there to join him, staying, as they had in 1883, with James Walker. A man called Hayes and his wife were also visitors when Kipling joined the rest of the family there. He wrote in his diary, "Wish they wouldn't put married couple next door to me with one 1/2 inch plank between. Saps one's morality." Then, three days later, there is a carefully enigmatic note. "My own affair entirely. A wet day but deuced satisfactory."

These ambiguous words, indicating, seemingly, some sort of sexual experience, along with several other such notes, lead me to the firm conclusion that Kipling's "diary" was not a diary in the usual sense of the word, a personal record to be kept from others. His usual practice was to destroy all records that would reveal anything about himself, but he carefully preserved this "diary" and meant it to be read by others. As in the plots of many of his stories, he is saying, "Make what you like of it. I'm not giving you any information."

What an exotic place Simla was! The hill-station was perched on a mountaintop, seven thousand feet above the Indian plains. As it grew, and buildings were added, they clung to the edge of the steep hills. The only flat place in the town was the polo field. Rough roads ran about, with precipitous drop-offs at many a corner. Here, during the hot season, came the men who ruled all India.

The place abounded in "characters," mysterious foreigners, drifters, spies, mystics, and eccentrics of every type imaginable. In addition, fifteen or twenty thousand plainsmen came up with their masters, because the hillmen had a reputation for being poor servants. The native bazaars were full of intrigue and rumors. There was a shop run by a man named Jacob, a "healer of sick pearls." Several of the older houses were reputedly haunted by an impressive array of ghosts.

Simla had a long-standing reputation as a shady place. The Victorians found the grass widows almost inherently suspect, for wives lived alone there for almost half the year while their husbands were buried in work down on the plains and only joined their wives for a month, or at the most two months, of vacation. Stories, quite untrue, circulated that it was a place of bejeweled luxury and unbridled sex. Actually, while some love affairs undoubtedly took place, Simla was most notable for its social and cultural activities. Parties, dances, art exhibitions and, particularly, theatrical performances were constantly taking place. Sir Walter Roper-Lawrence, a talented man who had lived all over the world, said, "I look back on Simla society as the brightest, wittiest, most refined community I ever knew."[19]

From this remarkable place, and from the native and Anglo-Indian life in Lahore, came the raw material from which Kipling fashioned his early poems and short stories.

Flo Garrard had written that she was no longer interested in him— if she ever had been—but he continued to write her, professing his undying love. He also wrote long letters to his Aunt Edith, the youngest of the Macdonald sisters, and the only one who never married. In 1884 he and Trix wrote and published in a limited edition a short book of poems consisting of imitations and parodies of famous poets. They called it *Echoes*. He sent a copy to his Aunt Edith, with warm dedicatory verses on the flyleaf, but she, for reasons best known to herself, thought that dedication was meant for Kipling's love, Flo, and that she (Aunt Edith) was just getting a copy. She therefore merely thanked him accordingly, which annoyed him greatly. He couldn't seem to win with women.

Early in 1886 he had made the acquaintance of Kay Robinson, a young man who had come out to India to work on the *Pioneer* at Allahabad. Robinson had written some verse and signed it "K. R.," which many people assumed was a reversal of Kipling's "R. K."; for never, perhaps, was there a young author so addicted to pseudonyms as Kipling. He signed his work "Nickson," "Yussuf," "Esau Mull," "E. M.," and nearly twenty other ways. When Robinson's "K. R." was mistaken for Kipling's "R. K.," Kipling wrote Robinson, and the two became friends by correspondence in 1885 and 1886. Toward the end of 1886,

Stephen Wheeler returned to England, and Kay Robinson, to Kipling's delight, came to Lahore to take his place. Unlike Wheeler, Robinson felt Kipling's abilities should be given full rein, and Kipling began writing, as his mother put it, with both hands and a pen in his mouth. The space allotted to him was a "turnover"—a column that began on the first page and ended on the second—so he was limited to about 2,500 words.

It is to Robinson that we are indebted for the vivid pictures of Kipling in India that have come down to us. He recalls, "He was always the best of good company, bubbling over with delightful humor."[20] Their conferring about some aspect of the newspaper was usually in the midst of "fits of laughter." He remarks on

> the amount of ink [Kipling] used to throw about . . . by the day's end he was spotted all over like a Dalmatian dog. He had a habit of dipping his pen frequently and deep into the ink-pot, and as all his movements were abrupt, almost jerky,* the ink used to fly. When he darted into my room . . . I had to shout to him to "stand off"; otherwise, as I knew by experience, the abrupt halt he would make, and the flourish with which he placed the proof in his hand before me, would send the penful of ink—he always had a *full* pen in his hand**—flying over me. Driving or sometimes walking home to breakfast in his light attire plentifully besprinkled with ink, his spectacled face peeping out under an enormous, mushroom-shaped pith hat, Kipling was a quaint-looking object.

And yet, Robinson remembers, he produced an astounding amount of work.

> . . .[I]f you want to find a man who will cheerfully do the office work of three men, you should catch a young genius. Like a blood horse between the shafts of a coal wagon, he may go near to bursting his heart in the effort, but he'll drag that wagon along as it ought to go. The amount of "stuff" that Kipling got through in the day was indeed wonderful; and . . . I am sure that more solid work was done in that office when Kipling and I worked together than ever before or after.

*Note here he is also commenting on Kipling's clumsiness.
**Robinson here refers, of course, to a dip pen; fountain pens had only just been invented, and had not yet found their way to India.

V

"KUPPELEEN SAHIB" II

During this winter of 1886-87, Kipling, just turning twenty-one, began to write the verses and stories that later, as *Departmental Ditties* and *Plain Tales from the Hills*, won him his first fame. What had he written up to this point? Besides his work for his school newspaper, he had had three things published. While he was still a schoolboy, his mother had collected poems that he wrote and persuaded her husband to publish a small edition called *Schoolboy Lyrics*. She did this without obtaining her son's permission! He did not find out about their publication until some time after his return to India. He was so furious that he scarcely spoke to his mother for three days—justifiably, I would say. It shows how interested Alice and Lockwood Kipling were in his career, but it also shows how high-handed Alice Kipling could be. *Echoes*, the book he wrote with his sister, has already been mentioned. In 1885, after they had all been together for part of the hot season at Simla, they published *Quartette*, to which all four of them contributed. It contained two of Kipling's better pieces, "The Strange Ride of Morrowbie Jukes," and "The Phantom Rickshaw." But *Plain Tales from the Hills*, Kipling's first book of stories, holds the most interest for us. Published in 1888, almost all of the tales had first appeared on the pages of the *Gazette*. They are short, vivid, arresting stories, usually revolving around a striking incident or episode, rather like a tale told at a dinner table by a masterful raconteur. Almost half the stories are about the Anglo-Indian society at Simla during the hot season, written in a gossipy, scandal-mongering way that immediately attracted attention across India. In some ways they are the work of a beginner—he wrote one story, "The Gate of the Hundred Sorrows," when he was eighteen—but the beginner is obviously amazingly precocious. They are well written. An outstanding feature is the author's use of vivid visual detail. This brilliance of observation, occasionally at the expense of character, was to mark his work all his life. I suggest a relationship between his emphasis on visual detail and his preoccupation with blindness, dating back to his days in the hands of Mrs. Holloway. In the Outward Bound edition, *Plain Tales from the Hills* consists of thirty-eight stories. I wish to point out two elements; first Kipling's difficulty with identity, particularly racial identity, and second, his emphasis on vision, or the absence of vision—blindness.

Kipling's confusion about identity can be seen repeatedly in nine of the thirty-eight stories, where the tale turns on one man being mistaken for another, or one woman for another, or a white man for an Indian, or a man for a woman.* "His Wedded Wife" is an example. An inept young Subaltern "with a waist like a girl's"[1] arrives at a post in India; the other officers, down on him, nickname him "The Worm." A Senior Subaltern is particularly mean; and "The Worm" bets him he will be able to play a successful trick on him to pay him back. One night all of the officers are chatting together and the Senior Subaltern is boasting about his fiancée, soon to join him in India. Suddenly a woman comes out of the darkness and asks, "'Where is my husband?' Four men jumped up as if they had been shot. Three of them were married men," says Kipling, as if with a grin. He gives a photographic picture of the circle of startled men— "Another was chewing his mustache and smiling quietly as if he were witnessing a play." The sobbing woman throws her arms around the Senior Subaltern and tells, in spite of his protestations of innocence, how they were married in England a year and a half before. Everyone is

---

*Some of the titles are also suggestive, such as "In Error," "False Dawn," and "On the Strength of a Likeness." (And in looking at a random list of forty short stories by other writers at the time, I find no name suggesting difficulty in identity.)

horrified until, of course, the "woman" is revealed to be the "The Worm" in disguise.

The narrator is clearly Kipling. He dotes on the military, he suffers from the heat, he is a journalist who must get the paper out, he is unconventional in his wanderings about the city, he believes anything can happen in India, and he has an unconscious feeling that he has two mothers, one Indian and the other white. Surely a cautious "or anyhow, the narrator" is unnecessary.

In another story, "False Dawn," a man called Suamarez is interested in two sisters; most people at the station decide he prefers the elder one and arrange a picnic so that he can propose to her. (Was Kipling thinking of his parents? His father proposed to his mother at a picnic, and he had an unconscious feeling he had two mothers.) Everyone rides out to the picnic-ground, but after they get there, a dust storm sweeps in; at its height the younger sister comes stumbling to Kipling, gropes for her horse, and gallops away, very upset. Suamarez then comes and shouts in Kipling's ear that he has always loved the younger sister, but, blinded (there it is) by the storm, he proposed to the elder by mistake. Kipling rides off after the younger sister, who had overheard the proposal, and brings her back; Suamarez explains his mistake and kisses her, and everything is straightened out. "It was like a scene in a theatre, and the likeness was heightened by all the dust-white, ghostly-looking men and women under the orange-trees clapping their hands—as if they were watching a play—at Suamarez's choice."[2]

Two of the stories are about Strickland, a favorite character Kipling returned to again and again. As mentioned before, he could pass as a native among the natives themselves. He had "dabbled in unsavory places . . . among the native riff-raff. He educated himself in this peculiar way for seven years."[3] (This was just the sort of roaming among the natives that Kipling himself did during *his* seven years in India.) In one story, Strickland is in love with a girl whose parents forbid his seeing her. He then "turns native" and becomes her *sais*, or groom, who accompanies her whenever she is out riding. He protects her from a General who becomes a little too amorous, and reveals his disguise; the General is amused, and admits that he was acting out of line. He offers to go and put in a good word for Strickland with her parents. They reconsider, and give their consent to his marriage to their daughter. She makes him promise not to pull his trick of "becoming a native," however. Kipling goes on: "Strickland was far too fond of his wife, just then, to break his word, but it was a sore trial to him; for the streets and the bazaars, and the sounds in them, were full of meaning to Strickland, and these called to him to come back and take up his wanderings and his discoveries."

Carrington, the official biographer, merely mentions Strickland, and Angus Wilson dismisses him contemptuously as an "unconvincing Sherlock Holmes of all disguises."[4] Though it is true that Strickland may not be the most successful of Kipling's creations, we must fix our attention on him and what he represents. Sherlock Holmes made himself look like an old man, a cripple, a vagrant—but never a person of a different race. That, of course, is the whole point of Strickland's change. When he disguises himself as a *sais* in one story and a *faquir* in another, he becomes what might be termed "a man who seems to belong but does not"—and he is the direct literary ancestor of Mowgli, who in turn has a similar relationship to Kipling's triumph, Kim, the Little Friend of all the World, who lets us see both the white and native sides of India. Kipling's initial steps along this enchanting trail are visible in excerpts from other *Plain Tales*—an authority "did not know that no man can tell what natives think unless he mixes with them with the varnish off."[5] Or, "A man should, whatever happens, keep to his own caste, race and breed."[6] All his life, this theme kept recurring in everything he wrote because of his own confusing childhood.

Plain Tales from the Hills contains much of the violence, often verging on sadism, that Kipling had to guard against all his life. The cruelty is not dealt out by Fate, nor is it that of man toward animals, but rather is of one human being toward another—often a woman's cruelty toward a man. When he speaks of brutality to animals, it is merely as a symbol of brutality to humans. In "False Dawn," he states that "Very many women took an interest in Suamarez, perhaps, because his manner to them was offensive. If you hit a pony over the nose at the outset of your acquaintance, he may not love you, but he will take a deep interest in your movements ever afterwards."[7]

"Thrown Away" is a story that is frequently cited as an example of

Kipling's deep sense of pity. It begins with a short poem describing the "breaking" of wild horses:

> Some—there are losses in every trade—
> Will break their hearts ere bitted and made,
> Will fight like fiends as the rope cuts hard,
> And die dumb-mad in the breaking-yard.[8]

The story is about a young man, called The Boy (no proper names are used throughout), a sensitive, overprotected lad who gets bogged down with details about his work after arriving in India. He becomes depressed and upset; and "*the* thing" that finally sinks him is a "cruel little sentence" that a woman throws at him. He asks for leave to "shoot big game" near an isolated house some miles away. Kipling and "the Major" ride out to check up on him and hear, from inside the house, "the brr-brr-brr of a multitude of flies." The Boy has "shot his head nearly to pieces with his revolver." Kipling and the Major are touched by the suicide note; the Major weeps openly. Then begins a "grimly comic scene" wherein the two concoct "a big, written lie, bolstered with evidence, to soothe The Boy's people at Home." They decide to pretend he died of cholera, and Kipling drafts a letter to this effect. Choking with emotion, Kipling finds himself laughing, and both men begin drinking whiskey. They decide to send a lock of the boy's hair back, but "there were reasons we could not find a lock fit to send." He cuts off a bit of the Major's hair since he, like The Boy, has black hair, and the family will be fooled. They go outside and walk, and Kipling "know[s] now exactly how a murderer feels." They bury The Boy, and the Major tells how "he himself had once gone into the same Valley of the Shadow as The Boy . . . so he understood how things fought together in The Boy's poor jumbled head." They return to the military post and their story of The Boy's death is believed, though they feel "more like murderers than ever."

Pity is there, no doubt about it; Kipling tells the tragic story of a young life that is "thrown away" (because of a woman), but in the laughter, the whiskey, the "feeling like murderers," the deception, there is a sense of participation, an unfortunate relish at the horrible death, that weakens the story as a whole. Throughout Kipling's life he struggled, usually successfully, to prevent the element of violence, the bullying, the pleasure in inflicting pain, from contaminating his work.

We can understand why the cruelties described in the *Plain Tales* are more commonly inflicted by women than by men. As seen in his relationship with Flo Garrard, he felt ineffectual around women. He saw them as fascinating but frightening, delightful but dangerous, an exaggeration of what we so often see in teenagers. And, again, if Kipling looked like thirty, he often felt and acted like fifteen. His attitude, indeed, was strikingly similar to the style of these stories as a whole—condescending, extremely cocksure and know-it-all, implying secret knowledge—attitudes that appeared in his writing and in his personal life over the next fifty years, often to an unfortunate degree.

Kipling's two main women characters in these stories are Mrs. Hauksbee and Mrs. Reiver. Although there are times when they are kind and helpful, for the most part they are manipulative, powerful, and evil. (Their names are significant. By "Hauksbee," close to "hawksbill," Kipling meant to suggest a sharp-eyed ferocity, and a "reiver," in Scottish dialect, is one who plunders and robs.) They could be termed "vindictively maternal." They refer to the men about them as "boys" and make them powerless. One man is "bound hand and foot"[9] and later learns "to fetch and carry like a dog, and to wait like one, too, for a word from Mrs. Reiver." (These women are portrayed as so malignant and castrating that one critic commented, "Only a man who knew nothing of women and was totally blind to sex could have devised Mrs. Hauksbee.")[10]

Gradually, over the years, Kipling was able to transcend this terrifying female image, which of course comes from his childhood experiences with Mrs. Holloway, and to portray women—white women, that is—as capable of loving and being loved.

His portrayal of Indian women is, as we might expect, very different. As in "Without Benefit of Clergy," the men and the women must suffer for their transgressions, the women more than the men. In *Plain Tales from the Hills*, one story, "Beyond the Pale" (with an intentional double meaning to the word *pale*, of course) tells of a man called Trejago, who, like Kipling, used to defy accepted behavior and wander all about the native parts of the city. In a dark alley he stumbles and falls, and a lovely laugh comes from behind a metal grate set in the wall. Trejago seeks its source and, concealed by a cloak, he finally meets Bisesa, a beautiful fifteen-year-old widow. The grating in the wall had been dislodged, leaving "a square of rough masonry into which an active man might climb."[11]

Then begins a period of dream-like bliss; he truly loves the childlike Bisesa, who knows little of the world outside her room. During the daytime he "put on his calling-clothes and called on the ladies of the Station; wondering how long they would know him if they knew of poor little Bisesa." He then has to fill in at a party and be with one of these women, talk with her at the Bandstand, and drive with her once or twice. He never imagines this would matter to Bisesa, but when she finds out, she orders him to leave, never to see her again. He goes off remonstrating, but returns after some weeks to the dark alley. He knocks at the grating. "There was a young moon, and one stream of light fell down . . . and struck the grating, which was drawn away as he knocked. From the black dark, Bisesa held out her arms into the moonlight. Both hands had been cut off at the wrists, and the stumps were nearly healed." A weapon is thrust out at him, wounding him in "the groin, and he limped slightly from the wound for the rest of his days." He cannot discover which house she lived in, and the grating "has been walled up." The story ends with Trejago "reckoned a very decent sort of man. There is nothing peculiar about him, except a slight stiffness, caused by a riding-strain, in the right leg." This theme of love between people of two races, a bit slick, "knowing," and precocious in its presentation here, was to return in full flower, with none of these faults, three years later, in "Without Benefit of Clergy."

The primitive life of India, the superstitions, the violence, the ever-present possibility of death, were all things of which the Home English were blissfully unaware. Kipling set about making them aware, in no uncertain terms, of what happened in the native quarters, the city of dreadful night.

Kipling's view of Indians was largely the conventional one of the times: the natives were inherently childish, irresponsible, and would always need the British to take care of them. Again he returned to the metaphor of vision when he described a typical Englishman's feelings about an Indian's inability to govern himself: "See!" said the Englishman, "he is blind on that side—blind by birth, training, instinct and associations."[12] If an Indian went to England, and attended, say, Eton and Oxford, it made no difference to Kipling and his contemporaries. He was then just a "hybrid, University-trained mule"[13] who was mouthing phrases and concepts that meant nothing to him.

Carrington states it is "unjust"[14] to claim that Kipling believed in "the absolute superiority of certain racial types." This is a denial of racism on Kipling's part. Yet there can be no doubt that Kipling was an out-and-out racist, along with the vast majority of Anglo-Indians. He may even have been a fanatic on the subject. He had been brought up by his *ayah* (whom he thought of as entirely under his command) and spoke Hindustani as his primary language. He may have been passionate in his conviction that the Indians were truly inferior; that they were too unreliable, too unpredictable, to be allowed to have authority over themselves. And yet he felt real love for the Indians—as long as they submissively accepted British rule. This was the loophole in Kipling's thinking; the Indians were admirable people, but only as subjects, never seen as equal to whites.

In contrast, the Liberals, steadily rising in power over these years, were anti-imperalist and antiracist and increasingly opposed his views. For the rest of his life Kipling, at the furthest extremity of the right wing, vehemently attacked the Liberals as intellectuals and spineless "softies" who were so naive that they believed that the Indians should be allowed to have self-government. In return the Liberals branded Kipling as a racist, one who believed that "pure blood," even in minute fractions, actually determines a man's behavior, and, sometimes, even whether he should live or die. This notion, so accepted one hundred years ago and so offensive now, is shown in "His Chance in Life." Miss Vezzis, a nurse, was part Portuguese and part Indian (like Kipling's *ayah*). She is courted by Michele D'Cruze, a telegraph operator, who "looked down on natives as only a man with seven-eighths native blood in his veins can."[15] Her parents consent to a marriage if he can raise his salary to at least fifty rupees a month—there being no prospect of this whatsoever. But Michele is sent to a remote outpost where, three weeks later, a riot breaks out between Hindus and Mohammedans. The local police turn to him for leadership, and, although terrified, he quells the disorder and telegraphs for help. However, the next morning, when meeting the white man sent to support him, Michele finds himself breaking into a "hysterical outburst of tears." "It was the White drop in Michele's veins dying out, though he did not know it." (But he gets the raise and is able to marry Miss Vezzis.)

Kipling's real love of Indians, particularly Indian children, emerges in "The Story of Muhammad Din." Kipling's man servant, Imam Din, asks for and is given an old polo ball that his "little son"[16] wants for a toy. Kipling lovingly describes tiny Muhammad Din, the little son, and his delighted arranging of the half-buried polo ball in the middle of an area, a circle of flowers stuck around it, a square of bits of brick and shell about that, and finally a mound of sand around the whole. But Kipling, taking an evening's stroll, does not see (blindness again) the spot and destroys it by walking through it. He tells the tearful Muhammad Din that he can make whatever he pleases, and the child begins even bigger and more elaborate creations. A sea-shell is added, and Kipling expects this to be used in some truly splendid way. "Nor was I disappointed. He meditated for the better part of an hour, and his crooning rose to a jubilant song. Then he began tracing in the dust. It would certainly be a wondrous palace, this one, for it was two yards long and a yard broad in ground-plan. But the palace was never completed." The next day there was no Muhammad Din to greet him as he returned from work. Told that he is ill, Kipling gets medicine and an English doctor, who says, as he leaves his patient, "They have no stamina, these brats." "A week later, though I would have given much to have avoided it, I met on the road to the . . . burying-ground Imam Din . . . carrying in his arms, wrapped in a white cloth, all that was left of little Muhammad Din."

Toward the end of 1887 Kipling was transferred from the *Gazette* in Lahore to work at the *Pioneer*, much larger and more important—in fact, the leading newspaper in India—in Allahabad, six hundred miles southeast in what is now north central India (Lahore is in present-day Pakistan). Going to Allahabad, on the Ganges, also meant a change from Muslim India to Hindu India. It meant leaving his family to whom he had become so devoted; but he was now more self-confident, eager to make his mark in the literary world, and was not homesick for Lahore. He was no longer limited to 2,500 words as he had been on the little *Gazette*, and began to pour out three and four thousand words a week. Since the paper would take anything their young genius produced, some of it was of the worst quality. He missed the restraining influence of his parents.

In Allahabad he fortunately had an excellent Muslim servant, for Kipling was absent-minded, disorganized, and needed someone to keep things in place. He joined the local Masons, carefully choosing the one organization that was most multi-racial in its makeup. Here is an example of the contradictions typical of Kipling, who could sneer at Michele D'Cruze's drop of English blood fading away and leaving him in hysterics, nevertheless joined the Lodge with the greatest variety of races in among members. India was home, but it wasn't. His *ayah* was his mother, but she wasn't. His childhood confusion appears again and again.

Soon after his arrival he met Mr. and Mrs. S. A. Hill. "Alec" Hill was a professor of science at a college in Allahabad; his wife Edmonia, who had the nickname "Ted,"* was to play a curious and important role in Rudyard Kipling's life. She was then twenty-nine, seven years his senior. She was an attractive, charming American woman, intelligent, soft-spoken, and, unlike many Victorian Englishwomen, unafraid to state her opinion if she disagreed about something.[17] Her dark hair met on her forehead in a widow's peak. She wrote her sister Caroline back in Pennsylvania that Rudyard Kipling

> looks about forty, as he is beginning to be bald, but he is in reality just twenty-two. He was animation itself, telling his stories admirably, so that those about him were kept in gales of laughter. He fairly scintillated, but when more sober topics were discussed, he was posted along all lines. . . . Evidently the rising young author had marked me for an American, and, seeking copy perhaps, he came to the fireplace where I was standing and began questioning me about my homeland. I am surprised at his knowledge of people and places. He is certainly worth knowing.[18]

A few weeks later, in January 1888, *Plain Tales from the Hills* was published, and he gave her a copy with a long introduction in verse that amused her. His friendship with her quickly became an intense one. He was a frequent dinner guest at their home. She immediately influenced what he wrote. He worked up plots from incidents in her life, and used names she suggested in his stories. In her straightforward American

---

*I usually put a nickname in quotation marks only when first used; when a masculine name, like "Ted" or "William," is given to a woman, to avoid confusion I will use them throughout.

way, she criticized aspects of his writing that she found disagreeable (one might guess that this involved the violence and sadism in some stories). This delighted him, although it produced no basic changes in his work.

Whenever he was free, he was with her. The two of them engaged in long, animated discussions. When the *Pioneer* sent him off to cover some event, he wrote her letters almost daily until his return. These letters, long and well written, describe his experiences but also contain pleasant remarks and jokes aimed at "Ted." Everyone was busy identifying the real-life people who had appeared as fictional characters in *Plain Tales from the Hills*, and Kipling had a fine time teasing her about her guesses. But, almost as if he had this in mind, they are letters even the most jealous husband could read without finding evidence that Kipling's warm feelings toward her had crossed the line separating friendship from romantic love. In March he was sent to Calcutta, the capital under British rule, where again his perceptive eye seemed to miss nothing. As always, he roamed the city at night, this time going so far as to make the rounds with the vice squad of the Calcutta police. They continued to exchange letters, in which Alec was seldom mentioned. After returning to Allahabad in April, in July he moved in as a guest with the Hills and stayed in their home for nine months, until March 1889, when he accompanied them to America. During the hot season, while they were up in the hills at Mussoorie, he stayed in their house alone.

In view of Kipling's daily attention and obvious feelings for another man's wife, nowadays we would ask why Mr. Hill didn't object to all this. The answer is that, so far as can be ascertained, he didn't mind in the least, and if this seems surprising, it should be explained that attitudes about this sort of relationship were very different a hundred years ago. They were a social phenomenon, now vanished, that can only be understood in the light of the customs and feelings of the Victorian era.

With the emphasis on class, social standing, "correct" behavior, and a horror of divorce, Victorian marriages were sometimes marriages in name only. When love between the partners disappeared, the husband or wife would often begin a deep, intense friendship with another woman or man in the community, often a person of high social standing about whom no question of impropriety would ever be raised. In this friendship the companionship and love that were lacking in the marriage would, to some extent, be found; and in view of the extreme emphasis on proper behavior it was understood from the beginning that no overt expression of love, or physical intimacy of any kind, would ever occur. Of course, the convenient rationalization "He or she is only a friend" allowed a lot of sexual feelings to emerge, some recognized and some not (as in Shaw's *Candida* and Marquand's *The Late George Apley*). We do not know what the real relationship was between the Hills. It is entirely possible, although there is no proof, that something of this sort was taking place; that love was lacking in their marriage and that she welcomed this young man's fervent, although adolescent, feelings for her.

When we look at Kipling's side of things, we find evidence that seems to support this hypothesis. He confided in her a great deal, more, it would seem, than in anyone else during his entire seven years in India. He told her about his schooldays, where "his great sorrow was that he could not enter the army, owing to his poor eyesight, and it was particularly hard for him to associate constantly with those who were preparing for the Service." But it was late in 1888 that he confided in her the most. With his parents up at Lahore—what did he think about their reading it?—he found himself writing "Baa Baa, Black Sheep." He was an unknown writer of twenty-two; he was about to set out on an eight-month trip to London with his friends the Hills; he did not know he stood at the threshold of one of the most successful literary careers in English history. In the midst of his tales of India, the military, the burning heat, the delicious scandals at Simla, there suddenly appears this passionate and moving account of a boy brought up in loving surroundings in India with his sister. The two are then left for years with strangers in a house in England where hatred and brutality reign. "Ted" described his writing the story:

> It was pitiful to see Kipling living over the experience, pouring out his soul in the story, as the drab life was worse than he could possibly describe it. His eyesight was permanently impaired, and as he had heretofore only known love and tenderness, his faith in people was sorely tried. When he was writing this he was a sorry guest, as he was in a towering rage at the recollection of those days.

He told her of being left in the house, reading every book there, and then, "forlorn indeed, having strained his eyes and being utterly alone, he entertained himself by measuring the whole house hand over hand."

As I have said, Kipling had always been haunted by the question, "How could they have done this to me?" It is significant that he told "Ted" that the reason why his parents had taken him and his sister to England and left them there was not the heat back in India, but the pernicious influence of native servants on Anglo-English children. They spoil them, he explained; the servant is "a slave to every whim, [and the child] grows too domineering to suit the fancy of an English parent. No self-reliance can be learned while under the pampering care of *bearer* or *ayah*." Now this explanation is accurate, although incomplete; Anglo-English parents in those days were indeed concerned about the influence of native servants on their children. If Kipling had stayed behind in Bombay, lord of his little world, he would probably have emerged spoiled and irresponsible, and not have become the writer he did. The years in the House of Desolation did not interfere with his creativity—indeed, they enhanced it. I will return to this later. But in his conclusions about servants, one can see the confusion of his childhood being compounded. For years he felt his "Asiatic" mother was good, his "white" mother bad; now the two are reversed. And although he arrives at a solution to the basic question of why he and his sister had to leave India, the other questions—why didn't you warn us, why didn't you say goodbye, why did you leave us with strangers, why didn't you come back in all those years?—are left unanswered.

"Baa Baa, Black Sheep" is a remarkable story, one of the most powerful Kipling ever produced. Down to the smallest detail it is autobiographical, under the thinnest veneer of fiction,* the only thing of its kind that Kipling ever wrote. Why did this man, who later in life had strong feelings about privacy, suddenly, in the midst of Indian stories, write about his childhood, the most upsetting time in his life? Present-day readers are not puzzled by this. We know that our most important memories from childhood "must out," be they happy or unhappy, and that the unhappy ones, the guilty ones, the ones we may be most de-

---

*He didn't mention the soul-saving yearly visit to his relatives; and in real life he may not have called the Holloways "Auntie Rosa" and "Uncle Harry," since their Christian names were Pryse and Sarah. The name Rosa, as Green has perceptively pointed out, may well have come from a song Uncle Harry used to sing about the Battle of Navarino, where "Rose" was the name of a ship of the line. In other places Kipling likens women to fighting ships. Their son's name, however, actually was Harry.

termined to hide, can be most counted on to be seen. Under the influence of "Ted" Hill, so warm and encouraging an audience, so unlike his sparkling but sharp-tongued mother, out they came. Like the central figure in one of his stories, "Wressley of the Foreign Office," "his heart and soul were at the end of his pen."

His feelings for "Ted" Hill—who, I presume, was the first American he ever knew—were very strong. They were never directly stated, but can certainly be seen in his actions and writing. At the time, a friend of Kipling's was having a love affair and used to drop by his quarters and pour out his feelings about what was going on till all hours of the morning. (The friend certainly spoke freely to the young journalist; one suspects he had fantasies of being immortalized in print, which, as a matter of fact, his listener immediately attempted to do.) Kipling, predictably, took it all in with fascination, and then wrote a detailed account to "Ted." He also used the material for a short novel called "The Story of the Gadsbys," which, set down in the form of a dialogue, is really more a play than a novel. Very juvenile and artificial, the story reveals how little the cocksure Kipling, who could tell you all about India and the military, understood women. "Ted's" letters to her mother and sister reveal that he asked her all sorts of questions about people in love, certainly suggesting a more-than-objective interest in the subject.

Then he began writing her about a person with whom *he* was in love. He referred to her as "My Lady." I worship My Lady; I will love her till I die; what a pang to the heart to know that My Lady does not love me as I love her—these are the sort of things he wrote "Ted." And who was My Lady? You probably think it's Tillie, he wrote; well, it's not. And it's not Miss Parry-Lambert; and you think it's Ethel? No, it's not Ethel. It becomes rather obvious who His Lady really was. It is possible that he addressed her in this fashion because, in a typically Victorian way, it expressed romantic love. But looking at other letters, one can see that his relationship with "Ted" was fundamentally a dependent one, that of a son to a mother, rather than that between a would-be lover and his beloved. In another letter some months later, he writes from Lahore, where he went to visit his family; he feels very bored; Mrs. Hill's pastry is far superior to his mother's; and he then recounts how he went to his father's museum and twirled the turnstile until it registered many more visitors coming in than actually did so.

This is the sort of prank that a ten-year-old might recount with glee to his mother, but hardly a man who had just become twenty-three. Accurately enough, Kipling himself refers to his "immaturity" at this time as being "indecent"[20] in degree.

As one might expect, he had accompanying preadolescent feelings about marriage—he was against it. He greatly admired the man of action, the brave soldier, the energetic administrator; but we hear little of their relationships with their wives. At this time he wrote the poem containing his well-known line, "A woman is only a woman, but a good cigar is a smoke."[21] He recounted with approval the edict of some commanding officers that no officer under them be married. In "The Story of the Gadsbys," the captain is presented as spoiling his career by falling in love and marrying, and a friend says decisively "A young man married is a young man marred."[22] The captain himself says, "Marriage—even as good a marriage as mine has been—hampers a man's work, it cripples his sword-arm, and oh, it plays Hell with his notions of duty." At the end of the story, Kipling sums up his feelings in a poem, with perhaps the first of his well-known lines:

> High hopes faint on a warm hearth-stone—
> He travels the fastest who travels alone.

In the gigantic subcontinent of India, a chaos of varying faiths, races, and cultures, the Army man—so erect, so trim, his uniform a model of correctness, who radiated a feeling of knowing his job—embodied solidity, a sense of belonging, that appealed to Kipling. The civil administrators had even greater responsibilities, but Kipling preferred the military—a group to which he knew he could never belong because of his poor eyesight. Nevertheless, that very eyesight enabled him to observe and leave a picture of military life that is unequaled—the beet-red sergeants bellowing orders, the loneliness, the heat, the heat, the heat. Others wrote about generals; Kipling wrote about "Tommy Atkins," the name given to the average British soldier, and made it famous.* It is unfortunate that his stories of this period, collected in two volumes of

---

*More than fifty years later, in World War II, the Germans sometimes still referred to their British opponents as "Tommies."

Soldiers Three and in *Under the Deodars and Other Stories*, are seldom read nowadays. They are excellent. He portrays the life of the average soldier with unsentimentalized truth: sent to India to do a difficult job, they do it well, in the face of depression, illness, and torment; they are "damned from here to Eternity."[23] His "soldiers three," Mulvaney, Learoyd, and Ortheris, emerge as three well-drawn characters, with their joys and sorrows, their hopes and memories. What holds them together and makes life possible is a sense of belonging, their companionship, and it is no coincidence that the first story in which they appear is called "The Three Musketeers."

Two other stories, "The Drums of the Fore and Aft," and "The Man Who Would Be King," should be mentioned. In the first, an over-confident regiment wavers and almost collapses in its encounter with the enemy. The day is saved by two drummer-boys, about fourteen, who rally the retreating men by marching alone straight toward the enemy, playing "The British Grenadiers." The regiment regroups and attacks; and defeat is turned to victory. But—a typical Kipling twist—the drummer-boys do this as no noble act of heroism. They are a pair of lying guttersnipes, foul-mouthed little devils who get away with whatever they can; and they march toward the enemy because they are so drunk with rum that they don't know what they are doing. They are cut down in the crossfire, and their part in the battle is carefully ignored in the official account.

"The Man Who Would Be King" is one of Kipling's best stories. Kipling tells of two men, Peachy Carnehan and Daniel Dravot (the latter's name was suggested to Kipling by Mrs. Hill), who decided to start a kingdom of their own, far in the north of India. Kipling tells the men their plan can only end in their deaths. Any such a Western notion of setting up their own kingdom defies ancient, immutable Eastern ways and beliefs. The men set off but three summers later Dravot comes crawling into Kipling's office a broken man, and tells of Carnehan's death in their kingdom; Dravot dies two days later. In India, Kipling is saying in both stories, death is very different from death in England. There death comes as an ending to a long life; it is inevitable and natural; to some extent it can be accepted. It would be seen as rare in anyone young and healthy. But in India death is everywhere, striking at random in its terrifying way. There is no accounting for it, no avoiding it.

Kipling learned this in his childhood when his brother died during the hot season, and when a child's hand was found in the Kiplings' garden in Bombay—the rest of the body, he found out from his *ayah*, having been eaten by vultures.

"The Strange Ride of Morrowbie Jukes" is another horror story of India. Far out in the desert, Jukes, a civil engineer, finds himself caught in a horseshoe-shaped depression, with sandy sides too steep to climb, and a quicksand across the mouth. Caught there with him are natives who tell him that he, like they, will remain there until he dies. In a moment Jukes is reduced from his lofty position as a white sahib, one of the ruling English, to being a helpless victim in the trap, worse off than the lowliest Indian. It is a living death, for there is no escape but death itself. (Though Kipling, in an unsatisfactory ending, provides a rescuer for Jukes.)

In a third story, "At the End of the Passage," Kipling tells us again that no white man can understand the mystery of death in India. In a remote outpost four men meet, having traveled great distances, for their weekly game of cards. The heat is overpowering. One man, Hummil, whose assistant has just died, talks of suicide. He is troubled (as Kipling was) by insomnia and this, along with fatigue, drives him back to "a terrified childhood."[24] He is tormented by an image of "A blind face that cries and can't wipe its eyes," a good line. Though treated by a doctor, Hummil dies, but the other men then see something on the surface of his eyes, something one of the men is able to photograph—presumably an image of the face Hummil spoke of—which causes the horrified photographer to destroy the film and to say shakily that the whole thing is impossible and best forgotten.

Other stories that Kipling wrote around this time shed light on his idyllic childhood in India.

In "The Story of the Gadsbys," women are described as "weak sisters" who interfere with masculine military duties. And yet, after the disappointing first three-quarters of the play, with its juvenile worship of the military, it comes to an effective climax when Mrs. Gadsby, who is due to give birth during the hot season, nearly dies, and the baby with her. Their lives are saved by the old family *ayah* who, wiser than the white doctors, alters the ventilation of the room at a critical moment which lowers the mother's fever and allows a safe delivery. This story recalls Mrs. Kipling's difficulties with childbirth, the death of Kipling's brother during the hot season, and the servants' intervention that was said to have ended her difficult labor with Kipling himself.

Besides "Baa Baa, Black Sheep," already discussed, there are two other stories about children in *Under the Deodars and Other Stories*. These are "His Majesty the King" and "Wee Willie Winkie." No one could read these stories and not know that Kipling loved children; he describes their toys, their views of adults, their toddling about, in long and affectionate detail. Their baby talk is reproduced at such length that it becomes tiresome to present-day readers (as it was also to those in 1888). Kipling's love of children came from a determination that they should never undergo the horrors he had to suffer in the House of Desolation (as he tells us in the incident about the bell-pull in his aunt's house.) These stories shift to a different question, never answered, "How could they have done that to me?" These two stories, then, are not as different from "Baa Baa, Black Sheep" as they might appear at first glance; they too are partly autobiographical, as is obvious on further examination.

In both stories, the main character is a six-year-old boy. (Kipling was five when he left India, and a few days short of six when he was left at the Holloways'.) In the case of Wee Willie, several reviewers have pointed out that his thinking and actions in the story would be impossible for a six-year-old (he effectively argues down a mob of savage natives, for instance), but Kipling didn't describe him as ten or twelve, Kipling was thinking of himself when he was six. In both stories, the boys talk partly in native dialect. "Speech in any vernacular—and Wee Willie Winkie had a colloquial acquaintance with three—was easy to the boy who could not yet manage his 'r's' and 'th's' aright."[25] His Majesty the King had picked up from his white nurse a "simple theology and welded it to the legends of gods and devils that he had learned in the servants' quarters."[26] (In "Baa Baa, Black Sheep," Punch "welded the story of the Creation on to what he could recollect of his Indian fairy tales").[27] Both children have loving mother-substitutes; Wee Willie has an *ayah* and His Majesty the King has the commissioner's wife and also his white nurse, who, when the children in her care "went over the sea to the Great Unknown, which she, with touching confidence in her hearers, called 'Home,' packed up her slender belongings and sought for employment afresh, lavishing all her love on each successive batch of ingrates."[28]

Both stories have the age-old theme of a rejected child saving adults. Why is this sort of story popular? Children often feel weak and inadequate when they compare themselves with adults, who seem to have the answers for everything. They—and we, remembering our childhoods—take particular delight in having the tables turned, and having the *child* be the omnipotent one for a change.

In the first story, Wee Willie Winkie, the son of a colonel of a regiment, knows of a lieutenant's love for a Miss Allardyce. He sees her take a forbidden ride across a nearby river—dry at this time of year—into an area inhabited by savage natives. Although his parents have restricted him to the house, he gets his pony, goes after her, and finds she has fallen off the horse and sprained her ankle. He sends for help and effectively handles a group of the natives that gather and threaten to kidnap them. Rescuers arrive, including the lieutenant and the colonel, and Wee Willie emerges as the hero of the day.

In the other story, "His Majesty the King," a child is neglected by his parents, who have drifted apart after quarreling over an imagined infidelity. The child turns for love to his nurse and to the commissioner's wife, a family friend. A package is brought to the house one day; he opens it and sees a sparkling jewel. He guiltily hides it among his toys. Then at night he becomes ill and, staggering and reeling from his fever, seeks out the grownups in the house for help. Taken back to bed, half in delirium—he "could hardly see distinctly"—he gasps out his secret to the anxious figures gathered around his bed. The jewel is from a would-be lover of the wife. The parents are drawn back together and devote themselves to loving the child.

This story of a child's bringing together quarreling parents is, again, an old one, and Kipling may well have simply dusted it off and used it here. It may be, however, that the broken home represents an answer to the question of why he was left in England: "Perhaps my parents deserted me because there was some trouble between them." Kipling describes the mother of the story so as to bring to mind his own mother: the child's mother (in the story) is described as "always getting into or stepping out of the big carriage"; and Kipling's own mother "would go out to Big Dinners."[29] A further point of resemblance is that it is the emergency of illness, with clumsiness and temporary blindness, that brings love to the child; Kipling remembered that it was a similar partial blindness (described as "phenomenal clumsiness")[30] that brought his mother to rescue him from the House of Desolation.

Here should be mentioned, along with things he *did* write, something he didn't, a novel that he never finished. Too often only an author's published works are studied; it is instructive to look at the things he or she struggled with, sometimes for decades, that never quite came out right and remained unpublished.

While still in his teens, soon after returning to India, Kipling began an "Anglo-Indian novel" he called *The Book of Mother Maturin*. It was a tale of an Irish woman, in the dregs of native society, who ran an opium den (a little like the memsahib in "The Gate of the Hundred Sorrows"), but who sent her daughter to be educated in England. She married a government official and, in touch with both worlds, was a channel for disseminating official secrets to the natives and native secrets to the officials—a sort of female Strickland. This is all that is known about the novel; after working at it off and on for fifteen years or more, Kipling finally destroyed the manuscript around the turn of the century, and the few people who read it are no longer living. But struggling with it was a blessing in disguise; years later, a good deal of it reappeared in *Kim*, Kipling's greatest work.

For our purposes, two points can be made. In *Mother Maturin*, there is again a preoccupation with racial identity: "Who is Indian and who is white?" This goes back to an unconscious doubt about his own race. Mother Maturin is white, but so deeply embedded in native society that she seems more native than the natives themselves; she combines both worlds, East and West. In Kipling's first ambitious work, he writes of a mother who is, in effect, both white and Indian, and manages to bring together both worlds, so that each knows the other's secrets. East was East, and West was West, but in this and many other works Kipling tried to find a way to make the twain meet.

The second point is that Mother Maturin married an official and sent her daughter to England to be educated. It appears that here Kipling again seeks an answer to his old question—"*Why* did my parents send me off to England?" Mother Maturin, in the gutter, determines that her daughter shall have better things, and sends her "Home" for her education. It presents an answer to his question: "My parents wanted to do this for my sake, so that I could be well-educated. It doesn't mean they didn't love me."

I now turn back in time and review his sister Trix's years in India. She had arrived in December 1883, more than a year after Kipling's return. She was then fifteen. She matured into a tall, beautiful young woman, with, her father said, a radiant, merry look about her. Kay Robinson also described her beauty and her astonishing grasp of English literature; she had entirely memorized several plays of Shakespeare. In the hot season of 1885, when the family was at Simla, they were admitted into the circle of the new Viceroy, Lord Dufferin and his wife, who came to delight in the Kiplings. "Dullness and Mrs. Kipling," the Viceroy often said, "cannot exist in the same room."[31]

Alice Kipling's sprightly personality often left Trix in the shade; Kipling described their conflict in his poem "My Rival." Trix was seventeen when he wrote it. About a year later, Lord Clandeboye, the Viceroy's son and aide-de-camp, was very interested in her and wished to have the relationship become a closer one. Alice Kipling disapproved of the match and put a stop to it with her characteristic firmness. One day the Viceroy called on Mrs. Kipling to discuss the matter. "Don't you think Mrs. Kipling, your daughter should be taken to another hill-station?" "Don't you think, your Excellency, that your son should be sent home?" It was Clandeboye who went and Trix who remained. In later years Trix wrote two novels, *The Heart of a Maid* and *A Pinchbeck Goddess*, both of which are transparently autobiographical. In the latter, she describes the heroine's love for her suitor being brutally ended. "Aunt Agatha . . . had . . . shattered the potentialities of the future in a very ruthless manner."[32] Soon after her affair with Lord Clandeboye was broken off, she became engaged, at nineteen, to John Fleming, a stolid, unimaginative, colorless officer in the Survey Department. Her parents again disapproved. This time even her father, an even-tempered man who seemed never to criticize anyone or anything, was moved to the most extreme statements I have ever seen from his pen. "I don't like it. . . . I can only hope with all my heart the child is right, and that she will not one day when it is too late find her Fleming but a thin pasture, and sigh for other fields."[33] One can understand their concern. Their daughter had climbed to the peak of the social ladder at Simla; the

Viceroy's son had wanted to marry her; she was interested in literature and writing. Why would she want to marry this dull man Fleming?

In her first novel, *The Heart of a Maid*, she portrays a young woman who does not get along with her strong-minded mother. (The "Family Square," firmly united by love, and so carefully described by all the biographers, existed for the first half of Kipling's years in India, but not for the second.) The reason the mother and daughter have little in common is that the daughter, after a few years of infancy, was sent to England and never really knew her mother until she was a teen-ager. "The enforced separation of parent and child, the alienation of years, cannot be done away with in a few months."[34]

Here, unwittingly, Trix is telling us why she wanted to marry Fleming. If childhood had been upsetting to Kipling, it was much more so to Trix, who was younger and more vulnerable. Trix sensed her mental illness before it could be seen by others. Behind her beauty, behind her brilliance, she probably felt an enormous insecurity, a basic feeling that "something is wrong." Life would not always be the exotic swirl of Simla, and she chose someone who, if not a social lion, was something she needed more—a steady, protective person with endless patience and understanding. She chose very well indeed.

After announcing her engagement, she broke it off, but a year later was re-engaged to Fleming, and they planned to marry in the spring of 1889.

Kipling was now half-way through 1888, his last full year in India. Part of the summer he was back at Lahore and the *Gazette*, since he had to fill in for Kay Robinson, who was away on leave. Robinson was not oppressed by the heat, but Kipling found it more and more intolerable each year. This time, besides the usual discomforts and sleeplessness, he had heart palpitations. That last hot season at Lahore seemed endless and forced a final decision he had been considering for some time; he would leave India. Opportunities for a young author would be far better in England than in India.

From the middle of June to the middle of July he was with his family at Simla, happy, but all the happier because he was writing daily letters to "Ted." Again, everyone wondered, "How that young Kipling knows so much about everything," and Kipling himself said that the proudest moment of his young life was when he rode up Simla Mall with

Lord Roberts, the Commander-in-Chief in India, who asked him what the enlisted men were really thinking and feeling.[35] Some people felt this smart young man was a little too smart. His articles on the Indian National Congress were so bitterly sarcastic that one supporter bodily assaulted the editor of the *Pioneer* (Kipling was up at Allahabad), which resulted in the filing of suits and countersuits. One of his poems, "One Viceroy Resigns," caused offense in high circles. So while several friends—and his family—were urging Kipling to leave for England, where there would be a much better market for a young writer, some people were hoping he would leave for very different reasons. This same impulsiveness and dogmatism were to cause him problems a few months later in America.

He returned to Allahabad and his room at the Hills' house. For some weeks he had the house to himself when they went on a trip to central India, and he resumed his daily letters to Mrs. Hill. In his writing he reveals a deep ambivalence about the changes English civilization was bringing about in the old India he loved so. He praises the new machines, the sanitation, the bridges, the laws, while at the same time expressing fury at some administrator attempting to alter the age-old customs, the mystery, the rituals of an India he can never understand. Perhaps only a Strickland, who administers the law but in an Indian guise, is the answer. Strickland worked from the inside out, not the outside in.

He now decided to return to England in March of 1889, before the hot season. He began to talk about the pleasures of going to the theater and the lovely borders of Epping Forest. (The reader will recall that it was to Epping Forest that his mother took him from the House of Desolation.)

Mrs. Hill had been ill, and was to return to America with her husband for her convalescence. What would be more fun than to go to England the long way around, east instead of west, and accompany them to America? It was arranged that he would send weekly letters to the *Pioneer*, which would help to pay for the trip. Family and friends gave him a dozen or more letters of introduction to people they knew scattered across the United States. Mr. F. H. Cook, the manager of the world-famous travel agency, was a family friend—at times it seems as though *everyone* was a friend of the Kiplings—and he saw to it that they would have no trouble getting their tickets.

In June of 1889 Trix married John Fleming. Kipling was notable by his absence. He had left three months previously in March, but if he had been there he would have been reluctant to attend the ceremony. He had always been protective of his sister, and was loudly disapproving of the attentions of Lord Clandeboye, of his successor, a young journalist, and now of John Fleming. Trix was hesitant about marriage. To Alice Kipling's annoyance, she usually sought out much older men, with whom matrimony was safely out of the question, and her prospects with Lord Clandeboye were dim—marriage between nobility and a commoner would have been frowned upon. Kipling seems to have sensed his sister's hesitation and urged her to wait until she could feel more secure about her plans for the future.

VI

THE WORLD OUTSIDE INDIA—AMERICA

Kipling left India in March 1889 with the Hills. Their ship went first to Rangoon, where they took a side trip to Moulmein. Kipling's vivid memories of the pagoda and of "a Burmese girl"[1] with whom, he jokingly said, he "deeply and irrevocably" fell in love, appeared in "Mandalay" a year later. Subsequently it was set to music and became, I suppose, the best-known song Kipling ever wrote. They planned to go on to Singapore, Hong Kong, and Japan, where they would stay a month, and then proceed across the North Pacific to San Francisco, where the Hills would leave him and proceed home, and he would pursue a leisurely trip across the United States. By July he would join "Ted" who was staying with her parents and younger sister, Caroline, at Beaver, Pennsylvania, near Pittsburgh; by this time Alec would have returned to India. Then, in September, "Ted" and Caroline would set out to join him there, and Kipling would accompany them across the Atlantic to London.

During most of this time he sent a running account of the trip back to the *Pioneer* in Allahabad. Casual, humorous, articles, they were meant to be printed in the newspaper in faraway India and forgotten; but a journalist in India at that time could not secure copyright, and after Kipling became famous, "pirating" of his early works forced him to reprint them and secure his rights. Reading these articles now, one gets a clear picture of Rudyard Kipling at that time. A short, dark-haired, chunky man, he had the prominent brow, mustache, and chin that were soon to become well known. Most observers also remarked on his eyes, quick and alert, behind the ever-present glasses. Usually quiet, particularly in any large group, with a few friends he could become very animated, and reveal himself as a fascinating conversationalist. He seemed to have a calm sense of his abilities, and was never immodest or boastful. Like many of us traveling in foreign lands, he found it hard to keep an open mind about new people and new customs. His insatiable curiosity helped him here; interested people tend to be more tolerant than bored ones. Although clumsy, he liked to take chances.

He was full of contradictions. For example, take his feelings about conformity. Unlike most Victorians, he had no hesitation in acting, dressing, or speaking in a highly unconventional way. Yet, on the ship, he was shocked beyond words that a white stewardess served the passengers, offering them tea, and thus "She . . . talks standing up, to men who sit down!" Enthusiastic, tireless, he had an endless interest in what went on about him. Kipling could not have walked past a man painting a fence; he would have characteristically started questioning him. Why do you use that brand of paint? How much lead is there in it? Is that a primer coat, or a regular coat? Do you have to use different kinds of paint for different kinds of wood? And so it would go. Over and over again people who knew him remarked, "I never heard a man ask so many questions."

He had lost the abruptness of his teenage years in India; there was an exuberance about him, an undirected energy that was appealingly boyish. His remarkable power of observation and ability to describe vividly a scene were as effective as ever. His descriptions of parts of Yellowstone National Park, written a hundred years ago and long forgotten, could be used today—though Kipling, by and large, was not interested in nature. Old Faithful and the mountains of Montana got nothing more than a passing glance.

If his energy was boyish, so too was his superficiality. He believed all he was told; took in everything about him with one glance of those gleaming eyes, and then would come to his conclusion. If he often had perceptive things to say ("A hundred years hence, India and America will be worth observing. At present the one is burned out and the other is only just stoking up"),[2] at other times he failed remarkably. His description of Utah is almost that of a man looking at it through a train window; the religion of the Mormons, their industriousness, their care of the elderly, their irrigation projects—all these things, about which he could have learned so easily, were lost to him. He showed a marked inability to accept a country for what it was, to alter the viewpoint of an Englishman who had been living in India. There, with the Indian empire at its high mark, he had known only order, peace, ritual, and stability. The comparative lawlessness and violence of the West—which, after all, was only forty years removed from the days of the forty-niners—shocked him deeply.

> When the hotel clerk . . . stoops to attend to your wants, he does so whistling or humming, or picking his teeth, or pauses to converse with someone he knows. These performances, I gather, are to impress upon you that he is a free man and your equal. . . .[For the men there were] provided spittoons of infinite capacity and generous gape. Most of the men wore frock-coats and top hats . . . but they all spat. . . . They deluded themselves into the belief that they talk English—*the* English—and I have already been pitied for speaking with "an English accent." The man who pitied me spoke, so far as I was concerned, the language of thieves.

Anyone visiting another country has difficulty adapting to it and appreciating it; indeed, Americans abroad used to have the worst reputation in this regard. But Kipling didn't just have difficulty; it seemed impossible for him to accept anything. In the articles he sent back to the *Pioneer*, he criticized American speech, manners, eating, drinking, politics, the army, the navy, and anything else that crossed his mind. The young nation was being raked over the coals as it seldom had before.

The remarkable thing is that Kipling did not really dislike America. This may seem hard to believe, in view of his bitter attacks. But he was always drawn to action, as opposed to thought, and there was much about the country, the energy and drive of the people, that appealed to him. His critical remarks are often followed by warm ones; at times he seems not to know how to feel. For example, soon after the ill-tempered attacks mentioned above, he wrote,

Let there be no misunderstanding about the matter. I love this People, and if any contemptuous criticism has to be done, I will do it myself. My heart has gone out to them beyond all other peoples; and for the life of me I cannot tell why. They are bleeding-raw at the edges, almost more conceited than the English, vulgar with a massive vulgarity . . . Cocksure they are, lawless and as casual as they are cocksure; but I love them. . . . They be the biggest, finest, and best people on the surface of the globe!

He actually seemed puzzled and hurt by the wave of resentment provoked by his criticism. Again, I think it is an example of his super-ficiality. He thought that readers would laugh, shrug it off, and forget it, a little as children can be bitter enemies one hour and then the best of friends the next. The grownup world refused to oblige, and a pattern was set that was to be repeated in the future.

Again, throughout these articles, there is an emphasis on race and "bloodlines" which is partly Victorian but mostly comes from his own childhood experiences. To cite one instance, after complaining on the ship that he had "met a lump of Chicago Jews and am afraid that I shall meet many more. The ship is full of Americans, but the American-German-Jew boy is the most awful of all,"[3] a few weeks later he was writing this accolade:

Wait till the Anglo-American-German-Jew—the Man of the Future—is properly equipped. He'll have just the least little kink in his hair now and again; he'll carry the English lungs above the Teuton feet that can walk for ever; and he will wave long, thin, bony Yankee hands with the big blue veins on the wrist, from one end of the earth to the other. He'll be the finest writer, poet, and dramatist, 'specially dramatist, that the world as it recol-lects itself has ever seen. By virtue of his Jew blood—just a little, little drop—he'll be a musician and a painter too. . . . Later on . . . he will produce things that will make the effete East stare. . . . There is nothing known to man that he will not be, and his country will sway the world with one foot as a man tilts a see-saw plank![4]

In India, he had felt a clash between the old and the new. Here in America, after his initial shock—and criticism—at the absence of an "old"—the lack of anything akin to English tradition and ritual— he was entranced at what might be made of the "new." He imagined the im-mense energy that he saw on every side (if it could be, Strickland-like, worked from within) resulting in a fantastic civilization. At his age, it is natural that this idea found expression in his views on the relationship between men and women. In the critical articles he sent back to India there was one group of people he always praised to the skies —the American women. He was used to a culture in which a wife seldom disagreed with her husband; "Ted" Hill, with her openness and direct-ness, had a great effect on him, and one is not surprised that a little over two years later he married an American.

He wrote of women in many different parts of the world, and concluded that "the girls of America are above and beyond them all. They are clever; they can talk. Yea, it is said that they think. Certainly they have an appearance of so doing. They are original, and look you between the brows with unabashed eyes as a sister might look at her brother." The racial element from his own childhood enters another description: "I roast a battered heart before the shrine of a big Kentucky blonde who had for a nurse, when she was little, a negro 'mammy.' By consequence she has welded on to Californian beauty, Paris dresses, Eastern culture, Europe trips, and wild Western originality, the queer dreamy superstitions of the negro quarters, and the result is soul-shattering."

In the running account he sent back to the *Pioneer*, he often men-tions Professor Hill, and parts of his articles sometimes consist of a discussion between "the Professor" and himself. But Mrs. Hill, so dear to him, is never mentioned once. Shyly, he leaves her out. It would seem his praise of American women was partly a reflection of his attraction to "Ted" Hill.

After arriving in San Francisco he presented a letter of introduction from his mother to a friend of hers, a Mrs. Carr, who had him meet many of her friends. He was pleasant but reserved; taken on a picnic to Lake Merritt, he seemed to prefer the company of the children to that of the adults.

He complained of the "filthy streets," but his curiosity for the seamy side held sway and took him to the slums of Chinatown in San Francisco. He explained that he "wanted to know how deep in the earth the Pig-tail had taken root." Having heard that "the tenements were constructed on the lines of icebergs—two-thirds below sight level," he went far down into smoky subterranean basements "past Chinamen in bunks, opium-smokers, brothels, and gambling hells" to the third level below ground, where, he says, he saw a Mexican shoot a Chinaman in a quarrel over a game of cards, and then quickly vanish. "All the tides of intense fear, hitherto held back by intenser curiosity, swept over my soul. I ardently desired the outside air. It was possible the Chinamen would mistake me for the Mexican." He ran up the stairs, and finally got out on the street. "I dared not run, and for the life of me I could not walk." With relief, he gained the safety of his hotel room.

Why this dangerous trip to Chinatown? Why the similar trips to the native quarters in Lahore and in Calcutta? It was certainly no idle whim that led him to such highly unorthodox behavior. I think that it represents his old attempt to find some stratum of society where he fitted and could feel at home. His fear of being mistaken for a Mexican reflects his confusion about the old problem of identity. A few days later, however, when fishing in Oregon, he acted so much the epitome of an Englishman the others nicknamed him "Johnny Bull." Scarcely one who resembles a Mexican!

After a brief trip into Canada, he turned eastward toward Yellowstone Park in Wyoming. In Livingstone, Montana, he saw the inhabitants gather to celebrate the Fourth of July. Although in one of the articles he sent back to India he describes this celebration very critically, in a later report he completely reverses himself and is very impressed with American patriotism. "The men and women set Us an example in patriotism. They believe in their land and its future, and its honour, and its glory, and they are not ashamed to say so. From the largest to the least runs this same proud, passionate conviction to which I take off my hat and for which I love them."

It was in Wyoming that, abandoning his usual lack of interest in nature, he wrote an excellent account of the industrious beaver, its house and habits, and how it altered and improved the environment with its dams and ponds. This was the first inkling of his remarkable animal stories to come in later years.

Kipling's preoccupation with violence, so often connected with women, reappears in his description of Chicago. A visitor there in 1889 might, I suppose, want to see the Academy of Fine Arts, or be given a description of the great fire of 1871, or of the stockyards; not many people would ask to see the slaughterhouse there, but Kipling did. His description lets us see it in all its horror; and again there is the unmistakable fascination that turns the scene from violence to sadism. He describes the pigs' throats being cut: "There awaited them a red man with a knife which he passed jauntily through their throats, and the full-voiced shriek became a sputter, and then a fall as of heavy tropical rain." And then he describes how

> women come sometimes to see the slaughter, as they would come to see the slaughter of men. And there entered that vermillion hall a young woman of large mould, with brilliantly scarlet lips, and heavy eyebrows, and dark hair that came in a widow's peak on the forehead . . . . She stood in a patch of sunlight, the red blood under her shoes, the vivid carcasses tacked round her, a bullock bleeding its life away not six feet away from her, and the death factory roaring all round her. She looked curiously, with hard, bold eyes, and was not ashamed.

Even his marked attraction to American women did not allay his old fears; and in describing her widow's peak he may have had "Ted" Hill in mind.

He went on to Beaver, Pennsylvania, where he stayed at "Ted's" parents' house for over a month, making a few additional trips from there to different points of interest in the East. Alec Hill had returned to India, so Kipling was the guest of Dr. and Mrs. Taylor, "Ted" Hill, and her two younger sisters, Carrie and Julia. Dr. Taylor was a Methodist minister, and a strict one; he was president of Beaver College. He and Mrs. Taylor were leaders in their own circle, among the most prominent people in town. All of this, of course, appealed to Kipling with his own Methodist background.

He was immediately struck with the beauty and tranquillity of Beaver. It reminded him of the orderliness—without the presence of death!—of his Anglo-Indian background. Of Beaver he wrote (using the name "Musquash"), "The little community seemed to be as self-contained as an Indian village." He admired the way young women were accepted as equals by young men; they were not merely relegated to the nursery or kitchen, as he felt they were in England. "The boys were nice boys—graduates of Yale of course; you mustn't mention Harvard here." He spoke with delight of picnics and boating on the Ohio, and even admired the local politics—perhaps for the first and last time in his life, since few things were more persistent in Kipling than his dislike of liberal politicians.

The Taylors gave a large reception for their oldest daughter and her distinguished guest. Caterers came from Pittsburgh, and Japanese lanterns were strung from trees for blocks around. It was the event of the summer; everybody who could dig up an evening gown or a dress suit came. The entertainment was conversation, music, and food. No liquor, no dancing. "Ted" wore a dress made in India, with panels of gleaming embroidery running up and down the front. On closer view each panel was seen to be made of hundreds of iridescent beetle-wing covers, each one sewn on by some patient Asiatic hand. No one had ever seen a dress like that! One of the witnesses to the reception, then a child, remembered in her old age reaching out with her finger to touch this marvelous dress.[5] Kipling was felt to be a novelty, with his English accent (which, of course, few had ever heard before), his bristling mustache, and his heavy glasses. At the reception, he was perfectly pleasant but reserved. People couldn't decide whether he was shy, bored, or uncomfortable being made the center of all this attention.

"He lived in his own way, disregarding the customs of the town." Beaver was "dry," and he certainly knew he would never get a drop at his hosts' home. He discovered you could get a drink by procuring a prescription from the local doctor and getting it filled at the pharmacy. Almost every day Kipling could be seen, usually wearing his white India suit and his pith helmet, being driven in the Taylor phaeton to the local drugstore. The driver would get the filled glass and bring it out to the carriage, and Kipling would sit there in the sun and leisurely sip his "medication."

His companions that July and August were "Ted" Hill's sisters, Carrie and Julia, and the sprightly Lida Dravo. One afternoon the four of them went off to Sewickley; after midnight when it was time to catch the last train back to Beaver, Kipling was nowhere to be found. Somewhat concerned, the others returned home and discovered that he had simply come back on an earlier train, by himself, without saying a word to anyone.

On another occasion the same foursome had gone out to play badminton but had to stop when a light rain began to fall. Kipling offered to take Lida home. They set off through the gathering darkness, sharing an umbrella. Kipling was silent, Lida was chatting casually about a variety of things. Just as they passed the town jail, Kipling stopped abruptly. "Here," he said, thrusting the umbrella into the startled young woman's hand, and walked off. Whereas nowadays we would think it normal to ask why Kipling took an early train back from Sewickley, in Victorian times one was less likly to question another person's behavior. It was customary to pass over things, to avoid "rocking the boat." On neither occasion did his friends ask Kipling any questions about his unusual actions. Lida's niece frequently discussed the incident with her aunt, who felt that Kipling was frightened; it was growing dark, there were few street lights then, and she knew that he had poor eyesight. She concluded that perhaps he was worried he might get lost. But if he was afraid of getting lost, he would stay with his companion rather than walk by himself; we might conjecture that walking in the dark with Lida, close to her, touching her, he felt anxious (the fear that Lida sensed) and—just as they passed the jail—he had to leave abruptly.

"Ted's" sister Carrie was a plump, animated person. She lacked her sister's long-limbed grace and her personality,[6] but Kipling, at an emotional age when all women seemed attractive, promptly fell for her. "Ted" may have been embarrassed at times by Kipling's attentiveness and pushed her sister in his direction. He wrote verses for her in the center of plates that he then had fired in a kiln. As so many others had been, Carrie and "Ted" were amazed at the way he could reel off the poems without a moment's hesitation. On the reverse of some other plates, in the smaller circular area, he drew pictures of things that referred to her initials—C.A.T.—like a cat-o'-nine-tails or a cat's cradle. When the whole group left for England, Kipling and Carrie considered themselves engaged, although Doctor Taylor had grumbled that "one Englishman in the family is enough."

From Beaver Kipling made trips to places in the East, from which he wrote back letters to "Miss Carrie." The things that appealed to him were the things demonstrating solidity—history and tradition—the sort of thing in which patriotic Americans took pride. He delighted in Philadelphia and the country around it, so closely connected with the birth of the nation. Visiting Lexington and Concord, he found himself choked with emotion. In Washington he had an animated discussion with military officers. He went to Niagara Falls, which were all right, but what he really enjoyed was watching a grain elevator work. This trip culminated in a visit to Elmira, New York, where he had an interview with Mark Twain. Awestruck, Kipling could not quite believe he was really in the presence of the man who had created Tom Sawyer and Huckleberry Finn.

Returning to Beaver, he joined Mrs. Hill, Carrie Taylor, and their cousin, Edgar Taylor, and toward the end of September they all went to New York from which they embarked for England. Arriving early in October, the others, after a brief sight-seeing stay in London, continued on to India, leaving him alone in the great city.

VII

THE WORLD OUTSIDE INDIA—ENGLAND

Although Kipling had no friends in London, he had relatives; his Uncle Ned and Aunt "Georgie" Burne-Jones (with whom he had spent those vital Christmas vacations when a child at Lorne Lodge) and his Aunt "Aggie" Poynter. (His Uncle Ned had begun to hyphenate his last name in 1885.) Their respective children, his cousins Phil Burne-Jones and Ambo Poynter, were about his own age. But the former was a liberal in politics and the latter preoccupied with climbing the social ladder. Neither held any interest for Kipling, so he could not feel close to either one. His strong sense of independence made him decide not to live near his relatives, nor near the familiar part of London from which he had left seven years before. Above all, he wanted to feel close to India, and he picked the one place in London where he could—a few doors away from the London office of the *Pioneer*. He walked the streets near the office looking for old Anglo-Indian acquaintances, and when he finally found one, he literally danced for joy.

He kept himself aloof from the literary figures in London. He did not, as one might expect, seek letters of introduction or the like, to get an "in" that would lead to publication. This was not a lofty refusal to kowtow to others; always modest, Kipling was not one to be superior. It was simply that he felt himself an alien, surrounded by strangers. He was Anglo-Indian, they were English. He refused to be influenced by prevailing ideas, to defer to anyone, to be controlled in any way. Current ideas, in any event, would be those of London, and his heart was in India. He knew what he wanted to write, and, if left alone, he was quietly confident of success. The Londoners, most of them comfortable, urban, leading civilized lives, didn't know that people died of heat, or were struck down by cholera, or gave their lives in administering India under the British flag. Well, he'd tell them.

Meanwhile, he was lonely, unhappy, and, for the only time in his life, almost broke. The last problem was not a serious one; he knew he would soon have sufficient money, and if some real emergency had arisen, he could have borrowed, albeit with a natural reluctance, from relatives. But his loneliness was real and desperate. We may presume that his friends' leaving him in London reminded him of his abandonment, eighteen years before, by his parents at Lorne Lodge; they had left and returned to India just as, now, the Hills and Carrie Taylor had. This memory deepened his loneliness and his homesickness for India. He had just parted from "Ted" Hill, an almost-constant companion for nearly two years (emotionally if not geographically; he had felt close to her even when they were in different cities), and her sister Carrie with whom he felt he was in love. The cold, dreary London winter closed about him, and he yearned for sunny India. When he had left seven years before, it was unwillingly, and he had been homesick for England. Now he was back in England and homesick for India. Often in his life he was to be caught in this way—leaving a place and yearning for it. Nothing ever quite suited him, for the confusion of his childhood had left him unsure of what he wanted.

He sent home pieces to his old favorite, the *Civil and Military Gazette*, among which was the following impression of London and Londoners:

> But I consort with long-haired things
> In velvet collar-rolls,
> Who talk about the Aims of Art,
> And "theories" and "goals,"
> And moo and coo with womenfolk
> About their blessed souls
>
> But what they call "psychology"
> Is lack of liver-pill,

And all that blights their tender souls
Is eating till they're ill,
And their chief way of winning goals
Consists of sitting still.

It's Oh to meet an Army man,
Set up, and trimmed and taut
Who does not spout hashed libraries
Or think the next man's thought,
And walks as though he owned himself,
And hogs his bristles short.[1]

Energetic, determined, Kipling was always to preach the value of action (as in the military), and to look down on aesthetes and dreamers—particularly when their dreams disagreed with his. The intellectuals he sneered at became the avant-garde of the Edwardian period, those who felt that pleasure was not of itself suspect, that propriety and conformity were sometimes used to cover up spontaneity, that to think was not less than to act.

His fame in India had, to some extent, preceded him, and a publishing firm offered to print an English edition of his *Indian Railway Library* ("Soldiers Three," "The Story of the Gadsbys," "In Black and White," and "Under the Deodars"). He went to their office and worked out an agreement with them to have the stories appear early in 1890. He later stated that this was the only time in his life that he directly bargained with a publisher; after this, he always worked through an agent. Perhaps this is said a little defensively, for he was certainly short of money, and might have been expected to drive a hard bargain for his work; after all, he could point to its proven popularity in India. Interestingly, he did not negotiate well; they paid him only a small amount. It would seem that Kipling, always modest about his work, could not be assertive in a situation like this.

He knew the best solution for loneliness and depression was hard work, so he was writing voluminously. Indeed, his basic philosophy of life, as evident in his school days and as seen in his work at the *Civil and Military Gazette*, could be summed up as "the only answer is to work hard and to do your best." This creed, which extends to "if everyone worked hard, there would be order instead of disorder," is ultimately simplistic and empty. It is like being told to "be good" or to "strive for perfection." It accounts for a certain dissatisfaction with Kipling's work, for critics' complaints that it is shallow. While we are given magnificently vivid pictures of life, the ideas behind the pictures are sometimes juvenile and unconvincing. The most famous criticism came from Henry James:

> Almost nothing of the complicated soul or of the female form or of any question of *shades* —which latter constitute, to my sense, the real formative literary discipline. In his earliest time I thought he perhaps contained the seeds of an English Balzac; but I have quite given that up in proportion as he has come steadily from the less simple in subject to the more simple,— from the Anglo-Indians to the natives, from the natives to the Tommies, from the Tommies to the quadrupeds, from the quadrupeds to the fish, and from the fish to the engines and screws.[2]

This is a criticism of Kipling's writing that was echoed repeatedly by others.

In November 1889 a story of his appeared anonymously in the *St. James Gazette*. Uncharacteristically, Kipling seemed unsure of himself in this initial venture and decided, apparently, that the story was a poor one. Subsequently, he attempted to deny that he had written it.* Then two long ballads were printed in *Macmillan's Magazine*. The second of these, in a December issue, was "The Ballad of East and West." Only two months after his arrival, he introduced a saying to the English language:

> Oh, East is East, and West is West, and never the
> twain shall meet,
> Till Earth and Sky stand presently at God's great
> Judgement seat;
> But there is neither East nor West, Border nor
> Breed, nor Birth,
> When two strong men stand face to face, tho' they come from the
> ends of the Earth![3]

Kipling published both ballads under the pseudonym "Yussuf," a disguised form of "Joseph," his actual first name. He had repeatedly

---

*This was "The Comet of the Season" (November 21, 1889), now generally agreed to be Kipling's work and ascribed to him in Livingston, F. V., *Bibliography of Rudyard Kipling*, Edgar H. Wells and Co., 1927, p. 72.

used names other than his own in India, and continued to do so until his fame was secure in England. Indeed, bibliographers have identified about twenty pseudonyms, the commonest being "Yussuf," "Esau Mull," and "E. M." It is not surprising that he used an Old Testament character for one of his pseudonyms, since Mrs. Holloway had made him memorize long portions of the Bible, and all his life he made frequent use of Biblical quotations. Another name, used much less frequently, was "Jacob." Why "Esau" and "Jacob"? In the Bible, Esau, the first-born, was twice tricked by his twin brother Jacob, robbed, and left with nothing. The use of the two names suggests that unconsciously Kipling felt like a twin; his sibling was his long-dead brother, John, who had been allowed to stay in idyllic India when Kipling was snatched away to his terrible life in England. (The fact that his brother was dead would mean little to the unconscious.) Also the hirsute Kipling, with his enormous vocabulary, probably knew that "esau" is Hebrew for "hairy." The "Mull," I suggest, has the meaning given in my dictionary: "to work mentally; to cogitate," as when we say we'll "mull something over." "Esau Mull," then, is "the hairy one, who thinks, who is wise." This *nom de plume* is the first example of a characteristic phenomenon: over and over, as I shall demonstrate, Kipling creates characters, whether people or animals, who stand for himself; they may be small, uncoordinated, and have visual difficulties, but they make up for these deficiences with the power of their minds.

To gain a deeper understanding of Kipling's use of the name "Esau," we must turn to the psychology of twins, about which a great deal is now known.[4] Briefly summarized, identical twins have a special need for each other, because a twin thinks of himself not entirely as an individual, but rather as half of a pair. Having another person who looks like you interferes with a secure perception of yourself. For one twin to attain success is often difficult unless the other twin can achieve it, too. I remember identical twin track stars who both ran the mile in college; they were among the very best in America at the time. Neither twin would race unless the other also raced. One was just a shade better than the other, and he usually would be in the lead as they came around the final lap. He would then slacken his pace until his brother caught up with him, clasp his hand, and the two would cross the finish line together. He would do this—to the coach's despair—

even if it meant that a competitor would pass them both and win the race.

This bond between twins sometimes becomes one of "love-hate," however, with one having all the "good" qualities, and other the "bad" ones. The malicious one, tired of needing his twin, will play tricks on him based on their looking alike. (Two years before, Kipling wrote a story, "Gemini," published in January of 1888, about identical twins. The first-born, the narrator, is tricked, robbed, and beaten by order of his twin, since the officers of the law mistake one man for the other.) When Kipling took his brother John's name in school, he showed something of the psychology of twins; John was his "Indian self," Joseph was his "English self," with all the feelings associated with that identity.

But why did he use so many pseudonyms? Partly it was the custom of the times; they were more commonly used than they are nowadays. For instance, John Galsworthy, one of Kipling's most noted contemporaries, published his first works under a pseudonym. But this custom would hardly be sufficient reason for a man to use twenty of them. And partly, perhaps, he doubted about how good his work really was; the beginner's thought that he could always hide behind a pseudonym and disclaim having written something. But this, too, does not seem to be the whole answer, for he was quietly self-confident and seemed to sense what a success he was soon to be.

Kipling used many pseudonyms because of an insecure sense of himself; for a person's name, of course, is an important part of his self-concept. We all become very attached to our names; the way we use them reflects how we feel about ourselves. If a person feels unsure of himself, he will often change his name. This commonly occurs in teenagers, who will suddenly wish to be known by a different name, usually a variation of the actual one. Another example is a criminal who uses an alias. It is certainly obvious that it would be wisest for him to change it radically, to make it harder to track him down. If his real name is John Smith, he should use a markedly different name like "Stanislaus Berkovsky" or "Peter O'Hara." But a glance at the wanted list in any post office shows that he doesn't; instead of John Smith, he uses "Jim Smith" or "John Schmidt." It is hard for him to give up his name.

In "The Ballad of East and West," Kipling's confusion about identity can be seen throughout the poem. In the first verse, which is repeated at the end, Kipling states that race, social position, and native land mean nothing, "when the chips are down." (What he says, incidentally, is just the *opposite* of the meaning usually given the quotation, when people shrug and say, "Well, it is like the old saying, 'East is East and West is West and never the twain shall meet.'") To be exact, Kipling is saying that they can never meet *except* when "two strong men stand face to face"; that is, in a life-or-death situation, when all superficialities and conventions are set aside—*then* they can feel as one. Again, it is an effort to understand his background, to feel that he could be European and Asiatic at the same time.

The ballad's story repeats this theme. Two men, a white and an Indian, are the bitterest of enemies at the beginning, but after seeing each other's bravery and skill they come to deeply respect each other by the end. East and West *can* meet, says Kipling: I *can* feel comfortable about my childhood, about myself.

In the cold, gray city Kipling was lonely indeed; and when Christmas came and then, five days later, his birthday, everyone else's exuberant holiday feelings made him feel even more alone. But this loneliness was self-imposed. He had been taken to the Savile Club and there introduced to many of the foremost English authors of the day. A year later, when his name came up for membership, he joined, but remained lukewarm about the club and its members. He could have gotten to know some of them better; he could have visited his aunt and uncle, the Poynters; he could at least have written his family (at Lahore his mother complained she never heard from him). In other words, he could have tried to feel more at home in England; but he was uninterested in doing this. At midnight of Christmas Day itself he wrote the Hills:

> There are five million people in London this night and, saving those who starve, I don't think there is one more heartsick or thoroughly wretched than the rising young author known to you as—Ruddy.[5]

It was India he longed for, and it was to Mrs. Hill that he wrote, but not as frequently as before, for he was now writing letters—and these were loveletters—to her younger sister Carrie.

And what letters! In a man whose life was filled with contradictions, these letters show one of the most startling ones. For the highly verbal Kipling could, as the reviewers were beginning to say with delight, express himself on any subject with equal felicity; everyone was beginning to talk about this man of the world who, amazingly, as the *Times* put it in a warmly favorable article, was "not yet twenty-five."[6] And yet the cocksure, here-let-me-show-you-how-to-do-it Kipling wrote loveletters that could have been improved upon by the average eighteen-year-old; they can only be described as floundering.

For example, when Carrie Taylor left for India in October, she sent him a last letter as the ship dropped the pilot and headed for the open sea. Kipling replied to it in part, "Heart o' mine, you, as well as I, must have discovered by this time that the writing of love-letters is no easy thing. I own that I laughed, disrespectfully, at the delicious one you sent off by the pilot—happy man was he."[7] This difficulty in expressing personal feelings, far beyond the usual stumbling incoherence we all experienced as teenagers, raises the possibility that Kipling may have found it hard to be tender, to express love, to *feel* love. It would not be surprising. After those first six childhood years he experienced such cruel rejection, such an utter absence of love (except for the annual visits to his aunt and uncle) that we might expect that he would seek the love of young women, and yet would find himself unable to utter that most important sentence that humans can say: "I love you." But what evidence we have indicates that this was not true in Kipling's case.

He continued writing Carrie in January 1890, when the two of them began to drift apart. This was hastened by a remarkable incident. Entirely by chance, he met on the street Flo Garrard, the girl at Mrs. Holloway's whom he had loved when he left for India seven years before. He immediately fell in love with her again—if, indeed, he had ever fallen out of love.

The meeting is described in a obviously autobiographical scene in *The Light That Failed*. Dick, the painter, is momentarily blinded by some smoke from a river-boat, and when it drifts away, there is Maisie. "Then, against his will, and before the brain . . . had time to dictate to the nerves, every pulse of Dick's body throbbed furiously and his palate dried in his mouth."[8] Kipling ardently pursued Flo, but she was as uninterested as she had been seven years before. His sister Trix, now married, arrived in England and quickly sought out her brother in his room on Villiers Street. He told her, "his face beginning to work,"[9] that he now realized he had never loved Carrie Taylor. It had become clear to him as soon as he saw Flo again. Trix described Flo as someone who was "naturally cold, and wanted to live her own life and paint her very ineffective little pictures." Looking at a sketch-book of hers that has been preserved in New York, one can certainly confirm the impression of her art. Both Flo and Kipling sketched in the book; hers are routine, art-class studies of hands and faces, pallid and unimpressive; his are stronger, bolder, and show more of a natural gift.

As before, the more passionately he sought her, the more she avoided him. Again, it seems he was pursuing her, not in spite of her unavailability, but *because* of it. This suggests masochism. Some people find it hard to believe that a person can be drawn to do precisely the wrong thing, just what is *not* in his best interests; it makes no sense. But feelings have next to nothing in common with reason and logic. The person involved may even have some awareness of what he is doing, and yet still feel compelled to do it. Of the many mechanisms possible, I will describe only one. The child who is given nothing but criticism, told everything he does is wrong, eventually is driven to embrace this view. He has a basic feeling that he is bad, whereas other people are good. Nothing he does can turn out well. He *seeks* failure; finds himself doing things that he knows will hurt him, and even gets a pleasure from self-defeat. The compulsive gambler, the alcoholic, the person who is "accident-prone" may all be working out this formula set in childhood. It is therefore not surprising to find Kipling exhibiting masochistic behavior in his relationship with Flo. Yet with all that Kipling suffered, he managed not to fall completely into masochism, but only to a minor extent in his relationships with women. His early years of bliss and security, the support his sister gave him during the time he lived at Mrs. Holloway's, together with some streak of inner fortitude, somehow saved him.

Early in the year, he had shaken off his depression enough to telegraph his mother in India, telling her of his amazing success and urging both parents to come to England. The telegraph message was a single Biblical reference: "Genesis 45, verse 9." The passage reads: "Haste ye, and go up to my father, and say unto him, Thus saith thy son Joseph, God hath made me lord of all Egypt; come down unto me; tarry not." (Note that again he referred to himself as "Joseph.") His parents arrived in May and were shocked—as Trix had been—at his appearance. He looked thin, wrought-up, and depressed. His father said he was writing "with a sort of fury." Being reunited with his family did not mean as much to him as it had when he was a teenager in India. Although he profited from his father's help with the remarkable short story "On Greenow Hill," he always sensed that the best answer to depression was hard work. Writing like a demon, he tried to forget his unhappiness. He nearly succeeded.

The result was Kipling's *annus mirabilis*, 1890, an amazing year in which, outdoing any other writer in living memory, he shot from obscurity to the very pinnacle of fame. In the first eight months of that year he poured out poetry and prose that, both in quantity and quality, would have satisfied almost any other writer as a whole lifetime's achievement.

In December he wrote "The Ballad of East and West." In January came "The Head of the District," on the first of March "The Courting of Dinah Shadd," in April "The Man Who Was"—like bursts of fireworks, they exploded over a delighted public. W. E. Henley, a lifelong invalid now best remembered for his poem "Invictus" and its lines, "I am the Master of my fate, / I am the Captain of my soul," had received a series of poems in an unknown hand. He is said to have stamped about the room, pounding the floor with his wooden leg in excitement at this new author. Henley was the editor of the *Scots Observer* and immediately began printing Kipling's work. Legend has it that the dignified Professor Masson waved the paper before his class, shouting, "Here's Literature! Here's Literature at last!"

Before the end of August, he wrote most of what are now included in the *Barrack-Room Ballads*, with such familiar pieces as "Gunga Din" and "Mandalay"; six short stories, all superior to his earlier *Plain Tales*, and his first novel, *The Light That Failed*. He confided in Henley on literary matters, but rigidly avoided any personal discussions. All this excess might have turned another author's head, but not Kipling's. He wrote Henley that he was determined to work at his own pace, to aim for quality rather than quantity, and to ignore the wild offers from other editors, eager to exploit him. His level-headed approach was backed up by his father; Lockwood Kipling, always calm, merely observed that each new boom was more portentous than the last.

The six short stories include several that have always been regarded as Kipling at his best. The chilling "At the End of the Passage" was accompanied by "The Man Who Was," a story of an officer in India who was captured and tortured by the Russians. Almost mute, a living skeleton, he somehow finds his way back years later to his old regiment which—a typical Kipling ingenuity—is entertaining a visiting Russian officer that evening. Kipling, who from his own past knew all too much about brainwashing, describes the officer cringing in fear at the sight of the Russian, and weeping "bitterly, hopelessly, and inconsolably as little children weep."[10]

"Without Benefit of Clergy" is perhaps the best of all. An English officer, Holden, falls in love with an Indian girl named Ameera and buys her from her "withered hag"[11] of a mother, who "would have sold Ameera shrieking to the Prince of Darkness if the price had been sufficient." Holden finds himself leading a double life. Part of the time he is a bachelor officer, in the routine, carefully conventional army; the rest of the time, behind the gate where Ameera and her grumpy mother live, he is in a kingdom of bliss, "for she was all but all the world in his eyes." She bears him a son, whom they name Tota.

Even the most fervent Kipling admirers concede that he had great difficulty portraying women. They come out as cardboard characters, mere foils for the men, or else are husky tomboys with masculine nicknames, men in disguise. (And this in an age that emphasized, to an extreme, the difference between the sexes: men ran everything, made all decisions; women were usually expected to be submissive and inefficient.) But even the most vicious Kipling critics concede that Ameera is Kipling's finest woman. Holden and she, with little Tota, lie back on the roof, count the stars in the velvet sky, and tell each other of their love. When Tota was born, the native watchman brought two goats and had Holden slaughter them. Then Holden repeated the Muslim prayer that a child's birth be balanced by the deaths of the two animals (echoing the ritual that accompanied Kipling's own delivery). For Holden, Ameera, and little Tota the months that follow are filled with absolute happiness. But we know Kipling will allow no such bliss to continue. In India, Death is perched on everyone's shoulder. First Tota dies, and then Ameera; the heavy rains thunder down, and the house looks as though no one has lived there for thirty years. The landlord says he will pull it down, a road will be built across it, "so that no man may say where this house stood."

Included in the *Barrack-Room Ballads* is "The Widow at Windsor," written in the Cockney accent many readers found tiresome:

> 'Ave you 'eard o' the Widow at Windsor
>   With a hairy gold crown on 'er 'ead?
> She 'as ships on the foam—she 'as millions at 'ome,
> An' she pays us poor beggars in red . . .
> Then 'ere's to the Widow at Windsor,
> An' 'ere's to the stores an' the guns,
> The men an' the 'orses what makes up the forces
> O' Missis Victorier's sons. . . .[12]

People who know nothing else about Kipling will tell you the tale that the offended Queen Victoria, that she refused to allow Kipling to be made Poet Laureate. Though totally untrue, the story persisted for decades. (It was taught to me as an established fact when I was a boy in school.) But there is no direct evidence that the Queen was angered, nor that the general public felt this brash young poet should not have written this way about a respected ruler. What information we do have, in fact, suggests that neither was the case. Only five years later, in 1895, he was offered the position of Poet Laureate, and in 1899, a knighthood (both of which he politely declined). We can be sure that the Queen approved in each case. Such offers would certainly not have been made without consulting her. So it is most unlikely that she was annoyed, yet the story persisted and with such strength! Why, out of all the stories that were told, and could have been told, about Kipling, did this one continue for so many years? The reason is not factual, but in the realm of feelings. He had difficulty in portraying women in any warm or loving way; they are usually cool and manipulative, controlling the men about them, like a cat toying with a mouse. Readers sensed his fear and hostility toward women and the tale about the Queen fell on receptive ears; "He hates women *that* much," was the message. It was repeated and believed, outlasting all the other stories. Factually, it was untrue; emotionally, it was true. Such persistence warrants a discussion of the concept of "psychic truth."

Psychic truth refers to a belief held for emotional reasons, sometimes over a long period of time, even when it is demonstrably incorrect. Factually, it is not true, but at the level of thoughts and feelings it really is true. For example, a most persistent story, accompanied by a knowing wink, went around England and the literary world for fifty years or more. This, to use the phrase of the times, was that Kipling was "four annas in the rupee"; i.e., he was part Indian. His father or (in some variants) his mother or a grandparent, had done a little "running around." Kipling himself was well aware of the story and jokingly used to tell his mother to shake the family tree and "dislodge the nigger in the woodpile."[13] His appearance contributed nothing to such a rumor; though his hair was dark, his skin was light and his eyes blue. The things about him that could be seen as Asiatic would only seem so to someone whose mind was already made up.

Hilton Brown, in his biography of Kipling, was indignant about the tale and puzzled at its persistence. He set out to demonstrate "its impossibility—a thing that can be done with very little trouble." No one on either side of the family "ever had [had] anything to do with India" and Kipling "was born within six months of his parents' arrival in the country." In four pages he presents extensive evidence for these two statements, and seems satisfied that he has refuted calumny once and for all. Yet the story persisted unchanged, because, I would argue, the reasons behind it were emotional, not factual, and emotions laugh at facts. One must look behind the facts. Again, it is not the factual truth that matters—of course it was untrue—but rather the psychic truth. For, as we have seen, here it *was* true. Emotionally, Kipling had two mothers, his own and his *ayah*; and unconsciously he felt he was part Indian, a feeling that is reflected in his actions and writing, and which was sensed by his readers, who perpetuated the tale. Intuitively, they were closer to the truth than the fact-finders.

Of the six short stories he wrote before the end of August, three involve the question "Is he white or is he Asiatic?" One, "The Mark of the Beast," is a good example of a story that at first seems not to have this theme, but does upon closer inspection.

The narrator, Kipling, comes home from a riotous party with Strickland and a man named Fleete, who is particularly drunk. They pass a native temple and Fleete runs in and stubs out his cigar on the forehead of the stone image. The priests are furious; then one of them, whose "body shone like frosted silver, for he was what the Bible calls 'a leper as white as snow'"[14] runs up and bites Fleete on his left breast. The priests, curiously, don't seem angry any more. The men take Fleete home, and all three go to sleep.

The next morning Fleete insists on having underdone chops, which he devours like an animal. The mark on his breast, a rosette of spots like the pattern of a leopard's skin, has now turned black; Kipling and Strickland wonder about it, and Kipling suggests that perhaps it is "a birthmark newly born and now visible for the first time." When they go near some horses, all of them rear and try to bolt when they see Fleete. Night comes, and Fleete gets more and more disturbed, snarling like a wolf, and finally has to be bound and gagged by the other two. His howls and cries, when he frees the gag, are answered from outside the house by the leprous priest, who makes a "mewing like a she-otter." Strickland gets some string, the barrels from an old shotgun which he heats in the fire, and other things, and says they must catch the leper and force him to remove the curse inflicted on Fleete. Kipling resolves "to help Strickland from the heated gun-barrels to the loop of twine—from the loins to the head and back again—with all tortures that might be needful." They grab the leper, drag him inside, and tie him up. Kipling "buckle[s] the leper comfortably to Strickland's bedstead." The torture with the red-hot gun-barrels begins; the priest has "no face"—from the leprosy—but "you could see horrible feelings passing through the slab that took its place" as they torture him. (As often happens in Kipling's writings, here the scene barely stops short of pathology, of pornography, and yet he never quite steps over the line.) The priest finally gives in and puts his hand on Fleete's breast. Fleete begins to improve, and the priest is released. In the morning a doctor, sure that Fleete is dead, brings a nurse for "what is necessary." To his amazement, Fleete cheerily sits up in bed and says, "Bring on your nurses." The mark on his breast has disappeared, and he has no memory of what he went through.

Kipling's preoccupation with violence, and with the victim being tied up, need no mention. The central character of the story is not Fleete but the priest, and there is something female about him, for he is heard "mewing like a she-otter" outside the house. His biting Fleete on the breast suggests the early mother-child relationship. He is a native, but he is white (from his disease). Kipling frequently makes dark people white or white people dark; he is asking himself, "Am I white? Am I Indian? Am I a mixture?" over and over again. The priest is faceless—and the face of course is the main physical determinant of identity. The story, which may at first strike the reader as merely being an effective account of the supernatural, has in it the deeper element of Kipling's confusion about his racial background.

Here Kipling also reiterates his conviction that no white man can really understand India. The country merely tolerates the British and accepts their railroads, bridges, and sanitation, as if to say these things don't count in the long run. European ideas and comprehension cannot be applied to India. When Kipling suggests that the spots on Fleete's breast are birthmarks, Strickland knows better, and when they send for a doctor, he says that what is killing Fleete cannot be handled by any doctor. Beyond the mere technological improvements the British introduced there is India's magic, her violence, her gift of a certain calmness and serenity. In Kipling's case he is saying moreover that if you've been born in India, "bought into India," have India in your blood, like any man's relationship with his mother it will shape your entire life. In this story Fleete, an ignorant "outsider", infuriates some priests by stubbing out his cigar on an image of their god, leaving a mark. A priest bites his breast, leaving a retaliatory mark. Only Strickland, as much of an "insider" as a white man can be, knows how to use India's brutal magic to undo the priest's death-sentence.

As usual, the "I" in the story certainly appears to be Kipling himself. This can be contrasted with E. M. Forster's *A Passage to India*, which begins with a group of Indians discussing whether or not it is possible to have a truly friendly relationship with an English man or English woman. Kipling, so far as I am aware, never writes from the Indian perspective. His point of view is essentially that of the outsider, commenting on the scene. This may simply be his preference, or what was customary at the time. But it is also a reflection of his feeling of identity, his concept of himself. To describe a discussion going on in a group of Indians requires the author, so to speak, to become an Indian for that part of the story, and this Kipling avoided. He had to keep reminding himself and the reader that he was white, not Indian, and though always influenced by the siren song of the East, his emphasis was on white rule, the glories of the (white) British Empire, the value of a (white) education and culture. Of course, we must remember that most Englishmen, and certainly most Anglo-Indians, like his own parents, would largely have agreed with him. But in the fierce intensity of his feelings, as in his political stance at the extreme right, we can see the influence of his childhood.

During those amazing first eight months of 1890, he wrote his first novel, *The Light That Failed*; it was completed by August and published just before the end of the year. Here a most unusual event occurred; two editions were released, with different endings.

It is the story of Dick Heldar, an orphan who is brought up with Maisie, another orphan, in the terrible home on the English seacoast, of a Mrs. Jennett, a widow who has "a natural desire to pain,"[15] i.e., to inflict pain on others. At the beginning of the book, the boy and girl are pistol-shooting out on the salt flats. One of Maisie's shots, fired dangerously close to Dick, momentarily blinds him with powder-grains and smoke. He tells her he is in love with her. Years later, he becomes an artist, making sketches to accompany newspaper accounts of fighting in Egypt. In one battle he gets cut on the head and in his delirium repeats the words he had spoken years before to Maisie. After recovery, lonely and poor, he returns to England. He nearly starves, but bravely holds out until his work achieves popularity. Then comes a chance meeting with Maisie on the street; again he is momentarily blinded, by some smoke. He realizes he still loves her, but, cool and self-centered, she shows no interest in him.

Dick's vision is now troubled by a "grey haze."* He finds out that the old cut is now affecting his optic nerves, and he rapidly becomes blind. In the version used in the collected works, he returns to Egypt, and, though blind, finds his way to the front lines of the English troops in action. He finds a friend and suicidally insists on standing at the front of the battle. He is hit and dies in his friend's arms. (In the other version, there is a conventional happy ending in England, with Dick and Maisie becoming engaged to be married.)

In the nine months preceding this book's appearance, the popular-

---

* The connection with Kipling's own visual problems at Lorne Lodge can be seen in "Baa Baa, Black Sheep" when Punch is also first troubled by a "grey haze."

ity of Kipling's work had shot past that of every other writer. Much of his previous Indian work was reissued, together with that prodigious output from the spring and summer of 1890, and a delighted public bought all it could lay its hands on and asked for more. His first novel, naturally, was eagerly awaited.

It proved to be, for many readers, a disappointment. The smart sneer of the time was to refer to it as "The Book That Failed." There are vivid scenes, yet they only shakily fit together into a plot. The characters seem shallow and inconsistent, and Dick Heldar an odd mixture of sentimentality and fury, a man who could be overcome with emotion in watching an outward-bound ship one moment, and threatening someone with violence the next.

Much of the novel is clearly autobiographical. To mention just a few points, the two children are orphans, which is how Ruddy and Trix had viewed themselves. Maisie is a combination of Trix and Flo Garrard, which again indicates the intensity of Kipling's early feelings for his sister. Dick and Maisie refer to their relationship as a brother-sister one. After the terrible years with Mrs. Jennett, Dick leaves England, goes overseas, begins his career, returns to England, starves, and then rapidly rises to the top of his profession—all like Kipling. Dick meets his childhood sweetheart, Maisie, by accident, just as Kipling met Flo when he was working on this novel.

Besides the general framework of the novel, the central themes of love and of an artist going blind are also drawn from Kipling's own life. Dick, a confused mixture of romance and anger, is full of information. "I'm an expert, let me tell you all about this" is his approach—a lifelong trait of Kipling's. Here again Kipling had difficulty in portraying love between a man and a woman. The passages in which he attempts to do so are almost embarrassingly ineffective. Dick faithfully trots along after the obdurate—and colorless—Maisie, worshipping the ground she walks on, while his male friends ponder at length if this is good or bad for him. Then, with relief, the discussion ends and the men get together and have good, hearty pillow fight.

More importantly, the artist going blind is of course linked to Kipling's own visual difficulties, which he associated with his torture at the hands of Mrs. Holloway and her son. This was inflicted by a woman on a man, as Maisie torments Dick. From his childhood, a side of

Kipling was forced to see women as dangerous, frightening harpies that can put men to the sword. The safest relationship with them is to be passive and submissive—in Victorian terms, like a woman oneself—blindness being seen as equated with castration, the loss of the penis.

In one of the few personal revelations that crept into his autobiography, Kipling tells how, when he was a schoolboy of twelve, his father took him to the Paris Exposition of 1878. There he "saw, and never forgot"[16] a picture of the burial of Manon Lescaut. When he was eighteen, in India, he read "that amazing" book, as he puts it. *The Light That Failed*, he tells us, was derived from his boyhood feelings about the painting.

Manon Lescaut is a novel written in 1731; from it came the famous opera *Manon*. It is easy to see why the book and the painting fascinated him. Manon is an alluring woman who captivates men. She delights in "letting them off the hook" and then making them crawl back to her. One lover goes off and becomes a monk; she makes him renounce his vows and return to her. Then, at the end, she is convicted of immoral behavior. When she is about to begin her prison term she is found by a faithful old lover and dies in his arms. The picture that the young Kipling saw in 1878 shows the Chevalier des Grieux, the lover, scooping out a grave for her body. For years she has tormented him; now, with mixed feelings of relief and loss, he buries her forever. He will never stop loving her; she has hurt him too much for that. A side of des Grieux is passive, wants to be tormented, to be helpless. *The Light That Failed* shows Dick as similarly under the control of Maisie, symbolically blinded by her, castrated and made into a woman.

An important element in our sense of ourselves is our sexuality. A man's identity is closely linked to notions of manhood, a woman's with those of womanhood. There has always been no quicker way to start a fight with a man than to tell him he is effeminate. In recent years there has been a perceptible change in sex-linked roles—a change the importance of which is hard to overestimate. We are beginning to be able to feel we should first of all try to be individual persons, in all our capacities, and only then women and men. There were Victorians, perhaps mostly writers, who felt this way, although they were fewer in numbers than nowadays. They could be flexible enough to see that every man has feminine inclinations, and every woman has masculine ones. Kipling and

110

The burial of Manon Lescaut

his parents, as far as I can determine, could not be said to be included in this group that allowed some minimal acceptance of bisexuality. It was therefore most unusual—beside being extremely intrusive—that his mother (when he was twelve, the same year he saw the painting) had written the headmaster about his "feminine" tendencies. Kipling would have been horrified at any such an idea. Over and over again he praised, in the highest terms, tough, pragmatic men "who got things done" (like the Anglo-Indians he had known in India), and sneered at thoughtful, sensitive men. The former he saw as strong and "masculine," the latter as weak and "feminine." And, of course, the more he loudly proclaims his admiration of the men, the more we suspect (and see) a hidden and feared identification with women. Kipling frequently spoke of things, and people, in terms that would have been used by a Victorian woman. When he was in America, he heard a Lieutenant Carlin—"such a big, brave, gentle giant!",[17]—give an inspiring speech, and wrote, "I, for one, fell in love with Carlin on the spot."

Other examples abound in *The Light That Failed*. After Dick goes blind, his friend Torpenhow takes him out for a walk and they pass the Palace Guards on parade.

> They approached as near to the regiment as was possible. The clank of bayonets being unfixed made Dick's nostrils quiver.
> "Let's get nearer. They're in column, aren't they?"
> "Yes, how did you know?"
> "Felt it. Oh, my men!—my beautiful men!"[18]

Years later *The Light That Failed* was dramatized by a female playwright who used the pseudonym "George Fleming." (Was she borrowing the name from Kipling's sister?) Max Beerbohm, who repeatedly attacked Kipling in savage caricatures, wrote a telling essay:

> "George Fleming," is, as we know, a lady. Should the name Rudyard Kipling, too, be put between inverted commas? Is it, too the veil of a feminine identity? If of Mr. Kipling we knew nothing except this work, we should assuredly make that conjecture. A lady who writes fiction reveals her sex . . . through her portrayal of men. . . . In *The Light That Failed* . . . men are portrayed . . . from an essentially feminine point of view. They are men seen from the outside, or rather, not seen at all, but feverishly imagined. . . . *"My* men —*my* men!" cries Dick Heldar when a regiment of soldiers passes his window . . . . [H]e had always doted on the military. And so has

112

Mr. Kipling. To him, as to his hero, they typify, in its brightest colours, the notion of manhood, manliness, man. And by this notion Mr. Kipling is permanently and joyously obsessed. That is why I say that this standpoint is feminine . . . Mr. Kipling is so far masculine that he has never displayed a knowledge of women as they are; but the unreality of his male creatures, with his worship of them, make his name ring quaintly like a pseudonym. . . .[19]

What I am saying here is that there was a large element of homosexuality in Kipling's sexual orientation. What he had suffered in the hands of Mrs. Holloway—having to submit to her cruelty, being constantly humiliated—left him with a fear of women that could only be solved by partly giving in and becoming like a woman; instead of fighting her, submitting to her, glorifying her, copying her. As stated earlier, probably only the support of his sister Trix, and some inner strength of his own, preserved his masculinity.

For something so obvious, it is certainly striking to see how Kipling's biographers have shied away from this subject. It is as if there was an unspoken gentlemen's-and-ladies' agreement to avoid the topic. This would be understandable if all the biographies had been written thirty years ago, but the omission is just as prominent in contemporary ones. Angus Wilson, in his excellent book, does not hesitate to suggest homosexuality in Flo Garrard. He points out that she shared a studio with a Mable Price in May of 1890, and was apparently still with this same friend thirty years later. This "may lead one to wonder whether he [Kipling] had not, by chance, embarked upon a romantic quest that was stillborn from the start,"[20] i.e., she was a lesbian. He raises this speculation about Flo on the flimsiest of evidence, and yet comments only briefly—and dismisses as irrelevant—the much more obvious indications of homosexuality in Kipling himself. And if Kipling's behavior up to this point indicates homosexual inclinations, what follows makes it even more evident. For now two Americans, a brother and a sister, entered his life and altered it forever.

VIII

KIPLING AND
WOLCOTT BALESTIER

To understand what is to follow we must examine Kipling's feelings about England and America—indeed, his impressions of any country except India. For that was the "magic country" of his blissful childhood, his *insula fortunata*, a dreamworld—which we all have—to which all other places, consciously or unconsciously, were compared. Returning there in his teens and early twenties, he saw a huge population tightly controlled by the British, a tiny minority. Decisions at the top were carried down for immediate execution without delay or red tape. The general mass of the Indian people, Kipling believed, contained too many ignorant, unscrupulous, or selfish individuals to be relied upon. It was necessary to have an all-powerful central authority in any worthwhile society. He scoffed at any concern for individual rights and freedom (although always insisting on his own absolute independence). He felt nothing but admiration for the Englishmen, civil and military, who governed the natives while gradually introducing modern technology to the country. His "worship of the expert" had one reservation; India must always be allowed to remain India. He strongly supported the traditional British rule, the building of railways and hospitals, but furiously attacked any attempt to alter the ancient Indian culture, caste system, and their status as a governed people. It was all very well to build bridges, but it was complete folly to attempt to bring in English ideas and concepts. Over and over again, he said, you cannot Westernize India; her ways are deep and mysterious and cannot be changed. The kind of expert Kipling admired, like Strickland (fictional, but based on a real person), would know enough not to try. Partly this was a political conclusion that he arrived at; but mostly he wanted the "magic country" of his childhood never to change. He sensed that to return to India as an adult would shatter that image, and in later years he consistently refused to do so, even under the strongest pressure.

In a series of short stories, Kipling heatedly put forth his basic belief that British ideas cannot be applied in India. The three best examples are "The Head of the District," "One View of the Question," and "The Enlightenments of Pagett, M.P." These were written in 1890, but he continued to express this point of view just as vehemently in years to come.

As might be expected from one whose heart still lay in India, his feelings about England and the Home English were bitterly critical. Politically, he felt that the general population, as in India, should have no voice in running the country. He was appalled by the internal conflict and compromise decisions so laboriously arrived at by the government. In "One View of the Question," Kipling portrayed an Indian visiting England—as he almost felt himself to be—and his horror at those who "despise the sword, and believe the tongue and pen sway all."[1] Members of Parliament, he says in the story, are influenced by women who are uninterested in marriage and having children. The most obvious proof of the Members' foolishness is their proposing an English type of government for India.

Kipling seldom ventured outside London—and when he did, he complained that it did nothing but rain—so his impressions are really limited to the city, although he did not hesitate to extend them to the country as a whole. He frequently referred to the choking fog, likening it to the evil of the inhabitants. In his letters sent back to be printed in the *Civil and Military Gazette* he referred to the British as "barbarians,"[2] "infidels" and "heathen." He saw the Home English as completely soft, spoiled, and lazy. The upper and middle classes in particular, he felt, were centers of "advanced" political and social thinking that questioned his own relatively narrow views. A furious Kipling—always intolerant—

attacked these intellectuals as indolent, worthless aesthetes whose ideas he saw—perhaps correctly—as basically opposed to the long-range maintenance of the British Empire. As just one example of his attacks on what he saw as the ignorant English, he describes a group of Londoners being shocked by the death of one of their number, although he died in advanced age, his family secure, his work done. Kipling sternly wrote that in India, frequently men at their healthiest, "thirty-five, with little children, died at two days' notice, penniless and alone."[3] When his exhortations were ignored, Kipling's hostility was such that he gleefully imagined an epidemic of cholera sweeping over England. *That* would show them what life was all about!

A complex of early life experiences contributed to Kipling's ambivalence toward England and the Home English. His preoccupation with death—a lifelong trait—had its roots in the sudden demise of his brother when he (Kipling) was four and a half. This sudden, bewildering tragedy was followed, a year and a half later, by his and Trix's abandonment, equally suddenly and bewilderingly, "at Home" in England. But Kipling could never use the phrase as other Englishmen did. Many years later, recalling his leaving India for the last time, in 1891, he said that it was "the only real home I had yet known."[4]

The only piece he wrote that expressed sympathy for the Home English is "The Record of Badalia Herodsfoot." The title character is a woman who has never known anything but life in the slums of London. In spite of her life in filthy poverty, she is a remarkable and intelligent person, the only one who understands how the grants of money provided by religious orders should be apportioned to the poor. Again Kipling is telling us, "Only the insiders know." He contrasts the rough-and-ready Badalia with the effete intellectuals he despised. She alone has standards by which she lives; when her long-absent husband returns and kicks her to death, Badalia tells lies on her deathbed so that he will not be apprehended by the law. In the face of death she is true to her principles. Only in this savage scene, more Indian than English, can Kipling find anything to praise in England.

His sympathy for the lower class is also shown in his going to the theater and feeling it was completely out of touch with the realities of life. In contrast, he was drawn to Gatti's, a music hall just across from his Villiers Street apartment, where the boisterous spontaneity of the audience was much more to his liking. In one of his articles sent back to India he told of writing a song for one performance with the punch line, "And that's what the Girl told the Soldier!"[5] It was a great hit, and he wrote that he went to bed "murmuring, 'I have found my Destiny.'" There is no way we can know how much of this is fact and how much fiction, but his attraction to the music hall is clear.

But again, although he could feel affection for the lower classes , he could never really feel himself one of them. His own middle-class status prevented that, and more strictly in Victorian England than anything we can imagine today.

His sympathy for Badalia and others like her did not extend to approving of any social upheaval to change the way they lived. The early steps of organized labor brought acid attacks from his pen. A working man, said Kipling, works for himself and his family, not for some hazy notion of improving his class as a whole. A laborer in America, he wrote, is "a nice person. He says he is a man and behaves accordingly."[6] The worker in England, by contrast, whines that he is one of the "poor, downtrodden helots—in fact, 'the poor workin'man'"[7] who feels he has an automatic right to education, employment, and housing. Unionism, Kipling felt, would result in chaos, and with the products of labor being not of the best quality, but of the worst. Labor unions would be the ultimate ruination of England.

His feelings about America, while mixed, were more positive than negative. One hundred years ago, there was a strong feeling that America was the "land of golden opportunity," a paradise that flowed with milk and honey, a place where, if a man put his heart into it, he could accomplish anything. This feeling of unlimited potential had always appealed to Kipling, and he had noted it when he traveled across the country in 1889. This belief in attaining all longings stems from a wish to return to the early infant-mother relationship, so important in Kipling's life. He had always yearned for the days of his childhood, where he had basked in the boundless love of his *ayah*. Here he felt like a king and, as he tells us, it never occurred to him that any wish would be denied.

Accordingly, there were two aspects of America that appealed to him; and these two were somewhat at odds with each other. In a place where "anything was possible" he could even make America, or a part of it, like India. There his children could have childhoods like Kipling's in Bombay. But he also longed to have had his *ayah*'s love flowing freely and instinctively from his biological mother, Alice Kipling. He had not wanted the barrier of race interposed. So this accounts for the theme of "who was my mother, Indian or white?" with all its multiple variations.

The second reason America appealed to him—somewhat opposed to the feeling of "newness"—was his love of tradition, of ritual, of things not changing. He was impressed with what he had seen in Beaver, Pennsylvania, and felt a respect for American writers, for the country's history and traditions, for the feelings that had made him choke with emotion when on the battlefield at Lexington.

Soon after Kipling's arrival in London in October 1889, he was introduced to Wolcott Balestier—pronounced "*Bal*-esteer"—an American a few years his junior who had come to Europe as a representative of an American publisher. It was his job to try to sign up some of the leading British authors and arrange for American editions of their works. Except for his childhood *ayah*, no other person in an entire lifetime influenced Rudyard Kipling as much as Wolcott Balestier did in a year and a half.

His grandfather, Joseph Balestier, had made a fortune and settled in Brattleboro, a small town in Vermont to which he used to come as a summer visitor. A son, Henry, Wolcott's father, married Anna Smith; they lived in Rochester, New York, with their four children. They often visited his parents back at Brattleboro, and some years after Henry died at a relatively early age, his wife moved back there with her family. Of the four children, Wolcott Balestier, born in 1861, was the oldest and the pride of the family. Charming and capable, he set out to make use of his unusual abilities as a writer, and did well from the start. Next came Caroline—known as "Carrie"—an efficient, clever little woman; next Josephine, the beauty of the family; and last Beatty, the spoiled, impulsive youngest brother. He was extremely likeable, generous with his money when he had any, but irresponsible and temperamental. The children around Brattleboro had been taught whenever they heard his sleighbells to scramble up to safety on the snowbanks at the side of the road, for he always went everywhere at a full gallop. Brattleboro abounded with "Beatty stories" and the subject of the stories liked nothing better than adding to the list. Alexander Wollcott, who knew him

Wolcott Balestier

well, described him as a "violent, warm-hearted, disorderly creature . . . a charming, contentious rattlepate."[7]

Wolcott Balestier, a thin, dapper young man, had gone to Cornell, where he had done well scholastically and was popular with his classmates. Lighthearted, full of energy and enthusiasm, he had a magnetism that is mentioned over and over again by his contemporaries. Behind his charm, however, was an iron will and a determination to get his own way. A contemporary in London described Wolcott as "difficult to get on with . . . electrical . . . a dictator . . . allows no one to stand in his way . . . a Czar in his family."[8]

When Wolcott first heard Kipling's name he was immediately curious: "Rudyard Kipling? What is it? Is it a real name? A man or a woman?"[9] Nothing came of their first casual meeting, until some months later, when they quickly became the closest of friends. One undocumented story has it that when Wolcott became fired with interest in his new friend, he went around to Kipling's apartment at seven in the evening, but found him out. Determined, he sat there until midnight waiting for his return, and then animatedly proposed to him that they collaborate on a novel.

The fact that they then did so, in view of Kipling's personality up to this point, is quite amazing. He had been a determined loner. Like his father before him, he was a craftsman in the tradition of William Morris, one who worked in the best way he knew how, took pride in what he produced, and considered that product sacrosanct and not to be altered or meddled with by others. Editors who wanted to change a word here or there got a sharp rebuff from Kipling: Print it as I wrote it or send it back. Besides this, now that he was famous, publishing houses had dug up his letters of the last year, that he had sent back for publication in the *Civil and Military Gazette* at Lahore. Since these letters were not covered by copyright, various American publishers were issuing "pirated" editions of them, along with other stories whose copyright was in question. Kipling was absolutely furious, but there was nothing he could do to stop it—the international copyright laws were only just beginning to be formed at the time. That he should become a close friend of an American sent over for a rather similar purpose—to arrange for cheap reprints in the United States of the work of leading European authors—seems odd and contradictory.

120

But, as described, Kipling felt little but disdain and fury for the Home English. This delightful American may have been seen as a pleasant change. Wolcott's background may have appealed to him; one of his ancestors was Paul Revere, another a signer of the Declaration of Independence, another the famous Judge Peshine Smith, who had controlled the international relations of the entire nation of Japan. This was the "old" America that Kipling always liked. But their friendship seems to have been largely based on Wolcott's remarkable charm, his amazing power over people. They became inseparable friends and in the summer of 1890, as soon as Kipling finished *The Light That Failed*, they began working on the novel.

In August of 1890 Kipling wrote "On Greenhow Hill," one of his better short stories. In it, three soldiers in India get to talking during a lull in action. One of them, Learoyd, speaks movingly of his love for a woman back in his native Yorkshire. But it is a hopeless love, for she is dying. Perhaps Kipling had in mind the fruitlessness of his own love for "Ted" Hill, her sister Carrie, and Flo Garrard.

A few months before a friend—it may have been Kay Robinson—had written him, encouraging him to strive for quality in his work and assuring him that success would then follow. Kipling's reply—repeating his philosophy of hard work—is one of those rare letters in which he expressed some personal feelings.

> It's the amazing selfishness of the White Man that ruins your counsel of perfection. "Money, fame and success" are to remain unto me? Surely 'tis as selfish consciously and deliberately to work for that Trinity as to lay siege to a woman or a glass of gin and porter!
>
> Where I come from they taught me (with whips of circumstance and the thermometer at 110 in the shade) that the only human being to whom a man is responsible is himself. His business is to do his work and sit still. No man can be a power for all time or the tenth of it—else would some of my friends who have died at their posts be those powers. Least of all can a man do aught if he thinks about it, and tries to add cubits to his stature, mental or physical. It's as bad as waltzing and counting the steps "One, two, three, one, two, three" under your breath.* Surely the young man does best to be delivered from "the public demand that walketh in the noonday and the cheque book that destroyeth in the study." For the rest his business is to

*Note that Kipling uses the analogy of someone with poor coordination.

121

think as little about his soul as possible for that breeds self-consciousness and loss of power. The event is in God's hands absolutely and no hawking or clutching for fame or any other skittles is the least use.

Recollect I've tasted power—such power as I shall never get this side of the water—when I knew all the heads of the Indian government—rulers, administrators, and kings—and saw how the machinery worked. Sunshine, colour, light, incident and fight, I've had poured into my lap, and now the chastened amusements of this bleak place don't bite . . . . Wait till you've been shot at and bossed a hundred and seventy men and walked "with death and morning on the Silver horns" in the Himalayas if you wish to know how far the smoking room, the club and the music hall and the cheap ormulu amourettes taste good.

This only do. Pray for me, since I am a lonely man in my life, that I do not take the sickness which for lack of understanding, I shall call love. For that will leave me somebody else's servant instead of my own.[10]

In all of Kipling's life these two years in London are the ones about which we have the scantiest information. As stated before, he felt only contempt for the Home English, and made no new friends in London— until Wolcott Balestier came along. Before this, he had been with his family, or worked with others in India, or traveled with the Hills. There are no similar sources of information for 1890 and 1891. Also, it may be a time about which he *wanted* us to know nothing, a troubled time. There are indications that this was the case.

In the fall of 1890, having begun *The Naulahka* with Wolcott, Kipling became upset and depressed over his copyright battle with Harper & Brothers. He followed the standard Victorian prescription for curing emotional problems—a sea voyage. According to one account, when in Paris, he had visited an old family friend, Lord Dufferin, who had been Viceroy when his parents had risen to the top of the social ladder at Simla. Lord Dufferin invited Kipling to visit him at his villa at Sorrento—he was now Ambassador at Rome—and Kipling gratefully accepted. Numerous newspapers coupled announcements of the forthcoming publication of *The Light That Failed* with statements to the effect that "Mr. Rudyard Kipling has broken down from overwork and has taken his doctor's advice to embark on a sea voyage." After a pleasant trip, Kipling arrived at Naples. With his usual "you-probably-don't-remember-me" modesty, he gave his name to the butler as "Mr. Lockwood Kipling's son." Lord Dufferin remembered him perfectly well on his own account. Kipling stayed with him for almost three weeks. Two old India hands, they talked endlessly about the one place that would always really be "home" for Kipling. He returned to England in November. With all his fame, publishers avidly seeking his work, everyone trying to get to meet him, his father noted that he seemed to care only for his mother.

He found himself confronted with the same problems that he had tried to escape. Kipling's anger over the pirated editions of his work was further inflamed by a letter that appeared in the *Athenaeum*, signed by the respected novelists Sir Walter Besant, Thomas Hardy, and William Black. In general, the letter, while deploring the lack of a good copyright law, supported the reputable American publishers. They try to treat their authors fairly, the writers argued, and to protect them from the out-and-out pirates that will do anything. The letter was a well-meant effort at appeasement, an attempt to pave the way for a workable international copyright agreement. It made no mention of the quarrel between Harper & Brothers and Kipling, and was not intended as an attack on him.

But Kipling exploded in wrath. Two weeks later, "The Rhyme of the Three Captains" appeared in the *Athenaeum*. It is a satirical poem that puzzled many a later reader, who did not understand that it was a personal attack on the three signers of the letter, whose names are referred to in the line, "The bezant is hard—aye—and black."[11] The skipper of a trading brig complains he was set upon by a Yankee pirate. The three captains reply with mildness and excuses. Then there is a description of what the skipper would like to do to the pirate. Kipling's poem becomes so savage it defeats its own purpose. The reader is so distracted by the juvenile ferocity that the central point—the desperate need for international copyright—becomes lost. All his life, usually in political causes rather than in personal ones, this happened to Kipling. Where a careful and reasoned reply would have helped most, he immediately launched an all-out attack, so vehement and excessive that the central point was forgotten. Any trigger could serve to release Kipling's backlog of anger.

> I had nailed his ears to my capstan-head,
>   and ripped them off with a saw,
> And soused them in the bilgewater,
>   and served them to him raw;

> I had flung him blind in a rudderless boat
>   to rot in the rocking dark,
> I had towed him aft of his own craft,
>   a bait for his brother shark;
> I had lapped him round with cocoa husk,
>   and drenched him with the oil,
> And lashed him fast to his own mast
>   to blaze above my spoil;
> I had stripped his hide for my hammock-side,
>   and tasselled his beard i' the mesh,
> And spitted his crew on the live bamboo
>   that grows through the gangrened flesh;
> I had hove him down by the mangroves brown,
>   where the mud-reef suck and draws,
> Moored by the heel to his own keel
>   to wait for the land-crab's claws!

In this matter, as in others, Wolcott Balestier came to his aid. The previous summer, William Dean Howells had written a condescending article in *Harper's Monthly* which had infuriated Kipling. Wolcott set about bringing the two men together—a task that most people would have found impossible, for Kipling was a man who carried grudges. He took messages back and forth between them, culminating in one from Howells that Kipling greeted with a shout of delight. After this, Kipling was friendly toward Howells and limited his hostility to Harper & Brothers.

That fall, Kipling was working on a long and ambitious poem, one that for the first time set forth his lifelong admiration for the British Empire and the responsibilities it demanded. Kipling states that his mother, listening to his fumbling with the opening words, said, "You're *trying* to say"[12] and the two lines easily came forth:

> Winds of the World, give answer!
>   They are whimpering to and fro—
> And what should they know of England
>   who only England know?[13]

The poem, "The English Flag," now largely forgotten, was immensely popular in its day, and the second line above was quoted for a generation.

Wolcott's sisters, brother, and mother (his father had died in 1870) came to England to visit him. Beatty characteristically had such a wild time of it he had to be sent back home to Vermont. It was Carrie, the elder of the two sisters, who made her presence most felt. Devoted to Wolcott, she took over his housekeeping, which she managed with her usual efficiency. Kipling, growing closer and closer to Wolcott, began taking his advice on business matters, to the intense annoyance of his literary agents, A. P. Watt & Son.

The Light That Failed was first printed in a magazine form in November 1890, with a conventional happy ending; we read that on the last page Dick and Maisie plan to marry. This version was also printed as a book in America by John W. Lovell Co. Four months later, however, when the British book edition was published, the novel was a third longer, and it ended tragically with Dick committing suicide and dying in his friend's arms on the field of battle. A one-sentence preface stands out from a nearly blank page: "This is the story of *The Light That Failed* as it was originally conceived by the writer."

The origin of the "happy ending" version becomes obvious when one learns the identity of the London agent for John W. Lovell Co., who printed the American book. It was Wolcott Balestier; he must have gotten Kipling to turn out the slick, "happy ending" version in an attempt to catch a bigger market. The Kipling who had fought like a tiger with editors over a changed word or comma had agreed to a marked revision of his first novel, with amputation of a third of it, purely at the urging of his new friend Wolcott.

They continued to work on their book, which was to be called *The Naulahka, A Novel of East and West.* ("Naulakha," as it should be spelled, is Hindustani for "nine lakhs," meaning 900,000; it was the name of a famous jewel in India, said to be worth nine lakhs of rupees.) During the collaboration both men were ill at times; just what was troubling them is not clear. Wolcott wrote a friend:

> Kipling and I have been wading deep into our story lately, and have written rather more than two thirds of it. It begins in the West where I have a free hand for several chapters. Then we lock arms and march upon India. The process of collaboration is much easier than one could have supposed. We hit it off together most smoothly.[14]

The resulting story is about Kate Sheriff, a Coloradan who, full of humanitarian impulses, goes to Rhatore, a fictional Indian province, as a nurse. Nick Tarvin, the other main character, also from Colorado, goes to Rhatore partly to continue his unsuccessful courtship, but also to steal a fabulous Indian necklace, the "Naulahka." He wants a railroad constructed to go through a certain town in Colorado and has promised the necklace to the wife of the railroad president as a bribe. After many adventures from which the clever, if dishonest, Nick emerges with the invulnerability of a comic-strip hero, he gets the necklace and wants to return to America with Kate. Realizing that she would not approve of what he has done, he returns the "Naulahka." Meanwhile, Kate's hospital has failed because of the natives' return to superstitious ways, so they escape and return to Colorado.

In many ways the novel is another version of *The Light That Failed*. Nick seems like an Americanized Dick Heldar.* Bold and reckless, he pursues the distant and preoccupied Kate, who reminds one of Maisie. However, Dick Heldar's worship of men and his vacillation over women have disappeared; Nick, decisive and energetic, knows he wants to marry Kate and goes to India hoping to do this. Kate seems, in Victorian terms, more feminine and submissive than the Maisie who symbolically blinded Dick, and in the end they marry—in India—and set out for home—in America—to "live happily ever after."

Looking at the book as a whole, it is, by general consent, the worst Kipling ever wrote. The reviewers at the time almost universally recommended that he avoid collaboration in the future. The plot is weak and irregular. Nick and Kate emerge as improbable, unreal characters, and there are all sorts of absurd episodes mixed with rambling dialogues that make it seem like something the two authors threw together in a month. Why would Kipling allow such poor work to be published? After all, they worked on it for a year and a half, and with his keen sense of values and his mother's sharp criticisms, Kipling must have known how bad it was. The book remains as a testament to his intense but conflicted feelings for Wolcott Balestier.

Their relationship was based on homosexual attraction. How else are we to see it? Kipling, always a loner, suddenly began to behave in ways he never did before, and never did again. Most people have had the

---

*The names are almost the same—Nick and Dick.

experience of suddenly finding themselves drawn to a person of the same sex. They think about him or her a great deal, feel very close, and have many daydreams about the person. Relationships like this are based on latent homosexuality, where feelings, but no acts, occur. The basis for it may even go quite unrecognized by the individuals involved.

For forty years biographers have edged closer and closer to an open discussion about the homosexual nature of the relationship between Kipling and Wolcott Balestier. Birkenhead, like so many other writers, chooses to ignore it—an example of the reluctance to discuss anything sexual when examining a person's life. Carrington hints at it when he says, "No man ever exercised so dominating an influence over Rudyard Kipling during the eighteen months of their intimacy."[15] Philip Mason discusses "the physical tenderness between men" but concludes that Kipling was primarily heterosexual. Leon Edel stated that "Between Balestier and Kipling it was a case of camaraderie and love, almost at first sight. Platonic, quite clearly. Both would have been terrified at any other suggestion."[16] Angus Wilson, in a brief and terse statement, denies that Kipling felt anything "unorthodox"[17] in his relationship with Wolcott. It remained for Seymour-Smith finally to call a spade a spade and discuss the question openly and, I think, fairly—a very considerable accomplishment.

He points out that Wolcott's conquest of Kipling—adding him to his string of authors—was absolutely amazing, since he (Kipling) had always been a loner; that he had always exhibited, both in his writing and daily life, a certain discomfort when dealing with women; that he had a definite longing for submission, and concludes that Kipling and Wolcott had latent homosexual feelings for each other but whether or not they went on to an overt relationship will never be known. But then he says, "Really we cannot say whether Rudyard and Wolcott made love. Who is in the least interested in what they may have done?"[18]

I, for one. The choice of behavior, when a homosexual or a heterosexual relationship becomes physical, is in no way random and involves some of life's most personal, important, and closely guarded secrets. Might they have masturbated each other? Might they have had oral sex? A sado-masochistic relationship? Might a dictatorial Wolcott have exerted a dominating role over a passive Kipling? Whatever happened must have been most revealing—if anything happened at all. And if no overt acts *did* take place, of course that is important too.

Kipling's homosexual feelings for Wolcott were made more conscious by his being drawn toward his friend's sister, Carrie, for she was becoming as important to him as Wolcott. There is a story that they met at Wolcott's London office, where she had gone to confer with her brother about household matters, the ledger of income and expenditures under her arm. In any event, they celebrated that day, November 28, as a special event every year for the rest of their lives. Apparently even their own children were never told what this date meant to them. A tiny, quick, determined person, neither warm nor outgoing, Carrie quickly laid plans to marry Kipling. He was interested, but of course felt this to be in direct conflict with his feelings for Wolcott. His parents' reactions are revealing; when his mother first met Carrie, she said, with evident distaste, *"That woman* is going to marry our Ruddy!"[19] Lockwood Kipling's remark was at once quieter and more devastating: "Carrie Balestier," he said dryly, "is a good man spoiled."

Let us now return to *The Naulahka* and its clues to this homosexual-heterosexual relationship among Kipling, Wolcott, and Carrie. It appears that roughly the first quarter of the book is mostly Wolcott's work, and the last three-quarters more that of Kipling, although careful studies have found no clear point where Wolcott stopped and Kipling began. As chapter headings Kipling uses bits of verse that indicate his being pulled in one direction by Wolcott and in another by Carrie. I will discuss these later. Of greater interest is a portion of chapter 8, when Tarvin is talking to the Maharajah. Tarvin feels friendship toward him; he was "more than a brother; that is to say, a brother of one's beloved."[20] But there is no such relationship in the book; the Maharajah has no sister in whom Tarvin is interested. The phrase is an unconscious expression of the feelings between the two authors. Kipling felt love for Wolcott, but also a conflicting love for Carrie. Here he attempts to solve this by saying, in effect, "There is no conflict. You only mean all the more to me because I love your sister."

Another fact should be noted. During 1890 and part of 1891, he continued to write to "Ted" Hill even after he broke off with her younger sister, and in these letters there is not a single reference to Wolcott. This omission certainly seems remarkable. For years he had written her every detail of his life; why not tell her about this new friend with whom he was writing a book? The obvious answer is that the relationship with Wolcott had about it a great deal of his old relationship with "Ted"; one was taking the place of the other, one was as intense as the other. Telling her would reveal conflictual feelings about being in love with a man as much as he had been in love with her.

Also, when his interest in Carrie Taylor faded, he had turned to Flo Garrard; and, when he got nowhere with her, he began to be interested in Carrie Balestier, although he felt conflicting homosexual feelings for her brother. As he grew closer to Carrie, his old romantic attachment to Mrs. Hill faded away. It had always been basically boyish, the kind of feeling one sees in school children and adolescents who desperately fall in love with someone ten years their senior. Usually, as Kipling did, they outgrow these intense, worshipping feelings and become interested in someone their own age. Kipling's maturing in this way was illustrated dramatically when Mr. Hill died suddenly in India, toward the end of 1890, about a year after "Ted" and the others had accompanied Kipling across the Atlantic to London. In December a sorrowing "Ted" and her sister Carrie passed through London on their way back to America. One can imagine that people who were "in the know" may have winked and wondered if, now that Alex was out of the way, Kipling might renew his attachment to "Ted." Perhaps they were surprised when he did not. Although he saw Mrs. Hill when she was in London, and wrote her occasionally in later years, the relationship cooled. If it surprised the family friends, it should not surprise us. Even if Mr. Hill had died a year or two before, Rudyard would not have wanted to marry "Ted." His relationship with her had been one of boy to woman, and he had now outgrown it; but he always remembered her with the greatest warmth. For the rest of his life, when a new book of his was published, he often sent her a copy, along with a friendly note.

Kipling apparently spent the winter of 1890-91 in daily contact with Wolcott, Carrie, and their mother and sister. In marked contrast with the amazing productivity of the first nine months of 1890, he did little writing. Apparently wrestling over *The Naulahka* with Wolcott, together with his personal problems, made any other writing impossible. There are continuing vague references to both men being ill.

Edmund Gosse, the noted writer and critic, was an enthusiastic admirer of Kipling, although more of the man, perhaps, than of his work. He referred to him as "the Star of the East" and wrote Richard Gilder, "His conversation and company fascinate me horribly."[21] Gosse had brought Wolcott and Kipling together; indeed, he was always convinced that he had introduced the two, although actually it is more likely that they first met at the home of the noted novelist Mrs. Humphry Ward. Gosse had praised Kipling in the highest terms when talking to Wolcott and was annoyed when Wolcott was unimpressed. The older man had retorted that Kipling was destined to be the outstanding writer of his generation. He was sure the two men could become close friends.

In May Gosse wrote an article in the *Century Magazine*, speaking highly of Kipling's work but, like so many others, cautioning him about publishing too much. He urged Kipling to slow down his writing and to go back to the Far East and then return ten years later with "another precious and admirable budget of loot out of wonderland."[22]

In June of 1891 Kipling, torn between Woolcott and Carrie, went, not to the Far East, but on an odd and furtive trip to America. His uncle, Frederic Macdonald, a Methodist minister, was going to visit his brother Henry, who had moved to America, where he had married but had encountered misfortunes in business and now serious illness. Kipling for some reason decided to accompany his Uncle Frederic on his trip. By now, with the Kipling boom well under way, he was constantly pursued by reporters. In America, which he had criticized so freely and where there was a great furor over the question of the pirated editions of his work, he could anticipate endless questioning. If we are repelled by the excesses of reporters nowadays, Victorians were infinitely more so. To this, Kipling added his own extreme views about privacy. With remarkable naivete, he tried to get to America as "Mr. J. Macdonald."[23] With his short figure, bushy eyebrows, mustache, and the ever-present glasses, he was instantly recognizable; one imagines the hoax lasted all of a few minutes.

When they got to New York, Kipling hurried with his uncle to the Brevoort House, where he registered as "J. W. Macdonald." If they recognized him on the ship, perhaps they wouldn't in the city. But they did; within two hours the clerks were saying, "Do you know who that is over there? That's Rudyard Kipling." Furious at being found out, Kipling—again naively—ordered that no one was to tell of his whereabouts. This ensured someone's being told, and the reporters descended on him; he avoided giving an extended interview, claiming laryngitis. He and his uncle found that Henry Macdonald had died while they were crossing the Atlantic, so Frederic Macdonald naturally offered to help the family in any way he could.

The usual account of what followed is that Kipling immediately returned to England, leaving his uncle behind in America. But according to a contemporary article in the *Critic*, what actually happened is that Kipling went on a short trip. He refused to check his trunk on to his next destination, knowing the reporters would use this as a way of finding out where he was going. He took a few things from the trunk and left it at the hotel to be picked up on his return. In response to the reporters' questions he would only say that he was going "to a secluded spot on Long Island."[24] Some days later he returned and sailed for home on the *Aller*.

> [The people on the dock] recognized him at once. A gray, ill-fitting suit covered his muscular figure. The soft hat was drawn down upon his forehead. Two or three people accompanied him. Kipling bade them good-bye in a few words, walked up the gang-plank with the tread of a nervous athlete and disappeared, as if he wanted to escape observation.

Surely there was more to this trip than what it seems on the face of it—that he kept his uncle company on the voyage and as usual wanted to avoid publicity. If it were only this, when Frederic Macdonald stayed on to help out Kipling would have stayed on also, and then returned to England when his uncle did.

To me the evidence is convincing that he went to see Mrs. Hill. Before he left England, as part of his elaborate plan to travel unrecognized, he carefully leaked a story that because of ill health he was going back to Italy. Mrs. Hill must have been part of this conspiracy, because at the same time, June 13, 1891, the *New York Herald* printed a note about sickness forcing Kipling's return to Italy, saying they had gotten the information from "a friend from Beaver (Pa.)."[25] A week later the *Herald* found out where Kipling really was when he appeared in New York with other passengers pointing him out. It seems most unlikely that he enlisted Mrs. Hill's aid just to throw the reporters off the scent, to prevent their knowing he was going to America. It would appear that he planned to travel incognito to America, for the purpose of seeing her, and had told her to keep this a secret and, in fact, to say he was going to Italy. When he was discovered, he disappeared to some place—perhaps on Long Island?—where he could be alone with her. The elaborate subterfuges, the use of aliases, his leaving his trunk at the hotel, were not merely instances of his dislike of publicity. This was a special trip, to see a special person, and above all he wanted to conceal his meeting with her.

If this hypothesis is correct, why would Kipling want to see Mrs. Hill? Not, as I have indicated, for romantic reasons. I think he faced a tormenting conflict between his homosexual feelings for Wolcott and his heterosexual ones for Carrie. He could not confide in his parents. The conflict and shame experienced nowadays by those who have homosexual thoughts or acts were multiplied a hundred-fold in Victorian times. He had to talk to someone. Perhaps he could to "Ted," now that he could see her as another adult, and not as an older woman with whom he had been in love. Contemporaries speak of her calmness, her open, direct way of speaking, her tolerance[26]—and that last quality was one that Kipling saw as being especially American.*

If he did see her, she gave him no solution to his problem. As occurred after his trip to Italy, he found himself back in England facing the same situation he had tried to escape. He spent July on the Isle of Wight with the Balestiers, and wrote a remarkable short story, "The Disturber of Traffic." It is preceded by a curious poem, "The Prayer of Miriam Cohen"; the last verse is:

> A veil 'twixt us and Thee, Good Lord,
> A veil 'twixt us and Thee —
> Lest we should hear too clear, too clear,
> And into madness see![28]

The prayer asks that we be spared a view of things as they really are; it would be too much for us. Part of this reality that we hope to avoid

---

*Poor "Ted" Hill! No one could have guessed what an unfortunate end awaited her. After she retired from her teaching at Beaver College, one by one the members of her family died, leaving her alone. Still the decades passed. Now without income, she spent her last years in a convalescent home, in her eighties and then nineties, utterly destitute. She had to sell her first editions and notes from Kipling in an attempt to make ends meet. She died in 1952, and if only I had begun this book a few years earlier, I could have been told, by the one person left who was truly close to him, about the young Kipling during his years in India.[27]

is insight into ourselves as we really are, our urges, our wishes, our feelings of which we are usually unaware. Kipling, tormented by his confusing heterosexual attraction for Carrie and his homosexual attraction for her brother Wolcott, was praying that he might be able to put his feelings aside and not confront them; he was saying, "I think if I really acknowledged what I'm feeling, I'd go mad."

Then he wrote a story about a man going crazy—the only time he chose this subject. He wrote several stories, in later years, like "The House Surgeon," "The Woman in His Life," and "In the Same Boat," in which people become insane, but they all recover; in fact, their recovery, and what brought it about, is central to the story. "The Disturber of the Traffic," in its expression of Kipling's sexual conflicts, is very different.

He is told this weird story by Fenwyck, a lighthouse keeper stationed on the English Channel. It is about another keeper, named Dowse, who manned a light in Flores Strait, near Java, half a world away. For a companion Dowse has a half-man, half-beast called an Orang-Laut (Malay for "man of the water," just as "orang-utan" means "man of the forest") named Challong, who has long hair and webbed fingers. Dowse becomes obsessed with the streaks and lines—foam and so forth—on the water running past the lighthouse. Through a crack in the planking he watches the streaks go by with each tide. In depicting this obsession Kipling skillfully portrays a person becoming psychotic. Dowse begins to believe—although he partly knows it's nonsense—that the passing ships are disturbing the streaks he feels he has to watch on the water. He and Challong set out beacons indicating wrecks and close the passage; the authorities come, remove the buoys, and take Dowse to England. We are not told if he recovers or not. For a time he joins the Salvation Army, but ends up working on a ferry from Portsmouth to Gosport, which is on the Isle of Wight where Kipling wrote this story. In the last two sentences, the dawn breaks, the fog disappears, and

A lark went up from the cliffs . . . and we smelt a smell of cows in the lighthouse pasture below.

So you see we were both at liberty to thank the Lord for another day of clean and wholesome life.

What does it all mean? Of course, Kipling doesn't tell us. He always liked to write obscure stories as if telling the reader, with a twinkle in his eye, "Make what you like of it." I think, as Angus Wilson has pointed out, that Dowse and Challong have a Prospero-Caliban relationship, although Dowse does not fit our usual image of the magician Prospero. But when Fenwyck has Kipling "put my coat on that chair," it appears to be an allusion to Prospero's putting aside his magic mantle and becoming human. And again, toward the end, Fenwyck twice orders Dowse, "Take off that jersey." Seemingly casual acts and remarks like this, in Kipling's obscure stories, are important. They are carefully chosen clues to the central meaning of the tale, and account for much of the fascination of his writing. Then when we notice that "Caliban" is very nearly an anagram for "cannibal," might "Challong" refer to "challenge"? Kipling wrote a great deal about challenges and the value of overcoming them—it could be said to be his central philosophy—and he certainly faced a challenge in choosing between his feelings for Carrie and feelings for Wolcott. But there comes a point where speculation becomes idle.

When I spoke of Dowse and Challong as having a Prospero-Caliban relationship, I meant this in the sense of a human-animal interaction, the clash between a controlled being and a wild one; and, especially since this was so much on Kipling's mind at the time, I feel he is here making a comparison between a heterosexual ("controlled") person and a homosexual ("wild") one. Seemingly he decides he is more sexually drawn to women than to men, and the story ends with thanks for the beginning of "another day of clean and wholesome life."

After "The Disturber" Kipling wrote another puzzling story, "The Children of the Zodiac." Here Leo, the Lion, and Virgo, the Girl, are among the gods who have come down to earth. They fall in love with each other, as they see men and women love, but are constantly haunted by the fear of death. Leo realizes that now he fears death for two—his wife and himself—and says, "My brother, the Bull, had a better fate . . . he is alone."[29] (I see this as a reference to Wolcott Balestier.) Leo becomes a famous poet and singer and reassures men that bravery and work are the answers to death. Then one day his wife, the Girl, finds her breast has turned hard, as Cancer, the Crab, had predicted. Soon afterward, as also predicted, Leo feels "the cold touch of the Crab's claw on the apple of his throat." He feels weak and cannot see the faces of those about him, and dies. Some of his lines are carved on the Girl's tombstone, and, writes Kipling:

> One of the children of men, coming thousands of years later, rubbed away the lichen, read the lines, and applied them to a trouble other than the one Leo meant.

At the time he wrote this, Kipling had laryngitis. All his life he had a deep fear of cancer. He once wrote "Ted" Hill that cancer of the throat was "the family complaint."[30] (This was not true.) In conflict over his love for Carrie, he wrote a story about death, and about a man finding a solution "to a trouble other than the one Leo meant." Surely this trouble was the Carrie-Wolcott-Kipling triangle.

In August he continued to stay with the Balestiers on the Isle of Wight. It would seem there was increasing tension between the three of them, with an atmosphere you could cut with a knife, and the prospect of open quarrels and accusations. Kipling could stand it no longer.

He set off on another ocean voyage, following the Victorian custom, this time a leisurely one, to take many months, perhaps involving going all the way around the world. The first two trips had provided no solution; now he would take a second, longer one. He was in an impossible dilemma. Carrie, who admired her brother but was not close to him, wanted to marry Kipling, who was interested in her but was writing a novel with this same brother toward whom he felt sexually attracted. It would seem these were the only conditions that would have necessitated Kipling's departure on a months-long ocean voyage to the other side of the earth. If he could have felt sure of his feelings about Carrie or Wolcott he would have declared himself one way or the other and the impasse would have ended. But he couldn't; there was no way to break this triangle. He could only leave the whole situation and see if time would make a change. He decided, in his own words, to "get clean away and re-sort myself."[31] (There may be a second meaning to the word *clean*, as in the last sentence of "The Disturber of Traffic.")

Before he left, he completed the first draft of a poem, initially entitled "L'envoi," and later changed to "The Long Trail." Three verses of it are:

135

There be triple ways to take,
    of the eagle or the snake,
Or the way of man with a maid;
But the fairest way to me is a
    ship's upon the sea
In the heel of the North-East Trade.
    Can you hear the crash on her bows, dear lad,
    And the drum of the racing screw,
    As she ships it green on the old trail, our own trail, the out trail,
    As she lifts and 'scends on the Long
        Trail—the trail that is always new?

Fly forward, O my heart, from the Foreland
    to the Start—
We're steaming all too slow,
And it's twenty thousand mile to our
    little lazy isle
Where the trumpet-orchids blow!
    You have heard the call of the off-shore wind,
    And the voice of the deep-sea rain;
    You have heard the song-how long? how long?
    Pull out on the trail again!

The Lord knows what we may find, dear lad,
And The Deuce knows what we may do—
    But we're back once more on the old trail,
    our own trail, the out trail,
    We're down, hull-down on the Long Trail—the
    trail that is always new![32]

Come away from that sister of yours, he is saying to Wolcott, and we'll set out in a man's world. Lock arms and we'll go off to the romantic South Seas. But when he left on August 22, he was alone.

Two months later, he published the final version of the poem just quoted. It is identical except that in place of the repetitive "dear lad" we find—"dear lass."[33] His feelings for Carrie were apparently winning out.

He planned to go south to Cape Town, spend a month or two there, and then make the long, six-thousand-mile trip eastward to Australia and New Zealand. After some time there, he wanted to go across to America, or back to India—his plans were vague.

He spent two weeks of September in Cape Town. According to one account, at a party he found himself in the same room with Cecil Rhodes but, ever unobtrusive, he did not meet the man who was to mean so much to him in later years. He was more interested in the British naval station at Simonstown, for this voyage was to be a change in more ways than one. For years he had been fascinated by the Army, and some of his best stories had been about soldiers. From this trip came his first naval story, "Judson and the Empire." It is actually not only about the Navy, but shows an odd mixture of emphasis on both Army and Navy, as if Kipling were reluctant to leave his soldiers. From this point on, Kipling slowly but steadily turned toward the Navy.

He left Cape Town on September 25 and set out on the long, lonely voyage across the bottom of the world to Australia. Almost three weeks later, the ship stopped in Tasmania, and then continued on a five-day run to Wellington in New Zealand. It was now mid-October. After two weeks there, Kipling left for only a few days in Australia, mostly in Melbourne.

His passage across the world was discussed in the correspondence between two perceptive people, Henry James in London and Robert Louis Stevenson in Samoa. The letters are separated by the weeks and months it took to communicate in those days.

James to Stevenson, March 1890:

> (We'll tell you all about Rudyard Kipling—your nascent rival—he has killed one immortal—Rider Haggard—the star of the hour, aged twenty-four and author of remarkable Anglo-Indian and extraordinarily observed barrack life—Tommy Atkins—tales.)[34]

Stevenson to James, August 1890:

> Kipling is too clever to live.[35]

Stevenson to James, December 1890:

> Kipling is by far the most promising young man who has appeared since— ahem—I appeared. He amazes me by his precocity and various endowment[s]. But he alarms me by his copiousness and haste . . . . At this rate his works will soon fill the habitable globe . . . . If I had this man's fertility and courage, it seems to me I could heave a pyramid . . . . Certainly Kipling has the gifts; the fairy godmothers were all tipsy at his christening: what will he do with them?

James to Stevenson, January 1891:

The only news in literature here . . . continues to be the infant monster of a Kipling.

James to Stevenson, October 1891:

That little black demon of a Kipling will perhaps have leaped upon your silver strand by the time this reaches you—he publicly left England to embrace you many weeks ago—carrying literary genius out of the country with him in his pocket.

However, Kipling concluded he did not have the time to get from southern Australia north to out-of-the-way Samoa to visit Stevenson, so he decided to turn northwestward to India and his parents. General Booth of the Salvation Army was a fellow passenger. Forty years later, Kipling remembered the boiling dark clouds and Booth "walking backward in the dusk over the uneven wharf, his cloak blown upwards, tulip-fashion, over his grey head, while he beat a tambourine in the face of the singing, weeping, praying crowd who had come to see him off."[36] They left Adelaide for Colombo in Ceylon (now Sri Lanka) and immediately encountered rough weather. Seas swept the ship from end to end, and since Booth's cabin was near Kipling's, "in the intervals between crashes overhead and cataracts down below he sounded like a wounded elephant; for he was in every way a big man." The next time Kipling saw Booth was when they both received degrees, years later, from Oxford. General Booth "strode across to me in his Doctor's robes, which magnificently became him, and, 'Young feller,' said he, 'how's your soul?'"

Besides the difficulty in getting to Samoa, there may have been another reason for his turning toward India. Somewhere around the middle of November—the exact date cannot be ascertained—Carrie Balestier apparently cabled him that Wolcott was ill. Toward the end of November Melbourne newspapers said Kipling would have to return to India (i.e., to England via India, the quickest route) since he had received "bad news." From Colombo he crossed to the southern tip of India, arriving the middle of December, and set off to visit his parents far up in the Punjab. For four days and nights the train took him the length of southern India, a strange, hot, flat, red India, where he said he couldn't understand a word spoken to him—for previously he had only been in the northern part of the country.

Wolcott Balestier had become sick about the middle of November and had gone to Dresden on business, perhaps also hoping that the change would would help him. Instead, he grew worse and was found to have typhoid fever. His mother and two sisters hastened over to take care of him, but he rapidly went downhill and died on December 8.

Mrs. Balestier and Josephine were heartbroken and Carrie, efficient even in such a moment as this, had to take over. She asked Henry James, a family friend, to come and help her, and sent word to the family back in Brattleboro and to Kipling in India. James, who had known Wolcott and had a warm liking for him, did all he could to help Carrie at this tragic time. His impressions are given in a series of letters.

> . . . I am working through my dreary errand and service here as smoothly as three stricken women—a mother and two sisters—permit. They are however very temperate and discreet—and one of the sisters a little person of extraordinary capacity—who will float them all successfully home. [37]

> The English chaplain read the service . . . . The 3 ladies came, insistently, to the grave. . . . By far the most interesting is poor little concentrated, passionate Carrie, with whom I came back from the cemetery alone . . . [She] is remarkable in her force, acuteness, capacity and courage—and in the intense—almost manly—nature of her emotion . . . . One thing, I believe, the poor girl could *not* meet—but God grant (and the complexity of "genius" grant) that she may not have to meet it—as there is no reason to suppose that she will. What this tribulation is—or would be, rather, I can indicate better when I see you. [38]

What is this "one thing" that Carrie couldn't face? It is something that Kipling could tell her, but "there is no reason to suppose" that he will. (James, in other letters of this time, refers to Kipling as a "genius.") It is something so shocking to James that he cannot refer to it in a private letter to a close friend, but must wait to whisper it face-to-face.

The letter quoted above was written to Edmund Gosse who, if not primarily homosexual, clearly had inclinations in that direction. For years he wrote love letters to a man named Hamo Thornycroft. Both Gosse and James, it would seem, recognized homosexual impulses in themselves and others and discussed this privately but in public kept a genteel and conventional silence on the subject. (Gosse, for example, exchanged many letters with André Gide but always carefully attempted to limit their discussions to literature.) James and Gosse knew both Wolcott and Kipling well and would have recognized and discussed any homosexual feelings between the two long before this time. One has to wonder, then, if the "one thing" that must be left secret was that the homosexual relationship between Wolcott and Kipling was overt, involving acts and not just feelings. If it had consisted only of feelings, now that Wolcott was dead it would have been speedily forgotten in typical Victorian fashion. Only these two sentences (omitted from the official biography) suggest that it was not.

IX

MARRIAGE

A week before Christmas Kipling had arrived in Lahore, where he was reunited with his parents and acclaimed by the community for his meteoric rise to fame since he had left them less than three years before. He appeared at a bazaar put on by the Lieutenant-Governor's wife and allowed a sketch of himself to be printed in his old newspaper, the *Civil and Military Gazette*. All this was dropped when Carrie's cable came, apparently the day before Christmas. Edmund Gosse said the wire read, "Wolcott dead. Come back to me."[1] Accounts differ as to whether he spent Christmas day with his family or dashed off immediately; in any event, he quickly took the train to Bombay and from there, as rapidly as he could, he rushed to England. Going by ship to Trieste and then overland, he reached London in fourteen days, practically record time in those days.

In Bombay he found time, however, to find the old *ayah* of his childhood (had he kept track of her since leaving India?); his "second mother" who meant so much to him, was, he said, "so old but so unaltered"[2] and she greeted him with "blessings and tears." As if he had sensed that he would never see India, his *ayah*, and Lahore again, he wrote, "This was my last look round the only real home I had yet known."

While he was racing toward England, word got out that he was going to marry Wolcott Balestier's sister; and the same information was making the rounds in Brattleboro, Vermont. But which sister—Josephine, the pretty one, or Carrie, the smart one? Interestingly, for several days no one seemed to know. Kipling's courting of Carrie had been so beset with extreme difficulties that family friends were predicting—many of them hopefully—that he would marry Josephine. With what we know of his experiences with women, and his preoccupation with dominating forceful ones, it will come as no surprise that it was Carrie who became his wife.

This is part of it; and yet why the confusion? It would seem that Kipling's family, and perhaps even Kipling himself, must have been in doubt about which one he wanted to marry; for if the family had known, surely they would simply have announced it, and that would have been that. It is almost as if, with Wolcott dead and gone, Kipling rushed to England to marry the sister—*either* sister, so long as she had Wolcott for a brother. His feelings for his wife-to-be would be reinforced by those he had had for Wolcott.

His actions, too, seemed to bear out this idea. With Wolcott dead, it was as if Carrie now had a double portion of his affection, and she and Kipling wanted to be married immediately. Considering the fact that they had been arguing about it for a year, it certainly must have been Wolcott's death that now made them positively dash into marriage, with such speed that a special license had to be obtained. At the hasty ceremony on January 18, Henry James gave the bride away; Ambrose Poynter, Kipling's cousin, was best man; and the entire congregation consisted of four people: William Heinemann, who had been Wolcott's partner, Edmund Gosse, and Gosse's daughter Teresa and son Philip, a boy of twelve. (About twice this number had been invited but an influenza epidemic had prevented their coming.) Philip, wide-eyed with excitement at the ceremony, years later remembered every detail about the bride: she was a little woman with tiny hands and feet, in a brown dress that buttoned down the front. Edmund Gosse had been quite overcome by Wolcott's death. He wrote Richard Gilder, "I know not how to get on without him—without his sympathy, his energy, his encouragement."[3] Looking back on it years later, however, Gosse spoke very differently of Wolcott. He wrote George Douglas, "You would have detested him. I should have detested him, but that he happened to like me very much."

Again and again, Henry James's letters expressed his doubts about the marriage:

[Carrie] was poor Wolcott Balestier's sister and is a hard devoted capable charmless little person whom I don't in the least understand his marrying. It's a union of which I don't forecast the future. . . .[4]

In another letter:

But Wolcott's ghostly presence was the thing that was most vivid to me— and the rest of the matter seemed a kind of ironic—though quite inevitable—dance upon his grave.[5]

Kipling's feelings about privacy, of course, extended to the events surrounding his marriage. One reason for the few people at the "dreary little wedding," as Henry James called it, was haste—and the flu—but another was secrecy. Kipling wanted no one to know.

W. E. Henley had known Kipling since soon after his arrival from India, and the *Scots Observer*, of which he was the editor, had been the first to publish some of the "Barrack Room Ballads." He had been closely associated with Kipling and could have laid some claim to being the person who launched him to fame. Kipling had brought back from his travels a poem called "Tomlinson," a set of verses about a man who dies and is judged in Heaven and Hell, and on his wedding day he wrote Henley about it. At the end of the letter he put in two terse sentences.

I have married Miss Balestier, the sister of the man with whom I wrote the yarn in the *Century*. I don't as a rule let men enter any part of life outside the working sections, but in this case methinks you are entitled to know.[6]

And after the wedding itself, as the Kiplings emerged from the church door, he saw a newspaper poster announcing the marriage "which made me feel uncomfortable and defenseless."[7]

The efficient Carrie had taken care of the sale of her brother's house and all other business matters left unfinished at his death. Whatever else the marriage meant, Kipling had gained the devoted care of an exceedingly capable person. She immediately took over all his business affairs, for Kipling had always been very disorganized in such matters, and ran them with meticulous care. She shielded him from publicity, watched over his health, and organized his working hours down to the last detail—at times, friends said, to an exasperating degree, as if he were a schoolboy and she an overprotective mother. If Kipling resented all this pressure, his sense of loyalty and the customs of the time almost always prevented any complaining on his part.

Early in February 1892 the Kiplings set out on a honeymoon, which, tentatively, was to take them around the world. The first stop was America and Carrie's family. On board ship Kipling was finishing up *The Naulahka*, which had begun to appear in monthly installments in the *Century Magazine*, and which had not been completed at the time of Wolcott's death. At this time, he wrote the chapter headings, which, as mentioned before, give clues about his feelings for Wolcott and Carrie.

Chapter 1 is headed:

> There was a strife 'twixt man and maide . . .
> 'Twas, "Sweet, I must not bide wi' you",
> And "Love, I canna bide alone";
> For baith were young and baith were true,
> And baith were hard as the nether stone.[8]

Chapter 8 is headed, in part:

> When a Lover hies abroad . . .
> Heaven smiles above.

But at the next chapter:

> I wait for thy command
> To serve, to speed, or withstand,
> And thou sayest I do not well? . . .
> And thou sayest 'tis ill that I came.

(Both were adjusting to their new relationship. The day after their marriage, Carrie had written in her diary with characteristic dry humor, "Jan. 19. We continue to be married.")[9]

Henry Adams happened to be on the same ship:

Fate was kind on that voyage. Rudyard Kipling, on his wedding trip to America . . . dashed over the passengers his exuberant fountain of gaiety and wit—as though playing a garden hose on a thirsty and faded begonia . . . and yet, in the full delight of his endless fun and variety, one felt the old conundrum repeat itself. Somehow, somewhere, Kipling and the American were not one but two, and could not be glued together. . . .[10]

They landed in New York where they spent a day or so. Full of gusto, energetic and observant, Kipling roamed around New York with his new wife. He delighted in the winter sunshine, but felt it was wasted shining on "the worst pavements in the world."[11] Always the impressionable journalist, he hated New York's "triply over-heated rooms, and much too energetic inhabitants," but loved "to walk round and round Madison Square, because that was full of beautifully dressed babies playing counting-out games."

They went up to Brattleboro on February 17, leaving behind "the roar and rattle" of the city, and Kipling, who had never experienced a really cold climate, was ecstatic at this sight of a New England winter. He wrote about it eloquently:

Thirty below freezing! It was inconceivable till one stepped out into it at midnight and the first shock of that clear, still air took away the breath as does a plunge into sea-water. . . . But for the jingle of the sleigh-bells the ride might have taken place in a dream, for there was no sound of hoofs upon the snow, the runners sighed a little now and then as they glided over an inequality, and all the sheeted hills round about were as dumb as death. Only the Connecticut River kept up its heart and a lane of black water through the packed ice. . . . Elsewhere there was nothing but snow under the moon—snow drifted to the level of the stone fences or curling over their tops in a lip of frosted silver; snow banked high on either side of the road or lying heavy on the pines and hemlocks in the woods. . . .

In the morning the other side of the picture was revealed in the colours of the sunlight. There was never a cloud in the sky that rested on the snow-line of the horizon as a sapphire on white velvet. Hills of pure white, or speckled and furred with woods, rose up above the solid white levels of the fields, and the sun rioted over their embroideries till the eyes ached. . . . [The snow for] the most part was soft powdered stuff ready to catch the light on a thousand crystals and multiply it sevenfold.

Carrie's brother, Beatty Balestier, had them to stay for three days at his seventy-acre farm, just given to him by his doting grandmother, Mrs. Balestier, who lived a couple of hundred yards away at

"Beechwood," the family home. Beatty's young wife, Mai, was charming and vivacious; but, as usual, it was to their tiny daughter Marjorie that Kipling lost his heart. Beatty himself seemed likeable to Kipling, who had always admired American energy and friendliness, though he must have been startled by his brother-in-law's wild ways. For Beatty was the town "character"; a back-slapper, friendly, loud, free with his money when he had any, a man whose every other sentence had a "goddamn" in it, he provided the town with plenty of gossip, all of which he thoroughly enjoyed. At his house he had a large bell which he periodically rang as an invitation for all who heard it to come in for a drink. He was also unreliable, impulsive, contentious, and constantly in debt—out of which his tolerant grandmother was forever bailing him. A person, in short, just the opposite of the reserved, disciplined Kipling, who avoided the limelight at all costs.

But the countryside was infinitely appealing. When he had crossed America before, in 1889, and stayed in Pennsylvania, he had often been bitterly critical. What has gone unnoticed is that his barbs were mostly aimed (as they were now at New York) at the cities and their inhabitants. Once Kipling was free to roam in Washington State, in Montana and Wyoming, above all in Pennsylvania, he tended to praise Americans to the skies. The ideal he always returned to was Mrs. Hill in Beaver, Pennsylvania. In that small town he found peace, a stratified, indigenous society, privacy, and Carrie Taylor's love—all in a place he immediately likened to an Indian village.

Much has been made of the idea that he imagined a union of the best aspects of America and England. This we can safely say is incorrect—on a factual level. (The psychic truth was that yes, in England, or America, or a blend of both, he was searching for a home, for his background.) As described, he felt nothing but contempt for the English in England. He had found them smug, out of touch with reality, weak and selfish. Their writers were lily-livered aesthetes. But America! Here—in the rural areas—there was energy, a frontier toughness, "Ted" Hill's openness and honesty—here anything was possible. Among American writers were Mark Twain and Bret Harte, and Herman Melville who had died only the year before in 1891; all three had been favorites of Kiping's since he was a schoolboy. Everything was as new and fresh as the snow sparkling in the sunshine. In this magic land he could create something of the India of his childhood. Not from the outside in; not in appearances only. The last thing he would have done is build some Victorian edifice, gingerbread and all, and perch it, Simla-like, on a Vermont mountaintop. He would build, like Strickland, from the inside out. Knowing the Indian world, he would have the things he valued there—the security, the love of a close-knit family, an ordered society, life measured out in comforting rituals, and the satisfaction of hard work well done.

The second day, exploring the lovely countryside, the Kiplings came to a quick decision. They must buy a share of the family property, one with a view of Mount Monadnock which reared "like a gigantic thumbnail pointing heavenward" twenty-five miles to the east. Beatty, with his casual generosity, was all for giving it to them on the spot as a wedding present, but the careful Carrie, who knew that a lot of contentiousness lay behind her brother's munificence, wanted to work out a legal agreement. They all went down to New York, talked it over with the family lawyers, and arrived at a compromise. By legal contract, Beatty gave them about ten acres of land for a dollar, but kept certain rights—mowing and the like—for himself. It was a perfectly friendly agreement; it almost seemed unnecessary to make it a legal one. Who could imagine that it would all end in the bitterest of family quarrels?

After visiting several friends in and near New York, they set out on their interrupted honeymoon. They headed west to Chicago—not the stockyards, this time—and then swung up to St. Paul. Kipling wrote a running account of their travels as he had in 1889, but now a much more lucrative one. It was printed simultaneously by the *Sun* in New York and the *Times* in London, and Kipling loyally allowed it to appear also in the *Civil and Military Gazette* for old times' sake. No matter how far away he went, something of him always remained in India.

It is interesting to compare Kipling's remarks about America with those written about three years earlier; he was now married to an American and was strongly considering living in America. He was considerably more temperate; the wild swings he made before are largely absent; but he still retained his old superficiality and susceptibility to snap judgments. New York City was a "long, narrow pig-trough." Here the three "pillars of moderately decent government, [which] are regard for human life, justice . . . and good roads," were sadly neglected. Returning to his old hatred, politics, he expressed his contempt for the men, "chiefly of foreign extraction, who control the city." But when he got to the "most excellent municipality of St. Paul," he was filled with enthusiasm. The city was "all things to all men." The people were so friendly, the houses so attractive; the Americans were "a hundred years ahead of the English in design, comfort, and economy, and (this is most important) labour-saving appliances in his house."

But they did not continue on across America; and despite his enthusiasm for New England and St. Paul, it was with a sigh of relief that Kipling and his Anglophile bride crossed into Canada at Winnipeg: "Her Majesty the Queen of England and Empress of India has us in her keeping." He noted with pleasure a Canadian Mountie on the train. "One wants to shake hands with him because he is clean and does not slouch nor spit, trims his hair, and walks as a man should." They continued westward over the prairie—Kipling described Medicine Hat and compared it with how it had looked three years before—the magnificent Rockies, and on to British Columbia, "perhaps the loveliest land in the world next to New Zealand."

At Vancouver, they boarded the *Empress of India* and set off for Japan. Most of their time there was spent in Yokohama. They planned to go on to Samoa where Kipling at long last could meet Robert Louis Stevenson. But it was not to be. Kipling went to the Yokohama branch of his English bank one morning and cashed a small check. The manager urged him to take more, but not taking the hint, Kipling answered that he "did not care to have too much cash at one time in my careless keeping."[12] He returned in the afternoon to find that the bank had failed. Kipling and his now-pregnant wife were stranded, almost penniless, in Japan. The plan to go on to the South Pacific had to be given up. The Kiplings, happy and full of zest, were not alarmed at this predicament, but took it as an adventure. They got the money from their now-canceled ship reservations, and they already had their return-trip tickets to Vancouver. In July they left Japan—Kipling did not know it, but it was to be the last time he was to be "east of Suez," that part of the world that, deep down, had such meaning for him.

Even on his honeymoon he kept working. Besides writing his accounts of their travels, he put the finishing polish on some old Indian stories and on "Judson and the Empire." His stay in Japan led to his well-known poem "The Rhyme of the Three Sealers."

> Away by the lands of the Japanee
> Where the paper lanterns glow . . .
> They tell the tale anew
> Of a hidden sea and a hidden fight,
> When the *Baltic* ran from the *Northern Light*
> And the *Stralsund* fought the two.[13]

On the return voyage across the Pacific those aboard had a rare treat. Kipling, happy on his honeymoon, read from his works at gatherings of the ship's passengers. This was unusual, the kind of thing that, in spite of frequent requests, he seldom did. He had always admired American friendliness; perhaps he was now trying to copy it.

They went across Canada as special guests of the chairman of the Canadian Pacific Railway. In Montreal, Carrie's mother got in touch with them, with news of a house they could rent in Brattleboro. A Mrs. Bliss, who owned a farm nearby, had a small white frame house on her property, generally used by the hired man, that she offered them for ten dollars a month. They came down to Brattleboro the end of July, stayed with Beatty—where Kipling could again adore little Marjorie—and, after taking a look at the Bliss Cottage, as it was called, took the offer. It was less than half a mile south of the land they had gotten from Beatty, where they already had plans to build a fine new house of their own.

For a year they lived in the Bliss Cottage, a simple and very happy life—perhaps the happiest year of their marriage. As Rice has pointed out,[14] the French translator of Kipling's autobiography unwittingly came closest to the truth when he rendered the name "Bliss Cottage" as "Maison de Bonheur."

> We took it. We furnished it with a simplicity that fore-ran the hire-purchase system. We bought, second or third hand, a huge, hot-air stove which we installed in the cellar. We cut generous holes in our thin floors for its eight-inch tin pipes, (why we were not burned in our beds each week of the winter I never can understand) and we were extraordinarily and self-centeredly content.
>
> As New England summer flamed into autumn, I piled cut spruce boughs all round the draughty cottage sill, and helped to put up a tiny roofless verandah along one side of it for future needs. When winter shut

down and the sleigh-bells rang all over the white world that tucked us in, we counted ourselves secure. Sometimes we had a servant. Sometimes she would find the solitude too much for her and flee without warning, one even leaving her trunk. This troubled us not at all. There are always two sides to a plate, and the cleaning of frying- and saucepans is as little a mystery as the making of comfortable beds. When our lead pipe froze, we would slip in our coon-skin coats and thaw it out with a lighted candle. There was no space in the attic bedroom for a cradle, so we decided that a trunk-tray would be just as good. We envied no one.

My first child and daughter* was born in three foot of snow on the night of December 29th, 1892. Her Mother's birthday being the 31st and mine the 30th of the same month, we congratulated her on her sense of the fitness of things, and she throve in her trunk-tray in the sunshine on the little plank verandah. Her birth brought me into contact with the best friend I made in New England—Dr. Conland.[15]

Though Kipling speaks of piling boughs and working around the house, it is unlikely that much of this took place. His extreme clumsiness was quickly noted by his neighbors. Some years later, a visitor asked if Kipling had helped to build a stone wall at his place, only to be told by a former hired hand, "He couldn't have put one stone on another, much less build a wall!"[16]

This happy year was also a productive one. After returning from Japan he was entranced with something seen nowhere else in the world—the colors of a New England autumn.

No pen can describe the turning of the leaves—the insurrection of the tree-people against the waning year. A little maple began it, flaming blood-red of a sudden where he stood against the dark green of a pine-belt. Next morning there was an answering signal from the swamp where the sumacs grow. Three days later, the hill-sides as far as the eye could range were afire, and the roads paved, with crimson and gold. Then a wet wind blew, and ruined all the uniforms of that gorgeous host; and the oaks, who had held themselves in reserve, buckled on their dull and bronzed cuirasses and stood it out stiffly to the last blown leaf, till nothing remained but pencil-shading of bare boughs, and one could see into the most private heart of the woods.[17]

And in November of 1892 he wrote "Mowgli's Brothers." This was the first of the famous stories which make up the two volumes of *The*

*Named Josephine, after Carrie's sister.

Jungle Books, completed in March 1895. These were Kipling's "best sellers," enormously popular books in their time, still read nowadays a century later.

That fall, too, work was begun on their new house. Ever since their return to America they had been talking with an architect about the exciting plans. The resulting house, about ninety feet by thirty feet, was built on the side of a long hill, with large windows facing east. On the west side was the main entrance and a long corridor, on each of the three floors, connecting the various rooms. It was called "Naulakha," spelled correctly now, unlike the book's title *Naulahka*, given it by Wolcott Balestier. It has been suggested that this was simply a mistake on Wolcott's part. This seems hard to believe. He and Kipling had used the word repeatedly in their early collaboration; it seems more likely that Wolcott (possibly in reaction to Kipling's departure around the world?) had, in his peremptory way, altered this foreign word, decided that it sounded better his way. Kipling was delighted with the house, the only one he ever built in his lifetime. He enjoyed looking at it from a distance, seeing "our Naulakha riding on its hillside like a little boat on the flank of a far wave."[18] And indeed, looking at the architect's drawings, it does have rather shiplike lines.*

Other people had less pleasant memories. On the ground floor, after the kitchen and dining room, there was a lounge, into which you stepped when entering the front door. The next room was Carrie's. Her desk faced the door as you entered the room, and as business manager for her husband no one, and she meant *no one*, ever got past her without her permission to open the next door, the one to Kipling's study.

Very unwisely, they hired Beatty as contractor in the building of the house. At first, all went smoothly; he had the foundation built of stones from old walls on the place, in the fall of 1892. In the spring, when the snow had gone (in those days it was common practice to let the foundation of a house remain untouched over a winter, so that it could settle), he hired a gang of carpenters and began the building of the house itself. While the major part of the construction was going on, it involved

---

*The house is still standing, as is the Bliss Cottage, although the latter has been remodeled and moved a short distance.

rather large sums of money, and, therefore, good-sized commissions; and Beatty, always in debt, could certainly use them. What exasperated him was the way the business end of the Kipling household—his sister—gave him his money. For the careful Carrie, horrified at the disorderly way Beatty lived, resolved to "help" him. When he came to the Bliss Cottage three or four times a week to discuss construction of the new house, she pointedly gave him his commissions in little driblets, five dollars one day, two dollars and twenty-five cents another, all meticulously noted down in her diary. She treated him as if he were a willful and irresponsible child, taking just the opposite position from that of his forgiving grandmother. The fact that Carrie's viewpoint was a rather realistic one made it no easier to accept.

That summer, with Naulakha almost finished, they were delighted to get a visit from Kipling's father, Lockwood, who had now retired after nearly thirty years of work in India. (Kipling's mother had not accompanied him; he greatly enjoyed travel, but she did not.) In the usual Victorian fashion, Kipling had put in a word for him to the current Viceroy, through a former Viceroy, and his father was given a pension for the remaining twenty years of his life.

The Kiplings, father and son, made a delightful pair, both full of information, both interested in everything, each stimulating the other's thoughts. Lockwood Kipling, however, had a far greater tolerance than his son, who struck some people as being perpetually indignant over something or other. "The Pater" also had a far better sense of continuity. He helped his son with the plot of some of his best stories, most notably *Kim*. He was the only man (always excepting Wolcott Balestier) whose advice Kipling ever sought. An inability to see "the whole picture" was a problem for Kipling throughout his career. Once he told a friend that it would always be a mystery to him how anyone could ever see the beginning, middle, and end of a long story; that he had plenty of ideas, but could not string them together to form a coherent tale. His classmates had noticed this when he was a schoolboy. In July, Kipling worked on "The Bridge Builders," in which the sure handling of the multitude of native deities suggests that his father helped in writing this story. It is the only one (with the exception of "The Sutlej Bridge") that centers in construction, no doubt because he was watching his own home being built at the time.

MARRIAGE

Kipling had a fine time with his father. The two of them, with some agility, managed to slip away on a brief trip to Canada just when everything had to be moved from Bliss Cottage to the newly finished Naulakha. One can imagine Kipling, with a mischievous glint in his eyes, laying plans with his father for a rebellion. Carrie was fuming, all the more so because, when moving-day arrived with the men gone, she faced insurrection in the ranks. The cook had been objecting to a certain cap that was part of her uniform. Carrie, never one to compromise, had flatly ordered her to wear it. The cook then quit the morning of moving-day and the maid left with her, so Carrie had to supervise the move by herself. In August the two men returned and Lockwood Kipling—skilled in any form of art—carved, in the bricks over the fireplace, a quotation from the Bible: "The Night cometh when no man can work,"* where it can still be seen. The professional quality of the lettering is striking. Kipling's next collection of stories was called *The Day's Work*.

In October after his father's departure, Carrie noted in her diary—one of the rare times she wrote down anything personal—that Kipling said that he felt enormously creative, a "return of a feeling of great strength, such as he had when he first came to London and met the men he was pitted against." [19] Then, lonely and depressed, he had had his back to the wall, and with characteristic stubborn courage, had produced in an amazing nine months several remarkable stories, poems, and *The Light That Failed*. Now, married, happy, and the father of a child he adored, he felt again this awareness of his tremendous abilities, an enthusiastic feeling of confidence. In his four years in America, Kipling wrote the works for which he is best remembered today—several of his poems and stories such as "McAndrew's Hymn," "The Rhyme of the Three Sealers," and "L'envoi" ("When earth's last picture is painted," which has to be distinguished from *five* other poems that Kipling called "L'envoi" at one time or another), the two *Jungle Books*, *The Day's Work, Part II* (notably ".007," "The Maltese Cat," "The Brushwood Boy"), and *Captains Courageous*; and it was in America that he did much of the preliminary work on *Kim*.

---

*The full verse (Gospel according to St. John, King James version, IX, 4) is: "I must work the works of him that sent me while it is day: the night cometh when no man can work."

Here we must ponder the mystery of a man whose two most productive periods in his entire life came when he was most miserable, and when he was happiest.

Pollock's work offers an explanation. After studying the mourning process following a loss, he noted that "it is found in all cultures throughout the world and throughout time, is a cornerstone of man's religious belief system, and is a fundamental adaptation to change and loss."[20] The person who successfully works through mourning experiences a sense of liberation, of being freed from a past which no longer exists. Creative people, Pollock believes, experience a burst of energy at these times, and he impressively demonstrates the effect of a loss in the work of Goethe, Mahler, Van Gogh, Schliemann, Lenin, De Quincey, and Barrie. It is possible that Kipling in London, desperately homesick for India, gradually came to terms with this loss and produced that amazing amount of work in his first nine months in England. After Wolcott Balestier's death, we have seen with what a mixture of grief and joy Kipling and Carrie, as Henry James put it, performed a "dance upon his grave." Perhaps in both cases Kipling mastered feelings about a loss and felt the resultant energy described by Pollock, though in the case of Wolcott's death he certainly felt relief as well as sadness.

As 1894 began, Kipling could look back over two years of happy accomplishments. "I have time, light, and quiet, three things hard to come by in London,"[21] he wrote a friend. Their new home was a delight; little Josephine, now a year old, healthy and precocious, was a constant joy; and Kipling's work was achieving solid recognition the world around. For it was during his four years in America that he began to achieve great financial success. Early in 1893 he was getting $10 per thousand words for his prose; by 1894 he came close to doubling that; Scribner's gave him a record $500 for a single poem, "McAndrew's Hymn," and during that year he made $25,000 (roughly the equivalent of $500,000 nowadays).

But they were having problems locally. A. Conan Doyle, whose "The Sign of the Four" (the second Sherlock Holmes story) had been one of the few pieces to compete with Kipling's outpouring in early 1890, came to visit them for Thanksgiving the previous November. Beatty, always friendly, came by and swept them all down to his house for one of his huge, delightful dinners. In Brattleboro he is quoted to this day as having said firmly, "No one would want to keep Thanksgiving in an Englishman's house." They all went down and had a fine time. He and Kipling went in to town by sleigh together daily for the mail, and Marjorie would come up to Naulakha to play with Josephine. But Beatty was becoming more and more of a problem. When the Kiplings had been building Naulakha he had a steady source of income from them; now that the house was finished he had only odd jobs on which he could get a commission, and he kept on trying to live in his same extravagant way. Not always sober, he took to hanging around the place, a source of embarrassment to the Kiplings and their guests; but no hints could be dropped, since, by their agreement, he had legal rights to mow and otherwise use certain parts of their land.

From Beatty's viewpoint, we can understand how it galled him to see this little Englishman in two years vault from being the penniless tenant of a hired man's cottage to being one of the richest men in town. And Carrie's condescending attitude only made it worse.

Many townspeople shared his feelings. Rural Vermonters looked askance at this "furriner" who had married "the Balestier girl." They lived a hard life, on marginal land that was steadily going downhill. Perhaps it was natural that they envied, and were suspicious of, a man who could make a fortune with a pen and some paper.

It should be emphasized that a good half of the fault lay with the Kiplings. He had moved there with the idea of creating a magic spot from his own childhood. There were the bokhara rugs he had brought from India, a big watercolor of the desert, military drawings, on the mantelpiece the carved figures of animals from *The Jungle Books* given him by Joel Chandler Harris, the tiger skin used as a sleigh-rug. Just as he had previously compared Beaver, Pennsylvania, and England with India, now he did the same thing with Brattleboro. "I live in the southern part of the state of Vermont," he wrote a soldier in India, "in a country not at all unlike the Doon if you have ever been there—the hills below Rajpur."[22] There was never any thought of accepting Vermont as Vermont. The Kiplings always remained totally aloof, never entering the community life in any way. They left others alone, and wished to be left strictly alone themselves, stating this "so loudly and so often," says van de Water, "that it became a challenge."[23] If a new neighbor paid a friendly call, Carrie would have a few words with him at the door—and that would be as far as he would get. One biographer claimed that they only made four friends in the four years that they lived in Vermont. A carpenter who worked for them said, "The Kiplings were nice people to work for, but you could never get real close to them, not like you and I are chatting together now."[24] It should be noted that the local people—presumably prejudiced in Carrie's favor—nevertheless felt that Kipling was more friendly than his wife.

In the spring of 1894 the Kiplings decided to take a long vacation, first going to Bermuda and then, after returning to Vermont, crossing to England for a long visit with Kipling's parents. On their way to Bermuda, Kipling asked the young women in the cabin next door, "Do you mind if I fasten your door? The banging is disturbing my wife."[25] This was the first meeting with Julia and Edith Catlin, who were friends of the Kiplings for the next forty years.

Edith Catlin, who had the nickname "Tommy," wrote poetry, and asked for Kipling's help and advice. She observed that he always began with a tune and then fitted words to it. He did this with the familiar hymn, "The Church's One Foundation," which is the rhythmic base for his poem "McAndrew's Hymn." "John Brown's Body" is used the same way for "Boots." Many people have left accounts of his humming a tune, tapping it out with his fingers, and then gradually attaching words to the meter until the poem was finished. His well-known "A School Song" is set to the rhythm of "Pop! Goes the Weasel"! "Tommy" said of Kipling's poems, "In their making he always sang them as he wrote them down. He used to tell me: 'Sing your verses and then other people can read them aloud.'" It is interesting that Kipling thought of his poems as being addressed to an audience, out loud, not read by a person sitting in a chair. Large numbers of his poems are called "Hymn of Such-and-Such," "The Ballad of So-and-So," or "The Song of This-and-That." (There are twenty-eight of these last.) Kipling himself usually referred to his works as "verses," not "poems." We are reminded of his delight in Gatti's, the music hall across the street from his flat in London, and of his fascination with the power of hundreds of voices, all chanting the same intoxicating rhymed words. His mental picture of having his poems heard, rather than read, may be linked, like so many other things, to his lifelong awareness of his own visual defect.

Of course, there is nothing inherently wrong with using a popular tune to form the meter of a poem. What counts is the poem that results. But Kipling's method of beginning with a tune did put an emphasis on rhyming, with some ludicrous results. In "Pan in Vermont," written the year before, in 1893, to get a rhyme for "road," he used half of the word "Zodiac:"

> It's forty in the shade today the spouting eaves declare;
> The boulders nose above the drift, the southern slopes are bare;
> Hub-deep in slush Apollo's car swings north along the Zod-
> iac. Good lack, the Spring is back, and Pan is on the road![26]

They soon became good friends of the Catlins, and that spring Carrie wrote "Tommy" of the stay in Bermuda, "Those were rare days together. We value them as a great treasure."[27]

In March they returned to Vermont to find that Beatty, left in charge of Naulakha for a month, had run their accounts into debt, and Carrie had to straighten everything out before they could leave. Early in April they set out, leaving Josephine behind in the care of Susan Bishop, her nurse.

They arrived in England on April 10 and went to Tisbury, a tiny village on the Salisbury Plain where Kipling's parents now lived. Lockwood Kipling in retirement was busier than ever; in a workshop behind the house he had his "drawing portfolios, big photo and architectural books, gravers, modelling-tools, paints, siccatives, varnishes, and the hundred other don't-you-touch-'ems that every right-minded man who works with his hands naturally collects,"[28] as his son put it. They stayed in Tisbury for three months, leaving the first week in August, having had a fine time; Lockwood Kipling helped his son, again, with several stories. In "The Miracle of Purun Bhagat," written in Tisbury, we see the tightened plot and the encyclopedic knowledge of animals* and native gods that, as in "The Bridge Builders," show the hand of Lockwood Kipling.

When Rudyard Kipling arrived in England he sported an American accent that amazed his friends; but now he quickly became entranced

---

*In 1891 he had published a book, appropriately entitled *Beast and Man in India*, where the originals of many of Kipling's animals can be found.

with England in springtime. During his previous stay in London, as mentioned before, he had hardly ever ventured out of the city; and when he had, remembered only walking around soaked from a steady downpour of rain. His feelings began to change. Now he began to "love my country with the devotion that three thousand miles of intervening sea bring to fullest flower."[29] He concluded that in England "A man could camp in any open field with more sense of home and security than the stateliest buildings of foreign cities could afford," and began to think about having his cousin, Ambrose Poynter, draw up plans for a house. But Carrie vetoed this idea.

After wandering about the beautiful English countryside, Kipling found his love of Vermont shaken. When he had been in America, he had written about India, in his Army ballads and in the *Jungle Books*; now that he was in England, he wrote—besides Indian stories—about America, or Americans, in two stories* and a poem. A third story of this sort was written immediately after his return to Vermont. These works obviously reflect his mixed feelings about the United States. The basic message is anti-American. And yet, often in the same breath, he reveals his admiration of some aspect of American life, and seems to end up not knowing how to feel. He expresses praise, in "An American":

> Enslaved, illogical, elate,
> He greets th' embarrassed Gods, nor fears
> To shake the iron hand of Fate
> Or match with Destiny for beers.[30]

And he still clung to some of his old doubts about England and the Home English, as opposed to positive feelings about India. In 1894 he wrote a friend, "My affection for England is in large part for the Head Quarters of the Empire, and I cannot say the land itself fills me with comfort or joy."[31] And to another friend, "England isn't home to a child that has been born in India and it never becomes homelike unless he spends his youth there."

Kipling had always admired American get-up-and-go, the cheer-

---

*The title of one story, "My Sunday at Home," is significant. For Kipling, who had just built a house in America, "home" is England. It is much more revealing than his original title, "The Child of Calamity."

fulness, the gusto, the friendliness, the spontaneity, the energy—the boyish qualities of the young nation that appealed to the boyish side of Kipling himself. But he had also been appalled at the comparative lawlessness, turmoil, and social and racial heterogeneity. Vermonters, he felt, lived lives of "terrifying intimacy."[32] Seen through the eyes of an Englishman from India, where a few thousand white men ran a nation of two hundred million people—this, it must always be remembered, was Kipling's basic orientation—America, particularly the cities, seemed chaotic. He had never had any use for democracy—"The common people . . . have no dignity"[33]—and felt that monarchy was the only way to achieve "a civilized land which is really governed." The advantage of living in one is that "All the Kings and Queens and Emperors of the continent are closely related by blood or marriage—are, in fact, one large family." Now the peaceful English scene, so orderly, so serene, so predictable, emphasized by contrast the turmoil of life back in Brattleboro—where he could only imagine with horror what Beatty was up to by this time.

In "An Error in the Fourth Dimension," one of the stories he wrote in England, a wealthy American named Wilton Sargent decides to live there and become "more English than the English"[34] (the same expression Vermonters had applied to Carrie). Taught by his servants, he acquires the accent and all the proper manners and behavior, and passes for an Englishman. Owning several railroads in America, he would have thought nothing of imperiously flagging one down should the need arise. One day, at his new home in England, when in a great hurry, he stops an English train. It proves to be a famous express, always scrupulously on time, and the outraged authorities put him in jail overnight, ignoring his pleas that a quick word or two with the president of the line would set everything aright. Indeed, they then decide he must be insane and send a doctor* to him. When Wilton Sargent, confused and angry, describes the incident, we can see Kipling's feelings about race and background, and the inherent inferiority and childishness of Americans, very much as he had described Indians in India a few years before:

---

*The doctor appears to be a psychiatrist. If so, he is the only one every to appear in Kipling's works—he hated psychiatry.

There was no chance now of mistaking the man's nationality. Speech, gesture, and step, so carefully drilled into him, had gone away with the borrowed mask of indifference. It was a lawful son of the Youngest People, whose predecessors were the Red Indian. His voice had risen to the high, throaty crow of his breed when they labour under excitement. His close-set eyes showed by turns unnecessary fear, annoyance beyond reason, rapid and purposeless flights of thought, the child's lust for immediate revenge, and the child's pathetic bewilderment, who knocks his head against the bad, wicked table.

(There is an echo here of Kipling's childhood blindness; in "Baa Baa, Black Sheep," when the doctor was sent by the child's parents to check on his condition, Black Sheep came toward him and "charged into a solid tea-table laden with china.")[35]

Wilton Sargent gives up in disgust and returns to America. There you can see "with a complete installation of electric light, nickel-plated binnacles, and a calliope attachment to her steam-whistle, the twelve-hundred-ton ocean-going steam-yacht *Columbia*, lying at her private pier, [ready] to take to his office at an average speed of seventeen knots an hour (sic)—and the barges can look out for themselves—Wilton Sargent, American."[36]

In this story Kipling caricatures an American puzzled and frustrated by the orderly routine of British life. Wilton Sargent blithely thinks he can stop a famous train just for his own convenience. What is not generally known (although Rice mentions it)[37] is that around the time he wrote this story the Kiplings decided to withdraw even further from their Brattleboro neighbors. They discussed with railroad officials their being allowed to flag down the train at a spot below their house, whenever they wanted to take it. They could then get on the train about three hundred yards before it got to the Brattleboro station. What was all right for an Englishman to do in America was shockingly wrong for an American to do in England. Although admittedly the two cases are not quite the same, since Kipling caricatured the latter one, making it a famous train, invariably on time, it is striking how he totally ignored the customs and feelings of his fellow Vermonters. In first wanting his own railroad stop, and then, as will be described, his own post office, Kipling's failure to understand Americans certainly equals Wilton Sargent's failure to understand Englishmen. In four pieces about Americans—the three stories, "An Error in the Fourth Dimension," "My Sunday at

Rudyard Kipling in his study at Naulakha

161

Home," "A Walking Delegate," and the poem, "An American,"—we again see Kipling's old struggle about background and origin. His ambivalence toward America was not just the natural confusion of a man who has lived in two different countries, but was, besides this, an echo of his own mixed feelings about himself, his mother, and his home. America, for Kipling, always had connotations of India. It was here he dreamed of creating a little spot that would be forever Indian. But, try as he might, he could not isolate it from the state and country around it.

In the three stories we see the unpleasant vein of violence that comes to the surface periodically in his lifetime of writing, and in his behavior. In two of the three stories men fight, but the violence is most pronounced in the third, "A Walking Delegate," a political piece. Kipling was inspired by contemporary events: workers staged a great railroad strike in 1894. In Chicago the strike resulted in riots, bloodshed, and destruction of property, which ended only when President Cleveland sent in federal troops. The English were particularly interested because the year before, in 1893, the coal miners' strikes and lockouts had been accompanied by unheard-of violence. In Yorkshire, the government, too, had had to use troops to prevent the wrecking of buildings by strikers who had overpowered the police. Both Americans and Englishmen were shocked and bewildered by these events.

Kipling's story is a political fable. Several horses out at pasture are joined by a newcomer from a livery stable. He preaches a revolutionary doctrine about the inalienable rights of horses and their duty to rise against their owners. The other horses, hard-working and reliable, gang up and kick the daylights out of him. This is Kipling's answer to labor problems. Whenever angered—usually by political events, but also in other situations, as in "The Rhyme of the Three Captains" previously discussed—Kipling's response is an immature and childish eruption of violence and ridicule. It is the solution to the bullies in *Stalky & Co.*—the answer is to out-torture the torturers. This, of course, has its origin in his humiliation at the hands of Mrs. Holloway and her son. It left an unfortunate cutting edge to his angry feelings that spoiled some of the things he wrote, as it most certainly did "A Walking Delegate."

Happy with his parents in England, for the first time appreciating the beautiful countryside—or perhaps American friendliness had rubbed off a little—Kipling cautiously lowered his guard. He relaxed his strict rules about privacy, allowed his portrait to appear in *Vanity Fair* and accepted an invitation to be guest of honor at the ceremonies connected with the retirement of Cormell Price, his old headmaster at Westward Ho! He made a speech on this occasion praising the school and "Uncle Crom," and began to think of writing an account of his school days.

But much of America still appealed to him. In late July he wrote to Robert Barr, a friend in England:*

> A regular weather-breeder of a day today—real warmth at last, and it waked in me a lively desire to be back in Main Street, Brattleboro', Vt., U.S.A., and hear the sody-water fizzing in the drug-store and discuss the outlook for the episcopal church with the clerk; and get a bottle of lager in the basement in the Brooks House, and hear the doctor tell fish-yarns. . . . There's one Britisher at least homesick for a section of your depraved old land, and he's going, Please Allah! the first week in August. . . .[38]

Again, as in his works of fiction, his divided feelings are apparent; now he is critical of the English weather—at the end of July he notes "real warmth at last"—and he wants to be back in Vermont. He writes of a "Britisher" who is "homesick," which certainly means he wants to be in Great Britain; but to this one, "home" is America; then, a few words later, he refers to it, in affectionate contempt, as a "depraved old land." (And when he says "Please Allah!" he brings to mind where his confusion all began—in India.) No place could ever satisfy him; for what he was trying to solve was a problem from childhood.

In August the Kiplings crossed the Atlantic and returned to Vermont, where they were glad to find Beatty had not upset things as much as they had feared. Josephine, now almost two, was healthy and happy. She was a lovely child, with light hair and beautiful eyes, quick and intelligent. "Flat Curls" was one of Kipling's many nicknames for her. He wrote "Tommy" Catlin, "Flat-curls is in enormous form, learning a new word every ten minutes, playing with the coal scuttle, eating pencils, smearing herself, bumping her head, singing, shouting, bubbling from dawn till dark."[39] Kipling was utterly devoted to her and spent a

---

*His writing to Barr presumably stirred up some of his confusion about "Where is home?" for Barr, educated in Canada, had spent many years in Detroit and had returned to England only about ten years before to spend what was to be the second half of his life there.

great deal of time with her each day. He taught her Hindustani fables and folktales, probably the same ones he had been taught as a child. The next day she would remember them remarkably well. Like her father in his childhood, she never seemed to forget a name or a face. She delighted in stopping the Kiplings' carriage and asking about the health of each horse by name, not just the two there but also those back at the stable. In intelligence she was the equal of her cousin Marjorie, who was twice her age—which may not have sat well with the Balestiers. Kipling loved telling the two girls stories of a whale—like one he had seen from the ship coming back from England—that swallowed a shipwrecked mariner, and of an independent cat that walked in the "wet wild woods"[40] between the Balestiers' house and Naulakha.

As Kipling's business manager, Carrie took charge of signing all checks and writing all letters to publishers. Apart from Kipling's disorganization and her inclination to take over, his rise to fame made it necessary for Carrie to write the checks. For if he wrote a check for a small amount, it never came back cashed—the recipient having correctly decided that a check with Rudyard Kipling's autograph on it was worth more than the face value. In her letters to publishers, Carrie's tone is pleasant—more pleasant than one might expect considering the criticisms voiced by many who knew the Kiplings. She appears to have been firm and businesslike but overly preoccupied with details. Kipling's childlike dependency on her is apparent from something Kipling said when they were at the railroad station awaiting a train to New York. A friend who was seeing them off asked Kipling what hotel they would be staying at. He replied, "*I* don't know! When Carrie is in charge of an expedition, I am like a cork bobbing on the water."[41]

Their relationships with the community grew steadily worse. The Vermonters sniffed at the Kiplings' pretentious style of living; for now there were two maids in the house, as well as Josephine's nanny, and then a coachman was hired, Matthew Howard, an alert little Englishman, who drove the Kiplings around the countryside in a shiny phaeton. Howard, a short, thin man just Kipling's height—five foot six—was quick and efficient and the one person in town who was not impressed by, nor fearful of, Beatty Balestier. He quickly took over a variety of jobs about the place, and the more he did, the less there was to do for Beatty, who was now deeper in debt than ever.

They did make a few friends, the closest ones being Dr. Conland, their physician; Charles Eliot Norton of Harvard, and his family; John Bliss; and Will and Mary Cabot. Mrs. Cabot was one of the very few women with whom Kipling was really friendly. He used to confer with her about his work, and she stated that once she heard him reel off seventy new lines of poetry without pausing a single time. A friend by courtesy was the Reverend C. O. Day of the Congregational Church. Although the Kiplings did not attend religious services, in Victorian times one was always friendly with the local minister. He came out to Naulakha a few times and tried winter golf with Kipling. The balls were painted red and, since the slopes were steep and icy, a drive could go for a mile.* Of Kipling's golf, Reverend Day tactfully said that he was a better poet than a golfer.

It was during this winter that an uncle of mine happened to see Kipling in the railroad station at Boston. Kipling made a beeline for some shelves featuring books for sale, including some by himself, for a dollar a copy. He pulled out a book and examined it. People in his vicinity began recognizing him, and murmurs could be heard—"Look, there's Rudyard Kipling." "Really? Why, so it is." He replaced the book, looked at the small crowd around him, growled, "The best way to ruin a book is to sell it for a dollar," and walked off.[42] (Meaning the books were overpriced—about twenty-five dollars each, by present-day standards.)

Early in 1895 Carrie scorched her face when she opened the furnace door. She gradually recovered but then developed an inflammation of her eyelids. Dr. Conland urged them to take a vacation in a warmer climate, so they went to Washington, D.C., for six weeks. Kipling was fascinated by the old Smithsonian Institution. "The nation's attic" was perfectly suited to his varied interests and insatiable curiosity. He met President Cleveland and several government higher-ups; predictably, the man who had a lifelong distaste for politicians of any type was repelled by Cleveland and his portly associates. Kipling was always one for action as opposed to thought and discussion. The perfect antidote for

---

*The clubs and faded red balls, along with the books, furniture, and other things from Kipling's days can still be seen in the house.

Cleveland was Theodore Roosevelt, whom he met at a stag dinner. Roosevelt, with his love of manliness, efficiency, and the strenuous life, was just what Kipling wanted. "I liked him from the first and largely believed in him."[43] The liking was reciprocated; the two men delighted in going to the Washington Zoo, where Roosevelt naturally steered them toward the bears.* Kipling preferred the industrious beavers that he remembered from Wyoming. He even thought of stocking some tributary of the Connecticut River with them. He planned to write about the animals of New England, and if he had, surely the industrious, disciplined beaver would have come first. Another American animal that delighted Kipling was the box turtle. Having a hinge across the front and back of its lower shell, it can close itself up so tightly that even a bit of straw cannot be poked anywhere in the crack. Such perfect privacy was a condition that was always important to Kipling—isolating himself so that no one would ever control him as he had been controlled and humiliated in his childhood.

Kipling set his animal stories in places where he really felt at home, and there is a close connection between these stories and his feelings for children. A few of his animal tales, like "The Mother Hive" and "A Walking Delegate," were political fables for adults, like Orwell's *Animal Farm*. But most, although they can be enjoyed by adults, were written for children—or perhaps, for adults to read to children. As in all great children's literature his stories explore the violence/peace, death/life, hatred/love, and security/helplessness conflicts that all children experience. Since they are connected with his own childhood, where he truly felt at home, it is not surprising that almost all the animal stories in *The Jungle Books* are set in India. (The "Just So" stories take place on a variety of continents.) If we knew nothing else about Kipling, the fact that throughout his four years in America he never wrote stories about animals native to America (not counting "A Walking Delegate," a purely political tale) would tell us he never really felt at home here. The stories about beavers and box turtles, alas, never got written. A similar lack of animal tales can make us suspicious about his cries of enthusiasm for his later home in Sussex. He praised the English countryside in such insis-

---

*The expression "Teddy bear" came from Theodore Roosevelt and his interest in bears.

tent terms we begin to doubt their sincerity. He wrote almost no English animal stories the last half of his life. This indicates, despite all his protestations, that he didn't feel wholly at home there.

In February he had written Charles Eliot Norton:

> Work has been going easily. I have a yearning upon me to tell tales of extended impropriety—not sexual or within hailing distance of it—but hard-bottomed unseemly yarns, and am now at work on the lamentable history of a very fat Indian administrator who was, in the course of a survey, shot in his ample backside by a poisoned arrow: and his devoted subordinate sucked the wound to the destruction of his credit as an independent man for the rest of his days. The administrator always liked being toadied to. . . . One can't be serious always.[44]

The entire passage from the word "yarns" to the beginning of the sentence "One can't be serious always" is omitted from the official biography written by Charles Carrington, without the ellipses I have used to indicate missing words. Access to the Kipling papers was reluctantly granted by Mrs. Bambridge, Kipling's only surviving child, to Birkenhead and Carrington. The papers were then burned. As noted before, Mrs. Bambridge did not hesitate to censor words in Carrington's biography that she felt reflected discredit on her parents. But this is more than only individual words. It is an entire story that amused and interested Kipling, a tale of an assistant who "sucked up" to his superior. And if something this innocent had to be suppressed, how many other stories and ideas were deleted? Mrs. Bambridge was notorious for being fiercely protective of her father's image, and anything that offended her had to be destroyed or, if published, angrily denied. This letter would have been burned if she'd gotten her hands on it.

It was while staying in Washington that some of the last of the stories in *The Jungle Book* were written. These remarkable tales were begun in 1892 in the Bliss Cottage. Among the very best things he ever wrote, they tell of Mowgli, a tiny child lost in the jungle, who is befriended by a mother wolf and then allowed to join the pack and be brought up in the mother wolf's family.

> Father Wolf taught him his business, and the meaning of things in the jungle, till every rustle in the grass, every breath of the warm night air, every note of the owls above his head, every scratch of a bat's claws as it roosted for a while in a tree, and every splash of every little fish jumping in

a pool, meant just as much to him as the work of his office means to a business man.[45]

Mowgli is taught different animal dialects, and the strict "Law of the Jungle,"—which emphasizes obedience—by Baloo, a wise, rotund old bear, and how to hunt by Bagheera, a powerful black panther.

> When he was not learning, he sat out in the sun and slept, and ate, and went to sleep again; when he felt dirty or hot he swam in the forest pools; and when he wanted honey (Baloo told him honey and nuts were just as pleasant to eat as raw meat) he climbed up for it, and that Bagheera showed him how to do. At first Mowgli would cling like the sloth, but afterward he would fling himself through the branches almost as boldly as the gray ape.

Mowgli owed a special debt to Bagheera, for the panther had gotten him admitted into the wolf pack when a tiny infant by offering a newly killed bull to the wolves—reminiscent of Kipling's own difficult birth, which the servants said was brought about safely through the sacrifice of a young goat to a Hindu goddess. With Bagheera, Baloo, and another friend, Kaa, a thirty-foot rock python, Mowgli has all sorts of adventures. Children enjoy them as much today as they did a hundred years ago. They produced a host of imitators, the most successful one being, of course, *Tarzan of the Apes.*

The Jungle Books, like any great piece of writing, do not arouse our feelings at merely one level. The interesting idea of being able to talk to animals is carried—unlike the Dr. Dolittle books, inferior for this reason—much further, into two themes: the creation of a new family, and the learning of self-control and cooperation.

Every child feels dissatisfied in some ways with his/her family, and imagines what it would be like to belong to another family that can fulfill the child's daydreams. Children are uncomfortably aware of their small size and inexperience; adults seem to have all the answers. The commonest element, perhaps, in all children's stories is that of the child achieving importance; he puts his finger in the dike and saves the town, or moves to different surroundings or a different symbolic family and plays an adult role—"One more step, Mr. Hand, and I'll blow your brains out."* These new surroundings abound in all the sensory stimuli, violent activity, and love that loom large in a child's life. In *The Jungle Book*, Mowgli is brought up in an utterly new family, and indeed has three sets of parents; Father Wolf and Mother Wolf; his biological parents, Messua and her husband, and, I think it can be asserted, Bagheera and Baloo. Bagheera, the epitome of violence and power, teaches him the "masculine" activities of tree-climbing and hunting, and it is to him that Mowgli goes when first troubled by sexual feelings at puberty. Bagheera reassures him about these. The rotund old Baloo, on the other hand, has taught the Jungle Law to Mowgli and to generations of wolves in the pack. He addresses Mowgli as "dearest of all to me"[46] and says, "Come to me!" when Mowgli, realizing he is becoming a man and must leave the jungle, is weeping. Then "Mowgli sobbed and sobbed, with his head on the blind bear's side and his arms round his neck, while Baloo tried feebly to lick his feet." A maternal figure, certainly; and it becomes even more certain when it is recalled that, early in his teaching, it was Baloo who used to beat Mowgli when he would forget what he had been taught. (The ambivalence Kipling always felt toward women—they love you but then they beat you—came from the years at Mrs. Holloway's.)

Mowgli, then, has a fascinating family—or even three families—in which he grows up. And it should be noted that, predictably, the "mothers" are more prominent than the "fathers" (with the exception of Bagheera). We hear little of Father Wolf, as compared to Mother Wolf; Messua's husband is hardly seen at all, and is never even given a name.

In addition to the theme of the fantasy family there is a deeper ethical message in *The Jungle Books*. These stories are fables; they carry unobtrusive but telling morals. First, members of a society must obey laws made for the common good. Having firmly said this, it is as if Kipling added, "but there are plenty of exceptions." Kipling, with his love of action that revitalizes society, was also in favor of breaking the law, when impatient with its complexities, or when harrassed, as a sort of safety-valve. He described the Law of the Jungle (and its obvious

---

*If the reader has not read *Treasure Island* lately, this is what Jim Hawkins says from his perch in the rigging of the *Hispaniola*.

allegory to human beings) but in many stories ("A Deal in Cotton," for example) he then advocates breaking it. Moreover, he makes it quite clear that the law varies in its application; the inner ring (one thinks of the British in India), those who are seen as uniquely qualified, are laws unto themselves.

Second, freedom demands responsibility. The monkeys that are called the Bandar-Log by the jungle animals are portrayed as contemptible, uncivilized beings. They have no sense of rules, do not participate in the Jungle Law, and have no leaders and no goals. They are childish and irresponsible.*

> They were always just going to have a leader and laws and customs of their own, but they never did, because their memories would not hold over from day to day, and so they settled things by making up a saying: "What the Bandar-Log think now the jungle will think later;" and that comforted them a great deal.[47]

Their impulsive and uncontrolled lives are portrayed in marked contrast to the rest of the jungle animals. In the wolf pack, the wolves learned the jungle laws and obeyed them, followed the leadership of the old wolf, Akela, and have prospered. Then many of the wolves, particularly the younger ones, begin to talk glibly of wanting "freedom" and start to follow the bullying tiger, Shere Khan. They trick Akela into being deposed as leader, but then things go badly with the pack. Many of the wolves become ill, and some get trapped or shot. The pack then returns to Akela and asks him to lead them again, saying:

> "Lead us again, O Akela. Lead us again, O Man-Cub, for we be sick of this lawlessness, and we would be the Free People once more."
> "Nay," purred Bagheera, "that may not be. When ye are full-fed the madness may come upon ye again. Not for nothing are ye called the Free People. Ye fought for freedom, and it is yours. Eat it, O Wolves."[48]

The emphasis upon submission to law in *The Jungle Book* is a reflection of Kipling's dismay at the comparative chaos of American society, as compared to England's. At the time he was writing these stories

---

*I feel quite sure that Kipling intended the Bandar-Log as a caricature of Americans, although he never explicitly equates the two.

there was indeed a contrast between the two cultures, at least in the upper-class level in which Kipling lived. In England there was widespread respect for the law, and social stability untroubled by racial diversity. It was a time of relative tranquility in England. If war is defined as a conflict in which at least a hundred soldiers die, England had only two wars—small ones—between the Indian Mutiny near the middle of the century and the Boer War near its end. In contrast, America was a young nation whose frontier had just closed. It had suffered violent disruption during the Civil War, which ended the year Kipling was born. It was the era of the "robber barons"—America's political structure, at the upper levels of society, was slipshod compared with that of England. Kipling always emphasized his belief in the necessity— clearly Anglo-Indian in origin—for a rule by the elite. During his first year in the United States, Kipling sarcastically characterized the Americans as the "freest people in the world"[49] and had a phrase for America: "ignoble broil of Freedom most unfree."[50] He had always admired the American's energy, friendliness, and ability to consider new and imaginative ways of doing things. However, he could never be tolerant of the raw young nation's casual attitude toward politics in the last century, its lack of self-control and respect for the law. These views of America, as we shall see, played a vital role in the family quarrel in which he soon became involved.

Kipling's emphasis on self-control and the rule of law, besides indicating the contrast between England and America at the time, was also an expression of a need to control himself, to keep a tight rein on his anger and on his sexual feelings.

Kipling was an angry man. This is obvious both in his writings and in his behavior. It was this barely controlled hostility that lay behind his vicious attacks on those who disagreed with him, his depressions, his anti-Semitism, perhaps even his gastric ulcer that finally killed him. These statements do not at all conflict with the impression many people have left us of a Kipling who was outgoing and delightful, a man who was the life of the party, who loved to roar with laughter. For we have always sensed the connection between joy and sadness, between laughter and tears, perhaps most obviously in the figure of the tragic clown. Pagliacci sings "I laugh with tears in my eyes" and Jack Point, the clown in *The Yeomen of the Guard*, has the punch line "They don't blame you so long as you're funny." Sometimes wit represents a desperate attempt to avoid depression, and when the wittiest and most enjoyable people become overwhelmed with gloom, their depressions are profound and difficult to treat. I think Kipling was a case in point, and that a great deal of his humor was a defense against his depression and anger.

His sexual impulses were both heterosexual and homosexual. In 1891, four years before, he had felt deep conflicts about his love of Wolcott Balestier. Now Wolcott was dead and Kipling was married to his sister. Kipling was comfortable in a heterosexual relationship, whereas he had been uncomfortable in a homosexual one. He experienced same-sex urges as frightening thoughts he could not avoid, shameful impulses that were alarmingly strong. He could now put most of this behind him. But he had married Carrie, a martinet, a tense worrier, with whom life would never be easy. He seemed to need a little punishment in his marriage to satisfy his guilt about his love for his wife's brother.

Both his rage and his sexual confusion resulted from the abuse he had suffered as a child. He had been taken away from his *ayah*, who had given him the support and love every child desperately needs, and been abandoned in the House of Desolation, where Mrs. Holloway had beaten and humiliated him. She tried to rob him of any feelings of identity as an individual, as someone whose needs and wishes as a person were respected and taken into account. Instead she treated him as an annoyance, something that interfered with her daily life.

To survive what he went through, as Shengold describes so accurately in his book,[51] throughout his life Kipling did three things commonly seen in the victims of abuse. First, he tried to deny the impact of his torture by joking about some of it (as he did in his autobiography), and by rationalizing it, as if to say, "Well, in some ways it was helpful." (Although actually I think that the abuse did help him as a writer.) Second, his rage at what he suffered was turned outward and directed at others. It has often been noted that victims of child abuse frequently become child abusers themselves. This was certainly not true of Kipling—on the contrary, he made every effort to make sure no child would ever feel as he had felt. But, as demonstrated, he bore an enormous burden of simmering anger which, like a flame thrower, he periodically turned on liberals, civilians, politicians, Jews, Americans, and anyone else within range. Third, the victim of child abuse takes on some of the guilt that should have been felt by his or her tormentor. This guilt can be seen in the modest, self-effacing, gloomy Kipling, who disowned pride and joy in accomplishments, saying his success was just the work of his "daemon," that all he did was write out the words. All three of these defenses are reflected in his insistence on following the law and on having control of one's impulses.

To return to *The Jungle Book*, I have already commented on the emphasis on the mother-figures in Mowgli's three sets of parents. My final observation is that in these stories the issue of identity is pervasive. Kipling, who emotionaly had both an Indian mother and a white mother, returns again to the question "Who am I?" Mowgli runs with the wolf pack and refers to them as "brothers," but he is a human, not a wolf. Yet, when he tries to join the world of men in a native village, he has stones thrown at him and is forced back to the woods. Eventually, in the story "In the Rukh,"* Kipling, in a rather artificial and forced way, has Mowgli successfully join the world of men. He retains his contact with his animal "brothers," but works as a forest ranger for the government,—a contrived and unsatisfying ending.

The other stories in *The Second Jungle Book*, such as "The White Seal," "Rikki-Tikki-Tavi," and "Toomai of the Elephants," are among the most popular Kipling ever wrote. Surely there is no story about snakes in the English language that compares with "Rikki-Tikki-Tavi." "The White Seal" is another well-known story. In the tale, a seal called Kotick is born in the midst of a huge seal herd. Kotick is albino, and none of the other animals has ever seen a white seal. He grows up with the other seals and has all sorts of adventures. Then, one day, Kotick sees men come, drive off part of the herd of seals, and then kill and skin them. In trying to find a way to prevent this, he is told that the only hope is to find an island where men will never come, and the seals can breed in peace. He tries to interest the other seals in finding such an island, but can get no help.

He searches all over the world and finally finds a secluded beach, protected by reefs far out to sea and by steep cliffs toward the mainland.

---

*This tale finishes up the "Mowgli" stories although, curiously enough, it was the first one written. Did Kipling have to get the end straight before he could begin?

This beautiful place can be reached only by a tunnel, entered deep underwater through a hole in the face of a cliff. Kotick returns and tells the other seals of this safe place, but they are skeptical; so he then has a fight with the entire herd, helped by his father, and forces them to accompany him through the Sea Cow's tunnel to the hidden islands. The story ends with the seals living happily "in that sea where no man comes."[52]

Present-day readers will recognize the symbolism of the protected breeding-place. The murderous attack of the men upon the seals symbolizes men's imagined sexual aggressiveness toward women, and not merely cruelty to animals. The hidden island, a breeding ground reached through the Sea Cow's secret tunnel, has a dual meaning in being safe from men: The seals are protected from the hunters, and the child's mother is protected from his father. This is a common theme in children's stories, seen in "Jack and the Beanstalk," for example. J. M. S. Tompkins, in her account of having *The Jungle Book* read to her as a child, remembers "It was certainly a happy ending; *why* did I feel so sad?"[53] This meaning to the story—protecting the child's mother from the father's sexual advances—would seem to account for her feeling of sadness. There comes a time in a child's life when he/she realizes that sexual relations between adults is all but inevitable, and love can take the place of the cruelty and violence the child imagined.

Again we have the theme of identity. Kotick is a seal. But he is an albino, different from all the other seals. Once more the question of origin arises, and the confusion about being white or Indian.

With some relief, Kipling finished the last of the Mowgli stories and immediately began a new tale, "William the Conqueror." It recounts the heroic efforts by a group of administrators to handle a famine that sweeps over a section of India. The sister of one of the men, an efficient, energetic, manly sort of woman—as the Victorians would have used the words—has the nickname "William." She works side by side with the men, and gradually falls in love with one of them, who has been feeding the children goat's milk. The figure of "William" is well drawn. She is one of the best women in all of Kipling's works; but even she, it cannot be denied, is shaky enough. It would appear that in this efficient woman we see something of the personality of Carrie Kipling; one is reminded of Henry James's description of

Carrie as "manly." Again we see with what difficulty Kipling portrayed his women.

In April 1895, with Carrie fully recovered, the Kiplings returned to Vermont and Naulakha, where the beauties of a New England spring were just getting under way. They gratefully settled down in their home, but troubles continued to assail them. The townsfolk respected their desire for privacy, and, as is traditional in New England, let them go their own way. The summer visitors were a different lot. Kipling was now at the height of his fame, and carriage-loads of tourists would ask to be driven past his house, to his intense annoyance. Every morning's mail contained requests for his autograph. Typically, Carrie came up with a scheme that would drive off the autograph hunters and make some money for charity at the same time. The *New York Tribune* was sponsoring a drive for the "Tribune Fresh Air Fund" to aid underprivileged children, and Carrie had a card printed up that was sent to those requesting autographs. It stated that when the applicant's name appeared as a contributor of $2.50 or more to the Fund, then Kipling would send his autograph. The Fund certainly profited from it, since he sent out over two hundred autographs. But Carrie's plan, some people felt, seemed manipulative and condescending.

Another example of Kipling's lack of coordination occurred when he attempted to move a horse and carriage from one position to another near the front door of the house. A visitor—a woman—saw him in trouble, red-faced and sawing at the reins. She offered to help, climbed up on the seat, and moved them easily.

As summer work began about the place their difficulties with Beatty immediately increased. With misplaced kindness, they kept on using him as a general contractor for some of the projects, even though he had caused them many difficulties in the past. That spring he oversaw the construction of a tennis court, but then quarreled with Carrie about the terms of the contract under which it was built. Then there was another fight about his mowing hay, and about his draining one of the pastures. He had taken the money she had advanced him for these jobs and spent it on some of his wild activities with his friends. Even Beatty's grandmother, who always used to get him out of debt, now decided, rather late in the game, that this was not really helping him. In June they attempted to negotiate some sort of a working agreement with Beatty, but it did not work out. He was steadily going downhill, and drinking more as he did so; but the final chapter was not to be written until a year later. It was with relief that the Kiplings left Beatty and Vermont for their usual summer in England, in July and August of 1895. This time they did not have to worry about Beatty's handling of Naulakha, for the efficient coachman, Matthew Howard, was in charge. They had a fine time in England, again seeing Kipling's family, and again feeling torn between a home in England and a home in America.

Back in Vermont toward the end of August, they found that Matthew Howard had everything going to perfection; but things—perhaps partly for this reason—were even worse between Beatty and themselves. The families were no longer on speaking terms. In September, with the weather still hot, there arose a situation that would have been ludicrous had it not held some portents of what was to come. Naulakha had a water pump that Kipling had tried to keep in running order, but which was constantly malfunctioning. (The Kipling who could write to perfection about how machines worked was all thumbs when it came to trying to handle them himself.) The pump broke down and the house had no water; the nearest source was Beatty's Maplewood nearby, but with the families not speaking to each other, the requests for water and its delivery were carried out in a stiff exchange of notes.

More and more they drew away from the town. Their only regular contact had been Kipling's driving in to the post office to pick up the mail. But they took steps to avoid even that brief interaction in a manner not calculated to produce friendly feelings among their neighbors. They wrote to a prominent lawyer they had come to know in Washington who had the ear of the President; and before long a special post office, for the Kiplings alone, was set up at the home of one of their neighbors, the Waites. Triumphantly, Kipling—or, one rather suspects, Carrie— mailed out hundreds of postcards, noting the change of address "from Brattleboro, Vt., to WAITE, Windham County, Vt. Be careful not to omit the name of county."

As winter closed in, they saw less of Beatty and his family, and accordingly their troubles lessened.

After coming back from England, with a reawakening of the memories of his childhood there, Kipling began to spin out a tale that he called "The Brushwood Boy." An ingenious and memorable story, it was completed in two weeks, as if it had been on his mind for years. It is awash with sentimentality and a prudish attitude toward sex, which, even by Victorian standards, is extreme. It is the story of an English boy, George Cottar, who as a child has a recurrent dream wherein he meets a girl by a pile of brushwood. He goes on to school, where he is an outstanding athlete and leader, and into the Army, where he begins a brilliant career in India. He continues to have the dream, with further elaborations, so specific that he is able to draw a map of what he encounters. He is given a year's leave and returns to England, and on the voyage back has the dream again. The little girl in the dream has now become a woman, who at the end of the dream kisses him. In the story, he comes back home and is welcomed back into the heart of his family. A girl who lives nearby is invited to dinner and to stay for a while, and, from outside the house, he overhears her playing the piano and singing a song. The song describes the dream he has had all his life; she has had it in all of hers and has dreamed of him in her dream.

The dream is significant, for it is not made up of items picked by chance, but can be shown to be an account of incidents—or wished-for incidents—in Kipling's life up to the time that he wrote this story. At the age of six, the Brushwood Boy was "telling himself stories as he lay in bed. It was a new power, and he kept it a secret."[54] He "could not tell anyone for fear of being laughed at." Kipling described his own childhood some years later by saying, "I read a good deal . . . and I learned all sorts of verses for the pleasure of repeating them to myself in bed."[55] When the boy in the story is seven, he is taken to Oxford on a visit, and there introduced to the Provost of Oriel. In his autobiography, Kipling says, "Once I remember being taken to a town called Oxford and a street called Holywell, where I was shown an Ancient of Days who, I was told, was the Provost of Oriel," apparently when he was about seven. In the story, the Brushwood Boy goes off to a school that prepares its students for entrance into the military service, and which lays great emphasis on the simple, vigorous life. Here he becomes a leader and outstanding athlete, and "enjoyed the dignity of a study with two companions in it."[56] Kipling, of course, went to a similar school, and, although lack of physical coordination prevented it, all his life wanted to be athletic and a military man, and envied those who were. A turning point in Kipling's school days was when he was allowed to share a study with two other boys.

In the story, the Brushwood Boy, in his teens, goes on to Sandhurst, and then on to India, where he "tasted utter loneliness." One remembers how homesick Kipling was for England when he first arrived in India at a similar age. George Cottar spends seven years in India, just like Kipling. Kipling was shy and inhibited around girls; Cottar spends all his time at his military duties and at exercise, and "[Does] not care to have his tennis spoiled by petticoats in the court."* Like Kipling, he is troubled by insomnia in the heat of India, and is attracted to safe, motherly women who are older than himself. On the way back to England, when Cottar begins his year's leave, a woman ten years his senior is attracted to him, but he is so naive in such matters that he does not even recognize it. One night he again has his dream. The delightful companion whom he had never seen in previous dreams is now revealed as "a woman with black hair that grew into a 'widow's peak,' combed back from her forehead."[58] "Ted" Hill again! When in his twenties, Kipling had made an ocean voyage to England with Mrs. Hill (described this way)—who was seven years his senior. In the story, when the Brushwood Boy finally sees the girl, he is "filled with delight unspeakable." She kisses him and in the story George Cottar wakes with a start. The curtain in the door of his cabin is moving as if someone had just left, and it feels as though the kiss had been a real one. The story moves on to its ending when he returns to England, finds the girl who had had exactly the same dream all of her life, and they fall in love and plan to be married as quickly as possible.

In comparing "The Brushwood Boy" with "William the Conqueror," one can see something of Kipling's feeling for his wife compared to those he had for Mrs. Hill. "William" is manly, efficient, and energetic; in the story she is spoken of as being "as clever as a man" and "as direct as a man." In contrast, Scott, the hero, seems somewhat effeminate. The most memorable scene is when he is surrounded by children, and he does a better job at feeding them the milk than "William" does. There seems to be a confusion of roles; "William's" strength is emphasized—"her brother is weaker than she is"—while

---

*In the original manuscript, Kipling put it even more strongly: ". . . tennis spoiled by petticoats giggling about the court."[57]

Scott is given the nickname of "Goat" because he has fed so many children goat's milk. Here Kipling is describing his relationship with his wife: the efficient, no-nonsense Carrie managed everything and kept things running smoothly around the house for her creative—and disorganized—genius of a husband.* But in "The Brushwood Boy," a romance, Kipling gives a tender picture of a more feminine woman, the girl of his dreams, and here it is not Carrie, but Mrs. Hill. One can readily imagine Kipling having a dream of her kissing him, and awakening, wishing that it had occurred in reality. And then one wonders, did it?

The winter of 1895–96 came and went. Carrie's mother stayed with the Kiplings for Christmas, but found she could not help in the quarrel with Beatty. The families were still not speaking. A. Conan Doyle, who had spent the previous Thanksgiving with them, sent Kipling a pair of skis from Norway. We may presume that if Kipling tried them at all, he did so with greatest caution. When he had first tried a pair of snowshoes, four years before, he immediately fell flat in the snow.

A series of events then occurred, now mostly forgotten, which tended to widen the gap between Kipling and America. For some years the frontier between Venezuela and British Guiana had been the subject of acrimonious disputes between the two countries. In the summer of 1895, President Cleveland, invoking the Monroe Doctrine, publicly intervened and demanded that England submit to arbitration to settle the disagreement. The issue became more and more inflammatory, and a real crisis developed between the United States and England, with war so likely that Congress seriously considered instituting a national draft.

Kipling was deeply concerned, although he proudly felt that the might of the British Empire would prevail. He used to read newspapers, "smile a quiet smile" and make "mental comparison of the American and

---

*C.J. Hooper, who worked in a publishing house and had assisted in the initial sale of *Plain Tales from the Hills* in England, described Kipling's disorganization: "He was curiously contrary and careless with his work. He would take extraordinary pains to turn out a perfect manuscript and then would forget its existence."[59] Hooper once found "The Record of Badalia Herodsfoot" scattered in wild confusion on the floor. It wasn't published immediately and when Hooper returned for it, it couldn't be found. Later it was discovered lying on a book-case, dusty and forgotten.

English navies."[60] Another time, when Mary Cabot, invited for lunch, made a casual remark about the difficulty in Venezuela, Kipling waspishly asked her if she realized that the British Navy could wipe out every city on the Atlantic coast within a few days. When Mrs. Cabot, not taken aback, retorted that she did not and questioned the accuracy of this estimate, Kipling became so angry that he got up and left the house. The whole quarrel over Venezuela left him "sick and sore and sorry to my heart's core."[61]

Now the British encountered new difficulties, which increased Kipling's concern. In South Africa, Cecil Rhodes had a scheme—one of many—to pull off a coup in the trouble-ridden Transvaal. His right-hand man, Dr. L. S. Jameson, was to pounce on Johannesburg and bring about the fall of the Boer government. This famous "Jameson Raid" failed disastrously. He was quickly surrounded and had to surrender. The Germans then intervened. The Kaiser sent Paul Kruger, the Boer President, a congratulatory telegram—a direct insult to the British. In England, there was an outburst of indignation, talk of war, and an immediate mobilization of part of the fleet.

Kipling saw the very Empire threatened by the United States on one hand and by Germany on the other. As his own response to the Kaiser's telegram, he wrote his determined poem, "Hymn before Action," and he decided at long last that he should return to England for good.

> I seem to be between two barrels like a pheasant. If the American mine is sprung it means dirt and slush and ultimately death either across the Canada border or in some disembowelled gun boat off Cape Hatteras. If the German dynamite is exploded, equally it means slaughter and most probably on the high seas. In both cases I am armed with nothing more efficient than a note-book, a stylographic pen, and a pair of opera-glasses.* Whether or no, any way and inevitably, C. will be confined within the next three or five weeks** and till that time I am tied here by the leg.
>
> I have arranged things so that C. ought not to starve; and she has the house and all my copyrights to boot. You see it is obviously absurd for me to sit still and go on singing from a safe place while the men I know are on

---

*Note that he again connects helplessness with impaired vision.
**Carrie was pregnant with their second child at this time.

the crown of it; and it may be that when I am closer to the scene of action I may be able to help with a little song or two in the intervals of special correspondence. But it is borne in upon me by the inner eye that if trouble comes I shan't live to see it out: unless I bolt and hide myself in the wilds of Patagonia or the Pole. Even in that resort I should be dead or worse than dead.

All these things fill me with a deep love for Mr. Cleveland who is responsible for the letting in of the waters. I permit myself however to cherish a hope that the row or rows may be delayed till May when I can hope to pick up C. and the children (D.V.) [God willing] and take 'em to England. I shan't mind so much then; but whether it be peace or war this folly puts an end to my good wholesome life here; and to me that is the saddest part of it. We must begin again from the beginning and pretend that we are only anxious to let the house for a year or two. It's hard enough, God knows, but I should be a fool if, after full warning, I risked my own people's happiness and comfort in a hostile country.

Early in 1896, then, Kipling resolved to return to England. And almost predictably, Beatty Balestier, determined to have the last word, was, in one final battle, to decide just when that return was to be.

In January Kipling had been working on *Kim*. At least three times during his four years in America he got out the old manuscript of *Mother Maturin* which contained certain basic elements of *Kim*. He worked and worked on it, but it would not seem to come out right; and it was with some relief that he put it aside for a new project. Carrie's approaching childbirth again put them in touch with their family physician, Dr. James Conland,* "the best friend I made in New England."[62] Dr. Conland was one of the few people who was close to the Kiplings.** He had worked on Gloucester fishing schooners thirty years before, and loved to tell tales of the Grand Banks. Kipling, ever the journalist, was full of

*Perhaps Kipling, with his unconscious confusion about his background, was partly drawn to Dr. Conland because he, too, had been a homeless boy. An orphan, he had been given the name "Conland," meaning against, or opposed to, the land, i.e., the sea. Born in 1851, he was working on a Cape Cod farm at the age of seven, and at the Boston Naval Office during the Civil War. As a young man he worked as a deckhand in the Gloucester fishing fleet and later on larger ships that had gone to Europe and to Kipling's India.

**Another was Frank N. Doubleday, who had appeared at Naulakha on a wet autumn day a few months before. He represented a publisher, Scribner's, and was therefore received coldly at first. But this genial giant managed to break through Carrie's resistance and achieved something no one else ever did; he became both Kipling's publisher and close friend. Kipling usually began his letters to Doubleday with the salutation, "Beloved Effendi"—a play on the man's initials.

questions and had to find out, in the minutest detail, everything he could about commercial fishing. In what was to be his last year in America, he decided to write a story of the Gloucester fishermen, and setting *Kim* aside, he plunged into it. He listened by the hour to Dr. Conland's stories and the book grew steadily.

The story is of a multimillionaire's son, Harvey Cheyne, who at fifteen is insufferably spoiled and annoying to others. He falls off the ship that is taking him and his parents to Europe, and is rescued by the crew of a Gloucester fishing schooner, the *We're Here*. Since there is no way of getting in touch with his family, Harvey—after a clouting by the skipper, Disko Troop,—pitches in and works with the rest of the crew. He makes friends with Dan, a boy about his own age. Coming to respect the integrity and skill of the other men of the crew and their outdoor life of the Grand Banks, he matures from a selfish young brat to a responsible and likable young man.

"Tommy" Catlin has left us a description of a working day at Naulakha. After breakfast, the mail would be gone through; children were more likely to get responses from Kipling than adults. Then there was absolute silence in the house, enforced by Carrie, until lunch and again for a time in the afternoon while Kipling wrote. Josephine's nursery was over his study and a special double floor had been installed so that her noise would not disturb her father at work. "Sometimes a helpless call for Carrie was heard to assist him in finding a word or unearthing a rhyme."[63]

On February 2, a second daughter, Elsie, was born. Matthew Howard always said it had only taken him ten minutes flat to harness up the horses and set out for Dr. Conland.

Kipling worked away at the book, to be called *Captains Courageous*. Dr. Conland took him on three brief trips to Gloucester—one of these including a short trip on a fishing boat from Boston—but the main source of information was the doctor's fascinating stories of the fishing fleet. The result, in some ways, is a classic tale of the sea. We feel the slippery fish, taste the salt, hear the ship's timbers creak. But all this is undone by Kipling's failure to develop his characters. We learn a great deal—in fact, rather too much—about the mechanics of cod-fishing. The persons in the story are cardboard characters, never convincing, never lifelike. Over and over again, with the Disko Troop, with Harvey, with

Harvey's father—the railroad magnate*—Kipling starts out well, gives the reader a good picture of the person, and then becomes sidetracked in details of things rather than people. Of his trips with Dr. Conland to Gloucester, Kipling said,

> Charts we got—old and new—and the crude implements of navigation such as they used off the Banks, and a battered boat-compass still a treasure with me. . . . And Conland took large cod and the appropriate knives with which they are prepared for the hold, and demonstrated anatomically and surgically so that I could make no mistake about treating them in print. Old tales, too, he dug up, and the lists of dead and gone schooners whom he had loved, and I revelled in profligate abundance of detail.[64]

This mention of exactitude brings up a point. Contrary to popular opinion, in all his work Kipling tended to be inaccurate in technical details. Those who thought highly of Kipling frequently praised his wide knowledge. "McAndrew's Hymn," they said, was taken to engineers who examined every line and found only two very minor errors. They had similar choruses of praise for *Captains Courageous* and later stories throughout Kipling's life. They were mistaken. "McAndrew's Hymn" is full of errors; so are ".007," *Captains Courageous*, and many other stories. The most obvious example is the use of the word "knot," meaning a rate of speed, one nautical mile per hour. One says, then, that a boat is traveling at five knots. Until about 1890, general usage added an incorrect "per hour" to the "knots"—"five knots per hour." It was then pointed out that the "per hour" was included in the word "knot;" saying "five knots per hour" is really saying "five knots per hour per hour." It was just when Kipling was becoming popular that more precise thinking and writing led to "knot" being used correctly. Even though he loved jargon, he couldn't get it straight for more than twenty years. In

---

*An acquaintance of Kipling's, Mr. F. N. Finney, a railroad tycoon, supplied the information for Kipling's description of the parents' dash across country. Railroad buffs have praised this portion of the book ever since. Finney, an ardent admirer of Kipling, when building a railroad line in Michigan named two towns on it "Rudyard" and "Kipling." This evoked an unusual response in the modest Kipling; he wrote Finney at length about the towns, asked for photographs of them, and wrote a letter of instructions to the town of Kipling and an uncollected poem about the event ("My Sons in Michigan"). One could say that the Kipling who had sneered at American materialism was beginning to enjoy being wealthy and showing it off. Perhaps he was influenced by his wife. Carrie was a great one for putting on airs and insisting on being lionized.

his very first naval story, "Judson and the Empire," written in 1891, he has "a couple of knots an hour"[65] and continues to make this mistake through the 1890s and early 1900s. In 1904 he compounded the error by using "knot" as a unit of distance (rather than speed) equal to a mile: "Tim fetches her down once every thirty knots as regularly as breathing."[66] Around 1910 or so he got it straight; in "Sea Constables," written in 1915, and in subsequent stories, the word "knot" is used correctly. It may be objected that this is a minor error, made by many people before and after Kipling's time. It is true that general scientific knowledge was at a far lower level then. Newspapers at the turn of the century were full of glaring errors that would cause howls of derision nowadays. But look at Doyle, Galsworthy, Wells, Barrie—Kipling's contemporaries made no such errors. And these were years when Kipling was writing intensively about the Navy—attempting (and failing) to produce a naval version of his *Soldiers Three* stories—and priding himself on his accuracy.* In *Captains Courageous*, written in 1896, Kipling's only book about the sea, there are naturally places where the word "knot" is needed. He warily avoided using it at all!

This is not meant to disparage Kipling as a writer. His forte was in "giving you the picture," which he could do brilliantly. He could not be bothered to notice just which nut fitted which bolt. By that time he was on to a next sentence and a new idea. He strove to give the vignette, the impression of the moment; philosophical discourses were for the editor's page. He expressed plenty of opinions but, as described, many of these—hard work is its own reward, New York is a pig-trough—were often superficial. But before we dismiss him as a nothing but a talented journalist, let us remember, first, how well he could depict a depressed soldier, a woman with cancer, a teenage boy; and second, with what skill he wove his obscure stories about life, about death, about love.

Let us return to *Captains Courageous*, a good book that deserves more study than it has received. One can see Kipling's description of himself

---

*In his autobiography, Kipling said, ". . . I have had miraculous escapes in technical matters, which make me blush still. Luckily the men of the seas and engine room do not write to the Press, and my worst slip is still underided."[67] Surely the error about knots (especially with its hint about deck and engine-room) was his "worst slip."

near the end, when Harvey's father is finding out things about the fishing port:

> This Gloucester was a new town in a new land, and he purposed to "take it in" . . . . Men said that four out of every five fish-balls served at New England's Sunday breakfast came from Gloucester, and overwhelmed him with figures in proof—statistics of boats, gear, wharf-frontage, capital invested, salting, packing, factories, insurance, wages, repairs, and profits. . . . He coiled himself away on chain-cables in marine junk-shops, asking questions with cheerful, unslaked Western curiosity, till all the waterfront wanted to know "what in thunder that man was after, anyhow.". . . It was then that Harvey noticed and admired what had never struck him before—his father's curious power of getting at the heart of new matters as learned from men in the street.[68]

Several themes mentioned before reappear in *Captains Courageous*. One is the question of identity: Who is Harvey Cheyne? He is one person in the guise of another; for, of all the crew, only Dan knows Harvey's true background, which is revealed triumphantly at the end of the book when his multimillionaire parents dash across the country to Gloucester.

A related theme is confusion about one's parentage. Harvey's falling off the liner is described in a curious way:

> He was fainting from seasickness, and a roll of the ship tilted him over the rail on to the smooth lip of the turtle-back. Then a low, grey mother-wave swung out of the fog, tucked Harvey under one arm, so to speak, and pulled him off and away to leeward; the great green closed over him, and he went quietly to sleep.

One reader protested that he didn't seem to fall at all; did a wave wash him overboard? Kipling said that no, he clearly fell.

I think that Kipling put it obscurely because he was unconsciously describing a birth. (Birth is often depicted in mythology and dreams as accompanied by water, as in the stories of Moses and King Arthur.) A "mother-wave" . . . "tuck[s] Harvey under one arm" and then Manuel, a Portuguese Roman Catholic, pulls him into his dory—where he puts him in the bow—and takes him to the *We're Here*. The connections to Kipling's life are significant. Kipling described his earliest memory as being early morning walks to the Bombay fruit market with my *ayah* and later with my sister in her perambulator, and of our returns with our purchases piled high in the bows of it. Our *ayah* was a Portuguese Roman Catholic. . . .[69]

I think at this moment when Harvey is beginning a new life on the fishing schooner, Kipling evokes memories of his own origins, his own confusion about his birth. Manuel is one person who represents Kipling's childhood *ayah*.*

The cook, who is black, is another representative of Kipling's *ayah*. He is given a curious and special role in the story. At times, he is the deprecated "nigger."[70] Of one incident, Dan says, "There was only dad an' me aboard to see it. The cook he don't count." But on other occasions, he is elevated to being a man of mystery. "The doctor," as he is nicknamed, has second sight, can predict the future, and successfully tells when the catch will be good. These traits might possibly identify the cook with Kipling's *ayah*. But he also represents Kipling's white mother.

When speaking of the cook, I was going to state that, of all the crew, only he is unnamed. But I have found that I was mistaken. At one point he is given a name. At the end of the book, when the crew board the *We're Here* and sail off, the cook remains ashore; he is determined to become Harvey's manservant. Harvey's father laughs and agrees with the idea. "Let the man stay, therefore; even though he called himself MacDonald and swore in Gaelic." The reader will remember that Mrs. Kipling was one of the remarkable Macdonald sisters. The black cook has Kipling's mother's maiden name (though with a capital D). Again, we see the racial element in Kipling's confusion about his mother.

In this book, for the first time, a hidden side of Kipling is revealed; he was awe-struck and envious of the wealthy and their possessions. This is just the opposite of what we are told—he makes fun of Wilton Sargent, whose yacht, the reader will recall, has an "electric light, nickel-plated binnacles, and a calliope attachment to her steam-whistle," and all other such materialistic Americans. But it slips out, both in Harvey's "revenge" when he shows the *We're Here*'s crew all the splendor of the *Constance* (his

---

*Confirmation of this, perhaps, can be seen in the movie version of *Captains Courageous* where Manuel, rather than Disko Troop, is made the central figure influencing Harvey.

father's private railroad car), and when, at the end of the book, Kipling, impressed, describes "most expensive houses built of wood to imitate stone," and tells us that Harvey's horse "would have been cheap at a thousand dollars." There is a contradiction here. Kipling isn't quite practicing what he preaches. But it is so inconspicuous it doesn't mar what he wrote. Again, we may wonder if Carrie influenced him.

A final observation about this book concerns Kipling's characterization of Americans. Kipling had married an American, albeit an Anglophile. He settled in Vermont, built a house, and two of his three children were born in the United States. At least at the beginning of his four years in America, he intended to stay there the rest of his life. He liked American energy, the sense of infinite possibility, in contrast to the stuffy, conventional English attitudes he had experienced in London. Yet only in this book does he treat Americans sympathetically. Up to this point almost all his other stories with American settings had been political diatribes filled with bitter criticism. One exception, ".007," being purely about machines, could as well have taken place in England as America; it exemplifies Kipling's intense wish to belong to a group, to feel at home, equalled only by his fear of just that same situation. Though beset by family problems, and feeling himself in the midst of a hostile country, Kipling did not disguise his love of America; he could not leave without, so to speak, giving us a final kind word.

X

THE FIGHT

As spring approached in 1896, things grew even worse between the Kiplings and the Balestiers. Beatty had not held a regular job for a long time and was deeper in debt than ever. Kipling had bought two horses from him the year before, but the money had quickly disappeared. The two families were still not on speaking terms; Beatty was grumbling and complaining to everyone, whereas the Kiplings kept a dignified silence.

Then, early in March, Beatty filed a petition for bankruptcy. The Kiplings (apparently mostly the forceful Carrie) again came up with an idea that was supposed to "help" Beatty. Two versions of this plan are still told in Brattleboro, and since there is no documentation we will never know which one is accurate. The first is that the Kiplings offered to give Beatty the money he needed to leave the town and his cronies and to get a steady job in a nearby city, such as Boston. They would also support his wife Mai and daughter Marjorie during his absence. The second was that they agreed to finance his departure and job search with Mai accompanying him. Marjorie would be left behind with the Kiplings! This last offer, if indeed it was made, would of course have infuriated the Balestiers. It would have been tantamount to selling their daughter, with the added implication that they were not fit parents to bring her up. Even if only the first plan was offered, Beatty would have felt it to be condescending in the extreme. In any case, the offer was indignantly refused.

Even if these ideas were indeed primarily Carrie's, Kipling also behaved tactlessly. The subject of Beatty's behavior came up when Kipling was having a drink at Brooks House. Instead of refusing to discuss a family matter, Kipling said, in front of others, that he had "been obliged to carry him for the last year; to hold him up by the seat of his britches."[1] In a small town, a remark like this was of course bound to get back to the hot-tempered Beatty.

The Kiplings' decision to return to England after the baby's birth was now apparently set aside. They seemed to hesitate, to avoid deciding on a definite date and ship. They refused to discuss their departure with friends, and went on with changes and improvements around Naulakha as if they were going to stay. One gets the impression they were leaving with reluctance, hoping somehow they might not have to go.

In April the Kiplings took a trip to New York for a few days. Kipling took some lessons in bicycling and brought back a bicycle for use in Vermont.* His clumsiness, however, made him an unsteady rider. As the days turned warmer, things seemed better; Kipling always intensely enjoyed the coming of spring in New England. He sent an amiable set of verses in Irish dialect to the Kipling Club at Yale, regretfully refusing their invitation to dinner on May 14. He looked forward to a visit from Mr. Finney, the multimillionaire railroad man who had supplied data for *Captains Courageous*. But an eruption then occurred that changed everything.

On May 6, in the afternoon, Kipling was bicycling shakily down Pine Tree Road, which descends from Beatty's Maplewood and then turns at the Waite's house, where they had their own private post office. Beatty came galloping up behind him** in a buckboard and swung his

---

*The old-fashioned bicycle with a huge front wheel and a small rear one was used after the Civil War. The English called them "penny-farthings" because of the similarity, in comparative size, between these coins and the two wheels. Around 1885 the modern type began to appear, with equal-sized wheels and a chain drive. Bicycles, now safe and easy to ride, became very popular in the 1890s, which is why Kipling took up cycling at this time.

**There must be a dozen biographers who state that Beatty "met" Kipling on the road, as if they were going in opposite directions. Again, the psychic truth is that he did "meet" Kipling, in

team across the road; Kipling fell down, cutting his wrist. Freeing himself from the bicycle, Kipling got up, sucking the cut. Beatty, pulling up his team, yelled at him, "Hey! I want to talk with you!" Kipling quietly replied, "If you have anything to say, you can say it to my lawyer." Beatty cut loose with a torrent of invective and accusations, punctuated with oaths: Kipling had been spreading a lot of goddamn gossip about him (the "britches" remark); his wife had been out to cheat him left and right; the little bastard was no better than a goddamn liar and a coward.

What then followed varies according to the testimony of the two men. Beatty claimed that he had said, "You've got to take back the lies you have been telling about me, or by Christ, I'll punch the goddamn soul out of you!" Kipling claimed that he had been threatened with murder; that Beatty had said, "If you don't retract the lies you have been telling about me within a week, I'll blow out your goddamn brains."*

Whichever threat was made, Kipling's response was a quiet, "Then you will have only yourself to blame for the consequences." After further angry words, Beatty galloped home, and Kipling, too shaken to ride his bicycle, began to push it up the hill toward Naulakha. Both men might have shrugged it off and forgotten the quarrel, but this time Kipling decided to make a definite move. What he did is revealing, and reminiscent of the fight itself. Then the "uncivilized" Beatty in the buckboard, ranting and raving, had hurled curses at his brother-in-law, and the quiet "civilized" Kipling, never raising his voice, had told him to "say it to my lawyer." It is also reminiscent of his view of Americans as opposed to Englishmen—that above all, they are lawless. Kipling, the next morning, turned to the law. He went in to Brattleboro and swore out a warrant for Beatty's arrest because of the curses and name-calling, and the threat on his life. Again, he was behaving as if Vermont were a province in India. To Kipling, the Englishman, the law would be expected quietly to take over and Beatty would be controlled henceforward. It was a little as if a drunken native in India had bothered some of

---

the sense that he encountered him, that they had an eyeball-to-eyeball confrontation. The actual fact happens to be that Beatty passed Kipling, going at his usual gallop.

*The vast majority of people in Brattleboro never believed Beatty said this. They acknowledged that he was quick with his tongue and perhaps his fists, but they felt he would never go so far as to threaten murder.

the white sahibs, who would then whistle up a policeman. The native, perhaps, would be tossed in jail and told upon his release that if he tried anything like that again he would get a beating he would not forget. Kipling could never understand that in America, a family quarrel like this would be settled man-to-man.

In rough-and-ready Vermont, with a considerable pro-Beatty element locally, what Kipling got was justice—of a sort—and the publicity which he abhorred and in which Beatty delighted. Kipling might win the case, from a legal viewpoint, but Beatty would get all the attention; and he would moreover manage, in the only way he could, to make life miserable for Kipling and Carrie. Turning to the law was the worst step Kipling could have taken. Surely he must have had some idea of what would follow. But if he did, why did he take the matter to court? Perhaps he felt an unconscious need to bring the whole business to a climax.

Two days later, on Saturday, May 9, Beatty was arrested and arraigned. The two men appeared before William S. Newton, Justice of the Peace and Town Clerk of Brattleboro, who had issued the warrant for the arrest. Beatty seemed totally unperturbed; in fact, he seemed to be enjoying himself. Violence and public attention were just what he liked. Kipling, in comparison, was embarrassed and ill at ease.

After a brief review of the facts, Justice Newton announced that, it being Saturday, the matter would be put off until the following Tuesday, when the hearing would be resumed. Mr. Balestier would have to be held until that time, unless he could produce bail. Could he? Beatty, always the operator, quickly saw where he now had Kipling; he could imagine his reaction to the newspaper headline: "Kipling has brother-in-law put in jail." So Beatty, with a grin, said, no, he had no bail. Had everyone forgotten? He was bankrupt. Kipling pulled out a checkbook and offered to pay Beatty's bail—an absurd situation, doing this for the man whose arrest he had just requested! Beatty was quick to take advantage of this and, in injured tones, refused the proffered bail. After more discussion, he was released on his own recognizance to reappear in court the following Tuesday.

Kipling, silent and reserved, retreated to Naulakha; but Beatty rushed out and got in touch with all the newspapers he could think of. All his life he had tried to be the talk of the town in Brattleboro; by

Tuesday, if he played it right, he might be the center of attention of all America, and perhaps even of the English-speaking world.

Over the weekend nearly fifty reporters arrived. The town was buzzing. Beatty wined them and dined them, with his pretty wife, Mai, and pointed out Naulakha through the trees, where the Kiplings kept an aloof silence.

The hearing, which had to be moved to the Town Hall because of the size of the audience, was all that Beatty had hoped for, and all that Kipling had begun to fear. As the only witness, he was forced to go over all the family disputes that had preceded the fight on the hillside, since Justice Newton, well aware of local curiosity, allowed wide latitude in the questioning.

Kipling's manner toward the defendant was sympathetic—almost apologetic—rather than one of righteous indignation. In his testimony, Kipling admitted that Beatty was not in debt to him. He had been in the past, but had paid it all back. No, Beatty had never been assaultive. No, he had never carried a gun. But he repeated his statement that Beatty had threatened to kill him, that he feared for his life. Kipling also stated that a major reason for their settling in Vermont had been to keep a promise to Wolcott Balestier that Kipling would help his brother Beatty—who, upon hearing this, gave a derisive laugh in the quiet court-room.

Did Kipling mean that on his deathbed Wolcott had asked this of Carrie? This is hard to believe to be *factually* true. Wolcott was in the terminal stages of typhoid fever and presumably in a disoriented state. But some would say Kipling meant the request was made of him, months before. This is no easier to believe; Wolcott would hardly express any such wish, for he was utterly different from his brother and the two did not get along. Wolcott was a sensitive, charming aesthete, with a will of steel; Beatty was loud, earthy, and irresponsible, and had sneeringly given his brother the nickname "Delicate Touch" because he would ponder so long over the exact word to use when writing. (The nickname may be significant in view of my conclusion about Wolcott's homosexual tendencies.) For that matter, there was little love lost between any of the Balestier brothers and sisters.

It is scarcely credible that any such wish was *actually* expressed by Wolcott. But, once again, if we leave factual truth and turn to psychic truth, it becomes believable. Kipling wanted to care for Beatty, for he—like his sister, Carrie—was linked in his mind with the dead Wolcott, who had meant so much to him. Now we can understand what seemed contradictory before—Kipling's trips to town with Beatty to pick up the mail, his visits to Beatty's house. Their personalities were poles apart, and becoming brothers-in-law would not seem to explain their relationship. Kipling had Beatty arrested—and then offered to post bond for him. He was torn between feelings of hatred and affection. In his testimony against Beatty, Kipling referred to him as "this poor boy" and said, "I have done him no wrong, God knows." What kind of plaintiff testimony is this? It is only understandable if we see that in the crowded courtroom, as at Kipling's wedding, there stood the ghost of Wolcott Balestier.

At the end of a day's testimony, Kipling won a technical victory; Beatty was bound over for the next meeting of the County Court in September. Beatty was delighted. It would prolong the publicity and the obvious discomfort of Kipling and Carrie. He left the courtroom to seek out more reporters and to expand on the story which would fill the newspapers over the coming weekend.

For his part, Kipling, as usual, was loath to say anything at all, but confessed to a reporter that he was "dead sick of this whole business." He stated that he had absolutely decided "to leave this part of the country." The *New York Herald*, in a column sub-headline, printed "Goodby Green Mountains." The political scene and the passage of time had gradually made America seem less and less desirable, and the trips to England made that country seem more and more so. The family quarrel had added to Kiplings feeling of distaste, and now this glare of publicity was the last straw. By bringing the matter to court, he had allowed himself to be forced out of the United States. Many months before he had decided to leave the country, but, liking it deeply, he had hesitated as to just when he would leave. Now, so to speak, the decision was made for him, for he certainly did not want to wait until September and suffer further humiliations in the courtroom.

For the rest of the summer Kipling worked away at *Captains Courageous*, and went with Dr. Conland for one last visit to Gloucester. He knew he had to leave; but he left with a pang, and with the hope that he might someday return. In a letter to a friend dated June 4, he said:

I don't think quite of quitting the land permanently. It is hard to go from where one has raised one's kids, and builded a wall and digged a well and planted a tree.[2]

Kipling's years in America were the happiest of his life. Two of his three children were born in Vermont. Then a combination of events, topped by the family feud with Beatty, made him decide to return to England. America was always linked in his mind with India, as can be seen by his last days in Vermont.

On August 29 the Kiplings took the train to New York and left on September 2 on the *Lahn*. A few days before this, *The Seven Seas* came out, and he now wrote for it a significant dedication; it is addressed to Bombay, the city of his birth. At the moment of leaving Brattleboro, with its happy memories, his mind turned to a similar time when he had been forced to leave behind the happiness and security of his childhood with his *ayah* in India.

And on August 28, the day before they left Vermont, two friends had come to say goodbye. They found Kipling, rather upset, pacing up and down on the porch.

"There are only two places in the world where I want to live," he said, "Bombay and Brattleboro. And I can't live in either one."[3]

XI

THE RETURN TO ENGLAND

Upon arriving in England in September of 1896, the Kiplings went to their new home, a house near Torquay—on the western part of the south coast of England—where they lived for nearly eight months. It was a two-story stone building, with good privacy (always their first thought), called "Rock House." It should have suited them well; and yet Kipling felt strangely disturbed by the place. Something about the house was cold and malevolent. It seemed to bring on his old attacks of depression. These upsetting feelings were specifically connected with the house. If Kipling left it, he felt better; as soon as he stepped back in the door, they returned. The feelings were so strong that when he visited the house thirty years later, they immediately swept over him again. His story, "The House Surgeon," was written with Rock House in mind. It is about a house that exerts an evil influence on everyone in it, making them depressed. The narrator manages to remove this curse. He discovers that one of three sisters who used to live in the house fell out of an upper window and was killed. The other two believed she committed suicide; when he demonstrates it was just an accident, the depression vanishes.

Once again, Kipling was deeply homesick, this time for America. The cold grey house, seeming to exude evil, was so different from the warm friendliness of Naulakha. The fall climate was cold, cloudy and damp, and little Josephine—whom her father described as being wholly American—went about complaining that "This Englandt is stuffy."[1]* Kipling felt no relief at being out of a hostile America; on the contrary, he yearned for the humpy green mountains of Vermont, and the friends he had made there. In letters he contrasted the English scenery with the breath-taking view from Naulakha, the mountains with their beautiful Indian names, Wantastiquet near at hand and Monadnock, like some benign giant, showing his blue tip on the skyline.

In September, he wrote Dr. Conland:

> Today we are running into the climate of my native land—a thick greasy sky, wind from the southwest and a sullen, toppy sea. . . . Already I begin to think with sorrow of the fine clear, September morning on the hillside.

And in October:

> There are times when I'd give a good deal for the keen sniffs of an autumn morning up on the hillside, when the first frost has wilted things in the garden and the leaves are dropping of themselves. . . .

In a letter to C. E. Norton he said:

> I don't think we can stay out a whole year longer without coming over to have a look at things. It's an uncivilized land (I still maintain it) but how the deuce has it wound itself around my heartstrings in the way it has?
> C. and I sit over our inadequate English fire and grow homesick!

In another letter to Dr. Conland, in December:

> I wonder when we shall come back. There are times when I feel like taking the first boat and getting you up to dinner straight off. Keep an eye on the place for our sakes. I tried to offer it for sale once but I took damn good care to put a prohibitive price on it.

But with his usual reserve, he revealed his feelings only to close

*Meaning the word would sound this way if Josephine had a stuffy nose.

friends. Carrie wrote Mary Cabot, "Mr. Kipling never talks of Brattleboro or reads a letter from America. . . ."[2]*

Trying to settle into his new neighborhood, Kipling learned that the old square-rigger *Britannia*, a few miles down the coast, was used as a training ship for naval cadets. Kipling's interest in the sea, especially since his friendship with Dr. Conland and his writing *Captains Courageous*, led him to accept invitations to visit the *Britannia* several times, meet her officers, and observe the training. He sent accounts of all this back to Dr. Conland in Vermont.

Friends and relatives arrived to stay. A cousin, Hugh Poynter, came, and Kipling gave him a gun and accompanied him on rabbit-hunts. (Apparently he himself did not shoot, either from lack of interest or because of his poor eyesight.) His father, Lockwood Kipling, arrived with a seemingly endless amount of paraphernalia and started to work on the low-relief plaques that were to be used as illustrations in the forthcoming Outward Bound edition of his works that Scribners was to publish. And, in the spring of 1897, another cousin, Philip Burne-Jones, showed Kipling a vivid painting he was to put on exhibit toward the end of April. It was a startling picture, in arresting colors, of a sneering woman towering over a man lying helpless on a bed. Kipling wrote some verses to appear in the exhibition catalogue, from them came one of the lines for which he is remembered:

> A fool there was and he made his prayer
> (Even as you and I!)
> To a rag and a bone and a hank of hair
> (We called her the woman who did not care)
> But the fool he called her his lady fair —
> (Even as you and I!)[3]

"A rag and a bone and a hank of hair"—as savage and hostile a line about women as has ever been penned, a phrase whose very vehemence

---

*Note that, even to a close friend, her husband is "Mr. Kipling" — although that sort of thing was far commoner in those days. Perhaps Carrie was being cool to Mrs. Cabot, indicating that further letters would not be welcomed, for in actuality Kipling was reading, and writing, plenty of letters.

insures its immortality. Kipling's feelings about women again came to the fore.

Early that year, Kipling's mind turned back to his school days. He began writing "Slaves of the Lamp" and the other violent schoolboy tales that were later collected under the title *Stalky & Co.*, stories that some readers found exceedingly brutal.

This period in Kipling's life was marked by a sequence of four important developments: first, he left America, and felt extremely homesick; second, he felt strangely troubled by Rock House; third, he was moved to write a vindictive poem about women; and fourth, he started to write stories of his school days. We can understand why these things happened, and in this order. Kipling was reliving his feelings when, as a child of five, he was taken away from warm, sunny India and his loving *ayah*, and put in the House of Desolation, where he was tormented by a woman. From there he went to school. As we have seen, he felt that his leaving Brattleboro was like his leaving Bombay twenty-five years before, and he had the same feelings of homesickness after his arrival in England that he had as a child. In the frightening Rock House he had the same emotions that he had experienced in the House of Desolation, where he thought of suicide. In his bitter line of poetry ("a rag and a bone and a hank of hair") he again brings up his feelings for Mrs. Holloway—whom he had described as "bony"—"the woman who did not care." And finally he wrote the sometimes-violent stories of his days at school. The four happenings recapitulate the events of a quarter of a century before. The scars were still there.

Now he wrote the poem for which, perhaps, he is best known— "Recessional." The year 1887 had marked fifty years of Queen Victoria's reign; and now, in 1897, came her Diamond Jubilee. "Sixty Years Our Queen" said the signs amidst the bunting on every village square, and all England swelled with pride. A variety of elaborate ceremonies were planned, culminating in Jubilee Day on June 22.

Kipling, a quiet, modest man—though not shy—was not interested. He wanted no part of a ceremony where he might be recognized and bothered, and he planned to avoid London on Jubilee Day. The man who was later called "The Poet of the Empire" felt a deep respect for the Crown, but his feelings about women prevented his having any real sense of devotion for the person who wore it. He viewed "The Great

"A rag and a bone and a hank of hair"

199

White Mother" with the same mixture of love and hate that he felt toward his own mother, whom he had seldom seen in his childhood. She, he felt (more than his father), had abandoned him and his sister at Mrs. Holloway's. This always mystified him. Over the years he had been given a variety of explanations; that it was because he had been a bad, disobedient child, and Mrs. Holloway had taken him in out of pity; that it was because children couldn't stand the heat of sea-level India; that it was because of the bad effects *ayahs* had on the young in their care, spoiling them so excessively; that it was because their staying with relatives would have caused difficulties between those relatives and his parents. None of these reasons seemed adequate and therefore he could never fully understand her deserting him, so that he could accept it and put it behind him.

When he returned to India as a teenager he found his mother to be a charmer, the center of attention in any group, a person who was witty but who also could be caustic and skewer a victim with her sharp tongue. He came to feel genuine warmth and love for her, ascribed to her one of his better lines of poetry, and enjoyed being with her—up to a point, for he felt some of the awe and fear toward her that he felt toward all women, a fear that came from his years at Mrs. Holloway's. He certainly preferred to be with his father, a warm and gentle man whose interests in art and writing were so close to his own. Where he felt furious about Mrs. Holloway he felt confusion about his mother, just as he described in the ending of "Baa Baa, Black Sheep" in which the mother returns and rescues the children, but what they have been through scars them for the rest of their lives.

On Jubilee Day, then, he felt no great enthusiasm toward Queen Victoria. When she was succeeded four years later by King Edward VII, Kipling's feelings toward his monarch warmed perceptibly. A prolific writer and ardent imperialist, he hardly ever wrote about the towering figure of the Queen. What little he did write is a significant mixture of routine patriotism ("Ave Imperiatrix"* and "The Young Queen"), and of hostility and fear, seen in three other poems.

---

*This poem's meaning is controversial. Some have claimed, notably Beresford, that it was written tongue in cheek, mocking patriotism. Others, particularly Dunsterville, state that it was genuinely patriotic. Most biographers seem to agree with Dunsterville.

Back in 1887, Kipling, then twenty-one and working for the *Gazette*, wrote the poem "What the People Said" which depicted the average Indian's response to the Queen's Golden Jubilee. He described the people saying they couldn't care less about

> The sound of the Great Queen's voice:
> "My God hath given me years,
> Hath granted dominion and power:
> And I bid you, O Land, rejoice."
> . . . .
> And the Ploughman settled the share
> More deep in the sun-dried clod:
> "Mogul, Mahratta, and *Mlech* from the North,
> And the White Queen over the Seas—
> God raiseth them up and driveth them forth
> As the dust of the plowshare flies in the breeze;
> But the wheat and the cattle are all my care,
> And the rest is the will of God."[4]

And during the first year of his marriage, in that snowy winter in the Bliss Cottage, he wrote "The Widow's Party," a soldier's account of a battle which is sarcastically likened to a picnic given by a woman:

> And some was sliced and some was halved,
> And some was crimped and some was carved,
> And some was gutted and some was starved,
> When the Widow give the party.[5]

Seven years before, in 1890, he had written "The Widow at Windsor," which, people believed, was so disrespectful it cost him the position of Poet Laureate.

In that Jubilee year, however, everyone was urging England's most prominent writer to produce a poem for the occasion. To one of these, a Mrs. Tree, Kipling wrote in March, "I've never written anything about the Queen. It's rather outside my beat and if I tried I'm afraid I should make a mess of it."[6]

What he wrote for the Jubilee was a famous poem—"Recessional"—but one that contains not a single word about the Queen herself.

After vacating the Rock House and staying at two other places for a few weeks each—Kipling said he felt like a houseless gypsy—in June the Kiplings finally left Torquay and moved to Rottingdean, near Brighton. Here there were many relatives. Kipling's Aunt Georgie Burne-Jones let them use her summer house at one end of the village green, called "North End House," until Carrie, pregnant with their third and last child, delivered in August. At one side of the green lived the Ridsdales, whose daughter had married Kipling's cousin Stanley Baldwin; she was also expecting. In the middle, like an island, was a house called "The Elms" that Aunt Georgie urged him to buy. The Kiplings were now surrounded by Burne-Joneses, Macdonalds, and Baldwins, everybody related to everybody else. In this close-knit group he could almost feel at home, for it reminded him of month-long escapes from the House of Desolation to Aunt Georgie's winter house where he would go and tug at the bell-pull "on the wonderful gate that let me into all felicity."

In July Kipling was working on some children's stories that he used to tell Josephine back in Vermont, tales that later became the famed *Just So Stories*; on his poem "The White Man's Burden" (he liked to work at both poetry and prose at the same time) and on two other poems called "The Destroyers" and "Cruisers." These last two poems again evince Kipling's feelings of fear and hostility toward women.

"The Destroyers" is unusual in likening ships to women who lure men to their deaths.

> The strength of twice three thousand horse
> That seek the single goal;
> The line that holds the rending course,
> The hate that swings the whole:
> The stripped hulls, slinking through the gloom,
> At gaze and gone again—
> The brides of Death that wait the groom—
> The Choosers of the Slain![7]

In "Cruisers," Kipling likens them not just to dangerous women, but to prostitutes.

> As our mother the Frigate, bepainted and fine,
> Made play for her bully the Ship of the Line;
> So we, her bold daughters by iron and fire,
> Accost and decoy to our masters' desire.

> Now pray you consider what toils we endure,
> Night-walking wet sea-lanes, a guard and a lure;
> Since half of our trade is that same pretty sort
> As mettlesome wenches do practice in port.
> And when we have wakened the lust of a foe
> To draw him by flight toward our bullies we go,
> Till, 'ware of strange smoke stealing nearer, he flies—
> Or our bullies close in for to make him good prize.[8]

While working on these two pieces and what were to be the *Just So Stories,* he finished another notable poem, "The Explorer:"

> Have I named one single river? Have
> I claimed one single acre?
> Have I kept one single nugget—(barring
> samples)? No, not I.
> Because my price was paid me ten times over
> by my Maker.
> But you wouldn't understand it. You go up
> and occupy.[9]

The narrator goes and discovers an area of incredible wealth.

It is hypothesized that the urge that has always driven man to explore this planet, a yearning for the undiscovered, for a lost land "flowing with milk and honey" where all dreams come true, stands for the early mother-child relationship. I think it no coincidence that Kipling wrote a poem about the having the urge to explore when he himself had suffered such a confusing childhood.

As Kipling began work on a poem for the Jubilee, the refrain "lest we forget" kept going through his mind. Another well-known story, repeated by many a biographer, is that this poem, one of his most famous, was rescued from the oblivion of a wastepaper basket by an American friend.

In the middle of July, the Kiplings had as guests his Aunt Georgie (Lady Burne-Jones, in whose house they were temporarily living) and Sallie Norton, the daughter of his old friend from New England days, Charles Eliot Norton. One morning Kipling was looking through a pile of material, throwing some of it out, and chatting with the three women as he did so. Sallie Norton, who was seated next to the wastepaper basket, was curious about what was being put into it; and, with Kipling's permission, began to look at some of the rejected pieces. She was immediately struck by a poem about the Diamond Jubilee called "After," with the refrain "Least we forget—lest we forget." She protested that this certainly was too fine a piece to be thrown out. According to the story, Kipling was doubtful about it, but Carrie and Aunt Georgie agreed with her, so he set to work on it, reducing its length from seven to five verses. At Sallie's suggestion, the last couplet of the first verse,

> Lord God of Hosts, be with us yet,
> Lest we forget—lest we forget![10]

was added as a refrain to the second and fourth verses; Kipling took Sallie's pen for this, and wrote in the margin, "written with Sallie's pen—R.K." and still using her pen added "Amen" and his signature, and beneath that,

> done in council at North End House,
> July 16
> > Aunt Georgie
> > Sallie
> > Carrie & me.

Miss Norton was given this original; Aunt Georgie, who was returning to London that afternoon, took along a fresh copy and sent it to the *Times*, where it appeared the next day, with a new title—"Recessional."

The first three verses are:

> God of our fathers, known of old,
> Lord of our far-flung battle-line,
> Beneath whose awful Hand we hold
> Dominion over palm and pine —
> Lord God of Hosts, be with us yet,
> Lest we forget — lest we forget!

> The tumult and the shouting dies;
> The Captains and the Kings depart:
> Still stands Thine ancient sacrifice,
> An humble and a contrite heart.
> Lord God of Hosts, be with us yet,
> Lest we forget — least we forget!

Far-called, our navies melt away;
On dune and headland sinks the fire:
Lo, all our pomp of yesterday
Is one with Nineveh and Tyre!
Judge of the Nations, spare us yet,
Lest we forget — lest we forget!

Now, looking through the pages of the *Times* for 1897, one can get some impression of the impact of the poem on the English people, for the issues that Diamond Jubilee year are one long paean of joy and pride. Leading up to Jubilee Day, June 22, the columns grow longer and longer, expanding on the greatness, the power, the glory of the British Empire and its Queen. The carriages in the Jubilee Day procession are drawn before us in a wealth of detail—the numbers of footmen, the carvings, the coats of arms—in inimitable British fashion. It must have been a fabulous time; Rebecca West had

> . . . enchanting memories of such feasts for the eye as I do not think I knew again until the Russian Ballet came to dip the textiles of Western Europe in bright dyes. London was full of dark men from the ends of the earth who wore glorious colours and carried strange weapons, and who were all fond of small children and smiled at them in the streets. I remember still with a pang of ecstacy the gleaming teeth of a tall bearded warrior wearing a high headdress, gold earrings, and necklaces, a richly multicoloured uniform, and embroidered soft leather boots. There were also the Indian troops in Bushey Park, their officers exquisitely brown and still, and coiffed with delicately bright turbans, the men washing their clothes at some stretch of water, small and precise and beautiful. They came from remote places and spoke unknown tongues. They belonged to an infinite number of varied races. They were amiable, they belonged to our Empire, we had helped them to become amiable by conquering them and civilizing them. It was an intoxicating thought. . . .[11]

In the midst of all this, in the middle of the center page of the *Times* (the "lead" position), there appears "Recessional"—tiny, all by itself, but with a powerful appeal to a nation with a strong Puritanical streak. Stop and consider, it says: Be not proud. All is but "dust that builds on dust." An entire Empire, conscience-struck, stopped and looked at itself; it was like a dash of cold water in the midst of the furor of the Diamond Jubilee. Kipling did not turn out a routine poem of praise for the occasion; he neatly struck just the opposite note—and a telling one. This was partly his genius as a writer; but his humility, his Biblical intonation, and his mixed feelings toward the Queen can only be understood in the light of his childhood.

The poem appeals to the Lord to "be with us yet, lest we forget, lest we forget," that is, be with us, for fear that we become proud and vain and forget Him. But on close examination, as Carrington points out, in the third verse Kipling makes an error. He changed the refrain to "Judge of the Nations, spare us yet, lest we forget, lest we forget." If God is asked to be with us, for *fear* that we forget, He should be asked to spare us (be lenient, be merciful) *even though* we forget, *even though* we become proud and vain. I point out this minor error, unimportant in itself, because it may reflect something of Kipling's feelings about the Queen and about women. With the whole nation pouring out praise for her, he wrote a poem urging caution and humility, "lest (for fear that) we forget." And when the Lord should be asked to "spare us" (be merciful) "even though we forget," it comes out again as "lest (for fear that) we forget," perhaps phrased this way because it expresses his feeling, "I could never say 'even though I forget,' or that I might forget. I will never, never forget what I suffered at the hands of a woman."

Did Kipling really mean to throw the poem out? It makes a good story; as the writer Philip Wylie pointed out to me, the poem's emphasis on awe and humility is borne out by the incident, where Kipling is modestly doubtful about the value of the piece.

I'm afraid it wasn't really rescued from oblivion by Miss Norton. He had been working on it for a month; this, then, was but one of many versions that had gone to the scrapbasket, and there were presumably others on his desk—or in his head.

What was done to the manuscript tends to confirm this conclusion, for Kipling did not treat it like some first draft about which he had doubts. It should first be mentioned that his extreme feelings about privacy extended with a vengeance to any piece of paper on which he set his pen. What he wrote was for printing alone or, in the case of letters, for the reader alone.* Few friends ever got an autographed copy

---

*Just to give one example where many are possible: "In reply to your letter with copy of Cambridge Magazine. I can only express my regret—my present engagements will not permit me to avail myself of your kind invitation to contribute to your magazine," Kipling wrote. Even such a routine letter as this is marked "private."[12]

of a book, and autograph hunters themselves were avoided like the plague.

He kept a particularly secure hold on manuscripts. On just five occasions, to my knowledge, did he give them away to individuals and then only special ones, to the most special of friends—the manuscript of "Baa Baa, Black Sheep" to Mrs. Hill, the one of *Captain's Courageous* to Dr. Conland, the one of "Mowgli's Brothers" to Susan Bishop (Josephine's nurse back in Vermont), the one of the "happy ending" version of *The Light That Failed* to Frank Doubleday and the one described above, given to Sallie Norton. (He did, of course, give many manuscripts to libraries.) The description of the poem's composition, the noting of whose pen was used, the special gift of the manuscript to Miss Norton, all show Kipling's awareness that here he had something memorable.

Ever since his stay in America, with his "ship" house and the writing of *Captains Courageous*, Kipling's interest had gradually shifted from the land to the sea, and from the Army to the Navy. About half the *Just So Stories*, written during this period of time, involve the ocean or water as a key element. No longer did he tell of the Army's battles, nor delight in the intricacies of its equipment; and his boyish worship of the bachelor officer faded away during the years that he became a husband and then a father. His fascination with the military now centered on the Navy.

In 1892 the successful development of torpedo boats had so alarmed naval circles that they decided to devise a new type of vessel to handle them. The result was the "torpedo-boat-destroyer," the original term for today's destroyer, and Kipling was delighted when he was invited to be aboard one of the new ships when she was put through her paces. However, around the middle of August, Carrie delivered their child, a son, who in keeping with the family tradition was named John; so his being at the ship's trials, as he wrote a friend, had to be put off.

Ref.: t.b.d. trials. My attention is at present taken up by one small craft recently launched from my own works—weight (approx.) 8.957 lbs; h.p. (indicated) 2.0464, consumption fuel unrecorded but fresh supplies needed every 2 1/2 hours. The vessel at present needs at least 15 years for full completion but at the end of that time may be an efficient addition to the

Navy, for which service it is intended. Date of launch Aug. 17th, 1:50 a.m. No casualties. Christened John. You will understand that the new craft requires a certain amount of attention—but I trust ere long to be able to attend a t.b.d. trial.[13]

"The Navy, for which service [he] is intended." From the day of his birth, with his father's militaristic inclinations, it could be predicted that John would join one of the armed forces; though, as we shall see, it was to be the Army, and not the Navy, to which he went, and where he met his death.

In his autobiography, so aimed at concealing any intense feelings, the only time he mentions his son's name Kipling merely says, "my son John arrived on a warm August night in '97, under what seemed every good omen."[14] All the tragedy of his son's early death is hidden behind that one word "seemed."

It should be noted that in the letter humorously likening John's birth to a boat-launching, Kipling remarks, "No casualties." Not "launching proceeded smoothly," or something of the sort, but "no casualties." When we further note that it was a "warm" night, I think here Kipling is referring to his own childhood, when his mother, during the terrible hot season, gave birth to a child, also named John, who died.

Kipling wrote about his nursing son, "the boy John he says nuffin' and takes his vittles."[15] This is a reference to "The Tar Baby," the best known of Joel Chandler Harris' poems in which Mr. Fox makes a baby out of tar and uses it to catch Brer Rabbit, who comes by, talks to the baby, who "say[s] nothin',"[16] and then hits him and is caught in the sticky tar. The recurring sentence at the end of each verse is "Tar Baby, he say[s] nothin'." Describing this scene of a mother nursing an infant, so full of meaning for him, Kipling, without realizing it, refers to his son as a tar baby, black.

During the autumn of 1897 Kipling looked about for a house that would suit them, but nothing seemed quite right. In September he took a brief trip with another writer—an unusual thing for him to do—when Thomas Hardy went with him and offered suggestions. Together they went to see a country home where an elderly lady lived. While Kipling was upstairs, Hardy said to her, "Do you know who that is? That's Rudyard Kipling."[17] No response; she had never heard of Rudyard Kipling. A few minutes later, when Hardy was in another part of the house, Kipling said, "Did you recognize him? That person with me is Thomas Hardy." Again, no reaction; she'd never heard of Thomas Hardy either. The two men chuckled, on the way home, that they weren't going to get far on the strength of their names alone.

The Kiplings finally ended up moving to The Elms, near Aunt Georgie, with all his relatives about. The house provided excellent privacy, since it was surrounded by a high stone wall that turned it into a fortress, but even this was not enough for Kipling, who could never stand seeing some tourist pointing at his house. They lived at The Elms for the next five years.

They had a happy Christmas there, with both his parents with them. Carrie kept a careful if unrevealing diary, and on the last day of each year—which was also her birthday—Kipling always put a little note summarizing the last twelve months. It is noteworthy that at the end of the year before, the year of the disastrous battle that ended in their leaving America, Kipling had written nothing. It was a year to be forgotten, if possible. But now he wrote on the last page of the diary for 1897, "Here endeth the 6th Vol—which is within three weeks of the sixth year of our life together. In all ways the richest of the years to us two personally. 'She shall do him good and not evil all the days of her life.'"[18]

Now they decided on a trip to South Africa, and early in January 1898 the whole family with Kipling's father, two maids, and the three children's governess set out on a liner for Cape Town. Three weeks later they arrived in the blazing heat of midsummer and settled down, not at all comfortably, in a boardinghouse on the slope of Table Mountain.

His children, happy in the sun, reminded Kipling of his own childhood in India.

> Flying-fish about our bows
> Flying sea-fires in our wake:
> This is the road to our Father's House,*
> Whither we go for our soul's sake!

---

*At the very beginning of "Baa Baa, Black Sheep" there is a quotation about the House of Desolation: "When I was in my father's house, I was in a better place." I presume this refers to Christ's saying, "In my Father's house there are many mansions: if it were not so, I would have told you." (Gospel according to St. John, 14:2, King James version.)

They that walk with shaded brows,
Year by year in a shining land,
They be men of our Father's House,
They shall receive us and understand.

We shall go back by boltless doors,
To the life unaltered our childhood knew—
To the naked feet on the cool, dark floors,
And the high-ceiled rooms that the Trade blows through:

The wayside magic, the threshold spells,
Shall soon undo what the North had done—
Because of the sights and the sounds and the smells
That ran with our youth in the eye of the sun!

And the Earth accepting shall ask no vows,
Nor the Sea our love nor our lover the Sky.
When we return to our Father's House
Only the English shall wonder why![19]

At Cape Town there was another remarkable man whose name was known throughout the Empire. This was Cecil Rhodes, who made a fortune in gold and then, as if that wasn't enough, another in diamonds. At one point, his mines produced nine-tenths of all the diamonds in the world. He planned to control the entire continent of Africa "from Cape Town to Cairo," in the catchy phrase of the time.

A devious man who was immersed in one scheme after another, Rhodes had two qualities that certainly appealed to Kipling. First of all, his plans were on a gigantic, British-Empire scale. One of many wills he made left all his money for the formation of a Secret Society that would extend British rule throughout the world, taking over all nations and continents. (He even thought of occupying other planets.) With all the "Colonial Representatives in the Imperial Parliament" there would be no more wars. This followed his declared philosophy that "We are the first race in the world, and that the more of the world we inhabit, the better it is for the human race."[20] Secondly, he had a marked fear of women. A bachelor, he chose bachelors for his assistants, and any defection from the ranks into marriage was viewed with deep misgivings. Later in his life a Princess Radziwill, a manipulative adventuress, got herself into his company. He was completely incapable of handling her. On one occasion when walking beside him she feigned a fainting-spell, necessitating his catching her in his arms. An observer said he would "never forget the absolutely abject look of helplessness on his face."

But of course it was not these idiosyncrasies that Kipling, or most people, thought of in connection with Cecil Rhodes. He was an Empire-builder, a man of action, enormously wealthy and with incredible determination. Once he had fixed on a goal nothing, it seemed, could stop him. He was just the sort of person to whom Kipling took an instant liking—and it would not have troubled him that Rhodes had been quoted as saying that he "preferred land to niggers,"[21] just as it would not have troubled many other Englishman at that time. As in the case of Theodore Roosevelt, here was another powerful man of action, not just a man of words. The two men quickly became friends. Kipling tended to idolize both Rhodes and Roosevelt; as had happened with other men, he exaggerated their successes and ignored their faults. A powerful man has enormous appeal to one who has been made to feel helpless as a child.

Rhodes built the Kiplings a house near his own to be used by writers and artists, and the Kipling family stayed there every winter from 1900 to 1908. In later years, even though knowing he would never return to South Africa and was aware that in clinging to the house he was acting contrary to Rhodes' intentions, Kipling touchily refused to give it up. And so for a time the house stood deserted and empty, just as Naulakha stands today on a Vermont hillside.

Early in March Kipling took a trip, arranged by Rhodes, fifteen hundred miles up to Rhodesia. It was one of the relatively few times when Kipling was away from Carrie for more than a day or so. This new province that Rhodes named for himself had been acquired with doubtful legality from Lobengula, the chief of the Matabeles. (Poor Lobengula was conned into signing his lands away in a fashion similar to the United States' exploitation of the American Indian that was taking place at the same time.) Kipling's route became one of the best known in English literature, for:

He went from Graham's Town to Kimberly, and from Kimberly to
Khama's Country, and from Khama's Country he went east by north . . . till

at last he came to the banks of the great grey-green greasy Limpopo River, all set about with fever trees. . . .[22]

as recounted in "The Elephant's Child," a favorite with three generations of children, and a story that may outlast much of his more serious work. More will be said of this and the other *Just So Stories* later.

Early in April Kipling took a train back to his family at Cape Town, taking along a bundle of native curios, souvenirs of this fascinating new country. Later that month they returned to England, delighted with South Africa and planning to return there the following spring. Kipling had found a new home. Of the four places he had lived—India, England, America, and South Africa—he couldn't tell which was most appealing, as he expressed in his poem "The Fires":

> Men make their fires on the hearth
> Each under his roof-tree
> And the Four Winds that rule the earth
> They blow the smoke to me.
>
> Across the high hills and the sea
> And all the changeful skies,
> The Four Winds blow the smoke to me
> Till the tears are in my eyes.
>
> With every shift of every wind
> The homesick memories come,
> From every quarter of mankind
> Where I have made me a home.
>
> How can I answer which is best
> For all the fires that burn?
> I have been too often host or guest
> At every fire in turn.
>
> Oh, you Four Winds that blow so strong
> And know that this is true,
> Stop for a little and carry my song
> To all the men I knew![23]

They arrived in England to find that Spain and America were at war. Two months before, on February 15, the battleship *Maine* blew up as she lay in the harbor of Havana, with the loss of two hundred and sixty lives. America, young, strong, and "uppity," was flexing her muscles. She wanted Spain out of the Caribbean, which she hoped would become an "American Lake," and was not averse to finding an excuse for throwing her out. More importantly, a civil war had been dragging on in Cuba for years, and Americans were strongly sympathetic to the guerrilla revolutionists. America's idealism was heightened by an inflammatory press; a war would not be a war against Spain, but a crusade to free the downtrodden Cubans from the ugly grasp of Spainish. Had the explosion that wrecked the *Maine* been an internal one, from the ship's machinery, or an external one, from some mine or other explosive charge placed there by the Spanish? A dark rumor circulated that the harbor authorities had insisted that the *Maine* be moored at one particular spot, the inference being that this was where the explosives had been planted. An American board of inquiry issued their findings on March 21, stating, to no one's surprise, that the explosion had been an external one, blowing the ship's bottom in. "Remember the *Maine!*" became the rallying cry of the Spanish-American War declared a month later.*

With incredible ineptitude on the part of the Spanish and equally incredible luck on the part of the Americans, the war moved to a rapid, almost storybook ending. In May Dewey defeated the Spanish fleet in the Philippines. In June, with enemy warships safely bottled up in the harbor, U.S. troops arrived ~~landed~~ at Santiago, in eastern Cuba. In July, the Spanish vessels were sunk and the Americans successfully attacked Santiago and took Cuba. In August, a peace treaty was signed, less than four months after the war began.

To an outsider, it seemed as easy as that. All our armed forces, Army and Navy together, had less than 400 deaths from combat. The whole thing had a certain holiday look to it, a little like an oversized company picnic, with the added zest of an idealistic crusade against the Spanish. Particularly at the beginning, the Americans seemed to be playing at war; one governor, hearing that his state's militia was now camped out in the open, asked in all seriousness, "But what if it rains?"[24]

---

*Most authorities now agree that it is highly unlikely that the Spanish, well aware of America's belligerent feelings, would have been so foolish as to blow up a U.S. battleship. The hulk was raised in 1911, but the cause of the explosion was reputedly still unclear. Finally, in the 1970s, the Navy officially declared the explosion had been an internal one.

The outsider did not know what it was like to fight in sweltering Cuba, with little food, nor that, although the Army had only 350 deaths from combat, more than 1,900 died of dysentery and malaria.

Kipling watched it all with his usual lively interest, particularly when he heard about his old friend Theodore Roosevelt leading a charge near San Juan Hill, using a revolver recovered from the sunken *Maine*. British sympathies, unlike those of other European nations, were all with the Americans; and Kipling's were too. He particularly responded to the idealistic vision of America freeing a subjugated people to better their way of life, a theme that he was to emphasize in his poem "The White Man's Burden," on which he had been working for over a year. Now the two nations swung toward Anglo-American unity; forgotten was the border dispute in South America that had played such a part in Kipling's leaving Vermont. When a German naval squadron interfered in Manila Bay after Dewey's victory, the British commander present immediately sided with the Americans, and the Germans withdrew.

Kipling welcomed the Anglo-American friendship; it brought back to his mind warm memories of a country that, in some ways, he deeply loved. And the American victories in the war were so dashing, so full of zest, so like episodes in one of Kipling's own stories—and so pleasantly lacking in the horrors of drawn-out warfare and general carnage. Kipling, who wrote with such fascination about the military life, had never seen action himself. The "splendid little war," John Hay, then the American ambassador to the Court of St. James, had called it (one wonders if he got the phrase from his friend Kipling); and so it seemed to an outsider—the last war that could almost look like fun. The Americans' easy victory strongly influenced the British actions in the events that led up to the Boer War only a year later.

That summer Kipling published *The Day's Work*, a collection of short stories he had written back in Vermont, including the aforementioned 'Brushwood Boy' and 'William the Conqueror.' He also turned once more to *Kim*, which he had begun and worked at repeatedly during his years in America, and which itself was an outgrowth of his first novel, *Mother Maturin*, that he had written and rewritten back in India, but which never seemed to come out right. He repeatedly consulted his father, Lockwood Kipling, about *Kim*—one is reminded of Kipling's remark, "It will always be one of the darkest mysteries to me that any human being can make a beginning, end, *and* middle of a really truly long story"[25]—and with the senior Kipling's help it gradually began to take shape.

That fall he completed another one of the poems that made him famous, and that provided a familiar phrase—"The White Man's Burden." Some of its verses are:

> Take up the White Man's burden—
> Send forth the best ye breed—
> Go bind your sons to exile
> To serve your captives' need;
> To wait in heavy harness,
> On fluttered folk and wild—
> Your new-caught, sullen peoples,
> Half-devil and half-child.

> Take up the White Man's burden—
> In patience to abide,
> To veil the threat of terror
> And check the show of pride;
> By open speech and simple,
> A hundred times made plain,
> To seek another's profit,
> And work another's gain.

> Take up the White Man's burden—
> The savage wars of peace—
> Fill full the mouth of Famine
> And bid the sickness cease;
> And when your goal is nearest
> The end for others sought,
> Watch Sloth and heathen Folly
> Bring all your hope to nought.

> Take up the White Man's burden—
> And reap his old reward:
> The blame of those ye better,
> The hate of those ye guard—
> The cry of hosts ye humour
> (Ah, slowly!) toward the light:—
> "Why brought ye us from bondage,
> Our loved Egyptian night?"

Take up the White Man's burden—
Ye dare not stoop to less—
Nor call too loud on Freedom
To cloak your weariness;
By all ye cry or whisper,
By all ye leave or do,
The silent, sullen peoples
Shall weight your Gods and you.[26]

Imperialism has nothing to do with financial profit, says Kipling. It is not a matter of "painting another red square on the map." It is a sober assumption of responsibilities, the thankless task of managing the affairs of those less civilized than ourselves. This idealistic view was widely held in those days; it was a most important factor in the outbreak of the Spanish-American War. In addition, Kipling's own background influenced his point of view in this area. His main orientation was always of a white man in India. There the framework of British rule was the Indian Civil Service. It was composed almost entirely of Englishmen, with a mere token representation of Indians—about one or two percent in Kipling's day. And it was the finest civil service ever formed. The members were carefully chosen, often from the top-ranking families in England; being sent out to India was considered an honor. These men measured up impressively to the responsibilities entrusted to them; their efficiency and honesty has never been equaled in any similar organization. The system, in a way, worked; and Kipling believed in it wholeheartedly.

But "The White Man's Burden" is a poem that arouses indignation and fury now. The statement that the imperialist is not interested in his own financial profit and, in fact, is only striving for the native's economic success would bring a derisive snort from any former colony today. Then there is the unquestioned assumption that the white man's way is best; there is no thought of leaving the native alone, or of giving him a choice of who is going to "modernize" him. In the fourth verse, Kipling seems puzzled and annoyed at the natives' complaints at being colonized; they actually don't seem to know what's best for them, he grumbles. But it is the smug note of superiority that are most noticeable to the present-day reader. More than any other poem Kipling wrote, this one dates him. The native is "half-devil and half-child" who must be spoken to "in open speech and simple," and when the imperialist has nearly attained his goal of helping the natives, "Sloth and heathen Folly" will "bring [his] hope to naught"—referring, it would seem, to self-government, which Kipling always felt to be utterly beyond the capacity of the Indians.

He believed the white man to be inherently superior to the native; only he knows what is best, and how to carry it out. Kipling viewed the natives as humans, but as inferior humans. He could be sensitive to their feelings, but could never quite think of them as human beings like himself. He could praise Gunga Din's bravery in battle and say, "You're a better man than I am, Gunga Din!"[27] even though he would not eat at the same table with him and did not believe Gunga Din should ever be given the right to vote. Indeed, with his insistence on racial superiority, his contempt for the educated Indian, his chuckling amusement at native activities, and his secret and guilty memories of a childhood attachment to his native *ayah*, he reflects exactly many of the present-day attitudes toward blacks of a die-hard Southerner in the United States—or the more subtle but equally bigoted attitude of many Northerners.

The claim has been made that Kipling did not have racist beliefs— that by "white man" he only meant a civilized, educated man. As previously shown, this is untrue. If an Indian came to England and obtained an Oxford education, it made no difference to Kipling; he felt he was still, as mentioned before, an Indian underneath, a "hybrid, University-trained mule."[28] He could come back to India and occupy a responsible position, as did a character in another of Kipling's stories, but he would merely be displaying his unusual English vocabulary with no true understanding of what he was saying; he could talk about government, but he could never govern. He was not white.

But Kipling must be judged in the light of contemporary, not present-day, beliefs. Many Englishmen in 1898 would have agreed with his views, including, it would seem, his parents. But the Liberals, anti-imperialist and anti-racist, were a rising power in British politics and by 1906 were to win overwhelming popular support. A majority of the newspapers sided with Kipling, although one reviewer reminded his readers that Kipling had said of Cecil Rhodes that "He needs no morals; he is building an empire."[29] And one of our greatest presidents, Theodore Roosevelt, to whom Kipling sent an advance copy of "The White Man's Burden" soon after he was elected vice-president, wrote to a friend that it made "good sense from the expansionist viewpoint."[30]

Kipling, although he had a lot of support for his right-wing views, was fighting a losing battle. Liberal beliefs were steadily gaining acceptance, and he fought them tooth and nail for the rest of his life.

Trix Fleming, Kipling's sister, who had married a soldier years before, just after Kipling had left India with the Hills, had stayed on in India after her parents had moved to England. She had always been an extremely sensitive person, rather withdrawn, who read a great deal and had an almost alarming ability to remember, by heart, practically all she read. She had always seemed a little odd, a little fey, to friends of the family. John Fleming, her husband, was a solid, unimaginative, down-to-earth military man, the soul of stability, quite unlike anyone in the brilliant intellectual family into which he married.

Over the years, Trix had steadily become more and more withdrawn and silent. In the autumn of 1898 her husband, now truly alarmed, brought her to England and to her family, as she was suffering from what we would now diagnose as schizophrenia. This disease is characterized by a severe impairment of the basic ego functions—those of thinking, relationships with others, the handling of feelings, the assessment of reality, the concept of self. The damage may be extreme, with complete withdrawal from the world and the most bizarre thinking, or mild, with unimpaired functioning in society and only a faint feeling, sometimes, on the part of others, that "so-and-so is a little queer, somehow." Single attacks of this disease may disappear and leave one patient unharmed for fifty years, or may, with terrible persistence, consign another patient to the back ward of a state hospital for a similar period of time. A century of study has left us with little real understanding of schizophrenia.

Unfortunately, Trix's case, triggered by her terrible childhood years, was severe. Silent for long periods of time, she moved in a world of her own, and had to be placed under her mother's care in Tisbury. Three years later, in 1902, she improved a good deal, and even returned to India with her husband, but upon his retirement a few years later she again had to return to England and to her mother, who proved to be thoughtful and patient in caring for her. The two of them collaborated on a small book of sensitive poems. Trix could not be with her husband for any length of time; the result was always silent withdrawal or destructive outbursts. So for many years she was cared for by others and only occasionally visited by her husband who, with characteristic patience, never uttered a word of objection. To repeat, Trix had indeed chosen a good person to marry.

In January of 1899 the Kiplings suddenly decided not to go to South Africa for that winter but instead to travel to America. Kipling wanted to discuss copyright questions with various publishers, and Carrie was anxious to see her mother up in Brattleboro. And then there was Naulakha to visit and perhaps dispose of once and for all. But what about taking the three little children, Josephine, Elsie, and John, aged six, three, and eighteen months, respectively, across the North Atlantic in the coldest time of year? Kipling did not want to do it, and his mother also thought it would be unwise, but Carrie was determined to go, so off they went.

They had a miserable crossing, with icy winds from the east of near-gale strength, and when the *Majestic* docked at New York on February 2, both Elsie and Josephine had colds.[31] As usual, Kipling and his wife brusquely dismissed the reporters; the *Daily Tribune* noted that "Mr. Kipling looked rugged and healthy and happy, but he could not be induced to say a word about his plans." The *New York Times* of February 3 merely listed, among other arrivals the day before, "Mr. and Mrs. Rudyard Kipling and Miss Kipling." The "Miss Kipling" was little Josephine; perhaps her father included her as an affectionate joke.

They went to the Hotel Grenoble, where first the children and then Carrie had severe colds. Carrie's sister Josephine had married a physician, Dr. Theodore Dunham, who came and cared for them. After a few days they all improved. It had been bitterly cold but now the weather became beautiful. To Kipling's delight the sun shone as brightly on the new-fallen snow as it had years before on his first day in Vermont. He and Carrie busily went around town, trying to straighten out copyright disputes with publishers and making calls on friends. One lovely sunny day the whole family went for a walk in lower Central Park. They were taken for a ride in an electric car and Kipling was predictably fascinated by this new form of transportation. He repeatedly said how delighted he was to be back in America. Meeting a friend, Hamlin Garland, on the street in Manhattan, Kipling spoke enthusiastically about the United States. "All the dislike of American which he had hereto expressed went for nothing," Garland later recalled.

On February 20 Kipling came back to the Grenoble after dinner at the Century Club. Near the door of the hotel a man asked for his autograph. Kipling chuckled and called him a "fiend" but gave him the autograph and chatted for a minute before going in. He felt tired and feverish and ached all over. The next day Dr. Dunham diagnosed pneumonia and called in a specialist, Dr. E. G. Janeway. Janeway examined little Josephine, who had been running a high fever, and said she also had pneumonia. The full burden of caring for the family, dangerously ill in a downtown New York hotel, fell on Carrie, and all accounts praise her indomitable courage and untiring strength throughout this ordeal. Fortunately there were family members and friends anxious to help, most notably the faithful Frank N. Doubleday, who took over all correspondence and tried to assist Carrie in dealing with the reporters who filled the hotel lobby, clamoring for news.

Here he had difficulty, for a rigid, fussy, I've-got-to-run-everything side of her became apparent. She insisted that every scrap of information given to the hotel press had to be approved by her personally. She told the doctors she would release one bulletin a day regarding Kipling's condition (the reporters did not know Josephine was ill) and beyond that, not a word was to be given out. She had Josephine taken to the privacy of the home of a friend, Miss Julia B. de Forest, at 121 East 35th Street,* out of reach of the press. The bulletins Carrie wrote and issued were very brief, vague, and decidedly slanted toward optimism. The frustrated reporters, not allowed to talk to one of the doctors, could only turn to guesswork, studying the faces of everyone entering or leaving the Kiplings' rooms, quizzing bellboys and nurses, and sending in their conjectures to the newspapers. They had to write something. The best-known writer in the world was apparently dying not fifty feet away.

During those last days of February Kipling's condition went steadily downhill. His fever rose and his breathing became more and more labored. In desperation the doctors used oxygen to try to help his respiration.** By Sunday, when every breath sounded like his last, there was agreement on one thing. He was going to die.

---

*Not, as has been stated by Carrington, Wilson, and Seymour-Smith, to Long Island.
**In those days there was no way to remove the carbon dioxide from an oxygen tent. Giving oxygen was therefore a method of last resort.

As if the crowd sensed this—for Carrie's bulletins were still optimistic—there was a spontaneous demonstration of concern and affection that exceeded that shown for any writer before or since. Reflecting his enormous popular appeal, letters and telegrams came pouring in. Prayers were offered in many churches that Sunday, and people at the hotel were seen kneeling and praying for his recovery. Even the reporters, hardened to this sort of thing, were impressed; the *Tribune* man wrote, "If sympathy could cure a man, Mr. Kipling would have been well by now."

Miraculously, Kipling survived the night and the next day seemed a little stronger. The day after that he could breathe more easily. His temperature fell and, barring unforeseen complications, his recovery was now sure. His old friend from Brattleboro, Dr. Conland, arrived and told reporters there was now "good hope of pulling him through."

Even at this point Carrie kept an iron hand on the press. The doctors were forbidden to use the word "pneumonia" in connection with the case. It was obvious that is what he had; it was printed in the newspapers all over the world; but the doctors still could not use the word in the bulletins, and when asked if Kipling had pneumonia, had to reply, "He has an inflammation of the lungs."

All this time Josephine, who had had her sixth birthday a few days before they left London, was down at Miss de Forest's home on 35th Street, ill with double pneumonia like her father. The press was informed of this on March 2, and reassured that her illness was of "not as severe a form" as Kipling's had been. The *New York Times* reporter recorded his polite exasperation: "It is thoroughly illustrative of the reticence that has been shown in connection with the entire case, that the public received no inkling of the fact until yesterday . . ." that she was sick. There were rumors that her condition was becoming critical, but the doctors said that she was no worse and were generally reassuring. Actually, her life was ebbing away. A week after her father's crisis, early in the morning, little Josephine died.

It was a blow from which Kipling never fully recovered. He could never forget that his first-born child, his favorite, the girl who used to run barefoot through the woods at Brattleboro, was gone forever. Three years later, in 1902, he made his only reference to her death in a poem that accompanies "How the Alphabet Was Made," one of the *Just So*

Stories. Two of these tales involve Taffy, a little girl in a primitive tribe, and her father Tegumai. "Taffy" was one of the Kipling's pet names for Josephine. Some of the last few verses are as follows:

Of all the Tribe of Tegumai
Who cut that figure, none remain,—
On Merrow Down the cuckoos cry—
The silence and the sun remain.

But as the faithful years return
And hearts unwounded sing again,
Comes Taffy dancing through the fern
To lead the Surrey spring again.

In moccasins and deerskin cloak,
Unfearing, free and fair she flits,
And lights her little damp-wood smoke
To show her Daddy where she flits.

For far—oh, very far behind,
So far she cannot call to him,
Comes Tegumai alone to find
The daughter that was all to him.[32]

XII

THE BOER WAR

Kipling recovered slowly from his pneumonia, staying mostly in New Jersey. Part of his time there was spent with their old friends the Catlins in Morristown, said at the time to be the wealthiest community in America. Kipling, as usual, was not impressed. At the end of the street where they were visiting there lived a Mr. Tubbs, a pig farmer, and Kipling preferred rocking on Mr. Tubbs' porch and asking him questions about his pigs.[1]

Not until the end of the summer did they return to England. There Andrew Carnegie, a fervent admirer, offered him the use of one of his houses up in Scotland for his convalescence. They accepted the invitation and Carrie, who always had an eye on the checkbook, got the multimillionaire to make a contribution to the Boys' Social Club that Kipling had started in the village of Rottingdean.

During their tragic stay in New York, Carrie can be seen at her best and at her worst. Her steadfast courage and tireless devotion have to be balanced by her rigidity and her need to dominate those about her. The descriptions of her that have come down to us are quite universally those of a tense, demanding, abrasive person who like to boss others around, her husband most of all. She was chronically depressed, with meager inner resources; she could find few joys in life, and tended to look on the gloomy side of things. In her family her sister Josephine was warm and attractive; her mother had always treated her sons as her favorites and beside her sister, and these two striking brothers, the brilliant Wolcott and the life-of-the-party Beatty, tiny little Carrie, with her sharp, determined features, must have felt unloved, hurt, and angry. Though she was pleasant in social situations, she was a worrier and a complainer, often a burden to those about her. It's my impression that I've never seen a photograph of her smiling. She was at her best when it came to decisions and emergencies; she would have been the last one to cave in and lose control. If she felt unattractive and unloved, she tried to make up for this by her efficient control of things.

We may recall that Henry James, and subsequently many others, wondered why the Kiplings even got married, and James was openly doubtful about their future together. They seemed to have so little in common. Where she was meticulous and efficient, Kipling was casual and even careless; where she was a worrier, Kipling, though under the sway of a deep streak of anger and subject to periodic black depressions, was usually outgoing and loved a good laugh; where she lived to guard her husband, he lived to go his own way and to write (and accepted her inability to appreciate what came from his pen); where she was concerned with social status and was a snob, he cared about feelings and his writing, and was not snobbish; where she liked to dominate everyone, he deferred to her, and almost never complained.

If this sounds like a harsh judgment of her, she was not an evil, malicious person. And it should be noted that, the more I read about her, the better I liked her. I found it sad to see her depression go on, decade after decade.

Why did Kipling marry her? Besides the obvious things—they loved each other, Kipling gained a dedicated woman who would be the mother of the children they both wanted so much, he didn't mind her vaulting to a lofty social position—there were two other important reasons.

First of all, he married her because she was Wolcott Balestier's sister. In the union he would be continuing his relationship, in a sort of once-removed way, with Wolcott, whom he had loved. Carrie was a substitute; marrying her was a little like marrying her brother. As described, nothing could change while there was a triangle, where he loved both the sister and the brother; when Wolcott conveniently died, Kipling tore across Asia and Europe, and, in almost desperate haste, married Carrie in a nearly deserted church, a little as if in fear that when the minister came to the portion of the service that says, "If any of you can show just cause why they may not lawfully be married . . . ," Wolcott's ghost would pipe up from the back row. In those times, his love of Wolcott was a shockingly unacceptable, a secret that must be kept from everyone; by marrying Carrie, it suddenly, in a sense, became totally acceptable, although in a hidden, diluted form.

Second, Kipling married her *because* she was difficult and unloving. He did it out of guilt over his love of Wolcott. If much of his obsessive need for privacy, noted when he was a schoolboy, came from the humiliations he suffered in the House of Desolation, later in life this need found expression in keeping anyone from knowing about his feelings for Wolcott. This accounts for the Kiplings' withdrawal from others, for the most routine letters being marked "private", for the hatred of journalists, for the burning of every scrap of paper, for the general atmosphere of secrecy so evident in their household.

Kipling's guilt over his homosexual feelings made him seek punishment; the woman he married would have to be, besides a joy, a burden, a reminder of urges he thought of as sinful. She would be like the (white) women in many of his stories, somewhat distant, tough and controlling. He could dream of a tender, loving woman like Mrs. Hill (as he did in "The Brushwood Boy"), but when it came to marriage he avoided someone like the warm Josephine Balestier, also a sister of Wolcott's, who would have filled the bill in that respect. Meekly submitting to Carrie's wish to run everything filled a need he had for pain, for punishment, for a feeling that "things shouldn't go too easily." After his near-fatal illness in New York, he said with absolute sincerity that he owed his life to Carrie.

In Scotland they were visited by Edith Catlin, their old friend from the American years. Miss Catlin's memoirs are most unusual in that she praises Carrie without qualification. Unlike other accounts one reads of the Kiplings, there is not a word of criticism. She described Carrie as "sympathetic"[2] and "a wonderful mother" but that "Above all . . . she managed the vast amount of business in connection with the publishing of his writings."

She enjoyed playing practical jokes on "the C.R.K.s," as she called the Kiplings. (This, by itself, tells us a lot about her hosts; there were, and are, plenty of houses where any sort of practical joke is not welcome.) She prepared a malodorous mixture, mostly vinegar but with tea added to make it look like whiskey. Putting it in an empty Scotch bottle she excitedly said it had been sent as a present from their host. "How thoughtful!" "Good old Andrew!" and similar appreciative statements ceased with the first sniff.

In the evenings, at this time and on subsequent visits, she and Kipling played parlor games. Carrie never joined in, but "was the most impartial judge of our youthful occupations." (Note that Carrie, often tense, did not participate in the fun, but instead took the role of an arbitrator.) One game consisted of completing a word for which only one or two letters were supplied. She challenged Kipling when he filled in spaces beginning with an *a* and ending with an *o* with the word *aino*. "Why," he bluffingly insisted, "The Ainos are a species of small carnivorous birds living in northern Japan who lay hairy eggs." (Kipling had in mind the Ainu, the hairy aborigines from the northernmost Japanese islands, and seemingly decided with his usual kindness to pass it over as a joke rather than reveal her unfamiliarity with the word.) On a different visit, playing this game, "Tommy" discovered that a certain author was "despised by the C. R. K.s." Tactfully, in her memoirs she only states that his name began with a G; but one can be quite sure it was John Galsworthy. His interest in personality, in people's relationships with one another, in psychology, instantly set him apart from the action-oriented Kipling.* When "Tommy's" visit came to an end, Kipling dashed off an (uncollected) poem for the occasion.

That summer and fall a series of events led up to the opening of the Boer War. England had controlled the strategic Cape Colony in South Africa since 1806, when it was taken from the Dutch. In 1834 slaves were ordered to be freed in every part of the Empire. This resulted in the Great Trek by the Boers, as the South African Dutch called themselves. It was, and is, as celebrated in their folklore as the wagon trains of the

---

*Other possible candidates I can think of, like Edmund Gosse or H. A. Gwynne, were admired by Kipling.

forty-niners are in ours. Often split on political ideas, they were united on one: an absolute determination to deny political rights to any black. Seeing the emancipation of slaves as a step in this direction, five thousand Boers in 1835 moved across the Vaal river to the northeast.

Over the next sixty years British policy toward the Boers was weak and vacillating. Decisions to "go forward" (i.e., occupy the Transvaal) alternated with inactivity and a "wait and see" attitude. In 1886 gold was discovered in the Transvaal and English prospectors swarmed in, soon equaling the Boers in number. The scheming Rhodes and another multimillionaire, Alfred Beit, attempted to annex the Transvaal on their own, in the disastrous Jameson Raid. Fortunately for them, the Kaiser's congratulatory telegram to Paul Kruger, the Boer President, turned it into an international incident. (As described, this had contributed to the Kiplings' leaving Vermont.) There was a storm of indignation against the Germans, and Jameson, instead of suffering deserved disgrace, was proclaimed a hero and made the subject of a poem by Alfred Austin, who, while perhaps the worst occupant ever of that position, was undeniably the Poet Laureate. The political implications of the Raid were forgotten amid this brouhaha.

The Boers did not forget the Jameson Raid. Fearful of being outnumbered and losing control of their country, they refused the British immigrants any political rights. Indignant over this, and with the glowing example of the Spanish-American War before them, the English saw themselves as a modern nation, an all-powerful wave of the future liberating the outdated and obsolete ways of the past. In its complete misunderstanding of the basic issues, its disastrous miscalculation of the difficulties, and its deliberate withholding of facts from the press and the people, the ensuing war was the last century's Vietnam.

Almost no one suspected that the wealthy industrialists and exploiters, like Cecil Rhodes and Alfred Beit, were behind all this agressive plotting for war against a weaker nation. Initially, the idea of war had popular British support: the white man was about to take on a new burden. No one knew that the respected Alfred Milner, the Queen's High Commissioner in Cape Town, sent to bring a settlement between Boer and Briton, was a sly old fox. While talking peace, he was bent on war. With the secret backing of "the gold bugs"—Rhodes and Beit[3]—he indignantly rejected Kruger's reasonable offer of a gradual enfranchisement of the British and urged that military forces be sent to Africa to pressure the Boers. This, he knew, would be the one thing that would start a war.

Kipling's feelings about these events are predictable. Like so many Victorians, he had tended to be opinionated in his thinking. His enemies usually got unforgiving hatred; his friends, unswerving loyalty. He was not one to question what he read in the newspapers. (These, with one exception, sounded a shrill note of jingoism and demanded military action.) He believed implicitly in Milner, Jameson, and Rhodes. If they said the Boers were forcing war on the British, then that's the way it was.

His feelings for England, however, were changing. The best way to understand this change is to see it as yet another restless urge for a place he could call home. Back in India, really home and yet never home, he had indignantly felt that the bureaucratic powers in London neither understood nor appreciated the Army and Civil Service overseas. He took these feelings with him when he went to London in 1889. His intense antagonism toward the Home English, reflected in his writing at the time, was equaled only by his intense identification with the Empire English. Where could he feel at home? His trip across America and the influence of American friends—the Hills and the Balestiers—drew him temporarily toward the United States. He married an American and lived for four years in Vermont, which he compared favorably to India. As always, he liked American ambition, energy, and patriotism. He also respected American history. But he was horrified by what he saw as American lawlessness, violence, and political confusion and corruption. Significantly, he felt these were racial in origin; they were brought about by the influx of immigrants.

His Vermont years were ones of reconsideration; was England really that bad? Was America really that good? He kept in touch with friends in England and, visiting his parents there, for the first time became aware of the beauties of the English countryside. His former pride at being an Empire Englishman and Anglo-Indian no longer conflicted with his wish to be a Home Englishman as well. No, America wasn't that good. He began to write stories extolling the British love of tradition and their well-ordered way of life, contrasting these with what he saw as chaos in America. England, Kipling decided, was the preferred society because it was unified, racially homogeneous, efficient, and run by an elite class. Rigid social strata must be preserved. A person in one story learns that in England he has a "decreed position in the fabric of the realm"[4] from which he must not depart—again the opposite of the democratic ideal in America.

Kipling's lifelong need to belong, coming from his childhood experiences, now found some measure of fulfillment in England. Observing the Fleet in Channel maneuvers he wrote:

> And the whole thing was my very own . . . mine to me by right of birth. . . .
> The wind and the smell of it off the coasts, was mine, and it was telling me things that it would never dream of confiding to a foreigner. The short, hollow Channel sea was mine—bought for me drop by drop, every salt drop of it, in the last eight hundred years—as short a time as it takes to make a perfect lawn in a cathedral close. The speech on the deck below was mine, for the men were free white men, same as me, only considerably better. Their notions of things were my notions of things and the bulk of these notions we could convey one to the other without opening our heads.
> We had a common tradition, one thousand years old, of the things one takes for granted. A warrant officer said something, and the groups melted quietly about some job or other. That same caste of man—that same type of voice—was speaking in the commissariat in Burma; in barracks at Rangoon; under double awnings in the Persian Gulf; on the Rock at Gibralter—wherever else you please—and the same instant obedience, I knew, would follow on that voice. And a foreigner would never have understood—will never understand! But I understood. . . .[5]

And now this society, where he was just beginning to feel at home, was threatened; as he saw it, a small and backward nation was opposing the progress of the British Empire. These upstarts would have to be put in their places.

The negotiations with Paul Kruger broke down, and Boer and Briton alike prepared for war. Kipling contemplated the outbreak of hostilities not just with confidence, but with eagerness. Sure of England's military power and glad to see it put to the test, he had an especially high degree of confidence in the English officers, products of the public (actually private in American terms) school system. He saw them as sort of grownup characters out of *Stalky & Co.* who could outwit any border tribesmen and the officers of any European army. In one story, "Slaves of the Lamp, Part II," the boys from Beetle's school days

229

have graduated and gone out into the Empire. They meet on furlough in England and tell tales of their exploits. Stalky, the best of the lot, is not there but the others tell of his imaginative leadership of some soldiers in India. One of the men remarks, "There is nobody like Stalky," but Beetle (Kipling) immediately disagrees:

> "That's just where you make the mistake," I said. "India's full of Stalkies—Cheltenham and Haileybury and Marlborough chaps—that we don't know anything about, and the surprises will begin when there is really a big row on."
> "Who will be surprised?" said Dick Four.
> "The other side. The gentlemen who go to the front in first class carriages. Just imagine Stalky let loose on the south side of Europe with a sufficiency of Sikhs and a reasonable prospect of loot. Consider it quietly."[6]

Kipling was to learn, all too soon, that it was the English themselves who went to the front in first class carriages, and that it was the Boers who fought with Stalky-like ingenuity.

Again we can note that the question of the right of England to thus handle the affairs of others was something that Kipling did not consider. If the question had arisen, he may have felt that England's dominion over weaker peoples was sanctioned by God. In 1893, in his poem "A Song of the English," he had represented the English as the Chosen People, comparing their expansion over the earth with the passage of the Israelites through the Red Sea. In "Recessional," under God's hand, the English hold "dominion over palm and pine." It was the duty of the English, Kipling felt, to conquer and control the less-civilized nations of the world, by force if necessary, and thus bring to them the joys of civilization. Before reacting too harshly to Kipling's point of view, we should again remember that he was supported in those feelings by the vast majority of Englishmen of his time.

Just before the war broke out, Kipling published a poem called "The Old Issue," which depicts the coming struggle as a battle in England's age-old war against tyranny. President Kruger is seen derisively as "the old King,"[7] one of a long line of tyrants from whom England has gradually wrested her freedom over the centuries. Kipling urges that the English break "the old King's" reign, and argues that war would be good for England; a nation too long at peace grows soft.

THE BOER WAR

Give no ear to bondsmen bidding us endure,
Whining, "He is weak and far"; crying "Time shall cure."
(Time himself is witness, til the battle joins,
Deeper strikes the rottenness in the people's loins.)
Give no heed to bondsmen, masking war with peace.
Suffer not the old King here or overseas.

Now, in October 1899, the Boers finally attacked. It was a relief to Milner; it would justify the war in the eyes of the public back home. Filled with confidence, anxious to "teach the Boers a lesson," the British landed troops in South Africa and moved against the enemy. There was a general wave of optimism; the word went around that the war would be "over by Christmas." The Spanish-American conflict had only taken four months, hadn't it?

They soon found it was not to be another "splendid little war." The British were woefully unprepared for battle and went about it with a rigid, by-the-book attitude. What worked on the Indian frontier, they felt, would work in Africa. The Boers were equipped with smokeless powder and small-caliber, high-powered magazine rifles. From concealed trenches they inflicted slaughter on the advancing British. In the first few months of the war the English suffered humiliating defeats at Ladysmith, Mafeking, and Kimberley. Shock waves reverberated back to England—"But we're the strongest nation in the world and they're one of the weakest—how can this be happening?" The general public did not know the British generals were divided into two cliques, called "Indians" and "Africans" depending on where their service experience had been. Each had their supporters among the government leaders back in London. Bitter infighting between these two groups, both in the field and at home, led to endless problems in the war effort. Kipling, of course, was an ardent "Indian" and supporter of Lord Roberts, whom he had known in India, and who was now sent out with an ever-increasing number of troops in an attempt to end this frustrating war.

Kipling, filled with enthusiasm about the war and sure of a quick victory, threw himself into its support with all his usual energy. He organized a volunteer company of soldiers from Rottingdean. He also wrote a poem, "The Absent-Minded Beggar," which, set to music by Sir Arthur Sullivan, was sung from one end of England to the other.

Cook's son—Duke's son—son of a belted Earl—
Son of a Lambeth publican—it's all the same today![8]

The audience was asked to "pay—pay—pay!" and the income, a large sum, was used to buy tobacco and other such things for the soldiers at the front.

In January of 1900 the Kiplings, complete with nursemaid and governess for the two children, set out to spend the winter in South Africa. They arrived to find that the British were still suffering defeats. Kipling visited military hospitals, his pockets stuffed with plug tobacco for the wounded. He met an officer, unhurt but with his uniform ripped by bullets, whom he had known in India where he had the nickname of "The Sardine." Lord Roberts asked Kipling to be part of the staff of a newly started newspaper called the *Friend*. It was to contain army notices, news of British successes, and fiction and entertainment for the troops. He happily slipped into his old role as a journalist, and spent two weeks with the troops, working for the paper. Shown the office, he said delightedly, "It's quite like old times in India!"[9] Two of the other editors, H. A. Gwynne and Perceval Landon, became lifelong friends. Gwynne later became editor of the ultra-right-wing *Morning Post*, Kipling's favorite newspaper in years to come. In later decades they exchanged many letters mourning the dissolution of the British Empire. This group meant so much to Kipling that, back in England, he formed a dining-club of those he had worked with, called "The Friendlies," for which he devised a badge and an elaborate admission ritual, fantastically intricate and, even in his tiny handwriting, over one hundred pages long. It is another example of the importance of "belonging."

Toward the end of his stay with the troops, he was taken to the front and there saw military action for the first time in his life. He described it vividly:

> The enormous pale landscape swallowed up seven thousand troops without a sign, along a front of seven miles. . . . We went on into a vacant world full of sunshine and distances, where now and again a single bullet sang to himself. What I most objected to was the sensation of being under aimed fire—being, as it were, required as a head. . . . Then more cracklings and a most cautious move forward to the lip of a large hollow where sheep were grazing. Some of them began to drop and kick. . . . [E]very twenty minutes or so, one judgmatic shell pitched on our slope. We waited, seeing

nothing in the emptiness, and hearing only a faint murmur as of wind along gas-jets, running in and out of the unconcerned hills.

Then pom-poms opened. These were nasty little one-pounders, ten in a belt (which usually jammed about the sixth round). On soft ground they merely thudded. On rock-face the shell breaks up and yowls like a cat. My friend for the first time seemed interested. "If these are *their* pom-poms, it's Pretoria for us," was his diagnosis. I looked behind me—the whole length of South Africa down to Cape Town—and it seemed very far. I felt that I could have covered it in five minutes under fair conditions, but—*not* with those aimed shots up my back. The pom-poms opened again at a bare rock-reef that gave the shells full value. For about two minutes a file of racing ponies, their tails and their riders' heads well down, showed and vanished northward. "Our pom-poms," said the correspondent. . . . Then to the left, almost under us, a small piece of hanging woodland filled and fumed with our shrapnel much as a man's moustache fills with cigarette-smoke. It was most impressive and lasted for quite twenty minutes. Then silence; then a movement of men and horses from our side up the slope, and the hangar our guns had been hammering spat steady fire at them. More Boer ponies on more skylines; a last flurry of pom-poms on the right and a little frieze of far-off meek-tailed ponies, already out of rifle range.

"*Maffeesh*," said the correspondent, and fell to writing on his knee. "We've shifted 'em."

Leaving our infantry to follow men on ponyback toward the Equator, we returned to the farmhouse.[10]

He went back to Cape Town to find Carrie tense and upset by his absence. They all returned to England in April, with Kipling determined to throw himself into political causes, to champion his heroes, Milner and Roberts, Rhodes and Jameson. He wrote about two main themes: first—with real fury—the neutrals, and second, the ignorance and rigidity of the British officers.

As for the neutrals, he felt that they supported either side, only caring about how it benefited them. Most of all he hated the Cape Afrikaners—the local Dutch-speaking population who were British subjects but felt an understandable sympathy for the Boers. Kipling did not understand it. In "A Burgher of the Free State" and "The Sin of Witchcraft" he savagely attacked these people as traitors. This intense hostility toward neutrals was to reappear during the First World War. It was, I think, another example of a tendency toward oversimplification that sometimes marred his work. If there was a war, you fought on one side or the other. The more complex position of a neutral only made him impatient.

The war, he discovered—like Vietnam—no longer had popular support back home. Whenever he completed a story, he had long enjoyed going across the village green and reading it to his Aunt Georgie, "the beloved aunt" in whose house he had found refuge during those terrible childhood years in Southsea. Now he found, at least for his political pieces, he could no longer do this. When he read her "A Burgher of the Free State," she objected to his point of view and argued with him about it. The war that was dividing the nation divided his family as well.

He expressed his feelings about the deficiencies of the military in a series of stories that appeared in 1900. They were a far cry from his worship of the military during his years in India. In one of those, "Folly Bridge," a group of officers is on a vital mission when they are held up at a railway trestle by an obstinate, arrogant, small-minded railway staff officer who demands that certain passes be countersigned a certain way before the officers be allowed to proceed. This insistence on official procedures, in the face of common sense, was a phenomenon that Kipling frequently criticized during the course of the war.

Another similar story, called "The Outsider," deals with a young officer, Lieutenant Setton, who had gone through public school and Sandhurst—as Stalky had—but whose only qualifications for leadership are his money and social position. Setton—one can wonder if Kipling had in mind Sefton, one of the bullies set straight in *Stalky & Co.*—has minimal knowledge about his duties as an officer.

> For the rest, he devoted himself with no thought of wrong to getting as much as possible out of the richest and easiest life the world has yet made; and to despising the "outsider"—the man beyond his circle. His training to this end was as complete as that of his brethren. He did it blindly, politely, unconsciously, with perfect sincerity. As a child he had learned early to despise his nurse, for she was a servant and a woman; his sisters he had looked down upon, and his governess, for much the same reasons. His home atmosphere had taught him to despise the terrible thing called "Dissent." At his private school, his seniors showed him how to despise the Junior Master, who was poor, and here his home training showed again. At his public school, he despised the new boy—the boy who boated when Setton played cricket, or who wore a coloured tie when the order of the day was for black. They were all avatars of the outsider. If you got mixed up with an outsider,

you ended by being "compromised." He had no clear idea of what that-meant, but suspected the worst. His religion he took from his parents, and it had some very sound dogmas about outsiders behaving indecently.[11]

Kipling contrasts Setton with an "outsider," Jerry Thrupp, a hard-working engineer who had volunteered as a private. He is given command of a gang of men repairing a railway bridge, and is making good progress until Lieutenant Setton barges in and stops the work at a vital moment, which causes a long delay in the repair of the bridge. The point Kipling now realizes, of course, is that the man who can do a job should be allowed to do it, whether he is a private or an officer, an outsider or an insider. Kipling began to see that superior social station and wealth do not necessarily go along with ability, as they sometimes had in India. (All this was quite a contrast with his recently declared belief—which came from his anti-American feelings—that in England, no one should venture from his "decreed position" in society.)

He became more and more involved in politics. Twice he dined with Joseph Chamberlain at the latter's club, and he wrote several articles about the conduct of the war.

In a letter to Dr. Conland, Kipling spoke of the war in his usual breezy, know-it-all way.

Dear Old Man—

As you know we went down to South Africa (Cape Town) for the winter and there happened to be a bit of a war on, and I had the time of my life. Carrie and the children stayed at Cape Town and I sort of drifted up country looking at hospitals and wounded men and guns and generals and wondering as I had never wondered before at the huge size of the country, but it was all deeply interesting—specially when I met the people who had been through the Siege of Kimberley. You could always tell 'em by the way they looked around for a place to hide in whenever they heard the *whiz-boom* of a Cape Town trolley car. It reminded 'em of the noise of an approaching shell. I was mean enough to laugh at 'em first—but I don't do so any more since I got under shell-fire myself and heard the cussed things booming over the small of my back.

War is a rummy job—it's a cross between poker and Sunday-school. Sometimes poker comes out on top and sometimes Sunday-school—but most often poker. The Boers hit us just as hard and just as often as they knew how; and we advanced against 'em as if they were street-rioters that we didn't want to hurt. . . .[12]

In that summer of 1900 came the completion of *Kim*, his greatest book, on which he had been working, off and on, ever since his four years in Vermont. Indeed, we recall that in part it goes back to *The Book of Mother Maturin*, which he had begun at Lahore in 1885 but never completed. After many long conferences with his father who, one suspects, gave the story its coherence—the beginning, middle, and end that Kipling always found so difficult—it was finally declared complete and published the next year.

In December of 1900 they returned to South Africa, Kipling celebrating his birthday while at sea. He was now thirty-five, and unknowingly had passed into the second half of his life. Born in 1865, he was to die in 1936, at the age of seventy; the halfway point of his life fell neatly at 1900. (Actually, in the first few days of 1901.)

Gilbert, in a perceptive essay, remarked:

> People who are born, as Kipling was, in a year numbered sixty-five are so placed chronologically as to have their biblically allotted three-score and ten years life exactly bisected by the turn of the century, and to be often a little uncertain, therefore, about which of two centuries they ought to identify with. . . . Literary people are likely to have their own experience coloured by this fact, as, most famously, was Dante's, and in particular to think of the two halves of their lives as being—and perhaps even to act so as to cause them to be—radically discontinuous. Certainly Kipling's life was full enough of striking discontinuities to encourage any apocalyptic fancies he may have derived from his birth date, and to account for those two sides of his head for which he was so grateful. His first six years he spent with loving parents in the heaven of India, the second six with hostile strangers in the hell of Southsea, a hell from which he was suddenly and magically rescued by the return of his mother. In 1899 in New York he played out before the whole world a dramatic scene of his own near-death and resurrection, a resurrection immediately clouded by the death of his favorite child. . . .[13]

And, I would add, in 1900 he finished *Kim*, always acclaimed his greatest achievement. The grouping of these events at the turn of the century seems particularly notable.

In anthologies of writers of the nineteenth or of the twentieth centuries, he invariably appears in the first and is excluded from the second—always relegated to the 1800s. Mostly he is put there because of his racism, his imperialism, and his reactionary, far-right-wing views. When Queen Victoria died in 1901, it was said that her century died with her. The British Empire flourished in the last century and faded in this one; naturally the man who sang its praises is associated with the 1800s, and this accounts for the response I frequently have gotten when I've mentioned that he died in 1936: "Really? I thought Kipling died around 1920."

As mentioned before, Rhodes had previously offered to build a house on his estate to be used by writers, the first occupants being the Kipling family. He sent a carriage to meet them at the ship, with the news that the house was now completed and furnished. It was a long, one-story Dutch colonial building, named "Woolsack," which was a delight for all of them. Kipling could relax and work on his next books, the *Just So Stories* and *Puck of Pook's Hill*. For the children, it was an enchanted land of burning sunshine and snowy beaches, far from the depressing English winters. But Carrie, most of all, adored it, every year looking forward to "dear Woolsack," which she enjoyed every winter from 1900 through 1908. There, one suspects, she could run things as she wanted to, without the Kipling relatives underfoot as they were at Rottingdean.

Rhodes knew his heart trouble meant his days were limited. He began to plan the Rhodes Scholarships, by which young men from every corner of the far-flung Empire, and from the United States, could have a period of study in England. He usually avoided all women like the plague, but he knew efficiency when he saw it, and he sought and accepted Carrie's advice on various matters. It was she who got him to increase the initial amount of the scholarships, which would not have been sufficient for a stranger arriving in England.

Kipling wrote Dr. Conland in February:

I never saw such a comic war in all my born days. Cape Town is full of rebels and is the only place where martial law is not proclaimed. A man gets as much as 12 months imprisonment sometimes for assisting the enemy, and six months for helping to blow up a railway culvert. And then we wonder why the war doesn't end. They make no secret of their intentions. They want to sweep the English into the sea, to lick their own nigger, and to govern South Africa with a gun instead of a ballot box. It is only the little Englanders in London who say that the Transvaal is merely fighting for its independence; but out here both sides realize it is a question of which race is to run the country.[14]

Soon after this, they returned to England, where the Catlins visited them. At their urging, Kiplings joined them on a trip to Paris, which they had not visited in years.

As always, as he had in Vermont, Kipling tried to find India in South Africa. His beloved India, the land of his idyllic childhood, the place of his dreams, where all things would be fulfilled—wherever Kipling lived he tried to imagine Indian scenes there, tried to make it into India—and always failed. It was altogether inevitable that he would write a story, "A Sahib's War," about a Sikh soldier who followed his companion, an English officer, to South Africa. The Sikh, Umr Singh, tells his story to a white man who speaks Hindustani—presumably Kipling. He learns that Kipling knows the Punjab, was "Born and bred in Hind, was he? . . . . The Sahib's nurse was a Surtee woman from the Bombay side? . . . . (T)he Sahib has sharp eyes. . . . The Sahib should have been in the Police of the Punjab."[15] Back with Strickland again!

Umr Singh tells of the loving, paternal relationship he had with the English officer, Corbyn—"Kurban Sahib"—whom he had cared for since childhood and who went off to England for his education and then returned to India. "He was a Sikh at heart. . . . When we were alone he called me Father and I called him Son." Now a captain in the cavalry, Corbyn arranges their transfer from India to South Africa when the war breaks out. There they join a regiment of Australians, the only people, says Umr Singh, who are fighting the war sensibly. He tells of local farmers who had affidavits signed by "foolish English Generals" that they were neutrals and should not be disturbed. As soon as they had a chance they put away the affidavits and shot at the English soldiers. In one such incident, a farmer and his family suddenly and treacherously attack and Captain Corbyn is killed. Umr Singh says he will mourn for the rest of his life for now he is "childless."

South Africa would not become India. Besides this, his life there was permanently soured by British ineptitude in the war. There is little feeling for the country and its people in his writings. Scenes of Africa, except for the *Just So Stories*, could just as easily be set anywhere else. And his descriptions of the soldiers there have none of the intimacy, the perceptiveness, that made his *Soldiers Three*—set in India—so successful. In addition, Kipling could no longer enjoy the terms of easy equality he had had with infantrymen when he was an unknown journalist. He was now a V.I.P., his name known to everyone. His appearance at a hospital, much as he tried to avoid it, was probably announced ahead of time and included deferential majors and colonels planning his day for him.

His Boer War stories and poems are therefore less personal—and less successful. He praises the average British soldier's courage, his tenacity, his maturity. Gone are the picturesque ruffians of his Indian days; these men are more interested in going home to their families and jobs than in beer-drinking and fist-fighting. And failures in the field are not their fault; the blame lies with the officers, particularly the ones at the top. His fury at those responsible for the way the war was being fought was expressed that summer in two poems, "Stellenbosch" and "The Old Men." The British had a system whereby men were decorated not only for heroism and brilliance, but also merely for having spent a certain length of time commanding in the field. In the first poem, Kipling portrays the generals avoiding combat and the risk of defeat so as to safely obtain the decoration. In the second, he caustically attacks the older officers who refuse to step aside and let the younger and more able men take their place. They merely sit back, he says, and smugly contemplate past achievements. "The Old Men" not only attacks generals, but by inference is aimed at older members of the government as well. There was a core of rottenness and weakness, he charged, that extended through the nation as a whole.

In December of 1901 they returned to South Africa. Just before he sailed he published "The Islanders," in which he bitterly attacked the British for wasting their lives in pursuit of pleasure, becoming militarily weak and morally indecisive.

> And ye vaunted your fathomless power,
>   and ye flaunted your iron pride,
> Ere-ye fawned on the Younger Nations
>   for the men who could shoot and ride!
>
> Then ye returned to your trinkets;
>   then ye contented your souls,
> With the flannelled fools at the wickets
>   or the muddied oafs at the goals. [16]

No poem of his ever evoked more antagonism. With the Boer War now unpopular at home, there was a wave of anger at Kipling's shrill scolding, and much shaking of heads in a nation that saw cricket not only as a game, but as a symbol of fair play, anti-jingoism, and tolerance between different points of view.

Rhodes' illness was now terminal; Kipling visited him every day, walking a path through a ravine set with hydrangeas, a solid mass of blue. On March 26 Rhodes died. No other imperialist had meant so much to Kipling, and when asked, he gladly gave advice about the funeral. At the private service, Kipling read a poem he had written the day before, the last few lines of which were carved on Rhodes' enormous—and, to a present-day eye, ugly—tomb at Bulawayo.

> The immense and brooding Spirit still
> Shall quicken and control.
> Living he was the land, and dead,
> His soul shall be her soul! [17]

About the middle of April they returned to England, having the pleasure of Dr. Jameson's company on the ship. The war was now winding down to an end. The guerrilla warfare that had seemed so interminable was finally coming to a close. The Boers sent a delegation to discuss peace, and in spite of Milner's secret attempts to prevent it, the terms were agreed to and signed Saturday, May 31. The news reached England the next day, Sunday, and a holiday was declared for rather subdued celebrations the following day. There was widespread opposition to the war and Kipling's Aunt Georgie was not alone in feeling the day was an occasion for mourning rather than for joy. She hung a large black banner from the window of her house that read: "We Have Killed and Also Taken Possession." Nothing was said about it during the holiday, but in the evening a crowd, some of whom had overly imbibed, gathered in protest. They tried to pull the banner down and threatened violence. This brought Kipling quickly from the Elms on the other side of the green. Although he disagreed with his aunt, he certainly would defend her. He spoke to the crowd, in spite of many interruptions, and persuaded them to disperse; much to his dislike, the incident was reported in the newspapers.

Other poems he wrote during the Boer War, such as "M. I.," "Lichtenberg," and his well-known "Boots," were published after the war was over, and therefore got less attention. Two stories, "The Comprehension of Private Copper" and "The Captive" appeared at the end of 1902. The first of these again shows Kipling's interest in people's racial and cultural backgrounds, coming, of course, from his own confusing childhood. In this story his emphasis on race is inappropriate and spoils it; in others, like *Kim*, it is an important part of the work's enormous success.

Private Copper is captured by one of the enemy. His captor, to his surprise, does not speak Afrikaans (the African version of Dutch) but English. He is "dark-skinned, dark-haired and dark-eyed"[18] and has an accent that Copper has heard before; his captor is of Indian descent. He speaks of Copper as a "po-ah Tommee" and the private remembers a similar sneer when stationed at Allahabad. But, confusingly, the condescending tone also reminds him of the young squire of Wilmington, back in Sussex, who had caught him poaching rabbits and kicked him. Kipling attempts to express his feelings about the Boers, his old yearning for India, and his anger at the upper class in England through a single character, but he does not succeed. Private Copper overpowers his enemy and takes him back to his platoon. When they are about to march the prisoner off, he begins to kick and weep, and one soldier remarks, "'E screams like a woman!" The vague political discussions between the men, supposed to maintain the reader's interest, fail to do so.

In the second story, "The Captive," Kipling returns to his interest in race and background. He wrote Boer War stories about South Africans, about the English, about a man of Indian descent, and now—predictably—about another prisoner, an American, who describes a field gun he invented, pouring out the techical terms Kipling loved to flaunt. The prisoner further tells of a meeting between a British General and a Boer Commandant. His story is full of references to race—"I put the brown man out of the question."[19] "[He] didn't love niggers. I liked him," "I'm a white man, and my present intention is to die in that color," among others.

It is in this story that a British general comes up with the oft-quoted sentence about the war, "It's a first-class dress-parade for Armageddon."

A few years later a novel called *Dingley*, written by Jerome and Jean Tharaud, achieved wide popularity and won the Goncourt prize. It is of interest because it is a caricature of Kipling and Carrie at the time of the Boer War. The novel as a whole reminds us of Cecil Rhodes' statement that "Kipling has done more than any other since Disraeli to show the world that the British race is sound at core and that rust or dry rot are strangers to it."[20]

Dingley, the protagonist, is a racist who glories in the war and is sure the superior British will win easily.

> Of all the events which had transformed the world since Rome, none seemed to him of greater consequence than the conquest of the planet by his race, and he felt himself chosen by Providence to be the herald of this great undertaking. A writer like himself, Disraeli, had conceived it. In his poet's garret he had written the novel of a man who, bringing all the English colonies together under the patriarchal robe of a glorious monarchy, loving and cruel like those of Oriental despots, had the Queen of Great Britain crowned Empress of India . . . .
>
> What a magnificent adventure for a man, to have written his life before having lived it! A Jew! And yet so typically English in his dual mastery of actions and dreams. Dingley was jealous of such complete glory and while conceding that Disraeli was the grand master of this plan, he savored his own role—that of being the effective spokesman of all British ideals.[21]

In Dingley's fascination with the military, subtle elements of homosexuality can be seen:

> The novelist contemplated admiringly, beneath the table, the wide feet of this man [an army sergeant], which had marched the length of the Empire.

He is struck by an idea for a story: an effeminate no-good who is transformed by enlistment.

> "Imagine, Jane," [he tells his wife], "a young man like the one I just saw; a wretch with deceitful eyes, scanty hair, pale, at the end of his rope, a long supple body, a beardless face, soft gestures, the look of a woman. If he stays in London, he will fall into the worst sort of dissipation. He enlists in the service of the Queen, not for patriotic reasons, but for a few guineas. And in military service, exposed to a profession, its laws and discipline, he will return a man!"

He praises a young Boer leader:

> He is young and he commands. These are the two supreme achievements. I have neither one nor the other. Any ability I do have is obscure, weak and feminine, and produces nothing worthwhile.

Dingley is shown as cool, extremely reserved, and so preoccupied with his writing as to be incapable of human warmth:

> "I don't understand you!" she said. "The suffering of a dog run over by a cart in the street makes you cry out, and the suffering of men attracts you."

In pointing at Dingley/Kipling's racism, feelings toward the military, his homosexual inclinations, and his extreme reserve, the Tharauds made some legitimate points that may have stirred up some discomfort in the Kipling worshippers. In their last claim, hinting that he was incapable of love, they were off the mark. Kipling's childhood had included those soul-saving first six years of his life, when he had experienced security and love. As an adult, he could give and receive love, unlike his sister who, traumatized at an earlier age, was never able to sustain loving relationships.

Kipling used to refer to his winters in South Africa as "my political times," and the Boer War certainly turned his mind more and more toward politics. It was an unfortunate path for him to take. From Swift to Orwell, those few who have been successful political writers have had the broadest of perspectives, an overall view of mankind that transcended the particular issues of their time, which lifts their work above mere diatribe. As Kipling himself said, this was his weak point. He was best at giving us a vivid picture of one moment; stringing a series of vignettes into a coherent whole was never his forte. From a literary view, his eye was far better than his ear—just the reverse of his actual bodily condition. Though he labored hard over accents, and used them constantly, they seem contrived and even tiresome. Critics sometimes quoted poems written in Cockney dialect, with the h's restored and the like, so as to make it standard English, and claimed the results were an improvement.

His political stories from the time of the Boer War are largely forgotten; but in subsequent years his fanciful accounts of Africa, of the North Atlantic, of the future, and, above all, of India, are among the very best things he ever wrote.

XIII

THE NEW CENTURY

The reader will remember that in 1900 *Kim* was finally finished. Kipling had been working at it, off and on, for fifteen years—in the 1880s in India, as *The Book of Mother Maturin*; in the early 1890s in Vermont, where it was set aside for *Captains Courageous*; and in the late 1890s in Africa. Now at last, in the summer of 1900 in England, it was finished. More than any other book, except *The Naulahka*, it was the product of joint authorship. Kipling took the manuscript down to Tisbury and spent hours going over it with his father. It seems probable that Lockwood Kipling helped give the book continuity, the "beginning, middle, and end" that was always such a problem for Kipling in a work of any length.

With *Kim* we see once more how Kipling's heart always lay in India. Over the years, he would work at stories and poems set in various parts of the world; but he would periodically return, as if refreshed, to write about India. It is not surprising that his crowning achievement, wherein he finally "put it all together" and wrote what is by all odds his best book, is set in India. Unforgettable, an enchanting book, rooted in Kipling's earliest memories as a child in Bombay, *Kim* is not so much a story as a series of brilliant pictures of India a hundred years ago—Kim, the contemplative lama, the heat and dust, the Grand Trunk Road, hilly Simla, the snowy peaks of the Himalayas, the red-bearded Mahbub

Ali—all linked together by the father-son love between lama and the Kim. No other book so immerses the reader in that enormous subcontinent. Senator Daniel P. Moynihan, a former ambassador to India, said his predecessor's advice to read *Kim* before going there was "the simplest and best advice" he got, and adds, "Would it had been read by more Presidents."[1]

We meet Kim, a thirteen-year-old boy, astride Zam-Zammah, the huge bronze cannon near Lockwood Kipling's school of art in Lahore. Kim, we are told in the third and fourth sentences of the book:

> . . . was English. Though he was burned black as any native; though he spoke the vernacular by preference, and his mother-tongue in a clipped, uncertain sing-song; though he consorted on terms of perfect equality with the small boys of the bazaar; Kim was white—a poor white of the very poorest.[2]

The half-caste woman who cares for him says she is Kim's mother's sister, but this is untrue: "his mother had been nursemaid in a colonel's family" (Kipling's *ayah* again) "and had married Kimball O'Hara, a young colour-sergeant. . . . " Like Tod, Wee Willie Winkie, "The Worm," Mowgli, Harvey Cheyne, Strickland, and a host of others, Kim is one sort of person, but appears to be another—again revealing Kipling's uncertainty about his background.

Both Kim's parents died and he grew up in the turbulent native section of Lahore. His father left him three papers—one is his birth certificate—and a tale that some day, two men would appear, followed by "nine hundred first-class devils, whose god was a Red Bull on a green field," whereupon Kim would be exalted and raised to power and wealth his father never had. The three papers were sewn in an amulet-case that Kim always carried around his neck.

He knew Lahore from one end to the other: "was hand in glove with men who led lives stranger than anything Haroun al Raschid dreamed of; and he lived in a life wild as that of the Arabian Nights." He begged for food, got prostitutes for young men, and, agile as a squirrel, could climb drainpipes and scuttle across the housetops in the heat of the night. Moslem, Hindu, Sikh, Jain, high caste, low caste—Kim knew everyone, and had the nickname "Little Friend of all the World."

He meets the lama, a holy man from Tibet, and takes him to the museum where he is shown around by a curator who obviously represents Lockwood Kipling. Kim decides to be the lama's disciple, or *chela*. The old man is on a lifelong search for a holy river, immersion in which will wash away all sins. While the lama sleeps, Kim changes into Hindu clothing; the lama doesn't recognize him when he awakens. Kim takes him to a crowded campground near the railroad station. There he knows he will meet Mahbub Ali, a red-bearded Pathan horse-trader he has known for years. Mahbub Ali failes to recognize Kim until Kim speaks to him in English. The horse-trader gives Kim a secret message concealed in a piece of bread to be taken to a colonel in Umballa.

Kim and the lama take the southbound train, stopping to spend the night in Umballa. There Kim delivers the secret message and hears orders given to dispatch eight thousand men, with artillery, to handle an uprising of five local rulers far to the north. Kim realizes Mahbub Ali is an intelligence agent for the British government.

Kim and the lama continue on the Grand Trunk Road. Elderly women often travel there in bullock-carts, going to see distant relatives. Kim sees one such cart, with hill-men in attendance, and talks to the woman; she invites them to join her as she travels. The next day, an English superintendent of police trots by and exchanges jests with the woman; she says he never learned to speak Hindustani so well since coming from Europe (that is, he must have been born in India). "Who suckled thee?" "A *pahareen*—a hill-woman of Dalhousie, my mother," he replies, and clops on.

They spend the next night by an open plain. Wandering out there, Kim and the lama see two British soldiers setting out flags to mark where an approaching regiment will make camp. The flag is a red bull on a green field—Kim's long-sought sign. He peeks in the officers' tent and is discovered by the chaplain, Mr. Bennett, who in catching him grabs the amulet of papers from around his neck. In English, Kim asks for their return. The chaplain calls for Father Victor, the regimental priest. He remembers Kim's father, having attended his wedding. Kim tells of his being a *chela* of the lama, who is brought to the tent and confers with the chaplain and priest. They say that Kim, as a white boy, should go off to school. Kim protests but the lama agrees that as a sahib, "Kim must go back to his own people," and offers to send money for Kim's education.

The lama returns to the travelers on the Grand Trunk Road and Kim, now dressed in English clothing, is taken off to school.

Four days later, he hails Mahbub Ali, who takes him away on horseback; they are joined by a Colonel Creighton; Kim recognizes him as the man to whom he gave the secret message in Umballa. Father Victor comes and tells how, to his astonishment, the lama has indeed sent money for Kim's schooling. He is taken off on the train and begins school. When the long summer holiday begins, Kim vanishes to the red-light district, where he finds Hindu costume and has a girl dye his skin brown. He disappears for a month, writing to Mahbub Ali that in due time he will rejoin him. One evening Mahbub Ali is taking care of some of his horses in Umballa when a Hindu boy begs alms, is sworn at, and replies in English—it is Kim. They change his clothes so that he now appears to be a Mohammedan. The "Little Friend of all the World" joins the horse-trader on his trip north.

Excitedly, Kim begins to understand the dangerous intelligence work in which Mahbub Ali is involved, and asks to become an agent himself. At Simla, the Pathan sends him to a man named Lurgan for further training in the "Great Game."

Lurgan's shop—he is a "healer of sick pearls"—is an exotic place, full of weapons, jewels, rugs, and a thousand other things from all over Asia. Lurgan is impressed when he tries to hypnotize Kim and cannot do so. He teaches him observation, memory, "body language," and how to look for what is unsaid besides what is said. Kim meets a Bengali named Hurree Chunder Mookerjee and learns he is another secret service agent. Hurree teaches him procedures and recognition codes between agents. Kim returns to school, where he does well; the lama visits him there from time to time. Mr. Lurgan and Mahbub Ali plead with Colonel Creighton to take him out of school and into intelligence work, and Creighton finally agrees to let him out for six months.

Mahbub Ali takes him to a blind woman who dyes his body so that again he appears Asiatic. Kim, now seventeen, and the lama head north on the train. Kim becomes involved in various adventures in the Great Game. At Delhi he sees another agent—named Strickland—who, Kim remembers, three years before rode by on the Grand Trunk Road and joked with the elderly woman. Some days later, they are joined by a drug vendor who argues with Kim and, when alone, says in English,

"How do you do, Mister O'Hara?" It is Hurree in disguise. He tells Kim that the Russians have been plotting to invade provinces far to the north and that he is going to investigate two agents there. He asks Kim to keep in touch and to assist him.

Many days later Hurree finds the two Russian agents and attaches himself to their party as an interpreter and guide. They catch up with Kim and his companion. One of the Russians grabs at the lama's drawing of the Wheel of Life, tears it, and hits the holy man. Kim attacks him; the coolies scatter in terror with the baggage. Kim manages to get the container with all the spies' correspondence and maps in it. The whole countryside turns against the agents for having hit a holy man. Hurree stays with the Russians for a time and when they leave, rejoins Kim and the lama. Kim takes the maps and letters to be sent to British Intelligence.

Returning to the plains, the lama finds his holy river; and Kim, after a struggle for his identity—"I am Kim. I am Kim. And what is Kim?"—finally feels sure of his goal of becoming a sahib in India. It is a struggle like Mowgli's in the jungle, like Harvey Cheyne's on the waterfront, the struggle of a person groping to find a secure sense of himself. Previously I have given examples where confusion about identity is symbolized by one person being in the guise of another. Indeed, so central is this theme that *Kim* really cannot be appreciated without its being recognized. It comes from Kipling's deepest roots; occasionally fails—as seen in "The Comprehension of Private Copper"—but here it is supremely successful.

In 1902 Kipling published his *Just So Stories* that he had been telling his children and polishing to perfection for five years or more. One of Kipling's strongest points is his versatility. He can tell you of Indian life, fishermen on the Grand Banks, old age, the military, and now, about the mind of a child. He is remembered today, perhaps, as much for his children's stories as he is for his writing for adults. It would seem that his own miserable childhood and his declared intention to give other children a happier time contributed to his lifelong love of children and to his ability to write for them.

These stories are free, imaginative, and involve magic. More myths than fairy tales, like dreams they abandon logic and reality and reveal things Kipling ordinarily kept scrupulously hidden—things about his family, about his childhood, about himself.

The stories are mostly about the origins of things. In "How the Leopard Got His Spots," for instance, Kipling tells how a man, for protective coloration, put on a dark skin and became black—color again—and by pressing the tips of his fingers on the fur of the leopard produced its characteristic spots. In most of the other stories he tells how animals came to have their various shapes and colors. Again, we see Kipling's intense curiosity, the way in which he asked himself all his life, "How does that work?" and "How did that come to be?" This curiosity goes back to Kipling's earliest days: to his being cared for by a native nurse, snatched from her, and put in a bewildering home where he was not loved by an Indian woman, but instead was beaten by a white woman. Again, we see the old confusion, at an unconscious level, as to who his mother was and as to whether he was white or Asiatic, and as to *how* his parents could have done such a thing as abandon him at the House of Desolation. His question "How did that begin?" originated as "How did *I* begin?"

The stories have a strong ritualistic element. Certain repetitive phrases occur again and again. Kipling told the first stories to his daughter Josephine when they lived in Vermont and published the first three of them in 1897. The name of the stories comes from their ritualistic nature—they must be told "just so." And, indeed, Kipling wrote them "just so," working over them and polishing them to an almost obsessive degree. Unlike most other writers, he illustrated his own stories. He must have spent hours on the drawings, which are excellent, and has a page of text accompanying each illustration describing many of the things in it. With a powerful magnifying glass, one can make out that the kangaroo's pouch (although the kangaroo is a male, Kipling gave him a pouch) is patented under the Federated Government of Australia. Another story, "The Cat Who Walked by Himself," begins with a large initial letter drawn on a bone. On the letter are tiny little marks which are actually runic, giving a message to anyone who has the patience to decipher it.

These stories are notable in several other ways. They present evolution from the Lamarckian, not the Darwinian, point of view—acquired traits can be inherited; when the Whale gets a constricted throat, no subsequent whales can swallow large objects. Before accusing Kipling of inaccuracy, we should reflect that it would be difficult, or even impossible, to imagine children's stories told from a Darwinian viewpoint.

It should be pointed out that these stories have a strong moral tone, a tone absent from other classics such as *Alice in Wonderland*. The camel is given his hump because he is lazy and misbehaved, the rhinoceros gets folds in his skin because he has no manners, and so forth. These are what Bettelheim calls "cautionary tales";[3] if you are bad, *this* will happen to you. In three of the stories, we are told about a Neolithic family composed of Tegumai, his wife Teshumai, and their daughter Taffimai (representing Kipling, his wife, and Josephine). Here we get a glimpse into the Kipling home. In all three stories the importance of obedience and good manners is emphasized again and again. The Kipling children were brought up lovingly but also firmly. Sadly, over and over again, we are told how close little Taffy was to her father. In one of the illustrations she is shown as a floating, ghost-like figure, and in the description on the opposite page Kipling notes, "Taffy is always drawn in outline—quite white."[4] At another point Kipling describes how "Taffy was very like Teshumai, especially about the upper part of the face and the eyes,"[5] just where Josephine resembled her mother.

On one or two occasions and only here, insofar as I am aware, in all that he wrote—in his correspondence as well as in his books—Kipling allows himself a wry comment on his wife's rigid and domineering nature. In one story, where the Head Chief and Tegumai are romping about with Taffy, they end up by:

> throwing the otter-skin cushions about and knocking down a lot of old spears and fishing-rods that were hung on the walls. At last things grew so rowdy that Teshumai Tewindrow came in and said, "Still! Still Tabu on every one of you! How do you ever expect that child to go to sleep?" And they said the really good-night and Taffy went to sleep.[6]

In another story we are told that:

> As soon as Taffy could run about she went everywhere with her Daddy Tegumai, and sometimes they would not come home to the Cave till they were hungry and then Teshumai Tewindrow would say, "Where in the World have you two been to, to get so shocking dirty? Really, my Tegumai, you're no better than my Taffy."[7]

In these stories, as in others, we see examples of self-percepts—animals and things that represent Kipling himself. With his small size, poor coordination, and bad eyesight, Kipling tended to feel physically inferior to those about him. Nick Tarvin, Mowgli, George Cottar, and many others could be cited as Kipling's physical ideal—tall, powerful, and well coordinated. Being small, Kipling turned to his mind for compensation. He may not have been athletic, but he was alert and intelligent. Here we see the Kipling who was "in the know," the person in his early stories who could recite all the parts of a regulation rifle—or thought he could—and in this way tried to feel a part of the British Army. A great deal of this stayed with him, and marred his writing, in later years.

In many of his previous stories, there is a small, smart animal, often one that is rather ignored and looked down upon by others, but who is wise and worth listening to. One thinks of Rikki-Tikki-Tavi, who begins as a half-drowned little animal but who ends up saving an entire family. There is also Limmershin, in "The White Seal." We are told that "Limmershin is a very odd little bird, but he knows how to tell the truth."[8] Even in a story that only involves machines, we see an example. In ".007," a new, small, and inexperienced locomotive, by diligence and intelligence, earns his acceptance into a fraternity of steam-engines. I can point to four examples in two of the *Just So Stories*. In "The Elephant's Child," we have two self-percepts. There is the elephant himself who is repeatedly beaten, as was Kipling, until he goes out, gets a long, powerful trunk, and then comes back and beats up all the other animals. There is also, however, the Kolokolo bird, the wise little animal who tells the elephant how to "Go to the banks of the great grey-green greasy Limpopo River, all set about with fever trees"[9] to get his potent trunk. In "How the Whale Got His Throat," there is a whale who eats all the small fish in the ocean except for a small, intelligent 'Stute Fish (that is to say, astute). Following his advice, the whale swallows a man who then jumps and thumps around in the "Whale's warm, dark, inside cupboards."[10] This obvious symbol of pregnancy is continued when the mariner forces the whale to deliver him—literally as well as figuratively—on "the Mariner's Natal-shore and the white-cliffs-of-Albion." Here we have two self-percepts, the small 'Stute Fish, and the Mariner. One part of Kipling always wished that he had been born in England so that he could feel secure about his mother-country and about his mother. His mixed feelings toward England are also shown by his making the Mariner an Irishman, a person who was English but was rebelliously trying to break away from England.

What is most interesting about the highly successful *Just So Stories*, however, is where they take place, or, rather, where they *don't* take place. With his happy childhood in India, his memories of the "stories and Indian nursery songs all unforgotten"[11] that his *ayah* had told and sung to him, and his familiarity with Indian animals, one might expect that several of these stories would be set in India. But they aren't. They take place in Africa, in the Atlantic Ocean, on an island in the Red Sea, in Australia, South America, and what are now Israel and Malaysia. It is almost as if he chose every place except India! Kipling seems to toy with the idea of using India a couple of times. In one story, he has a Parsee, Pestonjee Bomonjee—a real-life figure from Kipling's infancy who was a friend of his parents—on an island in the Red Sea, a place *on the way* to India. And when he drew an African elephant, it came out looking like an Indian elephant; but perhaps we shouldn't read anything into that. Asked to draw an elephant, he would naturally tend to draw the one most familiar to him.

Partly, having none of the stories take place in England or in India reflects Kipling's old confusion about his origin. At the beginning of a story about the Neolithic family—that is, his own—Kipling writes of the man, "He was not a Jute or an Angle, or even a Dravidian, which he might well have been, Best Beloved, but never mind why."[12] (Jutes and Angles were early inhabitants of England, as Dravidians were of India.) Again, he was saying, "Where was I born? England? India? I don't know."

But why do none of these stories, lovingly told to his daughter Josephine, take place in India, where he had his own enchanted childhood? I think the reason is the same one that explains why no stories occur in England or America. About these three places—and to a much lesser extent Africa—Kipling felt a basic sense of confusion. Each one seemed like home, but not strongly enough to give a really firm, secure feeling about his background.

Most people have a "magic land," usually one experienced in childhood, for which they always yearn. They carry with them delicious memories of mud under their toes in cold, briny water, the clear, dry air of the mountains, or flat wheat fields shimmering in the burning heat. Even if they live somewhere else for decades the "magic land" does not fade. Kipling's confusing background interfered a bit with such soothing memories. He came closest to having them about India, of course, which he portrayed magnificently in *Kim*. India was almost a "magic land." Years later, when the British government strongly urged him to accompany King George V on his 1911 trip to India, he knew better than to accept. Returning as part of an official delegation would shatter his loving memories. But the circumstances of his leaving it as a child— "How could my parents have ever done that to me?"—spoiled it just a bit as a true "magic land." When telling the *Just So Stories* to his children, he found himself veering away from India, to other parts of the world, *any* other part where things could be perfect. India, however loved, could never be quite perfect.

When in New York at the beginning of the disastrous year of 1899, Kipling was entranced with a ride in an electric car. At the end of the same year, back in England, an editor came to see the Kiplings in an early automobile and, after being taken for a twenty-minute spin, they immediately decided to get one of these fascinating new inventions. They rented a "Victoria-hooded, carriage-sprung, carriage-braked, single-cylinder, belt-driven, fixed-ignition Embryo which at times, could cover eight miles an hour."*[13] Complete with chauffeur, it cost them three and a half guineas a week (about twenty dollars, in present-day values). They withstood the fist-shaking and imprecations of the horse-drawn majority of drivers who disliked "those new-fangled contraptions." "Earls stood up in their belted barouches and cursed us."

Breakdowns in those days were very common, and with no service stations the chauffeur had to be a mechanic as well as a driver. Kipling himself, apparently, never drove or attempted repairs. He was interested in the jargon of machines, but his lack of coordination made it very difficult to actually run anything. (Driving your own car may not have been fashionable around the turn of the century, but certainly was by

---

*Note Kipling's confusion between speed and distance covered, previously seen in his misuse of the word 'knot.' His car could *cover* eight miles *in* an hour or *attain* a speed of eight miles *an* hour.

the teens and twenties; this was not the reason he avoided it.) The frustrating breakdowns continued. Many people felt that cars were just a passing fad and would never be reliable enough to replace horses and trains.

In 1900, upon returning from their winter's stay in South Africa, they bought an American steam-driven car called a "Locomobile." To their amazement, they could drive to a town fifty miles away and return, all in one day!

They took these drives all over Sussex because they were house-hunting. Even Rottingdean now had too many tourists for the Kiplings' taste. One day, when the Locomobile was being fixed, they took a train and then a carriage to the tiny village of Burwash (pronounced "*Burrash*") where they saw "Bateman's," a lovely Jacobean house of gray stone set by itself in a broad valley with a brook winding past it. Here was real privacy! Inside it was very dark, with original seventeenth-century oak panels. They instantly knew this was just what they wanted, the "very-own" house, as Kipling called it, that they had dreamed of, and they exclaimed, "That's her! The Only She! Make an honest woman of her—quick!" But while they discussed it someone else slipped in and rented it. In the summer of 1902, more than two years later, they were finally able to buy the house.

The next car they bought was a Lanchester, and the industry then was so pleasantly small that Mr. Lanchester himself brought the car to their door.

> When all was signed and sealed [about the house sale], the seller said: "Now I can ask you something. How are you going to manage about getting to and from the station? It's nearly four miles, and I used up two pair of horses on the hill here." "I'm thinking of using this sort of contraption," I replied from my seat in—Jane Cakebread Lanchester, I think, was her dishonorable name. "Oh! *Those* things haven't come to stay!" he returned. . . . In three years from our purchase the railway station had passed out of our lives. In seven, I heard my chauffeur say to an under-powered visiting sardine-tin: "Hills? There ain't any hills on the London road."

Kipling wrote "Steam Tactics" about the Locomobile and soon after that "The Muse amongst the Motors," verses involving automobiles.

On September 3, 1902, they moved into Bateman's, sure it would be, as it proved, the last move in their lives. Carrie was upset—changes were hard for a person of her inflexible nature—and she noted in her diary: "Sept. 3. Go to Bateman's to meet chaos and black night. Labour and struggle to put things right. 4. A hopeless day. 5. Fought with workmen and cleaners all day long. A terrible day."[14] Not until the end of the month could she begin to enjoy their new home.

Kipling wrote Charles Eliot Norton in November:

> We left Rottingdean because Rottingdean was getting too populated, though we didn't want to part from Aunt Georgie. Then we discovered England which we had never done before . . . and went to live in it. England is a wonderful land. It is the most marvelous of all foreign countries that I have ever been in. It is made up of trees and green fields and mud and the gentry, and at last I'm one of gentry—I'll take a new pen and explain.
>
> Behold us owners of a grey stone lichened house—A.D. 1634 over the door—beamed, panelled, with old oak staircase, and all untouched and unfaked. Heaven looked after it in the dissolute times of mid-victorian restoration and caused the vicar to send his bailiff to live in it for 40 years, and he lived in peaceful filth and left everything as he found it.
>
> It is a good and peaceable place standing on terraced lawns nigh to a walled garden of old red brick, and two fat-headed oast-houses with red brick stomachs, and an aged silver-grey dovecote on top. There is what they call a river at the bottom of the lawn. . . . Its name is the Dudwell, and it is quite ten feet wide.[15]

The brook had an ancient mill that had ground flour for centuries, the site of Kipling's story "Below the Mill Dam." He wrote of his delight at digging a well and finding "a Jacobean tobacco-pipe, a worn Cromwellian latten spoon and, at the bottom of all, the bronze cheek of a Roman horse-bit."[16]

Now attempting to feel fully at home at Bateman's, he finally decided to sell the long-empty Naulakha back in Vermont. Keeping it this long suggests that he always dreamed that somehow, someday, he would be able to move back there, although knowing it was realistically impossible. He had written to Dr. Conland that he had offered it for sale "but I took damn good care to put a prohibitive price on it,"[17] so that it wouldn't be sold. Now he sadly offered Dr. Conland his old fishing rods and anything else he wanted, and "I want to ask you, if you will, to go up to the house and get the old hog-yoke [a sextant] that you gave me and pack it up carefully (Howard wouldn't know how to do it,) and send it to me here . . . I want that old yoke 'for to keep' as the kids say."[18] A few months later, in January of 1903 he wrote, "I feel I shall never cross the Atlantic again."[19] He sold Naulakha to the Cabots for $8,000, considerably less than it was worth. This may have happened partly because Beatty Balestier, his old enemy, upon hearing that the house was to be sold, indicated he might start legal proceedings claiming it belonged to him. Kipling wanted no opening of those old wounds.

Toward the end of 1903 and the beginning of 1904, he wrote four remarkable stories: "A Deal in Cotton," "Mrs. Bathurst," "They," and "With the Night Mail." The first two are the last of his African stories. In 1903 Kipling published *The Five Nations*, poems mostly about the Boer War, and with relief turned his attention away from South Africa in what he wrote thereafter.

"A Deal in Cotton" marks the last appearance of Strickland, the policeman Kipling had been using in stories for fifteen years or more. Here was a man who could so cleverly disguise himself that he could mix unnoticed with the natives, becoming one of them, and in this way expressed Kipling's lifelong unconscious feeling that he was part Indian.

In the story, Strickland has married Miss Youghal—also from an early story—and they have a son, Adam, who is on convalescent leave from an administrative post in Africa. With his father and mother Adam, thin and weak, comes for a stay with Kipling and another of his old Army friends. Adam is supported by a body-servant, Imam Din, who is "one of old Strickland's Punjabi policemen—quite European"[20] and who refers to himself as a "white man"—i.e., in contrast to the blacks with whom he and his master have been working.

At dinner, with Imam Din standing in the shadows, young Adam tells of introducing the planting of cotton in his district, having begun with fifty acres—"I had the labour done by cannibals." His mother doesn't want to hear grisly details about cannibals and retires to the music room to play. Adam describes the cannibals as openly offering "you four pounds of woman's breast, tattoo marks and all, skewered up plantain leaf before breakfast," but his superior said that they could take action when a white man was eaten. There was also one Ibn ʿah in the district, a man who dealt in slaves and was the terror of tive.

One day, Adam recounts, a near-dead man was brought to his camp; he and Imam Din nursed him back to health—most of their treatment consisting of an enema—and the man, who went by the name of the Hajji, later tells how one of Ibn Makarrah's men has been openly running slaves through the district "in the Fork" (with a forked stick around their necks). If a slaver ran slaves through the territory and pretended they were servants, that was all right; but "hawkin' 'em around in the Fork" is too much, and Adam, now down with a raging fever, sends off Imam Din and some policemen to apprehend the slaver. They bring him back; the slaver freely admits his guilt and, oddly enough, worsens his case by openly trying to sell some cannibal slaves to the British themselves. He pays a fine of two hundred and ten pounds and departs. Because of the fever, Adam only hazily remembers the trial, getting the fine—which he immediately puts away to start his cotton field—and freeing the slaves, who gratefully volunteer to work for nothing on the cotton. Later he goes out with the Hajji and finds the cannibals' village had been struck by lightning and burned to the ground, and discovers it was this, not gratitude, that induced them to ask to work in the cotton fields. Tired by telling the story to Kipling and the others, Adam is taken off to bed by Imam Din who, when he returns to the dining room, tells them all what really happened.

When Adam became ill, the Hajji listened to his feverish ramblings, expecting to hear him speak of women, although Imam Din had assured him that the Sahib's "virtue was beyond belief" and that all he was interested in was this plan to introduce the cultivation of cotton. The Hajji then whispered to the sick man that a slaver was in the territory, and Adam sat up in bed, ordered his arrest, and then lapsed back into unconsciousness. The Hajji and Imam Din, convinced that getting the cotton started will help Adam's recovery, set off to catch and fine the slaverunner "in all respects conformable with the English Law." Adam was left in the care of an old woman of the Hajji's who was told that if he died, she would die. The Hajji, who "loved our Sahib with the love of a father for his son," boldly led the way into cannibal territory, ordered the terrified cannibals to yoke up six of their members as slaves, and to burn their own village to the ground. Imam Din began to realize that the Hajji was none other than Ibn Makarrah. The Hajji then told the cannibals that a white man will come by in a few days, planting a new crop, and ordered that they, and their children after them, must work for him. He and Imam Din picked up some other men, who hastily agreed to act as witnesses, and, with the fake slaves, they all returned to the town where Adam lay in his bed. (The Hajji was, in effect, arranging for his own "trial.")

"His (Adam's) eyes were very bright, and his mouth was full of upside-down orders, but the woman had not loosened her hair for death," says Imam Din. They and Adam—from his bed—carried off a "trial" keeping the "witnesses," "slaves," and "prisoners" all in the next room, "Yet—*yet* because no man can be sure whether a Sahib of that blood sees, or does not see, we made it strictly in the manner of the forms of the English Law." (None of Kipling's readers, nor the author himself, saw anything peculiar in this strict adherence to "the English Law" when the judge is disoriented, nor in the natives, in effect, being changed from one form of slavery to another.) The Hajji paid a fine of two hundred and ten pounds, and about all Adam remembered was locking up the money, so vital to his cotton scheme. ". . . [T]he gold wrought on him as a strong cure" and he quickly improved. He went out with the Hajji to see where his cotton was being started, and found that the cannibals' village had been burnt to the ground ("by lightning," the Hajji told him) and they were working away at the cotton crop. After their return to camp, the Hajji told Imam Din, "God has given me as it were a son in my old age, and I praise Him. See that the breed is not lost!" He gave Adam a gold and amber amulet and they parted, each saying the other's name was engraved on his heart.

In this story, Kipling is back in India where he had lived thirty-five years before. It is another of the *Plain Tales from the Hills*. Strickland, Adam, Imam Din—they are all right out of India, and there is no mention of the landscape or the people to remind you that the story is supposed to be about Africa. The Hajji had even "been to Bombay." In Adam, we again have the Kipling hero, chaste and pure, like Bobby Wick and George Cottar. When Adam is talking feverishly, the Hajji doesn't hear mention of women; all that's on his mind is starting the cotton. There is the old worship of the ruling English in India; Imam Din respectfully speaks of "a Sahib of that blood" and the Hajji admonishes, "See that the breed is not lost!" Again we see, Kipling's sadistic feelings toward women; Adam talks about the cannibals—his mother leaves at this point to play the organ—offering "you four pounds of woman's breast, tattoo marks and all, skewered up in a plantain leaf." He cured the Hajji with an enema composed, Kipling is careful to tell us, of "shaving soap and trade gunpowder, and hot water."

What of the servant, Imam Din? He is Asiatic, "one of old Strickland's Punjabi policemen," but we are also immediately told that he is "quite European." He refers to himself as a "white man." He is Asiatic, but he is white; it is Kipling's old confusion about race that goes back to his earliest years. Imam Din, the "body-servant," who is nursing Adam back to health, who cares for him (while his mother plays the piano) as Kipling's *ayah* did; who at the end of the story takes his mother's place at his bedside to "rub his feet till he sleeps," urges that Adam return to his post:

> The breed should not be lost. It is not *very* hot for little children in Dupé and as regards nurses, my sister's cousin at Jull—

In Imam Din we see Kipling's old feelings about his mother, divided between his real mother and his native *ayah*, between a white woman and an Asiatic one; Imam Din, who says "it is not *very* hot" where they live, further points to whom he represents (Kipling's *ayah*) when he suggests someone in his family who could be a nurse for Adam's children. It reminds us of Kipling's own birth, supposedly brought about by the natives sacrificing a kid to Kali, and Kipling's account of this in "The Story of the Gadsbys," where the *ayah* intuitively knows how to save the woman in labor during the terrible heat. That child, like Kipling, is symbolically born of two mothers, one white and one Asiatic.

The second story, "Mrs. Bathurst," is complex, in fact so complicated that there exists quite a large literature of attempts to understand it. A little like a dream, Kipling deliberately does not let us see what it means.

The narrator of the story is sitting with a friend of his, Hooper, in an empty railroad car in South Africa, when another friend, Pyecroft, arrives, bringing an acquaintance, Sergeant Pritchard. The four men sit and talk, as they drink beer, about a Boy Niven, who once lured several young seamen into walking around an uninhabited island near Vancouver. He deceived them with promises of property. Then Pyecroft tells about a man named Vickery who, because of a woman, deserted from the Navy only a year and a half before his pension was due. Pyecroft says that the woman involved was Mrs. Bathurst, a name that Pritchard immediately recognizes. She was left a widow at a young age, never remarried, and had the deepest respect of all the noncommissioned officers who went to her bar and hotel in Hauraki in New Zealand. She was an unforgettable woman whose effect on a man who fell for her would be that he "goes crazy—or just saves himself."[21] Pritchard tells a story that illustrates her steadfast loyalty.

Pyecroft then tells of being ashore at Capetown where he met Vickery, who insisted that he go to see some motion-picture clips with him, paying for his ticket. Pyecroft, while watching a scene filmed at a London railroad station, suddenly sees Mrs. Bathurst for a few seconds on the screen. Vickery, highly excited, said that he had brought Pyecroft to make sure that it was, indeed, Mrs. Bathurst whom he had seen. After leaving the movie, Vickery, very upset, drinks heavily and for five consecutive nights drags Pyecroft to the movies, where they watch the few seconds of film in which Mrs. Bathurst appears, and then go out and drink. Only once did Pyecroft venture to ask Vickery something about her, where upon Vickery threatens to assault him. Vickery then goes and speaks to his captain, and subsequently receives orders to go up-country alone to take care of some supplies. Before he leaves he tells Pyecroft that "I am *not* a murderer, because my lawful wife died in childbed six weeks after I came out." He then disappears; they presume he deserted.

Hooper then picks up the conversation. He tells of going up-country where he found "a couple of tramps" who had been struck by lightning. ". . . (T)hey were both stone dead and as black as charcoal." From identifying marks on one of the bodies Hooper, who had always wondered who it had been, now finds out that one of the tramps, who had been standing up when struck by lighting, was Vickery. Prichard is very upset to hear this; covering his face, he says, "And to think of her at Hauraki. . . . with 'er 'air-ribbon on my beer . . . Oh, my Gawd!"

This is the end of the story; we are never told the identity of the second tramp. Many critics have concluded that it was Mrs. Bathurst, and that love drove Vickery to his death. Kipling carefully avoids telling us anything, even regarding gender, about the second tramp. The two are merely spoken of as "tramps." One was standing up, and "the other" was squatting down. The standing one is referred to as "he" and is therefore male, and the other is described as "his mate." Going by the meanings of the words alone, one might conclude that "his mate" was a man. When one refers to "two tramps" (and when one referred to them in 1904), one tends to think of two men. At one point Hooper says, "The men who was standin' up had the false teeth." This may imply that the man who is squatting down did not. But we never know; we are left in doubt.

What does it mean? We have a picture of Mrs. Bathurst, generous, caring, and unforgettable. Both Pyecroft and Pritchard repeatedly say that if there was any violence or murder, "It wasn't her fault," though Pritchard adds at one point, "She never scrupled to feed a lame duck or set 'er foot on a scorpion at any time in 'er life." What had gone on between Vickery and Mrs. Bathurst, that he become so distraught, got drunk, and had to see her repeatedly in the movie? We only know Pyecroft's guess that "There must 'ave been a good deal between 'em." In the film Mrs. Bathurst seemed to be looking for someone; and Vickery says of this, "She's lookin' for me." But all questions about the story come down to this—who was the second tramp?

Much of what has been written in the last sixty years (the critics began discussing the story in about 1930) is summarized nicely by Crook.[22] C. A. Bodelsen and Elliot Gilbert agree that the early motion pictures, with their flickering, gray, ghost-like images, serve as a metaphor for the entire story. Also, with the invention of movies, for the first time people could be seen in action when the observer knows very well that they are dead. Bodelsen and Gilbert further agree that a clue lies in Kipling's epigraph, entitled "From Lyden's *Irenius*," wherein a man is to be hanged. A woman caused this death, but she "knew not that she did it, or would have died ere she had done it. For she loved him."[23]

Bodelsen at first thought that Mrs. Bathurst was a revenging angel of death, angry at Vickery for having deserted her after she went to London, but later (significantly; I will return to this presently) changed his mind and decided she had saved Vickery's soul. Mrs. Bathurst is the second tramp, but how had she gotten from New Zealand to England and then to South Africa? Bodelsen concluded that "Vickery had an hallucination by which he believes that the tramp is Mrs. Bathurst's ghost."[24] Surely there must be a simpler and more satisfactory answer then this.

Gilbert concluded that Mrs. Bathurst destroyed Vickery, but unknowingly. Had she realized what she had done, she would have sooner laid down her life. Pritchard's shock, then, is in realizing the power women have over man. Gilbert further points to a sentence from *Irenius*: "Not an astrologer, but would ha' sworn he'd foreseen it at the last versary of Venus, when Vulcan caught her with Mars in the house of stinking Capricorn."[25] Gilbert saw this as indicating the passionate relationship between Mrs. Bathurst and Vickery; he also pointed out that Vulcan makes lighting-bolts. In Gilbert's opinion the story is about man's search for order in a chaotic universe. The second tramp was not Mrs. Bathurst; he/she merely appeared on the scene and has no function in the story, illustrating further the random workings of fate.

But the majority of critics have felt that Mrs. Bathurst *was* the other tramp, and that there are many clues (the movie, *Irenius*) that point to this. Readers have recognized that the story is tightly woven, where no detail is superfluous. As Craig Raine said, "The story is as precise as a Swiss watch. Everything fits, but the reader has to wind it up."[26]

I will attempt to do just that. Kipling obviously meant us to be unsure of the gender of the person killed with Vickery. His wording has been examined minutely, but to little effect. Suppose Kipling intended us not to know, and that in itself was a clue to the identity of the second tramp? He/she is a bisexual person, like someone in a dream where we can't tell if it's a man or a woman. Invariably a person like this represents not a man or a woman, but rather stands for someone toward whom we have a mixture of feelings—a manly woman, or a womanly man. Vickery, who has feelings of guilt, finds death with someone who is both a man and a woman. Why both?

I think this refers to Kipling's marriage. He had had intense homosexual feelings for Wolcott Balestier, and fended off Carrie's determined efforts to marry him. While in Australia or New Zealand (where he met the original for "Mrs Bathurst"), he heard of Wolcott's illness. Then, his bonds to him cut free by his death, he dashed across the face of Asia and Europe to immediately marry Wolcott's sister. The tense, efficient, no-nonsense Carrie—all their friends wondered how Kipling could put up with such a controlling, "masculine" person.

"Mrs. Bathurst" is about the relationships between men and women, using the example of Kipling's own marriage. Some pro-Kipling writers, stung with accusations that their idol never once was able to portray a woman as warm and loving, have pointed in triumph at Mrs. Bathurst. She is indeed described as a kind, generous person. She put out a certain powerful magnetism; once seen, she was never forgotten. Kipling, making the first use of the word for sexual attraction, says that Mrs. Bathurst had "It." And any difficulties Vickery got into, the men in the story agree, were certainly not her fault.

But although she did not wish him any harm, and therefore cannot be held responsible for what happened, nevertheless his association with her led to his death. Kipling by now had gotten away from his teenage view of women as sadistic, scheming creatures who toyed with helpless little men. He portrays Mrs. Bathurst as warm and loving. But she is still dangerous; any close relationship with her, like some evil fate, leads a man to death. The woman does not wish this to happen, and would be tormented if she knew it was going to; and yet it happens. A remnant of Kipling's old fears is still there.

We see this when Pritchard, after telling warm memories of Mrs. Bathurst, adds, "She never scrupled to feed a lame duck or set 'er foot on a scorpion at any time in 'er life."[27] Kipling said he overheard this description of a New Zealand woman and "those words gave me the key to the face and voice [of a woman he had previously met] at Auckland, and a tale called 'Mrs. Bathurst' slid into my mind, smoothly and orderly as floating timber on a bank-high river."[28] The sentence he heard is the key to understanding the story. A kind and loving woman, who would help any hurt animal, could without hesitation set her foot on a scorpion. Squish! Can any reader freely imagine stepping on a scorpion? Mrs. Bathurst is loving and unforgettable, but she is also as hard as nails. This is what Kipling is telling us, that he deeply loved the woman so many found dominating and unlikable—his wife. (Here we see the significance in Bodelsen's hesitation between a conclusion that Mrs. Bathurst was an avenging Fury or one regarding her as a savior. She is both.) This theme is repeated when the "two tramps" are found; for of course the other tramp is Mrs. Bathurst. The main objection to this has been the realistic one that "it doesn't make sense"—how could Mrs. Bathurst get from New Zealand to England and then to the middle of Africa? True. But the story is successful precisely because it goes beyond reason.

Nora Crook comes as close as can be to the solution I propose when she says:

> It is not clear that Hooper's brusquerie *did* jolt the narrator out of his trance. Unlike "The Army of a Dream," where the entire story is a reverie from which the narrator surfaces at the end, Kipling has deliberately blurred the status of the narrative in "Mrs. Bathurst." Is what follows a vision or a waking dream? Has the narrator awoken from a false fairyland to a nightmarish truth?[29]

In "The Army of a Dream," as she says, the narrator awakens at the end; in this story he falls asleep at the beginning.

> The weight of the bland wind on my eyelids; the song of it under the car roof, and high up among the rocks; the drift of fine grains chasing each other musically ashore; the tramp of the surf; the voices of the picnickers; the rustle of Hooper's file, and the presence of the assured sun, joined with the beer to cast me into magical slumber. The hills of False Bay were just dissolving into those of fairyland when. . . .[30]

Note the things putting the narrator to sleep. They are: bland wind on his eyelids, song of wind under the roof, (song of wind) high in the rocks, musical drift (of sand), tramp of the surf, voices of the picnickers, rustle of the file, the sunshine, and the beer. These are all soothing, soporific images with, it seems to me, a notable exception—the phrase "tramp of the surf." It brings to mind a heavy, jarring, rhythmical beat; by deliberately avoiding some such words as "the murmur of the surf" Kipling is telling us two things; first of all, that he fell asleep, and all that follows is a dream. The Boy Niven incident, Hooper finding the "two tramps"—it is all based on the symbolism of dreams, not reality. The problem of Mrs. Bathurst getting to South Africa evaporates; anything can happen in a dream. However, we are told three times that she has a "blindish look" in her eyes—the connection between women and blindness dating back to Kipling's days at the hands of Mrs. Holloway.

Second, by calling the reader's attention to the word "tramp" he is of course telling us he is using it with different meaning; she is a woman, loving and therefore dangerous, who attracts a man who is helpless and guilty.*

When Kipling was four years old, his mother gave birth to a boy who died in a day or so—it was the hot season. We have seen how Kipling wrote of the imminence of infantile death in India in "The Story of Muhammad Din," "Without Benefit of Clergy," "The Story of the Gadsbys," and, in "Nursery Rhymes for Little Anglo-Indians," where he wrote of his brother's death. He also alluded to this, unconsciously, when he said there were "no casualties" at the time of his son's birth. Now in this story, Vickery says, "I am *not* a murderer because my lawful wife died in childbed" and he can therefore pursue Mrs. Bathurst (just as Wolcott's death, which Kipling heard of, perhaps in Australia, freed him to pursue Carrie). A child of four whose infant brother dies tends to blame, not some abstraction called "the weather," but the mother—she didn't deliver the baby as she should have. She doesn't want to cause the death, and would rather die herself (as stated above), but the baby died. Vickery is said to look like a stillborn fetus—"Those things in bottles in those herbalistic shops at Plymouth—preserved in spirits of wine. White an' crumply things—previous to birth as you might say." Mrs. Bathurst killed Vickery just as—to a child's mind—his mother killed Kipling's brother.

To return to the story, Hooper and his man find the bodies, struck by lightning and turned to solid charcoal, in the positions they were in when alive. Hooper can see the false teeth of the standing figure and the ashes of his tattoo marks. He takes the false teeth as a souvenir. The charcoal corpses fall to pieces as they bury them, but he sees the identifying tattoos looking the way "writing shows up white on a burned letter." (Black to white, this time.)

In this remarkable story Kipling tells of love being closely allied to hate; of how, as Edmund Wilson put it, only a man who has deeply loved a woman can become the person who most bitterly hates her.

---

*I quite agree with Crook[31] and Lisa A. F. Lewis[32] that the Boy Niven episode represents a homosexual encounter. The sailors Niven has "lured" were "very young an' very curious" and "lovin' an' trustful to a degree" (strange words for rough sailors to describe their relation to a boy) and when they all return, the authorities ignore the sailors' claim that they were led astray by Niven; these commanding officers say that *they* were guilty of deceiving *him*.

265

People who say of their marriages "We never had an angry word in all those years" are describing, not a good relationship, but a bad one. Marriage should be passionate, Kipling is telling us, as passionate as the love he felt toward his *ayah*, as passionate as the hate he felt toward Mrs. Holloway. Kipling further tells us that maybe his marriage to Carrie seemed to other people to be an unhealthy one; it suited them down to the ground.

In the third of the four stories, "They," Kipling describes how he drove his car through some hills and trees that formed a tunnel until he came upon a beautiful Elizabethan house. He sees two children in an upper window and he hears another one playing near a fountain. A woman comes out of the house and talks to him; he sees that she is blind. They talk about the children, and Kipling confides in her that he had a child who died. At her request, he drives the car the length of a stone wall and back again so that the children can see it. Again, he hears them, but they seem very shy and will not come out and take a ride in the car. Kipling and the woman talk about dreaming, and he says that he has "never seen the faces of my dead [i.e., Josephine] in any dream."[33] She replies, "Then it must be as bad as being blind." He leaves, and a butler, Madden, shows him to the nearest crossroads.

A month or two later he returns, and the car breaks down close to the house. He hears the children steal up, and spreads out a glittering array of tools to entice them closer. Again, the woman—her name is Miss Florence—comes and talks to him as he fixes the car, and gradually the children come nearer out of the woods; he can see them out of the corner of his eye. She speaks of suffering from the remarks of others, saying, "We blindies have only one skin, I think. Everything outside hits straight at our souls." They talk further, and she makes the puzzling remark that it is "curious" that he "[doesn't] understand."

An upset neighbor comes, saying her grandchild has become ill, and Kipling and Madden use the car to get a doctor from some miles away. Madden remarks that if he had had a car when his daughter "took sick, she wouldn't have died." He says, "She'd have been close on ten now."

Two months later, in early autumn, he comes again. A wet and foggy day makes the house even more mysterious. She invites him into its lovely interior. Miss Florence shows him around the upstairs rooms full of children's toys; he hears chuckles and the patter of feet, but can hardly see the children in the twilight. They come downstairs and have tea by the light of the fire, and he finally sees the children in the shadows behind a leather screen. He sits near the screen, while Miss Florence talks to a tenant farmer, who seems curiously terrified at being in the house. Kipling puts his hands behind his chair, still hoping to meet the children. He feels his hand taken in the soft hands of a child and is about to turn and make her acquaintance when the center of his palm is kissed. His daughter Josephine used to kiss his hand this way, and Kipling would close his fingers about the kiss as if to hold it. It was "a fragment of old secret code devised very long ago." He goes on, "Then I knew. And it was as though I had known from the first day when I looked across the lawn at the high window. I knew and I was content." When Kipling revised the story for book form, always careful to avoid any personal reference, he changed the "old secret code" to "mute code," and omitted the last sentence, "I knew and I was content."

He realizes that the house is a sort of Limbo for children who have died but are not quite ready to go to heaven, presided over by the loving Miss Florence, who loves them all the more because she has "neither borne nor lost" children herself. When she tells Kipling this, he says, "Be very glad then." Once Kipling wrote "Ted" Hill and used the same words, telling her she should be glad that she had no children, since she would never have to face the terrible tragedy of losing one. Kipling tells Miss Florence that it is right that she, burdened with her blindness, lovingly cares for these ghosts of dead children, but that for himself "it would be wrong." He must accept his loss.

His agony over Josephine's death found an outlet in this story. He began writing it precisely five years after the date of her illness. Kipling tells the woman how the death of his own child has led to his loving other children all the more, and the butler, Madden, tells how his daughter passed away not, as in Josephine's case, from pneumonia, but from "croup." If Josephine had lived, she would have been just the age of Madden's daughter, "close on ten now." Throughout the story, Kipling keeps almost seeing the children in darkened rooms, in doorways and behind bushes in the garden. One is reminded of his father's letter to a friend about how hard it was for Kipling and Carrie to return to The Elms after Josephine's death:

The house and garden are full of the lost child and poor Rud told his mother how he saw her when a door opened, when a space was vacant at table, coming out of every green dark corner of the garden, radiant—and heartbreaking.[34]

Josephine was always linked in Kipling's mind with America; tender feelings for the America where she was born, and bitter feelings for the America where she died. Although, when he lived in Vermont, Kipling for a time had many positive feelings about the United States, at heart he always felt he belonged in England—or in India. Josephine's death put the final seal on any warmth he may have felt toward America; he never returned to the United States after leaving in 1899, and he became increasingly critical toward America in subsequent years. More and more he turned to a deep love of England and of her past. Any mention of things American became rare in his works. In this story about Josephine's death, we find some references to America that do not appear in his stories written around the same time. On the first page, when driving his car, he goes past "that precise hamlet which stands godmother to the capital of the United States."[35] The second time Kipling goes to the house, he tells Miss Florence that one of the children has been shyly hiding and "watching me like a red Indian." As recounted in "The Tabu Tale," Kipling used to play Indian games with Josephine back in Vermont.

The traumatic years at Mrs. Holloway's left him with lifelong scars even though, unlike his sister, he had the soul-saving advantage of his five happy years before that in India. But these terrible experiences were an asset, not a liability, for him as a writer. He suffered terrifying and confusing losses in childhood. To make up for these he turned to his remarkable ability to create imagery by his writing. Now he could call into being new people, new relationships, whole new worlds that could compensate for the deprivations of his early years. His books have even achieved immortality and in this sense have overcome the forces of loss and death. As we have seen, in what he wrote there appear the feelings of confusion (Am I white or Asiatic?) and fear (Am I going blind?) that he experienced as a child. Writing gave him a way to cope with these questions, as outlined in the Loss-Restoration Principle described in the preface of this book.

In a similar way, tragedies he suffered as an adult were also woven into stories. In "They" and in "The Gardner" (to be discussed later) he wrote about the deaths of two of his three children. In creating, as it were, alternatives to his own losses, he could find some answers to the questions that haunted him—How can I endure life without my child? Why did this have to happen to me? How can I make any sense out of this?—and was able to conclude, "I knew and I was content."

Within a day or two after finishing "They," Kipling was hard at work at a new subject. Turning away from Josephine's death, he began to write in a new genre, one as different as possible—science fiction, perhaps more popular ninety years ago than is generally realized. His story, "With the Night Mail," is set in the year 2000, and describes a transatlantic flight of an airship going at the then-unimaginable speed of two hundred knots. An unimpressive story, it usually merely received mention as the precursor of a much more imaginative tale written three years later, "As Easy as A.B.C." I describe it here because both stories reveal something of Kipling's old pro- and anti-America feelings, so snarled, so contradictory, so full of his old question, "Where is home?"

At first glance, the story seems entirely anti-American. In crossing the Atlantic, the airship goes from London to Quebec—not the more usual New York or Boston. As it approaches North America, other aircraft of various nations are seen and described—but just one from the United States. The only other reference to America, so pointedly ignored, comes in a section after the story, where Kipling gives notices and advertisements from a flying magazine of the year 2000. The Aerial Board of Control has grounded three pilots for "obstruction and quitting levels";[36] two of the three lawless ones are Americans.

Another notice in the same post-story section reveals Kipling's old enmity toward democratic government. England was of course a democracy, but deep in his bones Kipling's basic trust was in the centralized authority he had known in India, where the all-wise district officer had charge of everyone beneath him. The notice explains that, as of 2000, Crete was until recently "the sole surviving European repository of 'autonomous institutions,' 'local self-government,' and the rest of the archaic lumber devised in the past for the confusion of human affairs." Tourists flocked to be amused by the "annual pageants of Parliaments, Boards, Municipal Councils, etc." All this changed, however; the A.B.C. (the Aerial Board of Control) took over "the administration of

Crete on normal lines; and tourists must go elsewhere to witness the 'debates,' 'resolutions,' and 'popular movements' of the old days."

"With the Night Mail" has distinct connections with *Captains Courageous*. There is the same wealth of detail, the same fascination with the extreme competence of the men. There is even an encounter with an "ancient, aluminum-patched, twin-screw of the dingiest" reminiscent of Abishai's old craft. The aircraft captain threatens to have her towed "stern first to Disko," the island after which Disko Troop told of being named. Later, they fly over a hospital boat, and hear in the distance the patients singing a morning hymn, rather as Harvey heard the crew of the Frenchman sing after one of their shipmates had died in a storm. Kipling's old mixture of feelings come out; along with his avoiding mentioning America, and portraying American pilots as careless and uncivilized, he has some unconscious allusions to *Captains Courageous*, the one book where he spoke positively of the United States.

One wishes we knew more about Kipling's relationship with his parents in those years after his father's retirement. The general picture is that they settled down in Tisbury, where he visited them from time to time and conferred with his father about poetry or prose he was working on. Further details are somewhat obscure. It is known that if Alice Kipling was content to lead a rather isolated life in the country, Lockwood Kipling was not. He greatly enjoyed travel—even more than his son did—and Alice Kipling just as greatly disliked it. He wrote a friend, "I have a fidgetty craving for society, for somebody fresh to talk to."[37] When Kipling lived in America, Lockwood—but not Alice—crossed the Atlantic to visit him. And in January of 1898 only "The Pater" accompanied the Kiplings on their first trip to South Africa. At the end of that year Trix's mental illness became serious and she had to be placed in her mother's care. In 1899, after Kipling's near-death in New York, it was Lockwood who came over to America, stayed with them for a time, and then helped the family return to Europe—even if Alice had wanted to come, caring for Trix would have prevented it. Later in the same year, Lockwood also joined the Kiplings when Andrew Carnegie generously loaned them his home in Scotland during Kipling's convalescence from pneumonia.

When speaking of these years in his autobiography Kipling repeatedly praised his father's wisdom and advice, but there is never a word about his mother. Partly this is because his father, an artist and something of a writer himself, was more involved with Kipling's work and would naturally be mentioned more often. But I think it likely that Kipling could never feel wholly at ease with his mother and was always a little afraid of her. In trying to cope with how his parents could have left him and his sister, when children, with complete strangers, I would surmise that he blamed his opinionated, no-nonsense mother rather than his gentle, kind father, whom he saw more as a victim, caught in the middle of a disastrous situation, just as he viewed the sympathetic Mr. Holloway.

In 1904, Kipling wrote an abbreviated version of *A Midsummer Night's Dream* for his two children to act out. John played the part of Puck and, with a paper donkey's head on, Bottom; in addition he mastered the lines for three fairies. Elsie, with a wreath of columbines, was Titania. They rehearsed their parts over and over again with their loving but careful father until they could run through the play without a mistake. The place they chose for the play was a grassy rise that led away from the brook, called "Pook's Hill." From this came Kipling's "Puck" stories, which were enormously popular in the early years of this century. A brother and sister, Dan and Una, have a spell cast on them by a fairy called Puck and are taken back to Viking times, or Norman times, or Roman times, in England—and, in two interesting stories, to America—where they hear tales told by the actual participants. And as the *Just So Stories* were told to Josephine in Vermont or, after she died, with her in mind, so the 'Puck' stories were for John and Elsie, the "Dan" and "Una" in the tales. The mischievous little storyteller who makes it all possible, Puck, the small person who lives by his wits, like Limmershin, like the 'Stute Fish, like the Kolokolo bird, like Rikki-tikki-tavi, of course again suggests Kipling's view of himself.

The "Puck" stories are in two books. The first, *Puck of Pook's Hill*, contains stories told to John and Elsie when they were about eight and nine. The second, *Rewards and Fairies*, came out when they were close to thirteen and fourteen. It would be interesting if the stories told to the children corresponded in content with episodes in Kipling's own childhood when he was the same age; that is, if the first book had stories of cruelty inflicted by women (Mrs. Holloway) and the second violence at the hands of men (*Stalky & Co.*). But there is no pattern this specific;

Kipling and Carrie

rather, we see Kipling's lifelong preoccupations—his confusion about his mother, his fear of women, his bent toward violence—all now set in stories in which he ecstatically praised the sense of history, so solid, so reassuring, evoked by the English countryside. At last he felt—he told himself—that he had really found a place he could call home. And yet, his praise of Sussex, his delving deep into its history, is a little shrill and overstated, as if he "doth protest too much." Perhaps it is no accident that several of the "Puck" stories, full of praise of England's history, were written in South Africa, when the Kiplings continued to go to Woolsack every winter, and we have the slightly odd picture of Kipling looking up descriptions of medieval England in the Cape Town library.

But even if the "Puck" stories did not quite let him feel he was at last putting down roots in Sussex, they are memorable in their own right. One story, "The Wrong Thing," gives us a picture of John Kipling; the next, "Marklake Witches," one of Elsie, who is shown as a demanding, hostile person, somewhat like her mother. The three stories of Parnesius, a Roman army officer, "A Centurion of the Thirtieth," "On the Great Wall," and "The Winged Hats," are all successful. His deep sense of honor, and devotion to duty, were key parts of Victorian thinking more than of Roman.

Other successful stories are "Weland's Sword" and "The Knights of the Joyous Venture." The verses that accompany the "Puck" series are memorable, especially "Puck's Song" and "A Charm." The latter comes before "Cold Iron," which is set first in the book—always an important indication of Kipling's feelings about the piece, and indeed he described two night-scenes in it as "the best in that kind I have ever made."[38] It is an excellent story marred by a weak ending. A boy, brought up by Puck, bears a curse: whenever he first encounters iron, that piece of metal will determine his life. If he should pick up an iron-bound book, he would become a scholar; if a sword, he would end up as a knight. What he does pick up, and fastens around his own neck, is the iron collar of a slave. Kipling seemingly then said to himself, "Now, how am I going to end *this* story?" and does so in a hasty fashion.

"And what happened to him?" asked Dan.

"When morning came, Cold Iron was master of him and his fortune, and he went to work among folk in housen. Presently he came across a maid like-

273

minded with himself, and they were wedded, and had bushels of children, as the saying is. Perhaps you'll meet some of his breed, this year."[39]

Hardly a satisfactory ending! He's a slave, but a happy slave?

Kipling's old confusion about origins, and his fear of women, can be seen in several stories, but most clearly in "The Knife and the Naked Chalk."

Dan and Una are out on the bare downs, and fall asleep under a magic spell while talking to an old shepherd. Puck appears with a prehistoric man who is making a flint arrowhead. He is carrying an iron knife, which he says was made by the "Children of the Night."[40] When asked what it cost him, he puts his finger to his cheek; his right eye is gone. He tells how he belonged to the People of the Worked Flint, "the one son of the Priestess." When he was young, their tribe was tormented by attacks from wolves that preyed on their sheep and even the tribesmen as well, and could not be driven off by their weak bows and brittle flint arrowheads.

One day, he saw a man from a different tribe, the Children of the Night, being chased by three wolves, but he easily killed one and drove off the other two with an iron knife. The man who tells the tale describes how he wanted to get knives like this for his tribe, but feared the Children of the Night would "change [his] spirit." He told his mother, the Priestess, "I go away to find a thing for the people, but I do not know whether I shall return in my own shape." She answered, "whether you live or die, or are made different, I am your mother." Fearfully he went into the forest and found the tribe called the Children of the Night hammering their iron knives. "They were cruel. They asked me many questions which they would never allow me to answer. They changed my words between my teeth till I wept."*

He was then taken to their Priestess. He offered to trade meat, milk, and wool from his tribe for some iron knives from theirs. She replied that their "God says that if you have come for the sake of your people you will give him your right eye to be put out" and the exchange can take place: otherwise, not. "I said, 'Be quick, then!' With her knife

---

*Compare with Kipling's accounts of the "torture" at Mrs. Holloway's—"If you cross-examine a child of seven or eight on his day's doings (specially when he wants to go to sleep), he will contradict himself very satisfactorily."

heated in the flame she put out my right eye. She herself did it. I am the son of a Priestess. She was a Priestess." His eye healed, they agreed to the trade, and showed him how to make the iron knives. He returned to his own tribe, and showed them the new knife; all the wolves fled before it. The tribesmen, however, and even his own mother, said, "This is the work of a God." The next day he led them to the edge of the forest where they exchanged their goods for the knives.

> Their Priestess called to me and said, "How is it with your people?" I said, "Their hearts are changed. I cannot see their hearts as I used to." She said, "That is because you have only one eye. Come to me and I will be both of your eyes." But I said, "I must show my people how to use their knives against The Beast, as you showed me how to use my knife." I said this because the Magic Knife does not balance like the flint. She said, "What you have done, you have done for the sake of a woman, and not for the sake of your people." I asked of her, "Then why did your God accept my right eye, and why are you so angry?" She answered, "Because any man can lie to a God, but no man can lie to a woman."

He returned with his tribe, but they treated him like a god. They avoided stepping in his shadow, and even his mother tried to kneel in front of him. When he got angry, she said, "'Only a God would have spoken to me thus, a Priestess. A man would have feared the punishment of the Gods.' I looked at her and laughed. I could not stop my unhappy laughing." He fell in a faint ("my eye darkened"), and Puck asks, "And your wise mother?"

> *She* knew. As soon as I dropped she knew. When my spirit came back I heard her whisper on my ear, "Whether you live or die, or are made different, I am your Mother." . . . Neither of us wished to lose the other. There is only the one Mother for the one son.

The story ends, like all the others, with Puck lifting the magic spell from Dan and Una, who return to their present-day lives.

When Kipling writes, "There is only the one Mother for the one son," he is of course attempting again to straighten out his unconscious feeling that he had two mothers—a loving Asiatic one and a castrating white one who, in the story, puts out his eye. This act is accompanied with the words, "I am the son of a Priestess. She was a Priestess." Unconsciously, he is saying, "She was my mother, the Priestess." All his

275

life, Kipling struggled with the question: "My parents deserted me in Mrs. Holloway's house. How could they ever do such a thing?"

Kipling's childhood experience left him with an extreme feeling of vulnerability, and an insistence on absolute privacy.* His refusal of the post of Poet Laureate has been mentioned. He would not join any literary or artistic society; he never in his life wrote a review or allowed to be published any comment or opinion of another writer's work. When Edmund Gosse and others formed the British Academy and entreated him to be one of the original members, he encouraged their plan but refused to join. He had even turned down all offers of honorary degrees (with the exception of McGill in 1899), but in 1907 he relented, accepting degrees from Oxford and Cambridge, and planned to cross the Atlantic to receive a second one from McGill. He agreed to give a series of talks at six Canadian cities, the only time in his life he undertook a lecture tour. Carrie could see her mother, and Kipling, who was becoming increasingly disillusioned with events in South Africa after the Boer War, was interested in a look at the Canadian political scene.

Kipling's "magic land" of India was always on his mind. He kept doggedly insisting that things be as they had been in his enchanting childhood. When they would not, he would turn to a variety of alternative solutions and rationalizations to explain away this disappointment. Then some new issue would present itself and the process would begin again. In the present case, after the Boer War, Kipling wrote that British deficiencies would lead to a sober self-appraisal and great improvement in the military ("a blessing in disguise," as it were). Another idea he put forward was that after the hostilities British immigrants would settle down peacefully, work for their Boer masters. Then, perhaps with relief, he turned his attention to Canada.

In September 1907 Kipling and Carrie crossed the Atlantic. The *New York Times* noted their arrival at Quebec and reported the passengers had listened with "keen appreciation"[41] to an address Kipling gave the evening before on the ship. Well might they be appreciative; ever vigilant

---

*Max Beerbohm's opinion of those who viewed Kipling's obsession with privacy as being neurotic was to state that any sensitive person is touchy about his personal privacy. Again, we can merely ask if Kipling's "sensitive" contemporaries, such as D. H. Lawrence, Robert Louis Stevenson, or A. Conan Doyle, showed these feelings about privacy.

about privacy, Kipling very rarely did this sort of thing. "Mr. and Mrs. Kipling," the newspaper went on, immediately left for Montreal "by special train." Carrie, unlike her husband, always went for the red-carpet treatment. That afternoon they arrived at Montreal, to be welcomed by Mrs. Wolcott Balestier (Carrie's mother, up from Brattleboro). America, besides having other unpleasant memories, was now associated in Kipling's mind with the death of his oldest daughter Josephine, and he resolved not to set foot across the border.

Accounts of his trip were published as "Letters to the Family" and he said of them in a letter of 1908 to Lord Milner: "I write them with a single loving wish to annoy the Radicals in England. . . . I have just come out of a trough of blank bloody pessimism—a cold reasoned despair of the Republic. . . . "[42] (He also wrote, in the same letter, of his dislike of telephones, saying "I find it interferes with the peristaltic process, and Canada is a constipating land.") On this trip, except for a few biting remarks, he studiously ignored the United States. But in his autobiography, written nearly thirty years later, he said in recollecting the tour:

> Always the marvel—to which the Canadians seemed insensible—was that one side of an imaginary line should be Safety, Law, Honour, and Obedience, and on the other frank, brutal decivilization; and that, despite this, Canada should be impressed by any aspect whatever of the United States.[43]

Kipling said as little as possible to the reporters, and even deliberately misled them. (He always seemed unable to remember that he himself had once been a reporter.) The *New York Times* man continued, saying that "In the course of a brief conversation" (perhaps quite an understatement), Kipling said he expected to stay in Montreal "for a couple of weeks."[44] (He planned to stay, and did stay, for three days.) After this he was to go to the Pacific Coast and then return to Eastern Canada, "but after that his plans were undecided." Not a word about the lectures, the purpose of the whole trip. A few days later, in British Columbia, the reporters caught up with him with a quotation about his racist philosophy. Canada, he said, should aid in the immigration of "people of British stock."[45] This was a "desired reinforcement" as opposed to the "undesirable rush of races from whose instincts you are separated by thousands of years." (While we are repelled by any such a notion, we might think this sort of thing was commonly believed at the time, and must be judged in that light. It is for just this reason that the speech should be noted, for the *New York Times* devoted almost all of its space to these racist statements: they were not, therefore, commonly said and unworthy of attention.) It was not his beliefs, primarily, that attracted interest; it was how he stated them—so clearly and openly. In those days it was perhaps more common to conceal feelings on touchy issues.

Kipling was referring here to the immigration of Central and Eastern Europeans. By contrast—and not at all logically—he was in favor of an influx of Asians—Chinese and, especially, Indians, although they obviously would also be of totally different cultures. Their "instincts" would not be "separated by thousands of years"; they would have nothing whatsoever in common! How did he drift into this illogical statement? The answer, of course, is that he felt that Indians, being British subjects, were different, a mixture of white and Asian, as he unconsciously felt himself to be, and therefore superior.

The *New York Times* column ended by saying, "Mr. Kipling will return to England without visiting the United States on his present trip."

Such a terse statement only hints at the strong feelings America kindled in Kipling. His burning feelings of hostility, in this case directed at America, are shown in a story, "As Easy as A.B.C.," the first drafts of which he wrote that year. The story is one of the more savage things he ever produced in his life. His basic political orientation, one must always remember, was that of the English civil servant administering his area of India. As Kipling saw it, the population under his rule was childlike, incapable of organization or self-direction. Anyone who spoke up for self-rule or discussion was a troublemaker who must be removed as rapidly as possible by the all-wise administrator.

The important point is not that these ideas were formed by his childhood and youth in India; plenty of other conservative Anglo-Indians were saying the same thing. What is significant is that being snatched away from India and put in the clutches of Mrs. Holloway gave Kipling a streak of savagery and, indeed, passivity that is reflected in his life and writings. What is striking is not what he is saying but how he says it, and how his childhood experiences interfere with the literary quality of what he wrote. The strain of violence, of the harassed "good guys" who inflict an even more savage punishment on the "bad guys", recurs once more. Although intrusive and occasionally unpleasant, this savage streak is usually redeemed by Kipling's sense of artistry and his synthesis of the elements in a story.

"With the Night Mail" revealed indirectly some of Kipling's old love of America. But its sequel, "As Easy as A.B.C.," though savagely anti-American, is one of Kipling's better science fiction stories, which he marked as important by setting it first in the book.

The world, tired of endless bickering between nations and political compromises within nations, in the year 2065 is controlled by an international Aerial Board of Control. (It is very close to the "Colonial Representatives of Imperial Parliament" imagined by Kipling's old hero, Cecil Rhodes.) With no nationalistic strivings, war simply ceases as a choice of action. Scientific advances lead to control of the birth rate, so that problems of overpopulation no longer exist, and the span of human life is greatly increased. Any deviation from the Board's edicts, however, is swiftly and firmly corrected—one is reminded of the Viceroy and his chain of command controlling all of India.

Some people in northern Illinois (referred to as "Serviles," very much like the "proles" in Orwell's *1984*) have been engaging in "crowd-making and invasion of privacy."[46] This minority of agitators "who can't live without listening to themselves" begin to gather near a statue of "the Nigger in Flames." They want to "go back to the old Voodoo business of voting with papers and wooden boxes, and word-drunk people and printed formulas, and news-sheets!" A fleet of aircraft is dispatched by the Board to put down this intolerable insurrection; an international committee in the leading aircraft will only call in the others if necessary. After a brief encounter with a woman in a farmhouse who immobilizes them with electricity and laughs at them, they go on to hover over Chicago and subdue the entire population to helplessness, using piercing beams of light and high-pitched sound waves. (It should be noted that the light temporarily blinds the victims.) The troublemakers are released from "the water-tower" where they have been locked up lest the rest of the aroused and indignant populace kill them. One of them, says Kipling:

> . . . urged us to arise in our might, burst our prison doors and break our fetters (all metaphors, by the way, were of the most medieval). Next he

demanded that every matter of daily life, including most of the physical functions, should be submitted for decision at any time of the week, month, or year to, I gathered, anybody who happened to be passing by or residing within a certain radius, and that everybody should forthwith abandon his concerns to settle the matter, first by Crowd-making, next by talking to the Crowds made, and lastly by describing crosses on pieces of paper, which rubbish should later be counted with certain mystic ceremonies and oaths. Out of this amazing play, he assured us, would automatically arise a higher, nobler, and kinder world, based—he demonstrated this with the awful lucidity of the insane—on the sanctity of the Crowd and the villainy of the single person.

The Board members decide to remove the ten or twelve people guilty of "crowd-making" before the others—particularly the women—kill them. One woman says, "We women don't want our children given to Crowds. It must be an inherited instinct. Crowds make troubles. They bring back the Old Days. Hate, fear, blackmail, publicity." Before taking the prisoners on board, however, they decide to "wipe out that Statue" and the Mayor of Chicago, who has been helping them, orders an assistant to "Slag the Nigger before you go on to fuse the Market."

They take the twelve people on board, agree to send back other airships for their relatives and children, and set off for the return flight to London. Wondering what to do with the troublemakers—one person suggests "Open[ing] the bilge-doors" and letting them drop to earth— they hit on another idea and radio ahead to a theatrical producer in London. He is ecstatic with the idea of the captives putting on a continuous show of themselves.

> They weep, too. . . . Not a spark of shame or reticence in the entire installation. . . . They can get word-drunk, and make Crowds, and invade privacy in a genuine old-fashioned way; and they'll do the voting trick as often as you ask 'em a question.

Kipling presents a grim view of the future. Science conquers disease but all human activity is made secondary to transportation and its allied interests. Any gathering or discussion interferes with the airships and must be instantly stopped.

Being an honored visitor to Canada, with the United States in view just over the border, brought back to Kipling memories of his public humiliation with Beatty Balestier and, on his later visit, the death of his oldest and favorite child, Josephine. The fury he avoided revealing in public still burned within. Out comes a story where the Board has absolute rule over all the earth; people who "make Crowds" or "invade privacy"—never in his adult life was his privacy invaded as it had been at Brattleboro—or otherwise stray from Kipling's ideal of efficient silence and reserve can be snatched away, taken to England, and laughed at by the public like captured monkeys.

Other elements we have seen before return again. In a story that clearly reveals Kipling's childhood fury, the men of the airship are first imprisoned by a woman who laughs "mercilessly"; later one of the Board men, upset at what they are doing, is held by one of the other men, ". . . and I think he rocked him in his arms," and other incidents occur to show again Kipling's connecting women with violence.

And yet, two years later, his old warm feelings for America are seen in "Brother Square-Toes," a story about George Washington, in the "kindly, softly country there, back of Philadelphia among the German towns, Lancaster way."[47] Again, we can see that Kipling's anti-American feelings come out when he talks of cities and masses of people; his love of America when he speaks of the countryside, individuals, and small groups. The story comes from *Rewards and Fairies*, the second book of the "Puck" stories. In it Dan and Una, magically transported back to an earlier time in history, hear the tale of two Seneca Indians, Cornplanter* and Red Jacket, who go to talk with George Washington and observe his adept handling of the French. Each story is preceded and followed by a related poem. The one before "Brother Square-Toes" begins, "If you're off to Philadelphia in the morning" and brings to mind the delightful weeks Kipling spent with "Ted" Hill and her family in Beaver, Pennsylvania, in August and September of 1889. The poem after the story is "If—", one of Kipling's best-known:

---

*Cornplanter, a remarkable Seneca chief, was reputedly born in 1730, did in fact meet Washington, and lived until 1836. Kipling loved American initiative and energy; beyond that, as a conservative Englishman, he admired our history, and the prominent Americans of his day, particularly those whose families reflected our past as a nation, such as Charles Eliot Norton of Harvard or President Theodore Roosevelt. It was, perhaps, this second aspect that brought a man like Cornplanter to his attention.

If you can keep your head when all about you
Are losing theirs and blaming it on you;
If you can trust yourself when all men doubt you,
But make allowance for their doubting too:
If you can wait and not be tired by waiting,
Or being lied about, don't deal in lies,
Or being hated, don't give way to hating,
And yet don't look too good, nor talk too wise;
If you can dream—and not make dreams your master;
If you can think—and not make thoughts your aim,
If you can meet with Triumph and Disaster
And treat those two impostors just the same:
If you can bear to hear the truth you've spoken
Twisted by knaves to make a trap for fools,
Or watch the things you gave your life to, broken,
And stoop and build 'em up with worn-out tools;
. . . .
If you can talk with crowds and keep your virtue,
Or walk with Kings—nor lose the common touch,
If neither foes nor loving friends can hurt you,
If all men count with you, but none too much:
If you can fill the unforgiving minute
With sixty seconds' worth of distance run,
Yours is the Earth and everything that's in it,
And—which is more—you'll be a Man, my son!

As all biographers have duly noted, Kipling in his autobiography states that the lines refer to the statesman Jameson, a close friend throughout the winters the Kiplings spent in South Africa. But Kipling's autobiography is mainly devoted to self-concealment; as pointed out before, he never mentions Mrs. Hill or Wolcott Balestier, or even, by name, his own wife! In a volume in which, in effect, he says, "I won't tell you about this or this or this; I'm concealing as much as possible," we have a right to doubt him when he says, "Now I *do* tell you about this; these lines refer to Jameson." All the other verses, in Kipling's careful manner, refer to the stories that come between them;* it is not like Kipling to make exceptions. The poem "If—" refers to George Washington. Jameson may well have been on Kipling's mind—he visited the Kiplings a few months before the poem was written—but if all the other

---

*J.M.S. Tompkins, in discussing Kipling's putting descriptive poems before and after his stories, correctly notes, "In *Puck of Pook's Hill* some of the stories are supported on both sides by verses, and in *Rewards and Fairies* all of them are."[48] "Brother Square-Toes" is in the latter volume.

verses refer to the stories, why doesn't this one as well? And it would be just like Kipling to attempt to conceal his old warm feelings for America and her history.

A discussion of *Rewards and Fairies* leads to examining a curious and unique theme that appears in a story in this book and reappears in all of Kipling's work. It might be summarized as "a man (or men) made helpless with laughter." This often happens to the onlooker, who is telling the tale, but sometimes two or even more men are involved. Women are invariably excluded. The man (or men) begins roaring with laughter, weeping, gasping for breath, rolling on the floor—helpless with mirth.

In most cases, this outpouring forms the end of the story but sometimes just accompanies it, the ending being fashioned in some other way. An important point is that these paroxysms of laughter are appropriate as part of a humorous piece, like "In Ambush," one of the *Stalky* stories, or "Beauty Spots," one of Kipling's farces, written thirty years later. Here there are a series of increasingly comical events, culminating in the person or persons collapsing in unrestrained mirth. The reader may not feel it is a successful ending, but at least it is an understandable one. In the stories referred to, it is not. The episode of hysteria—Kipling used the word often—occurs after a tragedy, or an armed attack, or a supernatural event, in a way that seems out of place and, indeed, often spoils the story.

A story from *Rewards and Fairies*, "The Wrong Thing," for example, is about two craftsmen, Hal* and Benedetto. Hal is the more skilled of the two, and Benedetto is consumed with envy. Hal is rewarded by the King by being knighted, not for the excellence of his craftsmanship but because he saved the King from the loss of some money and from an argument with a woman. This is the last straw for Benedetto, who attacks Hal with a knife and says he is going to kill him. Hal tells the whole story leading up to his being knighted. Benedetto begins to laugh, and drops the knife; Hal begins laughing also; they both become helpless

---

*Kipling avoided using the name "Harry," that of the Devil Boy son of Mrs. Holloway. It does not occur applied to a single one of his major characters. In this story, and in another, "Hal o' the Draft," he lets Hal be called "Harry" a few times, but for the most part he carefully used variations of "Harry," like "'Arry"[49] in "The Wish House," and "Henry"[50] in "Their Lawful Occasions." "Harry" brought back too many memories.

with mirth. "When he began to roar and bay and whoop in the passage, I haled him out into the street, and there we leaned against the wall and had it all over again" (retold the story). Another man "laughed till he rolled on the new cold pavement."[51]

The following examples—not a complete list—are taken from the entire span of Kipling's work, a period of forty-five years. The first three are from *Plain Tales from the Hills*. In "A Germ Destroyer," when clouds of smoke fill the building, the Viceroy is "prostrate with laughter."[52] Dicky Hatt, from "In the Pride of His Youth," when a tragedy is resolved, "burst into laughter—a laughter he could not check."[53] When the subaltern in "Thrown Away" commits suicide, first Kipling and then the Major have a "laughing-fit."[54] In "A Conference of the Powers," an officer throws himself on an enemy in bed. Both became tangled in the mosquito net. Another officer, seeing this, "laugh[s] till [I] couldn't stand,"[55] and says, "If you'd seen 'em both tangled up together on the floor in one kicking cocoon, you'd have laughed for a week." After the curse has been lifted in "The Mark of the Beast," Strickland begins to laugh wildly. The narrator, too, "laughed and gasped and gurgled just as shamefully as Strickland."[56] In "Judson and the Empire," there is the "disgraceful spectacle of two men reeling with laughter on the quarter-deck of a gunboat."[57] The story "My Son's Wife" has Midmore laughing "till he can scarcely stand,"[58] and Mr. Sidney laughs "in roars." In the "Pyecroft" stories, to be discussed later, the onlooker (quite clearly Kipling) laughs until he is "long past even hysteria."[59] In "The Miracle of Saint Jubanus," at a church service, a man and two boys become entangled in an umbrella. "The central effect, Monsieur, was that of an undevout pagoda conducting a *pas de trois* in a sacred edifice"[60] while the congregation roars with laughter.

There are three interpretations that may explain why Kipling put in these bizarre and inappropriate scenes. First of all, they gave him a way to end a story—often a problem for him. In "The Wrong Thing," for example, how is he to end it? Hal and Benedetto shake hands and part friends? They leave and the hatred continues unchanged? Neither sounds satisfactory. Perhaps the guffaws of mirth simply provided him with an ending.

Second, Kipling loved a good laugh. Over and over one finds accounts of how he delighted in roaring with laughter, especially with children or a very few friends. (In a gathering of any size, this was not true; he tended to be much quieter, listening to the conversation and occasionally tossing in some question to keep things rolling.) In a memory from his childhood, he recalls staying with his Aunt Georgie for a month each year, that all-important escape from Mrs. Holloway's. There, at bedtime, he would lean over the bannister upstairs and "listen to the loveliest sound in the world—deep-voiced men laughing together over dinner."[61] Kipling, then, may be using the catharsis of a good hearty laugh to dispel any unpleasantness in the story he has just told.

Lastly, and most significantly, it suggests a male homosexual encounter. The intensity of the description—the men lose control, roar, weep, gasp for breath, gurgle, fall on the floor—gives this impression. Occasionally, Kipling uses words like "shameful" and "disgraceful" in describing these scenes that he might well have thought of in connection with homosexual acts. Women are carefully excluded; in "The First Letter," the men roar with laughter, but the women do not.

Probably all three aspects are involved, the last most importantly. When Kipling needed an end for a story, and wanted it to be pleasurable, his homosexual urges found expression in the wild scenes described.

From 1898 through 1908 the Kiplings spent every winter in South Africa, a trip they always eagerly anticipated. The voyage south, away from the grim English winter, and the delightful time spent at Woolsack were parts of an annual routine, all the more pleasant for being so familiar and unvarying. Kipling settled into a middle-aged life, with none of the shocks and ordeals of his childhood, and with a sense of security that found expression in numerous stories about the therapeutic stability of the beautiful Sussex countryside.

His daughter Elsie left her impressions of their trips south.

Every winter the family left for South Africa just before Christmas, accompanied by large, black, dome-topped trunks, boxes of books, two faithful maids and the children's governess.

Things went according to a fixed routine. First the experienced appraisal of the ship and passengers by the two children, then the unpacking and stowing away of their travelling possessions in the tiny cabins of those days, and then their hunt to discover if any of their numerous friends among the stewards and crew were in this particular ship. A "good trip" meant one on which several friends, from the captain downwards, happened to be on board. One special crony was a certain grizzled cabin steward, who could always be counted upon for escorted visits to the otherwise forbidden parts of the ship, as well as plates of dessert after the grown-ups' late dinner.

The first few days through the Bay were generally chilly and sea-sick misery. But once Madeira was passed the sun gathered strength daily, the twilights shortened as the semi-tropical nights shut down swiftly, and the first lifting of the Southern Cross above the horizon was eagerly looked for. It was all familiar, yet ever exciting.

R. K. always worked during these voyages, mostly in a tiny cabin opening on to the noisy promenade deck, but sometimes seated at a small folding table on the deck itself. He was quite oblivious to the noise and movement round him, and would pace the deck, come back to his writing pad for a few moments, and pace the deck again, just as if he had been in his own study. His fellow passengers interested him enormously and he invariably made many friends, specially with some young soldier or mining engineer just going out to start a career, or perhaps with a ship's officer. The delights of the captain's table were always courteously offered and as courteously declined, and the family had a small table just inside the door of the dining saloon.

R. K. was always quite unconscious of the interest that his presence aroused among his fellow-passengers. One chilly evening, going below to get his overcoat, he absent-mindedly put on the first thing that came to hand in his cabin, which happened to be a brown camel-hair dressing-gown. As he came on deck a young acquaintance diffidently drew his attention to the mistake; but R. K. simply remarked that the dressing-gown kept him very warm and that was what was needed! The young man went away muttering, "Fancy being the sort of man who can do a thing like that and not have it matter."

Often old friends were on board, Dr. Jameson, Abe Bailey, Baden-Powell, mining engineers, and many of the big men who were shaping the destiny of South Africa at that time; endless talks and deck pacing went on in their company. Often after tea and before bed-time his children would collect various small friends, and sit in an enraptured circle round him on the sun-warmed deck in some quiet corner while he told them stories.

The end of the three-weeks' voyage to Cape Town meant the joyful arrival at the lovely, small, single-storied, white house, set under the shadow of Table Mountain, which Cecil Rhodes had given to R. K. for his life. A wide veranda or stoop ran on two sides of it, and there was an open court in the centre on to which all the rooms opened. Huge oak and pine trees sheltered the house, and the garden tumbled down the hillside, ending in a vast view across flat country to the Drakenstein mountains. Myrtle and plumbago hedges, oleander and fig trees, wild cannas and arum lilies, roses and violets grew under the lazy eye of Johnston, the Malay gardener, while a hedge of banana plants gave the children the daily fun of hunting for an unsplit banana leaf, the finding of which unknown treasure was never accomplished.

After lunch a siesta was the custom of the house, and R. K. was often read to sleep by his small daughter. Careful pronunciation of words was insisted upon, until he was too sleepy to bother about it; but when a specially long or difficult word had to be dealt with, the ruthless, wide-awake child would rouse her father to ask how it should be pronounced!

At an early age the two children were taught a proper respect for the use of words, and an appreciation of poetry. Very often in the evenings R. K. would sit in the nursery, intoning rather than reciting poetry by the hour. Wordsworth, Longfellow, the Sagas of King Olaf, the *Lays of Ancient Rome*, *Percy's Reliques*, and the old Border ballads became so familiar to the two small and eager listeners that quotations from them became part of their everyday talk. Misquotations were frowned upon, and the careful learning of verse insisted upon. "The man took trouble to find the exact word to fit into the line; the least you can do is not to change it," was his point of view. A feeling of fury at misquotation remains with his daughter to this day, and when a certain official of the B.B.C. in quoting four lines of verse by R. K. on the air managed to make three mistakes, it was with difficulty that she refrained from angry protest.[62]

In 1902, however, Rhodes died; Lord Milner's plans for the reconstruction of South Africa ended when he returned to England in 1905, and the Liberals came into power. In 1906 the House of Commons voted to censure Lord Milner. Winston Churchill was prominently involved and this, together with his liberal policies, earned him Kipling's bitter and lifelong enmity. Churchill did not return the feelings; on the contrary, he said that Kipling had greatly influenced his life, and a case could be made for the claim that Kipling was his favorite author.[63]

With the self-government given them, the people voted Dr. Jameson out of office in 1907.* Rhodes' house was bought by a Liberal; the Kiplings felt themselves increasingly in disagreement with their neighbors. Then, too, John was getting to an age when he would be going off to boarding school, and could not take the leisurely midwinter vacation.

---

*It is striking, in view of Zimbabwe's (formerly Rhodesia's) recent state, that Kipling wrote a friend in 1907, after hearing of Jameson's defeat, "Remember that Rhodesia *must* be kept out of the federation and our ploy must be to develop Rhodesia as well as we can. It's the last loyal white colony."[64]

In 1908 the Kiplings sadly decided that they would never return to South Africa. Kipling must have felt that another "fire on the hearth" was burned out, that he had lost another "home." He was sure that inefficiency and dishonesty would soon set in. He wrote a friend that the handing over of a higher civilization to a lower was a heartbreaking job.

All these years "Trix" Fleming, Kipling's sister, had been under her parents' care in Tisbury. She had become completely psychotic in 1898; then improved and returned to India to join her husband in 1902; but some time later, upon his retirement, she had to return to her mother's care in England. Preoccupied with the occult, she believed in spiritualism and crystal-gazing. She was most at ease with her parents. After the First World War, she seemed calmer; now a widow, she lived in Edinburgh, and would often go to the zoo and talk to the animals in the Hindustani of her childhood. Outliving Kipling, she died in 1942.

She had her brother's facility for writing, reeling off a poem like this, after seeing a painting of St. George, as fast as she could write it:

> He lost his way at eventide
> And wandered where the paths divide
> He found a goblin by his side
> > A satyr child
> > Whose look was wild.
> The day drew on to eventide.
> Ah! Good St. George at eventide
> Choose not a goblin for thy guide,
> For things of terror may betide
> > Before moonrise
> > Beneath thine eyes;
> Go forth alone where paths divide.
> St. George knew well the goblin lied
> But yet he took him for his guide
> And on through shadows dappled pied
> > He led the Knight
> > At fall of night
> Until they reached the water side.[65]

And so on, for six more verses. The difference, of course, is that it is poor poetry. Artistic creations require both sensitivity and discipline; the poet may be struck by a painting, moved by it, let it evoke feelings in him, but when it comes to setting them down, he must put aside his emotions and possess the sense of order to sift through what he writes, weighing this phrase against that, filtering out the imperfect, so as to attempt to arrive at the essence of what he tries to communicate. Like many schizophrenics, Trix had all the sensitivity but none of the discipline.

In November of 1910 Kipling's mother, now aged seventy-three and suffering from heart trouble, died in Tisbury. As if in haste to follow her, Lockwood Kipling died two months later. Kipling's Aunt Georgie wrote that he loved his father so much he could even rejoice at his death, realizing how empty life would have been for him once his wife was gone. After the funeral service Kipling said to his "beloved Aunt" Georgie that he felt "the loneliest creature on God's earth today."[66]

One does not know how to interpret these statements. They may be more or less routine expressions of filial devotion, or actual feelings of agony at the death of a loved one. We do not know and never will know how Kipling really felt about the death of his parents. I think, however, that of the two, he was more upset at the loss of his father. Here was a warm and gentle person with whom he had shared numerous travels, a fellow-craftsman (to use Kipling's own term) who had worked closely with him on *Kim* and on such stories as "Hal o' the Draft." His mother, in so many ways her husband's opposite, was a charming but sharp-tongued person, with a mind as quick as a trap. Kipling had had a confusing series of mother-figures in his life, first his *ayah* and then Mrs. Holloway, and had only gotten to know his biological mother and father, slowly and cautiously, when he was just short of sixteen. He obviously developed an intimate and loving relationship with his father. But his childhood experiences with women, together with Alice Kipling's personality, which on occasion could be formidable, prevented his ever feeling truly close to her. And it should be noted that while Kipling's wife Carrie always delighted in Lockwood's company, she and Alice, two dominating people, avoided each other whenever possible. One can be quite sure that Kipling mourned his father's death more than his mother's.

About 1910 Kipling wrote "An Habitation Enforced" and "My Son's Wife," two stories with a common theme, that a troubled person can be helped by the calmness, the unchanging rural rituals, and the sense of history of the English countryside. In the first story, a wealthy

American, George Chapin, has a nervous breakdown and is sent with his wife Sophie on a trip to England to recover. They are shown a rundown Georgian mansion and buy it, gradually falling in love with the place and overcoming initial resistances—George speaks of "[doubling] the value of the place in six months"[67] and says "One could always sell it again" and Sophie accuses him of wanting to "lay out a Morristown [golf] links" on the farms. They learn the local customs with delight; where they had drifted apart in their relationships with each other they now find a new closeness between them. Sophie finds that her mother's family originally came from that very part of England, but—with something of Kipling's own feelings about privacy—she does not reveal this, but lets their neighbors find it out for themselves. They express their appreciation for her reserve and accept the Chapins wholeheartedly, in contrast to an even wealthier newcomer called Sangres, a Brazilian by birth,* who is socially "pushy" and unappreciative of the countryside.

In the second story, "My Son's Wife," this time it is an Englishman (though he has the very American name of Frankwell Midmore) who is leading a dissolute life and then inherits a house and some land. He too is uninterested at the beginning, wishing to sell the house as quickly as possible. Then the beauty of the country and the delight he finds in learning the local customs—mostly from Rhoda, an old family retainer who, he finds, was his nurse when he was a child—begin to appeal to him as they did to George and Sophie. When he first arrives, he hears a girl sing "about ships and flocks and grass"[68] as she passes his house in the dark, and later, after the emergency of a burst dam has been handled, he meets and falls in love with her, having found the poem and learned it himself. (In this detail, it is sort of an updated version of "The Brush-wood Boy.")

Both stories deal with Kipling's love of the English countryside, and its healing effects on the American couple and the troubled Englishman. It is the same comfort he felt when visiting England from America

---

*In 1904 Kipling wrote "With the Night Mail," which as previously stated has subtle pro- and anti-American touches in it. One of the latter was a listing of three reckless pilots; two were American, one Brazilian. Now in this story the offensive person, as opposed to the "good" Americans, is Brazilian again. I think it reflects Kipling's old conflicts about race ("Sangres" is Spanish— but not Portuguese—for "bloods"); one of the tenants refers to the Brazilian as "that nigger Sangres."

in 1894, more than fifteen years before, when he wrote, "A man could camp in any open field with more sense of home and security than the stateliest buildings of foreign cities could afford."[69] But it is also the attraction he felt for Vermont, where a snow scene was "beautiful beyond expression"[70] and where one is "set down to listen to the normal beat of [one's] own heart—a sound that very few men have heard,"[71] or, to repeat, how he felt when he returned to India when nearly sixteen— "My English years fell away, nor ever, I think, came back to full strength."[72] India was his real home—or was it England? or America? Where was home? And behind this question, as we have seen, lies "Who was my mother?"

For some years the suffragettes of England had been agitating for the franchise. The thought of women having an equal voice with men in national affairs, together with his life long feelings about them, can be seen in his poem, "The Female of the Species."

When the early Jesuit fathers preached to Hurons and Choctaws,
They prayed to be delivered from the vengeance of the squaws,
'Twas the women, not the warriors, turned
    those stark enthusiasts pale.
For the female of the species is more deadly than the male.

She can bring no more to living than the powers
    that make her great
As the Mother of the Infant and the Mistress of the Mate!
And when Babe and Man are lacking and she strides
    unclaimed to claim
Her right as femme (and baron), her equipment is the same.

Unprovoked and awful charges—even so the she-bear fights,
Speech that drips, corrodes, and poisons—even so
    the cobra bites,
Scientific vivisection of one nerve till it is raw
And the victim writhes in anguish—like the Jesuit
    with the squaw!

So it comes that Man the coward, when he gather to confer
With his fellow-braves in council, dare not leave
    a place for her
Where, at war with Life and Conscience, he uplifts
    his erring hands
To some God of Abstract Justice—which no woman understands.

And Man knows it! Knows, moreover, that the
    Woman that God gave him
Must command but may not govern—shall enthrall
    but not enslave him.
And *She* knows, because She warns him, and Her
    instincts never fail,
That the Female of Her Species is more deadly
    than the Male.[73]

Among the people offended by this poem was Kipling's daughter
Elsie, now seventeen. Indeed, some letters arrived threatening to burn
Bateman's to the ground—a threat that Kipling ignored but that caused
Carrie, a worrier, a great deal of concern.

The children had had governesses when young, but now they
needed tutoring for school, especially John, and more expert help was
needed. Miss Dorothy Ponton, an experienced multilingual teacher and
secretary, was hired and left this account of the prewar years with the
Kiplings:

At this time (1911) Rudyard Kipling was forty-five years of age, short, but
well-proportioned. He had a pronounced cleft in his chin and very dark,
bushy eyebrows, beneath which his blue eyes glowed through his spectacles. In the country he usually dressed in "plus-fours" with a remarkably
shabby cap, or a Trilby hat. After working in his study most of the morning, he often did a little gardening before lunch. He was also fond of fishing
and, in wet weather, usually donned leather gaiters and tramped across the
fields with Mrs. Kipling to inspect the farms on the estate. [In a similar
account, Elsie wrote, "'Farm walks' were often taken and while C. K.
discussed with the foreman ditches to be cleaned out, barns to be repaired
or crops to be sown, he stood by listening and only sometimes making a
suggestion."][74] Mrs. Kipling, in spite of a rather hard face, had a kindly
smile. She was between forty and fifty years of age, short and stout and had
very small feet. Her hair was almost white, and her eyes were grayish and
shrewd. Elsie, the daughter, was a well-developed girl of sixteen years with
nut-brown hair fastened loosely at the back with a black bow. Her dark
hazel eyes were bright and intelligent. She had been brought up simply and,
except for three months' holiday during the winter when her parents took
her abroad, saw little of society. John, a typical schoolboy of thirteen [ac-
tually fourteen], was dark and thin and wore glasses.

During the school holidays there were usually young visitors at "Bateman's." Mr. Kipling was fond of children and was adored by them, so they
had great times together. But there were moments when Mrs. Kipling found

them rather too boisterous and exacting. As soon as Elsie had settled down to her term's work, Mrs. Kipling asked me to give one hour's "holiday work" to the other children (Oliver Baldwin and his sister) before lunch, so that they might be kept quiet. The day when these lessons were to commence, Mr. Kipling took his young relatives mushrooming, and I met them hilariously carrying back the harvest in his hat. [75]

These were their days of peace before the nightmare of the war.

XIV

THE WAR

As the war clouds gathered, Kipling, curiously, was more concerned with Ireland, where civil war threatened, than with the Continent. He was an ardent backer of the Ulster Covenant, which pledged resistance against any attempt of the Catholic south to take control of the Protestant north. In May of 1914 he made a political speech, one of the few in his life, in support of the Conservatives and furiously attacking the Liberal leaders. When Kipling's hostility was unleashed, and expressed in his fanatical far-right-wing views, the results were startling. He made a personal attack on the Liberals, who, he said, were like fraudulent lawyers or swindlers, only out for what they could steal.[1] Newspapers quoted at length from this "wild outburst,"[2] as the *Manchester Guardian* described it. Even in those days of violent politics, Kipling's speech was seen as so extreme, so childish, and so unfair that it was an embarrassment, not to the hated Liberals, but to Kipling's own party, who did not invite him to speak again.

On August 4, 1914, World War I began; within six months there were air-raids on England and unrestricted submarine warware. In October, Kipling wrote "Swept and Garnished," in February 1915, "Sea Constables," and in March, "Mary Postgate."

"Swept and Garnished" portrays a German woman named Ebermann. Feverish and delusional, she hallucinates that children, the victims of atrocities in invaded Belgium and France, are in her bedroom. As the story ends, her nurse finds her on her knees, scrubbing at the floor—a little like Lady Macbeth—trying to wipe out the spots of blood the children have left behind. (Kipling was quick to believe the wild tales of German atrocities then being circulated. This story includes a reference to one—that German infantrymen were chopping the right arms off little boys, so that they could never become soldiers in the future.) It is striking that Kipling chose a Berlin woman to hallucinate the victims rather than a soldier who had been directly involved.

"Sea Constables" is a different tale, exclusively masculine. Four men, eating a comfortable dinner, recount how they have been watching a neutral vessel on their patrols, suspecting it of transferring fuel to German submarines. (The neutral is unspecified, but sounds American.)* The last speaker casually tells the end of the tale; the neutral captain comes down with pneumonia and begs to be taken to England—"Why, if you leave me now, Mr. Maddingham," he said, "you condemn me to death, just as surely as if you hanged me."[3] The English captain coldly reminds him that there's a war on and says, "I can do nothing for you. . . . He died. I saw his flag half-masted next morning." The men finish their meal with a final toast: "Damnation to all neutrals!" and depart. It is a story of hostility, of cruelty—deliberate, calm, unruffled masculine cruelty, as Tompkins points out—unlike the feverish Frau Ebermann and unlike the central figure in the next story, "Mary Postgate."

Mary Postgate is an old maid, the middle-aged companion of the ailing Miss Fowler, a quite unremarkable person whose "speech was as colourless as her eyes or her hair."[4] She is pleasant and loving, gets along with everyone in the village, and is "sort of a public aunt to very many small children of the village street." When Miss Fowler's eleven-year-old nephew Wynn is suddenly orphaned and joins her home, Mary Postgate devotes her life to him. She buys his clothes, arranges his schooling, and without revealing it adores him with all of a mother's love. With the ingratitude of the young, Wynn calls her "Gatepost" and "Packthread,"

---

*He is referred to as "Uncle Newt" (i.e., "Uncle Sam").

holds her strictly accountable for every sock and shoe, and generally makes her his "butt and slave."* He has affection for her—takes and keeps a picture of her, tells his friends about her—but hides this beneath his demands and his teasing. He joins the Flying Corps and soon is killed in a trial flight. Miss Fowler, his aunt, says she had expected it adding:

> "I'm sorry it happened before he had done anything."
> The room was whirling round Mary Postgate, but she found herself quite steady in the midst of it.
> "Yes," she said. "It's a great pity he didn't die in action after he had killed somebody."[6]

This is the clue to the rest of the story—the murderous hostility of the nurse-mother whose beloved has been snatched from her. Mary Postgate, on an errand in the village, sees a child killed by a German bomb. "Bloody pagans!" she says to herself, a phrase Wynn "had applied to the enemy." Back home, Miss Fowler and she decide to burn Wynn's old books, toys, golf clubs, and all other personal possessions in the garden incinerator. Mary Postgate takes load after load down to be burned, puts coal and sticks underneath, and methodically pours paraffin over the whole pile:

> The shrubbery was filling with twilight by the time she had completed her arrangements and sprinkled the sacrificial oil. As she lit the match that would burn her heart to ashes, she heard a groan or a grunt behind the dense Portugal laurels.**

---

*One is reminded of the nurse-child relationship in many of Kipling's stories, such as "His Majesty the King," written nearly thirty years before in India. There, readers will remember, the nurse, when the children grow old enough to leave her and go "Home" (i.e., to England), "packed up her slender belongings and sought for employment afresh, lavishing all her love on each successive batch of ingrates".[5] Behind both stories, of course, is Kipling's childhood love for his *ayah*, toward whom he was similarly imperious and demanding, and from whom he was snatched when he was taken to the House of Desolation. In dwelling on the nurse-child relationship, Kipling is working through his own feelings of loss and guilt: "If only I hadn't teased her so; if only I had appreciated her love while I had it." Note also that Wynn joins the family and gains Mary's love at the age of eleven; it was at this age that Kipling escaped from the House of Desolation when his mother came and took him away.

**Why "dense Portugal laurels"? It is a distracting detail, interfering with the flow of the story. As one critic said, "Another writer would have simply written 'shrubbery.'"[7] But in one of Kipling's most powerful stories about a nurse and her child, we might expect that unconsciously some allusion to his Portuguese *ayah* would come in.

By the light of the "pyre" she sees a severely injured German pilot, whose fall from his plane was broken by branches of the tree against which he is sitting. He begs for help and asks for the "toctor." She goes to the house, not for help but for a revolver:

> Again the head groaned for the doctor.
> "Stop that!" said Mary, and stamped her foot. "Stop that, you bloody pagan!"
> The words came out quite smoothly and naturally. They were Wynn's own words. . . .

She then abandons herself to the exquisite passion of hate. Wynn is dead, so now the German must die, and she will watch it happen. She wields the poker with a fury, making the fire blaze, humming contentedly to herself. None of the critics seem to understand—or rather they seem reluctant to understand clearly—the sexual nature of Mary Postgate's anger. A frustrated, inhibited woman finds an outlet in hostility for long-repressed sexual feelings; her pleasure at the moment of the airman's death is quite clearly equated to an orgasm:

> The exercise of stoking had given her a glow which seemed to reach to the marrow of her bones . . . She thumped like a pavior through the settling ashes at the secret thrill of it. The rain was damping the fire, but she could feel—it was too dark to see—that her work was done. There was a full red glow at the bottom of the destructor, not enough to char the wooden lid if she slipped it half over against the driving wet. This arranged, she leaned on the poker and waited, while an increasing rapture laid hold on her. She ceased to think. She gave herself up to feel. Her long pleasure was broken by a sound that she had waited for in agony several times in her life. She leaned forward and listened, smiling. There could be no mistake. She closed her eyes and drank it in. Once it ceased abruptly.
> "Go on," she murmured, half aloud. "That isn't the end."
> The end [i.e., the death of the German] came very distinctly in a lull between two rain-gusts. Mary Postgate drew her breath short between her teeth and shivered from head to foot. "*That's* all right," she said contentedly, and went up to the house, where she scandalised the whole routine by taking a luxurious hot bath before tea, and came down looking, as Miss Fowler said when she saw her lying all relaxed on the other sofa, "quite handsome!"

As recounted previously, when his son John was born in 1897 Kipling described him in a letter to a friend as "one small craft recently launched from my own works. . . . The vessel at present needs at least 15 yrs. for full completion but at the end of that time may be an efficient addition to the Navy, for which service it is intended." Given his father's fascination with the military, John Kipling was thus from the day of his birth destined for the armed forces of his country.

When the war broke out, John was sixteen, a few days short of seventeen. He immediately went up to London by himself and attempted to obtain an officer's commission. Being only sixteen, and with poor eyesight, he was rejected. Like his Uncle Beatty Balestier whom he so resembled physically, he was thoroughly likable but was no scholar; he had to leave Wellington, a school with a strong military tradition, and go to an "Army Crammer"—just the sort of arrangement that Stalky and Co. had sneered at during the years at Westward Ho! Like almost every other young man in Britain, he was burning to join up, and he proposed that, with his father's permission, he enlist as a private. Kipling appealed to his friend, Lord Roberts, who at once gave John a commission as a second lieutenant in his own crack regiment, the Irish Guards. (It is ironic that as a private he might have survived the war. A second lieutenant, unless he were wounded so that he could not return to duty, had almost no chance of survival.)

A year went by, as John, stationed near London, chafed to go overseas—which was not permitted until he reached eighteen. A broad-shouldered, lean boy, at five feet seven inches the tallest in his family, he did not look in the least like the rest of them. A comparison of photographs shows how close a resemblance he bore to his Uncle Beatty over in America—the uncle he had never seen and whose name was almost never mentioned in the Kipling household.

In August of 1915 John turned eighteen and went to France. Carrie wrote a touching note in her diary: "John leaves at noon for Warley. He looks very straight and smart and young, as he turned at the top of the stairs to say, 'Send my love to Dad-o.'"[8]

He said this because his father was not at home, having gone—why at *this* time?—on a brief trip to write an account of life in the trenches. One can be very sure that visiting civilian big-wigs were taken only to sections of the trenches that were safe, with absolutely no action anticipated. And some people were impressed when told in a whisper,

"You're only twenty-five feet from the Germans." Kipling certainly was. He came back home bursting with a "now-I've-*really*-been-there" pride. He wrote Carrie, "When I return be prepared for a new Domestic Tyrant. I'm somebody, and I've pulled the whiskers of death and don't you forget it."

To John, now in combat, he wrote an all-knowing letter that, in the light of subsequent events, makes unpleasant reading:

> 22 Aug. 1915
>
> Dear Old Man:
>
> I hope you'll never get nearer to the Boche than I did. The quaintest thing was to watch the NCO gesticulating to his Colonel and me to keep quiet. . . . Also, I hate to be in a town with stone pavements when same is being bombarded. It's a grand life though and does not give you a dull minute. I found boric acid in my socks a great comfort. I walked 2 hours in the dam' trenches.
>
> Don't forget the beauty of rabbit netting overhead against hand-grenades. Even tennis netting is better than nothing.[9]

John Kipling never got his hands on tennis netting. At that time the life of a second lieutenant at the front lasted, on an average, six weeks. Some died their first day; others survived for weeks or months, but only a very few came through unscathed. John did not even get six weeks. Just over a month after Kipling posted his letter John was dead. In the Battle of Loos, in which ground was gained, lost, regained, and lost again over a four-day period, the British lost twenty thousand dead. John Kipling, like many others, simply disappeared, his body never found, probably blown to pieces by shellfire. Kipling thought of a more merciful end; in "The Gardner," surely thinking of his own son, he described Michael's fate at Loos:

> . . . a shell-splinter dropping out of a wet dawn killed him at once. The next shell uprooted and laid down over the body what had been the foundation of a barn wall, so neatly that none but an expert would have guessed that anything unpleasant had happened.[10]

In the story, Michael's body is found. The Kiplings were not so fortunate. On the second of October they had first received word that John was "wounded and missing." Kipling was ill with gastritis, and

Elsie's friend Isobel Law was visiting her on the day that Carrie received the telegram. She at once decided not to say anything until Isobel had left, and forced herself to go through the rest of the day appearing as though nothing had happened. Three days later, Kipling still too sick to accompany them, she and Elsie went up to London but could get no details. For the next two years the Kiplings sought out wounded men of John's battalion and, clinging to the hope he was a prisoner, made inquiry through the Red Cross, neutral channels, and the Vatican, all to no avail. John had simply vanished, his fate unknown, his body never found.*

Kipling wrote to Brigadier L. C. Dunsterville, the "Stalky" of his school days:

12 Nov. 1915

Our boy was reported "wounded and missing" since Sep. 27—the Battle of Loos and we've heard nothing official since that date. But all we can pick up from the men points to the fact that he is dead and probably wiped out by shellfire. However, he had his heart's desire and he didn't have a long time in trenches. . . . It was a short life. I am sorry that all the years' work ended in that one afternoon but—lots of people are in our position—and it's something to have bred a man. The wife is standing it wonderfully tho' she, of course, clings to the bare hope of his being a prisoner. I've seen what shells can do, and I don't.[12]

Again the all-knowing Kipling—"I've seen what shells can do" and the unusual statement, "It's something to have bred a man."

The mourning of his son's death is expressed in the poem, "Gethsemane":

The Garden called Gethsemane
In Picardy it was,
And there the people came to see
The English soldiers pass.
We used to pass—we used to pass

*His name was subsequently inscribed with all the others on the Loos Memorial to the Missing. Remarkably enough, according to one source, Kipling asked that John's name also be included among the dead of the *Indian* Army, a request that was granted.[11] If this is true—it has not been verified—it is yet another example of Kipling's feeling that he—the pronoun can refer to either Kipling himself or to John—was part Indian.

300

Or halt, as it might be,
And ship our masks in case of gas
Beyond Gethsemane.
The Garden called Gethsemane,
It held a pretty lass,
And all the time she talked to me
I prayed my cup might pass.
The officer sat on the chair,
The men lay on the grass,
And all the time we halted there
I prayed my cup might pass—
It didn't pass—it didn't pass—
It didn't pass from me.
I drank it when we met the gas
Beyond Gethsemane.[13]

All his life Kipling had been devoted to his children and wanted most of all to have them grow up happier than he had been. Now two out of the three were dead. An aching sadness settled on Kipling and Carrie, as on so many English families, and the best antidote for that, as he had so often said, was work. He accepted two appointments—the very first ones in his life (in 1917 he was fifty-two). One was that of becoming an Imperial War Graves Commissioner. The Commission had the enormous task of exhuming, identifying, and reburying under appropriate inscriptions and in new, permanent cemeteries, a million British dead. The second was to become a Rhodes trustee, participating in the disposition of the huge fortune Rhodes left so that young men from every corner of the Empire, and from every state in America, would have the opportunity to study at Oxford. A third task, begun in 1917, was to write the history of the Irish Guards, John's regiment. These three jobs, particularly the last, took up almost all his time for the next five years.

The Irish Guards in the Great War is unlike any other account of a military unit I've ever encountered. I took it up expecting the "usual thing"—maps, accounts of engagements with the enemy, outstanding years, successes and failures, giving the whole story from their arrival in France until the Armistice. It does give these things. But in addition, there is a curious light-hearted quality about it all. Every few pages there is an account of a humorous incident. Opening one of the two volumes at random I soon came to an account of a raid against the German line:

The 2nd July was the day for the raid itself, and just as Battalion Head-quarters were discussing the very last details, an urgent message from Bri-gade Headquarters came in to them—"Please hasten your report on Pork and Beans rations."[14]

A page later:

At the last minute, one single unrelated private, appearing from nowhere in particular, was seen to push his way down the trench, climbing over the raiders where they crouched waiting for the life-or-death word. Said an Officer, who assumed that at the least he must bear vital messages, "Who are you?" "R.F.A. Trench-morter man, sir," was the reply. Then, "Where the devil are you going?"—"Going to get my tea, sir." He passed on, mess-tin in hand, noticing nothing that was outside of his own immediate show; for of such, mercifully, were the Armies of England.

It could be argued that this is an effective way of telling the history of a military unit, for it lightens an otherwise routine account and so much of war is so contradictory, so absurd, that it almost seems to have a crazy sort of humor about it. This explanation does not seem sufficient. I think Kipling's inclusion of amusing episodes seems queer and inap-propriate and detracts from his history. Perhaps he felt this way himself, for in the introduction he attempts to explain it:

It is for the sake of these initiated that the compiler has loaded his records with detail and seeming triviality, since in a life where Death ruled every hour, nothing was trivial, and bald references to villages, billets, camps, fatigues and sports, as well as hints of tales that can never now fully be told, carry each their separate significance to each survivor, intimate and incom-municable as family jests.[15]

Somehow, these reasons also seem insufficient. It is only when one asks oneself, "How else might he have done it?" that the answer appears. For better or for worse, Kipling simply was incapable of producing the "usual thing." In writing an account of the Irish Guards, he becomes caught up in it, recording with boyish enthusiasm unnecessary details and anecdotes as he tries to feel a member of a unit that, as a noncom-batant, was precisely the one in which he never could fit. Again he is asking himself, Where do I belong? Who is my mother?, as we have seen him do all his life. Corroboration for this can be seen in his own expla-nation, just quoted, where the amusing anecdotes are "intimate and incommunicable as family jests."

Is it possible Kipling felt a twinge of guilt over his son's death? For twenty years, perhaps more than any other writer, he had sung the praises of the Army and the Navy. From the day of John's birth he had declared that his son would be a military man. Then the war began and John, a pleasant, not-too-bright schoolboy with poor eyesight, got a commission—because his father interceded with Lord Roberts—and a little over a month later, quite predictibly, his life was snuffed out on the front. Did Kipling feel any remote sense of responsibility? He set all other writing aside so that he could concentrate on the history of the Irish Guards; was this an act of penance as well as wanting to work on a memorial?

I think that all evidence points to the fact that it was not, and that Kipling felt no guilt whatsoever over John's death. To believe he had some such feeling would be to imply that he was in some measure a war-monger, that he helped begin the war in the first place—an untenable view. Yes, Kipling always exalted the military, but not war. In fact he consistently pointed out British restraint and contrasted it with the aggressive expansion other nations would have undertaken if they had possessed similar power. In getting John a commission he was, after all, helping him obtain what he wanted most. Now, more than seventy years later, we are aghast at the carnage of what was then—naively— called the Great War. Hundreds of thousands of men died in endless struggles, back and forth, for possession of a few hundred yards of torn-up earth. We wonder if the military build-up before 1914 could have been prevented in any way. But this is not the way most people saw the war then, and most assuredly not the way Kipling saw it. It was civilization defending itself against barbarism, and John's death was that of a warrior doing his duty, offering his life as a contribution to victory. During the war nationalistic fervor ran high. Orchestras stopped playing German music; universities stopped language courses in that hated tongue; the city of Bismarck, Ontario, changed its name to Kitchener; and at times women handed out white feathers to any man not in uniform.

In general, Kipling would have sympathized with these views. He was not a profound thinker and definitely not an introspective person. I do not make these statements critically. (Indeed, I think that these qualities account for some of his success as a writer. When he fixed his attention on some subject, be it heroism, childhood, or the supernatural, he approached it with fascination, with a boyish enthusiasm, undistracted by other thoughts, and could then write about it vividly, somewhat reminiscent of Einstein's statement that when pondering a problem he tried to think of it as a child would.) Kipling was terribly affected by his son's death, but guilt was not part of what tormented him.

The years of America's neutrality provided an outlet for his old angry feelings toward the United States. He wrote bitterly to friends—particularly Theodore Roosevelt, now out of office—that under Woodrow Wilson's leadership America was sitting back and shirking her duties. In his replies, Roosevelt agreed to some extent about his political foe Wilson. He told Kipling that shirking duty was an old story with Wilson, his entire family had avoided fighting in the Civil War.* However, his letters frequently contain a note of caution against Kipling's hasty and violent judgments.

When America did enter the war, Kipling's attacks naturally ceased. Alexander Woollcott described an incident that, if accurate, would have made a good story:

> During the heyday of the AEF (American Expeditionary Force) Kipling, momentarily placated by our having sent two million soldiers to France, gave the *Stars and Stripes* the privilege of being first to publish one of his poems. In acknowledgment, we sent a courier, accompanied by a blushing young orderly, to deliver the first copy off the press. Kipling received them, and it, at Brown's Hotel. The courier acquitted himself as instructed, and the incident was about to close, when the private, whose name I've forgotten and who was breathing heavily and obviously bursting with excitement, suddenly stepped forward, shook the gifted hand and said: "My, Mr. Kipling, it will be a great day when my folks in Georgia hear that I actually met the man who wrote *The Rubaiyat of Omar Khayyam*."[16]

Unfortunately there is no record of Kipling's having contributed to *Stars and Stripes*.

Kipling visited a U.S. Army camp and even made a speech of welcome to seven thousand newly arrived soldiers—an extremely unusual thing for him to do. He wrote warmly to Roosevelt, singing the

---

*It is striking that Roosevelt chose this point on which to attack Wilson. Roosevelt's own father had avoided enlisting in the Union Army, and had paid a substitute to take his place—an incident about which Roosevelt had always felt guilty. We hate most in others what we fear in ourselves.

praises of the American Naval and Air Corps men. Roosevelt, the man of action, like Rhodes, had always been the object of Kipling's hero-worship, as opposed to Woodrow Wilson, the man of ideas, one of our greatest presidents, who only drew his utter contempt. Kipling acidly wrote to Roosevelt about Wilson, saying, "I am sorry that there is a schoolmaster, instead of a man at the head of the U.S. today" and that Wilson was less reasonable than "an ape looking down [from] a palm tree . . . ."

Gradually the war drew to a close. Before the days of radio broadcasts, and with no telephone at Bateman's, the only way Kipling and Carrie could learn of the war's end was to hear the distant ringing of all the church bells. Two months later Kipling received a real blow: in January of 1919 Theodore Roosevelt died. This largely broke his last ties with America. There only remained Frank Doubleday, the publisher, now a close and old friend, and "Ted" Hill, to whom he still wrote a friendly letter when he sent her a copy of each new volume he produced.

XV

THE YEARS AFTER
THE WAR

Kipling was busy until 1922 with his work on the War Graves Commission, and in writing *The Irish Guards in the Great War*. The "gastritis" that had first appeared after his son John went to battle had continued off and on ever since; no medical advice or treatment seemed to help. When Dorothy Ponton, who before the war had been the children's tutor, returned to Bateman's to be Kipling's secretary in 1919, she noticed a change: "Mr. Kipling had lost his buoyant step."[1] His gastrointestinal trouble, she felt, was more the result of emotional conflict than any organic problem.

He seemed old and tired and, though only fifty-four and destined to live nearly twenty years more, he wrote comparatively little between 1919 and his death in 1936. Intermittently troubled with abdominal pain, which the doctors were astonishingly slow to diagnose correctly as a gastric ulcer, he spent more and more time on rearranging his works for different editions. Predictably, he became entranced with the whole process. He drew illustrations that accompanied stories, and devices and symbols that appeared on title pages, on the book covers, and even as a watermarks in the paper. He specified vivid colors—he always said that when it came to colors, his tastes were florid—and the books were embellished in red, black, gold, and dark green. He took an increasing delight with each new edition.

As his health declined, Carrie guarded him even more fiercely than before. She opened and answered all his mail, paid all his bills, and supervised the farming of the estate with as watchful—and exasperating—an eye as she had kept on Beatty back in Vermont. It was the general opinion that her persnickety attitude cost the estate in the long run; she would waste pounds in order to save a few shillings. Like an overprotective mother, she followed Kipling with her eyes if he so much as got up and wandered about the room.

Her protectiveness was excessive, but its being occasionally necessary was shown by an incident in June 1922. Clare Sheridan was the daughter of neighbors, someone they had known for twenty years. Shallow, selfish, and manipulative, she had a well-deserved unsavory reputation. Greedy for publicity, she saw to it that hints of her love-affairs got into scandal-sheets everywhere. She was now a reporter for the *New York World*, and "resolved to be unscrupulous in order to satisfy my desire for efficiency,"[2] as she herself put it.

On the day in question she innocently dropped in at tea-time with her two children and was welcomed by the Kiplings; she waited until Carrie, who had also welcomed Isobel Law and her husband, was showing them the garden, and then questioned Kipling about American participation in the war. Always touchy about America, Kipling—according to her—cut loose with his usual violent feelings. America, he said, had entered "the War two years, seven months, and four days too late." The Americans had loaned England gold at eight percent; it was just "business as usual" for them. "They've got our gold, but we have saved our souls." The United States had forced "the Allies to make peace at the first opportunity instead of insisting upon finishing it in Berlin. America quit the day of the Armistice without waiting to see the thing through." America, he went on, was corrupted by low-class immigrants since her best blood had been lost in the Civil War.

The "interview" produced headlines in America, England, and France and provoked so much turmoil that the British and French governments issued official disclaimers. After a long period of silence, so did Kipling, denying that he said the things attributed to him. Mrs.

Sheridan, who probably hadn't told much more than the truth, took a verbal swing at Kipling in a subsequent book; he was, she said:

> a jolly little man with a school-boy humour. . . . He was wrung dry by domesticity. When he had a good story to tell, Mrs. Kipling always intervened to tell it better.

If Carrie had intervened this time, Kipling would have been prevented from telling his story at all. He was taken advantage of by somene who, off and on, had been a neighbor for years, and if one thinks of him as an innocent victim of an unscrupulous person, it is also striking how easily he let himself be trapped by Clare Sheridan. Everybody knew about *her*. A person who has a fear of being beaten—ultimately, castrated, losing his penis—by women has an unconscious urge to put himself in just the spot where this will happen.

In the summer of 1922 Kipling's health grew even worse.* In August he was hospitalized for extensive examinations, including X-ray studies, but no evidence of disease could be found. It was at least a relief that there were no signs of the cancer he had always feared.

In October his abdominal pains returned with increasing severity and in November he was operated on, apparently an exploratory procedure, although through Carrie's efforts the entire event was carried out with extreme secrecy and the reporters kept completely in the dark. Whatever the surgeon did, it helped; during the winter he improved rapidly, and in the spring of 1923 he began writing again, although he suffered from intermittent abdominal pain for the rest of his life.

Stories written during and after the war, and on into the 1920s, were collected in *Debits and Credits* in 1926, the first book published since 1923. In these stories written during and after the war, there is a new strain of tenderness and love that modifies the sadism evident in some of his earlier work.** Kipling was nearing sixty and had lost, as a tablet in

---

*The incident with Clare Sheridan had nothing to do with his condition; although she had seen him in June, she did not publish her account until September.

**One story, "On the Gate," written in 1918, describes the rush of the wartime dead arriving in Heaven. Rider Haggard, an old friend, described Kipling's reading to him "a quaint story about Death and Saint Peter, written in modern language, almost in slang, which his wife would not let him publish. It would have been caviare to the General if he had, because the keynote

the local church recorded, his "only son"[4] in the war. Now an element of compassion appears in his works. It finds a place in his philosophy which up to now had usually been the Victorian one of "duty and discipline." The first and last stories—always significant, for Kipling placed them to bracket the book and symbolize its contents—are, respectively, "The Enemies to Each Other" and "The Gardener." They show neatly two aspects of the older Kipling's feelings about women—one hostile and fearful, the other now warmer and more loving.

"The Enemies to Each Other" is the story of Adam and Eve. Each has a secret fear: "that the one of us might be made an enemy to the other."[5] At Eve's urging, they eat of the forbidden fruit; she accepts all the blame, but they are expelled from the garden, with the curse, "*Get ye down, the one of you an enemy unto the other.*" After pondering a long time, Adam is "enlightened," and he

> laughed without cessation and said: "By Allah I am no God but the mate of this most detestable Woman whom I love, and who is necessary to me beyond all the necessities."

Eve is similarly enlightened, and then they tear down the two altars, one for each, and erect a single one in its place, on which is written: "*Get ye down, the one of you an enemy unto the other.*"

When Kipling writes of his fear of women, as I have demonstrated, we can often find references to his blindness under the care of Mrs. Holloway more than half a century before. You look, and there it is. In the Garden of Eden, there is a

> Mole, whose custom it was to burrow in the earth and avoid the light of the Sun. His nature was malignant and his body inconspicuous but . . . he was then adorned with eyes far-seeing both in the light and in the darkness.

The mole spies on Adam and Even and returns telling of how they love each other and their baby, Cain. Instead of the expected reward, the mole is punished.

---

of it is infinite mercy extending even to the case of Judas."[3] The version Kipling published in 1926 was greatly altered.

"Be darkened hence forward, upon Earth and under Earth. It is not good to spy upon any creature of God to whom alleviation is permitted." So, then, the Mole's eyes were darkened and contracted, and his lot was made miserable upon and under the Earth to this day.

"The Gardener," at the end of the book, stands in marked contrast. It opens with the sentence, "Everyone in the village knew that Helen Turrell did her duty by all her world, and by none more honourably than by her only brother's unfortunate child."[6] The brother, "an Inspector of Indian Police," had "entangled himself with the daughter of a retired noncomissioned officer" and died a few weeks before the baby was born. The child is brought "from Bombay" and the unmarried Helen, after discharging the inefficient nurse in charge, brings up her nephew, whom she christens Michael. (Subtle hints are given, however, that he is actually her own illegitimate son.)

She gives him the same love and devotion Mary Postgate lavished on Wynn, who, be it noted, had also been orphaned and therefore brought up by his aunt. It represents Kipling's old feelings about his *ayah*, his childhood confusion, "Who is my mother?" The brother's being "an Inspector of Indian Police" and the mother taking the place of the nurse are allusions to his other question, "Am I Indian or white?"

Michael, like John Kipling, gets a commission and goes to the front at the Battle of Loos. He is posted as missing in action. Later, his body is found and buried in one of the vast military cemeteries. Helen Turrell goes there to seek out his grave, and tells someone she takes to be a gardener that she is looking for her "nephew's" grave. The man, "with infinite compassion," replies: "Come with me . . . and I will show you where your son lies." When she leaves, she looks back, "supposing him to be the gardener." (These last words refer to St. John's Gospel, where Mary Magdalene supposes the risen Christ "to be the gardener.")

This compassionate story at the end of the book balances "The Enemies to Each Other," at the beginning; written after the war, it also forms a counterpart to "Mary Postgate," written soon after it began. In each, Kipling shows us a middle-aged women's response to the death of her son—or, actually, the person she loves *as* a son. In "Mary Postgate," she is a nurse; in "The Gardener," Helen Turrell must always pretend Michael is her nephew. In one we see fury, hatred, and torture; in the other, compassion and the merciful lifting of a secret "one day in all the years, one hour in that one day." In the contrast between "Mary Post-gate" (or "The Enemies to Each Other"), and "The Gardener," we can also again see Kipling's lifelong conflictual feelings toward women: that they are vicious, tormenting creatures, yet also tender and loving.

The same ambivalence can be seen in another story from *Debits and Credits*—"The Wish House." Two elderly ladies sit and talk about their lives. One, Liz Fettley, plays a secondary role; by confiding in Grace Ashcroft, the principal character, she leads her, by nature a stolid, self-confident woman, to confide in return. It is the last meeting of these old friends; Mrs. Ashcroft has cancer, and Liz Fettley is "blindin' up"[7] (going blind). Mrs. Ashcroft tells of her love affair with Harry Mockler. After a time he left her. In her misery she suffers intolerable headaches, and a young girl, the daughter of a friend, tells her she knows a cure. The girl leaves and Mrs. Ashcroft's headache disappears within minutes; the girl returns, and now *she* has the headache. She tells Mrs. Ashcroft she did it by going to the Wish House nearby, a long-deserted house where a Token (ghost) lives. You ring the bell, the girl describes, and hear footsteps approach the door; ". . . (Y)ou say you'll take the trouble off of 'oo ever 'tis you've chose for your love; and ye'll get it"

Some time later, Mrs. Ashcroft sees Harry Mockler in the street, thin and pale, and learns that he is suffering from an infection and has "but a few months left." She knows what she wants to do, and goes to the Wish House. She rings the bell and hears the footsteps—"like it might ha' been a heavy woman in slippers." She speaks through the letterbox slot: "Let me take everythin' bad that's in store for my man, 'Arry Mockler, for love's sake." Through the door she hears an expiration—"She just breathed out—sort of *A-ah*, like." Mrs. Ashcroft returns home and soon afterward her leg becomes infected and will not heal. Indeed, the lesion later becomes cancerous. But she learns that Harry Mockler has made an astonishing recovery and is now well. Months later she hears he has been kicked by a horse and has to be repeatedly seen by the doctor. She deliberately stands all day to make her old leg infection worse, and sure enough, Harry recovers. She learns to coordinate her illness with anything that happens to him, and in this way takes all his misfortunes upon herself.

But she does this for a purpose. Here nearly all those who have written about this story make a striking error. Sensing the sadism in so much of what Kipling wrote, they turn with relief to a story that seems to indicate love and altruism. They see Mrs. Ashcroft's deed as pure self-sacrifice, the ultimate act of love. Carrington describes "a curse which is lifted from the back of one who is beloved but unworthy, and is faithfully borne by one who loves and forgives."[8] Tompkins speaks of her "sublime and unrewarded devotion"[9] and says, "She is still, in some measure, the unsanctioned Alcestis, who goes down into Hell to save her lover." Bodelson refers to the story's theme as that of "the victory of love over death."[10]

At first glance, as in the summary just given, it may appear to be just such a victory; but on closer reading one can see that Mrs. Ashcroft is more controlling and possessive than loving. After his first illness she remarks, "'Arry bein' *dead*, like, 'e'd ha' been mine, till Judgment. 'Arry bein' alive, 'e'd like as not pick up with some woman middlin' quick."[11] It is to control him, and prevent his taking up with another woman, that she learns to lessen his illnesses by becoming ill herself. When Liz Fettley wails, "But what did *you* get out of it, Gra'?" Mrs. Ashcroft replies, "But 'e's never looked at me, ner any other woman, 'cept 'is mother. 'Ow I used to watch an' listen! So did she." There is a close connection in the story, hitherto unnoticed, between Mrs. Ashcroft and Harry Mockler's mother. Mockler is a mama's boy. After the time he is kicked by a horse, a neighbor remarks to Harry's mother that it was a pity Harry had no wife to care for him; his mother, infuriated, says that he'd never looked at any woman in all his life, and as long as *she* was alive, she'd take complete care of him. Mrs. Ashcroft similarly controls Harry. She says to Liz, "The pain *do* count to keep 'Arry—where I want 'im."

Mrs. Ashcroft hates Harry's mother—they both want to "mother" and control him—and speaks of a conversation with Harry:

> "Thank ye kindly, Gra'," 'e says (But 'e never says "my woman"), an' 'e went on up-street an' 'is mother—Oh, damn 'er!—she was watchin' for 'im, an' she shut de door be'ind 'im.

Harry behaves like a child toward his mother, and toward Mrs. Ashcroft, too—"'e never says 'my woman'" but rather "Gra'." In her remark, "No odds 'twixt boys now an' forty year back. 'Take all an' give naught—an' we to put up with it," we are reminded of Wynn and Mary

Postgate, of His Majesty the King and his nurse Miss Biddums, of Kipling himself and his loving *ayah*. When Kipling, now nearly sixty, writes of love—with the sole exception of "The Gardener"—his old feelings about female domination come in, carried out through the Token that, significantly, is clearly described as being a woman. "The Wish House" is not a story of "sublime and unrewarded devotion." Purefoy is quite correct in saying that this

> woman didn't sacrifice her health out of unselfish love; it was a bargaining counter with Fate—her pain in exchange for Harry's keeping off other women, most of all off marrying.[12]

In his reactions to events in the twenties Kipling revealed again his obsessive need to imagine that everything would return to the India, America, and England of his boyhood and early years. He could do nothing but rant against a British Empire that was gradually changing to a liberal Commonwealth, and in 1925 when an internationalist was appointed to a vacancy on the board of trustees of the Rhodes Trust, Kipling resigned and insisted that the resignation be publicized, since it was necessitated by his principles.

One of the officers in the Irish Guards who had visited Batemen's often while contributing to Kipling's regimental history was Captain George Bambridge. He and Elsie announced their engagement in the spring of 1924, when the family was in Spain, and in October they were married. It is evident that Elsie was only too glad to get away from her parents, and it is no coincidence that she married an embassy official and knew she would probably be spending more time abroad than in England. She had always been rather close to her father and there was still a degree of intimacy between them. But she had had quite enough of her mother, who, she felt, was jealous and possessive, a person who dominated her father and herself unmercifully. She felt so strongly about this that she stated it explicitly in the epilogue to Carrington's biography of her father. Confirmation for her opinion can be seen in Carrie's behavior after the marriage; she was meddlesome and complaining and never ceased to criticize her daughter and son-in-law.

Debits and Credits was published in 1926, and Hugh Walpole, about to leave on a speaking tour in America, left a description of spending a wonderful morning with old Kipling in the Athenaeum. He was sitting surrounded by the the reviews of his new book, beaming like a baby. He talked to me delightfully about America, and when I said it was nice the eagerness with which they greeted one, he said: "Of course they are a marooned people!"[13]

Some time later he described Kipling at a house-party, meeting P.G. Wodehouse and asking him, "But tell me, Wodehouse, how do you finish your stories? I can never think how to end mine." He also left a fuller picture:

> Kipling at Fairlawne is like a little gnome. All sorts of people about. The Athlones—she with her funny little German governess who says not a word but suddenly breaks out once with "Ach, Thomas Mann—he's a splendid writer" and looks across the table scornfully at Kipling as though she'd like to tell him how inferior she thinks *he* is. And J. H. Thomas . . . catching Kipling's arm and chuckling in *his* ear some rather dirty joke about Labour Gentleman of the Bedchamber. Not that Kipling cares in the least about any of them. He is kindly, genial, ready apparently to be friends with anyone but keeping all the time his own guard.
>
> I asked him at luncheon whether he approved of censorship (apropos of this tiresome stupid *Well of Loneliness*).* No, he doesn't approve of the book. Too much of the abnormal in all of us to play about with it. Hates opening up reserves. All the same he'd had friends once and again he'd done more for than for any woman. Luckily Ma Kipling doesn't hear this—but she's had her ear to *his* keyhole for so long that, without hearing anything, she nevertheless suspects and turns her dull eye on to me as much as to say: "Now the moment you're tiresome you *go*, so if you want to stay with him you'd better behave." Nor do I blame her. She's a good strong-minded woman, who has played watch-dog to him so long that she knows now just how to save him from any kind of disturbance, mental, physical or spiritual. That's *her* job and she does it superbly.
>
> All the same he manages to tell me all about my short stories . . . and manages to leave a pleasant tingle in my cheeks.
>
> He does this, I fancy, with everyone. He's endlessly kind and end-lessly reserved. His black eyebrows, which today jut out like furry rocks over his eyes, keep guard. When I tell him that we were all amused about his mistake over Jane Austen and Scott,** he jokingly defends it, but she doesn't like my telling him of it and gives me another warning look.
>
> He really, I think, has no vanity. He's a zealous propagandist who,

---

*A book by Radcliffe Hall about a female homosexual relationship.

**Kipling wrote a poem, "Jane's Marriage," in which Sir Walter Scott welcomes Jane Austen in Paradise, when actually she died years before he did. Kipling later revised the poem.

having discovered that the things for which he must propagand are now all out of fashion, guards them jealously and lovingly in his heart, but won't any more trail them about in public.

He walks about the garden, his eyebrows all that are really visible of him. His body is nothing but his eyes terrific, lambent, kindly, gentle and exceedingly proud. Good to us all and we are all shadows to him.

"Carrie," he says turning to Mrs. K., and at once you see that she is the only real person here to him—so she takes him, wraps him up in her bosom and conveys him back to their uncomfortable hard-chaired house. He is quite content.

More than twenty years before, in the verses accompanying the Just So story "The Beginning of the Armadillos," he had written, "Oh, I'd love to roll to Rio some day before I'm old!"[14] In January of 1927 Kipling and Carrie set out for Brazil. His vivid account of the trip and of the places they visited was later published as *Brazilian Sketches*. If anyone had the thought that Kipling, now in his sixties, was losing his touch, the book would certainly set him right. His descriptions are as energetic and imaginative as ever.

On a ship that every day sailed deeper into the tropics, with many of the passengers and crew speaking Portuguese, one might anticipate that Kipling's mind would turn to his childhood and his *ayah*, (although she, of course, spoke Hindustani), and this indeed happened. In some introductory verses to the book he writes:

> I had some friends—their crowns were in the sky—
> Who used to nod and whisper when a little boy went by,
> As the nuts began to tumble and the breeze began to blow:
> And I haven't seen a Coco-palm since ever so long ago![15]

Here he alludes to the Mahim Woods, where, "When the winds blow the great nuts would tumble, and we fled—my *ayah*, and my sister in her perambulator—to the safety of the open." This is his ominous impression of the port of Bombay, from which he left India when he was five; in "Baa Baa, Black Sheep," Meeta tells him he will have to go "down to the sea where the cocoanuts are thrown" and be taken away to England in a ship.

Soon after their arrival in Rio he speaks of the plants:

> All things were in their places that should have been, and growing naturally in their own atmosphere—the fruits, flowers, trees, and smells that awaken

remembrance, sorrow, or delight, in all parts of the earth, from the twinkly-leaved mango, which in my early beliefs was inhabited after dark by "Things," down to jack-fruit—that durian which reeks like a corpse, but makes those who have once tasted eager as ghouls to eat again. . . . [There were also] bananas, of which one's *ayah* used to tell that, if you got up very early and found a single new frond, neither split by the wind nor dried by the sun, you could wish a wish and the Gods would grant it.*

He generally avoided references to America. Describing a railroad car, he said that "Except that it was more luxurious, the car might have been Indian, South African, or Canadian." Not American. But then, two pages later, they meet a delightful little wood-burning locomotive, ringing its bell, "coughing, sparking, and tolling as though it were back among the cornfields in ancient Vermont." Much as he hated America, he loved it too.

In some introductory verses to the last section of the book, when he speaks of his impressions of Brazilians in general, he writes

> E'en so it is; and, well content
> It should be so a moment's space,
> Each finds the other excellent,
> And—turns to follow his own race!

At the very end of the book, he tells of a group of Brazilians—not black, but singing a black song—and, speaking of how it moved him, says, "Most likely their *ayahs* had sung it to them when they were babies."

In 1927 and 1928 he worked at a new book, *Limits and Renewals*, published in 1932, which continued his postwar preoccupation with pain and suffering, with a man's breaking point and how it can be avoided. In "The Woman in His Life," Kipling tells of Marden, a former soldier who builds up a successful engineering business. Suddenly the "forgotten and hardly held-back horror"[16] of his wartime years returns; unable to work, he turns to drink, which only makes things worse. He was a "sapper" during the war, working in tunnels beneath the earth, and he begins to have hallucinations, one of which is of a small black dog pressed against the baseboard of his room; he feels that if the animal ever leaves this spot, "the Universe would crash down on him."

---

*Kipling told his own children this same tale, as Elsie recounted (p. 287).

Marden's former batman, now his manservant, brings a real black dog to the apartment, a "jet black" Aberdeen terrier called Dinah. Marden doesn't know if the dog he sees is real or a hallucination, and has conflicting urges to get his pistol and kill her or to get the shovel from the fire-irons and clean up the mess that Dinah proceeds to make in the corner. He does the latter and, losing his heart to Dinah, begins to improve. His manservant says she is pure-bred and pedigreed, "Not a white 'air on 'her! An' look at 'er boo-som frills!" They nurse Dinah through distemper and move her out to the country in the summertime.

One evening she does not return home and Marden fears she is caught in some sort of trap. He goes out searching for her in the darkness and finally hears her, deep in a cleft in the earth. He crawls in. With his flashlight he can see that the cleft becomes a tunnel that gets smaller and smaller, and all the wartime memories flood over him as he enters and wriggles forward, surrounded by the earth. The tunnel widens and he finally sees Dinah, caught not by a snare but by a root through her collar. He grasps the root, "shut[s] his eyes, and humour[s] it out by touch." He gets Dinah and himself out and, bruised and exhausted, staggers homeward, with "eyes unable to judge distance." After a hot bath and a good night's sleep he feels entirely recovered, and sings his usual black song to Dinah:

> Oh, show me a liddle where to find a rose
> To give to ma honey chi-ile!

Now cured of his psychosis, he energetically returns to his work, and all is well.

I need hardly point out that the "woman" in Marden's life is a bitch, that she is black, pure-bred, and has "not a white 'air on 'er," and that her master sings black songs to her after she leads him to recovery. A reference is made to her breasts. A black female saving a white male child—it is what we saw when Imam Din saved Adam in "A Deal in Cotton," when the wise *ayah* saved Ameera and her child in "Without Benefit of Clergy," all the way back to Kipling's own birth which, he was told, was made possible by the natives' sacrifice of a kid to Kali, and to his "good-Asiatic-mother/bad-white-mother" conflict. And, again, this is accompanied by references to visual disturbances.

XVI

THE FINAL YEARS

In 1928 Dr. and Mrs. William Beebe had tea with the Kiplings in London, one of several meetings in the large suite they invariably took at Brown's Hotel—one suspects Carrie's need to "do it up grand" might have been the reason. Dr. Beebe was one of the most prominent scientists in America in the twenties and thirties, and his books on natural history, written for the layperson, had achieved wide popularity. Kipling, always interested in everything, was already familiar with Dr. Beebe's publications, and there had been some correspondence between them. They therefore met almost as old friends and Mrs. Beebe, intimately familiar with the works of both writers, naturally expected to join in their conversation. But on this occasion, and on subsequent ones, Carrie immediately interposed her formidible self and Mrs. Beebe found herself firmly relegated to the far side of the tea-table, where she was compelled to make polite small talk with her hostess. She remembered it as "incomprehensible possessiveness"[1]—a somewhat different conclusion than Hugh Walpole had reached the same year. She also remembers envying the hearty laughter between the two men on the sofa that day, and later heard from Dr. Beebe a story told by Kipling—which he had never written but recounted that day with much laughter—about a little dog which had been born on a battleship at sea and had never seen grass.

Therefore, on his first trip ashore he didn't know what to make of grass—or what possible use it might be put to—since it tickled his feet and made him step rather high, to the amusement of his shipmates. During another trip ashore it was discovered too late that he had got into the ship's stores and licked up some siccative—paint dryer—which caused him to foam at the mouth. The entire naval station went into an uproar, fearing he had rabies.

Every winter the Kiplings journeyed to the south of France, to Egypt, to Spain, in search of the warmth that somehow always seemed to elude them. Carrie, afflicted with arthritis and diabetes, now needed these trips more than Kipling. Each voyage usually ended in Paris with a visit to Julia Catlin, who had first met them more than thirty-five years before on their trip to Bermuda.

In February 1930 they set off on a cruise of the West Indies, but in Jamaica Carrie was troubled with gastrointestinal pain that was diagnosed as appendicitis. Reluctant to have her operated on in Jamaica or on the ship, Kipling attempted to get her back to England; by the time they got to Bermuda, however, her inflamed appendix burst, fortunately forming an abscess rather than the general peritonitis that might have ended her life. Carrie had to go ashore and receive medical aid, and the ship sailed on without them. She was hospitalized but soon improved, was up and about, and could return to their hotel.

Kipling found that Dr. Beebe had set up an oceanographic field station on one of the small Bermuda islands and was there with Mrs. Beebe. When Sir Louis Bols, the governor of Bermuda, invited the Kiplings to luncheon, Kipling asked if the Beebes could also come. Sir Louis, whom the Beebes knew well, remembered Kipling from decades before in India as an "ink-stained journalist in a white suit." The lunch party was a small and informal one. Dr. and Mrs. Beebe were talking to Sir Louis and Lady Bols when the Kiplings arrived, and they were both startled and inwardly amused when Carrie made an entirely uncalled-for curtsey to the governor. At an informal lunch party, everyone knew no such ceremonious gesture was in order. But then, as they used to say in Vermont, Carrie was always "more English than the English."

At luncheon, Mrs. Beebe sat next to Kipling, and across the table from Carrie. When a lavish salmon mayonnaise was presented on a large silver platter, Carrie helped herself generously. Sir Louis, aware of her medical problems, asked anxiously if she was allowed to eat that much, and was brushed off. When the hot lamb entree followed, she had some of that too, and uneasy glances went around the table. Kipling said not a word, "doubtless," Mrs. Beebe concluded, "from unhappy experience." The next day Carrie was so much worse she was readmitted to the hospital, where she had to stay for several weeks.

Kipling had eagerly accepted Dr. Beebe's invitation to visit the island laboratory at St. George's and see the deep-sea fish that were coming up in the nets every day. Getting there and back only involved a carriage drive and a short trip in a launch and would not have consumed much more than an afternoon, between lunch and dinner. But no further word came from Kipling and no further request for the transportation which had been offered at lunch.

One day Mrs. Beebe came in to Hamilton on some errands and as her carriage went down the hill past the hospital, she saw Kipling trudging up the road toward her, his raincoat carried in a hooked thumb over his shoulder. Knowing his eyesight was uncertain, she stopped the carriage and turned back on foot, speaking his name. He turned and waited for her, and they sat down together on a low stone wall beside the road while she inquired about Mrs. Kipling and asked about his proposed visit to the laboratory. He explained patiently that he had given up on the idea of coming, because "she doesn't like to be left alone," inclining his head toward the hospital, so he went up during visiting hours to sit with her. They chatted for some minutes, and he mentioned his delight in Dr. Beebe's books and asked which were her favorites. She named the Guiana volumes, in which her husband had written of the ants, butterflies, and birds. Kipling, looking straight ahead through his thick glasses, said, "Yes—but I don't see birds." She always remembered his flatly saying "don't" rather than "find it difficult" or "have trouble" or some less absolute word. Separated from his wife—for almost the first time in thirty-eight years of marriage—he struck her as "gentle, low-voiced, sad and lonely." She returned to her carriage and he resumed his solitary journey up the hill to his wife's bedside.

Kipling was anxious to get Carrie back to England, but all the ships were running only to America. He refused to bring her to New York, even though it would presumably involve only getting off one ship and

320

onto another. She might have to seek medical advice there, which might be to have an operation, and that, he felt, would kill her.

> Also, (she says and I believe) New York would equally slay her. It's *not* a civilized country for the sick and they're just as likely to shove one into Ellis Island as any where else.[2]

Finally Kipling found a ship going to Halifax, and on June 1 they embarked. They then traveled to Montreal and from there back to England.

In the midst of the Depression, in 1931, Kipling wrote an American friend that Carrie's health was slowly improving. The world was in a mess, and it was the fault of the politicians. "There are not three pins to choose between your national indigestion (and flatulence) and ours."[3]

The same year, his old feeling about race can be seen in a letter about Edna Ferber's *American Beauty:*

> It's all right—very much so—and it has for me a personal interest, because we were in New England just as the outside invasion began, and the last of the old tough mortgaged-to-death white men were dropping off the naked farms. Mercifully, I didn't see the Poles move in. It was Italians in those days. They had finished laying down car tracks in the small cities and were starting shops and restaurants there. The farms were derelict. . . . And now—for her next job—how did the Swedes get into Minnesota *en bloc;* and what was (and is) their attitude to newcomers of (to them) alien extraction? Same with both Dakotas.[4]

Using the American term "gangster," Kipling assessed the danger of Hitler's rise to power. Writing to a friend that "the Leopard doesn't change his spots," he added, about Germany's refusal to pay reparations from World War I:

> The Hun will never pay any more unless and until he can be convinced that it's not a paying proposition for him to start rearming himself. He's the Leading Gangster of the world—a fact we've forgotten.[5]

Writing to Frank Doubleday in March 1932, he showed his reaction to Franklin Delano Roosevelt's most recent speech, together with a realistic assessment of how much he (Kipling) was out of touch with the times. We can presume he had in mind President Roosevelt's (for him a different President Roosevelt's) inaugural address of two weeks before, the famous speech of having "nothing to fear but fear itself." The American people, Kipling wrote:

> *do* need guidance between sullen apathy and false exultation. I'm so hopelessly out of touch with the present generation that my view of what is needed is useless.[6]

He wrote little and did little in the remaining four years of his life. Interestingly, he gave in to the urge many elderly people experience, and began his autobiography. But if he had an impulse to tell of his life, he had another one, almost as strong, to conceal everything about it. To the title, *Something of Myself*, some people jokingly added, *As Little as Possible.* It must be one of the more unrevealing autobiographies in the English language. He mentions his *ayah* from his childhood and Mrs. Holloway in the House of Desolation, but speaks of her in a defensive, joking fashion, to hide what he really felt. As quoted before, he describes undergoing

> calculated torture—religious as well as scientific. Yet it made me give attention to the lies I soon found it necessary to tell: and this, I presume, is the foundation of literary effort.[7]

The whole battle that led to his fleeing from America is contained in the single sentence, "So far as I was concerned, I felt the atmosphere was to some extent hostile." He does not speak of the deaths of two of his three children. Everyone has the urge to reveal, and the urge to conceal; nowhere, perhaps, can this be seen more clearly than in Rudyard Kipling's life and writings.

In 1934 and 1935 his old fascination with ships and machinery was reawakened. The huge *Queen Mary* was being built, and he plunged into technical discussions with Sir Percy Bates, who was in charge of her construction. Through these years he was in comparatively good health, although troubled with gastrointestinal pain at times. Carrie was in much worse general shape, with her arthritis and mild diabetes. In the summer of 1935, he and Carrie went to Marienbad in Czechoslovakia so she could take the cure at the baths. Passing through Germany was unpleasant, bringing back memories of John, but when they got to

Marienbad Kipling was delighted. He wrote Nelson Doubleday (Frank Doubleday's son), "I never saw—outside of Vermont—woods and hills to match these."[8]

In the autumn they returned to England, where Kipling became involved in something new—meeting in London with Hollywood agents and planning the filming of some of his work. In years past silent films had been made of a few of his short stories, but these had been mostly unsuccessful. Now initial steps were taken to make three films, one loosely based on "Toomai of the Elephants," to be called *Elephant Boy*, and two others, movies of *The Light That Failed* and of *Captains Courageous*.

Kipling and Carrie voted in the general election of 1935, which brought Stanley Baldwin into office with a clear majority. Kipling, however, had never been so disapproving of his cousin's ideas. Italy was preparing to invade Ethiopia (or, as it was called then, Abyssinia) and those few governmental figures—like Winston Churchill—who believed in being firm with dictators incurred Kipling's bitter anger. (Closing the Suez Canal to Italian shipping, in retrospect, would have brought the invasion to a screeching halt.) Kipling was adamantly opposed to anything like this. We would earn the enmity of the Italians for three generations, he said, by making threats which could be implemented with no weapon "more formidible than a surplice,"[9] and in December he sent a poem to the *Times* attacking any such sanctions. It was in the mail when the contents of the disgraceful Hoare-Lavall pact were revealed. These were so shockingly anti-Abyssinian and anti-League of Nations that Kipling's poem, although in general agreement, would presumably have looked pallid by comparison. With some difficulty he managed to retrieve it from the *Times* and destroy it before it could be printed.

The end of December was coming, and with it his seventieth birthday, which, he said, "Somehow seems to lack charm." Rather to his surprise, the event was widely noted and he and Carrie were inundated with letters and telegrams. On his birthday he wrote an American friend who had accused him of not understanding our country:

> Remember that I lived in the land for four years just as a householder. . . .
> As the nigger said in Court: "If Ah didnt like de woman, how come I'd take de trouble to hit her on de haid?"[10]

My hatred of America, he is saying, is accompanied by feelings of love; and again, it is put in terms of black and white.

Two weeks later, on January 13, he suddenly had pain and gastric bleeding in the middle of the night and had to be operated on immediately. For the next few days his condition wavered, but then death came early in the morning of January 18. Carrie, daughter Elsie, and Elsie's husband struggled with the waves of reporters, letters, telegrams, and callers. Elsie's husband accompanied the casket to the crematorium. Just ahead of him, there were several Indians singing "The Red Flag." By an eerie coincidence, the Indian Communist leader, Shahpurji Saklatvala, had been cremated just before Kipling and these were his followers. At his death, as through his whole life, there appeared this bond with the East, a link that had been forged between a native *ayah* and an Anglo-Indian child, seventy years before, in India.

REFERENCES

Except where stated otherwise, all references were taken from the Outward Bound Edition, first edition, Charles Scribner's Sons, New York, 1897–1937. I have tried to give references for all quotations and for all new information. Where several quotations are all from the same source, I have only given a reference for the first one; therefore if a reader looks for a reference, and finds no number, looking back to the last number given should provide the answer.

ABBREVIATIONS

CP —Catlin Papers
KJ —Kipling Journal
LC —Library of Congress, Rare Books Division
SOM—*Something of Myself*, Vol. 36.

PREFACE

1. Neiderland, W. G. "Psychoanalytic Approaches To Artistic Creativity," *The Psychoanalytic Quarterly*, Vol. XLV, No. 2, 1976, p. 185.
2. Pollock, G.H. "On Mourning, Immortality, and Utopia," *Journal of the American Psychoanalytic Association*, Vol. XXIII, 1975, p. 334.

INTRODUCTORY QUOTATIONS

I. "BOUGHT INTO INDIA"

1. Green, R. L. *Kipling and the Children*, Elek Books Ltd., London, 1965, p.13. Includes next quotation, p. 14.
2. Baldwin, A. W. *The Macdonald Sisters*, Peter Davies, London, 1960, p. 111. Includes next two quotations.
3. SOM, p. 40.
4. Baldwin, p. 111.
5. Macdonald, Frederic W. *As a Tale that is Told*, Cassell & Co., London, 1919, pp. 114–115. Includes next two quotations.
6. Baldwin, p. 107. Includes next quotation, p. 32.
7. Carrington, C. E. *The Life of Rudyard Kipling*, Doubleday & Co., Inc., New York, 1955, p. 87.
8. Baldwin, p. 126.
9. KJ, Vol. 24, 1938, p. 45.
10. SOM, p. 4. Includes next quotation.
11. Freud, S. "A Childhood Recollection from 'Dichtung und Wahrheit,'" Selected Edition, Hogarth Press, London, 1953, 17, p. 145.
12. SOM, p. 6.
13. Baldwin, p. 114. Includes next quotation.
14. SOM, p. 6. Includes next four quotations.
15. Green, p. 24.
16. Norton, C. E. *McClure's Magazine*, Vol. 13, 1899, p. 282.
17. "Baa Baa, Black Sheep," *Under the Deodars and Other Stories*, Vol. 6, pp. 324–326. Includes next four quotations.

II. THE HOUSE OF DESOLATION

1. "Baa Baa, Black Sheep," *Under the Deodars and Other Stories*, Vol. 6, p. 333.
2. Fleming, A. M. "Some Childhood Memories of Rudyard Kipling," *Chambers's Journal*, March 1939, p. 168.
3. "Baa Baa, Black Sheep," *Under the Deodars and Other Stories*, Vol. 6, p. 333.
4. Shengold, L. "An Attempt at Soul Murder," *Psychoanalytic Study of the Child*, 30, 1975, p. 683.
5. SOM, pp. 7–12. Includes next quotation, p. 7.
6. "Baa Baa, Black Sheep," *Under the Deodars and Other Stories*, Vol. 6, p. 337.
7. SOM, pp. 8–16. Includes next quotation.
8. The Beinecke Rare Book and Manuscript Library, Yale University Library. This poem, copied from the original manuscript in 1899, was never published but Kipling established copyright. With the emphasis on visual impact—the "dark walls" standing out against the "beaming lights," and the use of the technical details—the "stun'-sails set and royals too"—it certainly appears to be vintage Kipling.
9. SOM, p. 17.
10. SOM, p. 17. The last seven words, involving the card saying "Liar," were omitted from the Outward Bound edition. They may be seen, however, in several others,

such as SOM, American Edition, Doubleday, Doran, & Co., New York, 1937, p. 18. Includes next three quotations.

11. Fleming, A. M. "More Childhood Memories of Rudyard Kipling," *Chambers's Journal*, July 1939, p. 506.
12. Shengold, p. 183.
13. "Baa Baa, Black Sheep," p. 362.
14. SOM, p. 18. Includes next seven quotations, pp. 17–19.
15. Fleming, A. M. "Some Reminiscences of My Brother," KJ, No. 44, December 1937, pp. 117–118. Includes next two quotations.
16. "Baa Baa, Black Sheep," p. 368.

III. WESTWARD HO!

1. SOM, p. 23.
2. Beresford, G. C. *School Days with Kipling*, C. P. Putnam Sons, New York, 1936, pp. 1–3.
3. Dunsterville, L. C. *Stalky's Reminiscences*, Jonathan Cape Ltd., 1928, p. 30. Includes next quotation.
4. Fleming, A. M. KJ, Vol. 44, December 1937, p. 123.
5. Sale of Cormell Price letters, in Sotheby's Catalogue, December 1964.
6. Beresford, pp. 9–10.
7. Sale of letter, the *New York Times*, p. 58, December 2, 1964.
8. "Souvenirs of France, I," *War Writings and Poems*, Vol. 34, p. 290.
9. "The Moral Reformers," *Stalky & Co.*, Vol. 18, p. 176. Includes next nine quotations.
10. Sale of letter, the *New York Times*, p. 58, December 2, 1964.
11. Dunsterville, p. 22.
12. Beresford, p. 196.
13. SOM, p. 33.
14. Beresford, p. 213.
15. KJ, Vol. 195, 1975, p. 2.
16. Beresford, p. 47.
17. Carrington, C.E. *The Life of Rudyard Kipling*, Doubleday & Co., New York, 1955, p. 401.
18. SOM, p. 26.
19. Carrington, p. 32.
20. Beresford, p. 2. Also illustration opposite p. 124.
21. Tompkins, J. M. S. *The Art of Rudyard Kipling*, Methuen & Co., Ltd., London, 1959, p. 9.
22. Beresford, p. 266.
23. Wilson, A. *The Strange Ride of Rudyard Kipling*, The Viking Press, New York, 1978, p. 56.

IV. "KUPPELEEN SAHIB" I

1. SOM, p. 39.
2. Fleming, A. M. "My Brother, Rudyard Kipling," KJ, No. 84, 1947, p. 4.
3. Wilson, A. *The Strange Ride of Rudyard Kipling*, Viking Press, New York, 1978, p. 56.

4. SOM, p. 39.
5. "The City of Dreadful Night," *In Black and White*, Vol. 4, p. 35. Includes next six quotations.
6. Robinson, E. K. "Kipling in India," *McClure's Magazine*, Vol. 7, No. 2, 1896, p. 104.
7. Carrington, C. E. *The Life of Rudyard Kipling*, Doubleday & Co., New York, 1955, p. 41.
8. SOM, p. 40.
9. Fleming, A. M. "Some Reminiscences of My Brother," KJ, December 1937, p. 120.
10. SOM, p. 39–40.
11. Taylor, I. *Victorian Sisters*, Adler & Adler, Bethesda, Maryland, 1987, p. 144–145. Includes next five quotations.
12. "My Rival," *Early Verse*, Vol. 17, p. 170.
13. Adams, F. *Essays in Modernity*, John Lane, The Bodley Head,London, 1899, p. 91.
14. "Miss Youghal's Sais," *Plain Tales from the Hills*, Vol. 1, p. 32.
15. "A District at Play," in "The Smith Administration," *From Sea to Sea*, Part II, Vol. 16, p. 541.
16. "New Brooms," *Abaft the Funnel*, B. W. Dodge Co., New York, 1909, p. 91.
17. SOM, p. 52.
18. Houghton Library, Harvard University. Includes next two quotations.
19. Roper-Lawrence, W. *The India We Served*, Cassell & Co., London, 1928, p. 121.
20. Robinson, p. 163. Includes next three quotations.

V. "KUPPELEEN SAHIB" II

1. "His Wedded Wife," *Plain Tales from the Hills*, Vol. 1, p. 172. Includes next three quotations.
2. "False Dawn," *Plain Tales from the Hills*, Vol. 1, p. 55.
3. "Miss Youghal's Sais," *Plain Tales from the Hills*, Vol. 1, p. 32. Includes next quotation.
4. Wilson, A. *The Strange Ride of Rudyard Kipling*, Viking Press, New York, 1978, p. 65.
5. "Tod's Amendment," *Plain Tales from the Hills*, Vol. 1, p. 221.
6. "Beyond the Pale," *Plain Tales from the Hills*, Vol. 1, p. 189.
7. "False Dawn," *Plain Tales from the Hills*, Vol. 1, p. 56.
8. "Thrown Away," *Plain Tales from the Hills*, Vol. 1, p. 17. Includes next twelve quotations.
9. "The Rescue of Pluffles," *Plain Tales from the Hills*, Vol. 1, p. 69. Includes next quotation.
10. Frankau, G. "The Female of the Species," KJ, No. 17, 1931, p. 5.
11. "Beyond the Pale," *Plain Tales from the Hills*, Vol. 1, p. 193. Includes next five quotations.
12. "New Brooms," Burwash Edition, Vol. 23, p. 86.
13. "Tod's Amendment," *Plain Tales from the Hills*, Vol. 1, p. 225.
14. Carrington, C. E. *The Life of Rudyard Kipling*, Doubleday & Co., New York, 1955, p. 215. Includes next quotation.
15. "His Chance in Life," *Plain Tales from the Hills*, Vol. 1, p. 86. Includes next two quotations.

REFERENCES

16. "The Story of Muhammad Din," *Plain Tales from the Hills*, Vol. 1, p. 307. Includes next three quotations.
17. Moorehead, Mrs. Mary K., personal communication.
18. Hill, E. "The Young Kipling," *Atlantic Monthly*, April 1936, p.406. Includes next four quotations.
19. "Wressley of the Foreign Office," *Plain Tales from the Hills*, Vol. 1, pp. 327–328.
20. SOM, p. 70.
21. "The Betrothed," *Early Verse*, Vol. 17, p. 230.
22. "The Story of the Gadsbys," *Under the Deodars and Other Stories*, Vol. 6, p. 220. Includes next two quotations.
23. "Gentlemen-rankers," *Verses*, Vol. 11, p. 50.
24. "At the End of the Passage," *The Phantom Rickshaw*, Vol. 5, p. 350. Includes next quotation.
25. "Wee Willie Winkie," *Under the Deodars and Other Stories*, Vol. 6, p. 301.
26. "His Majesty the King," *Under the Deodars and Other Stories*, Vol. 6, p. 307.
27. "Baa Baa, Black Sheep," *Under the Deodars and Other Stories*, Vol. 6, p. 337.
28. "His Majesty the King," *Under the Deodars and Other Stories*, Vol. 6, p. 309. Includes next two quotations.
29. SOM, p. 4.
30. "Baa Baa, Black Sheep," *Under the Deodars and Other Stories*, Vol. 6, p. 359.
31. Carrington, p. 51. Includes the next quotation.
32. Fleming, A. M. *A Pinchbeck Goddess*, D. Appleton & Co., New York, 1897, p. 10.
33. Baldwin, A. W. *The Macdonald Sisters*, Peter Davies, London, 1960, p. 126.
34. Fleming, A. M. *The Heart of a Maid*, John W. Lovell Co., New York, 1891, p. 11.
35. SOM, p. 56.

VI.   THE WORLD OUTSIDE OF INDIA—AMERICA

1. "From Sea to Sea," *From Sea to Sea, Part I*, Vol. 15, p. 258. Includes next quotation.
2. "From Sea to Sea," *From Sea to Sea, Part II*, Vol. 16, p. 209. Includes next two quotations.
3. "From Sea to Sea," *From Sea to Sea, Part I*, Vol. 15, p. 292.
4. "From Sea to Sea," *From Sea to Sea, Part II*, Vol. 16, p. 208. Includes next thirteen quotations.
5. "Come with me to . . . Musquash, Pa.," *Beaver Falls News-Tribune*, Beaver, Pennsylvania, February 19, 1951. Includes next quotation.
6. Moorehead, Mrs. Mary K., personal communication. Includes next quotation.

VII.   THE WORLD OUTSIDE INDIA—ENGLAND

1. "In Partibus," *Civil and Military Gazette*, December 23, 1889.
2. James, H. Letter to Grace Norton, December 25, 1897, Houghton Library, Harvard University.
3. "The Ballad of East and West," *Verses*, Vol. 11, p. 61.
4. Arlow, J. "Fantasy Systems in Twins," *Psychoanalytic Quarterly*, Vol. 29, p. 175, 1960.

5. Carrington, C. E. *The Life of Rudyard Kipling*, Doubleday & Co., Inc., New York, 1955, p. 112.
6. The *Times*, March 25, 1890, p. 3.
7. Carrington, p. 106.
8. *The Light That Failed*, Vol. 9, p. 64.
9. Quoted in: Carrington, p. 121. Includes next two quotations.
10. "The Man Who Was," *Soldiers Three and Military Tales, Part 2*, Vol. 3, p. 403.
11. "Without Benefit of Clergy," *In Black and White*, Vol. 4, p. 103. Includes next three quotations.
12. "The Widow at Windsor," *Verses*, Vol. 11, p. 32.
13. Brown, H. *Rudyard Kipling*, Harper & Brothers, New York, 1945, p. 13. Includes next three quotations.
14. "The Mark of the Beast," *The Phantom Rickshaw*, Vol. 5, p. 173. Includes next eight quotations.
15. *The Light That Failed*, Vol. 9, p. 2. Includes next quotation.
16. SOM, p. 218.
17. *From Sea to Sea, Part II*, Vol. 16, p. 78. Includes next quotation.
18. *The Light That Failed*, Vol. 9, p. 219.
19. Beerbohm, M. *Saturday Review*, Vol. 14, February 14, 1903, pp. 198–199.
20. Wilson, A. *The Strange Ride of Rudyard Kipling*, The Viking Press, New York, 1978, p. 154.

VIII. KIPLING AND WOLCOTT BALESTIER

1. "One View of the Question," *In Black and White*, Vol. 4, p. 274.
2. "The New Dispensation, I," *Abaft the Funnel*, B. W. Dodge Co., New York, 1909, p. 313. Includes next two quotations.
3. "A Death in the Camp," *Abaft the Funnel*, B. W. Dodge Co., New York, 1909, p. 258.
4. SOM, p. 101.
5. "My Great and Only," *Abaft the Funnel*, B. W. Dodge Co., New York, 1909, p. 292. Includes next quotation.
6. "Letters on Leave," *Abaft the Funnel*, B. W. Dodge Co., New York, 1909, p. 218. Includes next quotation.
7. Woolcott, A. Typescript in LC.
8. Holbrook family papers, Brattleboro, Vermont. Letter from Will Cabot, June 1891.
9. Carrington, C. E. *The Life of Rudyard Kipling*, Doubleday & Co., New York, 1955, p. 137.
10. The Kipling papers, March 1890, as quoted in: Birkenhead, Lord. *Rudyard Kipling*, Random House, New York, 1978, pp. 125–126.
11. "The Rhyme of the Three Captains," *Verses*, Vol. 11, p. 105. Includes next quotation.
12. SOM, p. 87.
13. "The English Flag," *Verses*, Vol. 11, p. 143.
14. Wolcott Balestier to W. D. Howells, Feb. 18, 1891, as quoted in: Carrington, pp. 139–140.
15. Carrington, p. 137.

REFERENCES

16. Edel, L., "A Young Man from the Provinces," in: Gross, J. *The Age of Kipling*, Simon and Schuster, New York, 1972, p. 63.
17. Wilson, A. *The Strange Ride of Rudyard Kipling*, The Viking Press, New York, 1978, p. 278.
18. Seymour-Smith, M. *Rudyard Kipling*, Queen Anne Press, London, 1989, p. 159.
19. Carrington, p. 141. Includes next quotation.
20. *The Naulahka*, Vol. 10, p. 104.
21. Thwaite, A. *Edmund Gosse*, Secker & Warburg, London, 1984, p. 331.
22. Gosse, E. *Century Magazine*, 1891, May.
23. My account of Kipling's trip to America is taken from contemporary newspapers and from Macdonald, F. W. *As a Tale That Is Told*, Cassell & Co., London, 1919.
24. Unsigned article, "Kipling under an Alias," *The Critic*, Vol. 16, July 4, 1891, pp. 10–11.
25. The *New York Herald*, June 13, 1891.
26. Moorhead, Mrs. Mary K., personal communication. Mrs. Moorehead, an 1893 graduate of Beaver College, was acquainted with Mrs. Hill.
27. Mrs. Frederick Dunn, personal communication. Mrs. Dunn was a friend of Mrs. Hill's in the last years of her life.
28. "The Disturber of Traffic," *The Phantom Rickshaw*, Vol. 5, p. 258. Includes next four quotations.
29. "The Children of the Zodiac," *The Phantom Rickshaw*, Vol. 5, p. 362. Includes next two quotations.
30. The Kipling Papers, June 1906, as quoted in Carrington, p. 364.
31. SOM, p. 91.
32. Original version in Berg Collection, New York Public Library.
33. "L'envoi," *Verses*, Vol. 11, p. 168.
34. Edel, L. *Henry James Letters*, Harvard University Press, Cambridge, Mass., 1980, p. 272. Includes next two quotations.
35. Colvin, S. *The Letters of Robert Louis Stevenson*, Vol. II, Methuen & Co., London, 1901, p. 195. Includes next quotation.
36. SOM, p. 98. Includes next two quotations.
37. Henry James to Mrs. Mahlon Sands, Houghton Library, Harvard University, December 12, 1891.
38. Henry James to Edmund Gosse, Houghton Library, Harvard University, December 10, 1891. (The word "passionate" and the last two sentences quoted are omitted from the official biography.)

IX. MARRIAGE

1. Thwaite, A. *Edmund Gosse*, Secker & Warburg, London, 1984, p. 332.
2. SOM, p. 102. Includes next quotation.
3. Thwaite, p. 332. Includes next quotation, p. 333.
4. Henry James to William James, Houghton Library, Harvard University, February 6, 1892. (The word "charmless" is omitted from the official biography.)
5. Henry James to William James, Houghton Library, Harvard University, December 13, 1891.
6. Carrington, C.E. *The Life of Rudyard Kipling*, Doubleday & Co., New York, 1955, p. 151.

7. SOM, p. 103.
8. *The Naulahka*, Vol. 10, pp. 1, 102, and 119.
9. Birkenhead,Lord. *Rudyard Kipling*, Random House, New York, 1978, p. 134.
10. Adams, H. *The Education of Henry Adams*, Houghton Mifflin Co., Boston, 1918, p. 319.
11. "In Sight of Monadnock," *Letters of Travel*, Vol. 28, p. 3. Includes next fourteen quotations.
12. SOM, p. 104.
13. "The Rhyme of the Three Sealers," *Verses*, Vol. 11, p. 226.
14. Rice, H. C., *Rudyard Kipling in New England*, The Book Cellar, Brattleboro, Vermont, 1951, p. 15.
15. SOM, p. 106.
16. Mr. F. Cabot Holbrook, Brattleboro, personal communication. Mr. and Mrs. Holbrook owned 'Naulakha' when I visited it.
17. "Leaves from a Winter Notebook," *Letters of Travel*, Vol. 28, p. 119.
18. SOM, p. 114.
19. Carrington, p. 162.
20. Pollock, G. H. "On Siblings, Childhood Sibling Loss, and Creativity," *The Annals of Psychoanalysis*, Vol. 6, 1978, p. 443.
21. Carrington, p. 171.
22. Letter to J. H. Cooke, December 10, 1893. Offered by George F. MacManus Co., 1317 Irving Street, Philadelphia, Pennsylvania, Catalogue #249.
23. van de Water, F. F. *Rudyard Kipling's Vermont Feud*, Reynal & Hitchcock, New York, 1937, p. 11.
24. Carrington, p. 170.
25. CP. Includes next quotation.
26. "Pan in Vermont," *War Writings and Poems*, Vol. 34, p. 459.
27. CP.
28. SOM, pp. 133–134.
29. "My Sunday at Home," *The Day's Work, Part 2*, Vol. 14, p. 225. Includes next quotation.
30. "An American," *Verses*, Vol. 11, p. 288.
31. LC. Includes next quotation.
32. "Leaves from a Winter Notebook," *Letters of Travel*, Vol. 28, p. 8.
33. "Judson and the Empire," *Soldiers Three and Military Tales, Part II*, Vol. 3, p. 527. Includes next two quotations.
34. "An Error in the Fourth Dimension," *The Day's Work, Part II*, Vol. 14, p. 157. Includes next quotation.
35. "Baa Baa, Black Sheep," *Under the Deodars and Other Stories*, Vol. 6, p. 323.
36. "An Error in the Fourth Dimension," *The Day's Work, Part II*, Vol. 14, p. 181.
37. Rice, p. 38.
38. Carrington, pp. 168–169.
39. CP.
40. "The Cat That Walked by Himself," *Just So Stories*, Vol. 20, p. 203.
41. Mr. and Mrs. F. Cabot Holbrook, personal communication. Also in LC.
42. Mr. Gerald Morgan, personal communication.
43. SOM, p. 117.

REFERENCES

44. Letter to C.E. Norton, Houghton Library, Harvard University, Feb. 8, 1895.
45. "Mowgli's Brothers," *The Jungle Book*, Vol. 7, p. 1. Includes next quotation.
46. "The Spring Running," *The Jungle Book*, Vol. 7, p. 261. Includes next quotation.
47. "Kaa's Hunting," *The Jungle Book*, Vol. 7, p. 35.
48. "Tiger! Tiger!," *The Jungle Book*, Vol. 7, p. 109.
49. "Across a Continent," *Letters of Travel*, Vol. 28, p. 18.
50. "Quebec and Montreal," a verse of "The Song of the Cities," which is part of "A Song of the English," *English Illustrated Magazine*, Vol. 10, May 1893, p. 537. This verse is drastically altered in the Outward Bound edition, *Verses*, Vol. 11, p. 181.
51. Shengold, L. *Soul Murder: The Effects of Childhood Abuse and Deprivation*, Yale University Press, 1989.
52. "The White Seal," *The Second Jungle Book*, Vol. 8, p. 58.
53. Tompkins, J. M. S. *The Art of Rudyard Kipling*, Methuen & Co., Ltd., London, 1959, p. 56.
54. "The Brushwood Boy," *The Day's Work, Part II*, Vol. 14, p. 250. Includes next quotation.
55. SOM, p. 21.
56. "The Brushwood Boy," *The Day's Work, Part II*, Vol. 14, p. 256. Includes next quotation.
57. Ms. in Firestone Library, Princeton University.
58. "The Brushwood Boy," *The Day's Work, Part II*, Vol. 14, p. 279. Includes next quotation.
59. Hooper, C. F. "Kipling's Younger Days," *The Saturday Review*, 161, March 7, 1936, p. 308.
60. Rice, p. 36.
61. Letter to C. E. Norton, Houghton Library, Harvard University, January 8, 1896. Includes next quotation.
62. SOM, p. 110.
63. CP.
64. SOM, p. 125.
65. "Judson and the Empire," *Soldiers Three and Military Tales, Part II*, Vol. 3, p. 564.
66. "With the Night Mail," *Actions and Reactions*, Vol. 24, p. 130.
67. SOM, p. 204.
68. *Captains Courageous*, Vol. 12, pp. 211, 6.
69. SOM, p. 3.
70. *Captains Courageous*, Vol. 12, pp. 38, 24, 211, 204, 240.

X.   THE FIGHT

1. Mr. F. Cabot Holbrook, personal communication. My account of the entire feud with Beatty is based on contemporary newspapers and conversations with Mr. Holbrook and other Vermonters.
2. Letter to W. D. Howells, Houghton Library, Harvard University, June 4, 1896.
3. Mr. F. Cabot Holbrook, personal communication.

XI. THE RETURN TO ENGLAND

1. LC. Includes next four quotations.
2. Cabot letters, in possession of Mr. & Mrs. F. Cabot Holbrook.
3. "The Vampire," *War Writings and Poems*, Vol. 34, p. 470.
4. "What the People Said," *Early Verse*, Vol. 17, p. 266.
5. "The Widow's Party," *Verses*, Vol. 11, p. 45.
6. Letter to Mrs. Maude H. Tree, March 4, 1897, Houghton Library, Harvard University.
7. "The Destroyers," *The Five Nations*, Vol. 21, p. 13.
8. "Cruisers," *The Five Nations*, Vol. 21, p. 10.
9. "The Explorer," *The Five Nations*, Vol. 21, p. 51.
10. "Recessional," the *Times*, July 17, 1897, p. 13. Includes the next quotation.
11. West, R. "Miscellany," *The New Statesman and Nation*, June 25, 1936, p. 112.
12. Letter to C. K. Ogden, Kenneth W. Rendell Catalogue No. 62, 1981.
13. Letter to W. J. Harding, no date, quoted in Carrington, C. E., *The Life of Rudyard Kipling*, Doubleday & Co., New York, 1955, p. 209.
14. SOM, p. 132.
15. The Kipling papers, August 1897, as quoted in: Birkenhead, Lord, *Rudyard Kipling*, Random House, New York, 1978, p. 188.
16. Harris, J. C. *The Tar Baby and Other Rhymes of Uncle Remus*, D. Appleton Co., New York, N.Y., 1904, p. 9.
17. Carrington, p. 209.
18. Birkenhead, Lord, p. 189.
19. "Song of the Wise Children," *The Five Nations*, Vol. 21, p. 72.
20. Lockhart, J. G. and Woodhouse, C. M., *Cecil Rhodes*, Macmillan Co., New York, N.Y., 1963, p. 56. Includes next quotation.
21. *Time* magazine, Vol. 86, No. 19, Nov. 5, 1965, p. 42.
22. "The Elephant's Child," *Just So Stories*, Vol. 22, p. 71.
23. "The Fires," *War Writings and Poems*, Vol. 34, p. 427.
24. Friedel, F. B. *The Splendid Little War*, Little, Brown & Co., Boston, 1958, p. 33. Includes next quotation, p. 3.
25. Trevelyan, J. P. *The Life of Mrs. Humphry Ward*, Dodd, Mead & Co., New York, N.Y., 1923, p. 117.
26. "The White Man's Burden," *The Five Nations*, Vol. 21, p. 78.
27. "Gunga Din," *Verses*, Vol. 22, p. 19.
28. "Tod's Amendment," *Plain Tales from the Hills*, Vol. 1, p. 217.
29. Letter signed 'C.S.H.' in the *Outlook*, Vol. 64, Feb. 10, 1900, p. 2.
30. Lodge, H. C. *Selected Correspondence from Theodore Roosevelt and Henry Cabot Lodge*, Scribners, New York, N.Y., 1925, letter of Jan. 12, 1899, p. 384.
31. All details from this trip to America, except where otherwise noted, come from contemporary newspapers, especially the *New York Times* and the *Daily Tribune*.
32. "How the Alphabet Was Made," *Just So Stories*, Vol. 20, p. 173.

XII. THE BOER WAR

1. Miss Caroline Foster, personal communication.
2. CP. Includes next five quotations.

REFERENCES

3. Pakenham, T. *The Boer War*, Random House, New York, New York, 1979, p. 88. Pakenham's account of the war, quite at odds with the traditional view, seems totally convincing.
4. "An Error in the Fourth Dimension," *The Day's Work, Part II*, Vol. 14, p. 158.
5. "A Fleet in Being," *From Sea to Sea, Vol. II*, Vol. 5, The Seven Seas Edition, Doubleday, Page & Co., New York, New York, 1913, p. 257.
6. "Slaves of the Lamp, Part II," *Stalky & Co.*, Vol. 18, p. 330.
7. "The Old Issue," *The Five Nations*, Vol. 21, p. 104.
8. "The Absent-Minded Beggar," *War Writings and Poems*, Vol. 34, p. 408.
9. Wilson, A. *The Strange Ride of Rudyard Kipling*, The Viking Press, New York, New York, 1977, p. 214.
10. SOM, p. 153.
11. "The Outsider," *McClure's Magazine*, Vol. 15, No. 3, July 1900, p. 3.
12. LC.
13. Gilbert, E.L. *Silence and Survival in Rudyard Kipling's Art and Life*, English Literature in Transition, Vol. 29, 1985, p. 124.
14. LC.
15. "A Sahib's War," *Traffics and Discoveries*, Vol. 22, p. 86. Includes next three quotations.
16. "The Islanders," *The Five Nations*, Vol. 21, p. 129.
17. "The Burials," *The Five Nations*, Vol. 21, p. 63.
18. "The Comprehension of Private Copper," *Traffics and Discoveries*, Vol. 22, p. 177. Includes next quotation.
19. "The Captive," *Traffics and Discoveries*, Vol. 22, p. 2. Includes next three quotations.
20. McDonald, J. G. *Rhodes: A Life*, Philip Allen & Co., Ltd., London, England, 1928, p. 337.
21. Tharaud, J. and Tharaud, J. *Dingley*, Librarie Plon, Paris, France, 1923, p. 5. Includes next four quotations. (Translation by author.)

XIII.   THE NEW CENTURY

1. Moynihan, D. *Washington Post*, May 11, 1980.
2. *Kim*, Vol. 19, p. 3. Includes next six quotations, pp. 4, 5, 6, 124–5, 150, 359, 462.
3. Bettelheim, B. *The Uses of Enchantment*, Vintage Books, Random House, New York, N.Y., 1977, p. 27.
4. "The Tabu Tale," *Just So Stories*, Vol. 20, p. 252.
5. "How the First Letter Was Written," *Just So Stories*, Vol. 20, p. 137.
6. "The Tabu Tale," *Just So Stories*, Vol. 20, p. 255.
7. "How the First Letter Was Written," *Just So Stories*, Vol. 20, p. 130.
8. "The White Seal," *The Second Jungle Book*, Vol. 8, p. 29.
9. "The Elephant's Child," *Just So Stories*, Vol. 20, p. 67.
10. "How the Whale Got his Throat," *Just So Stories*, Vol. 20, p. 5. Includes next quotation.
11. SOM, p.4.
12. "How the First Letter Was Written," *Just So Stories*, Vol. 20, p. 129.
13. SOM, p. 169. Includes next four quotations.
14. Birkenhead, Lord. *Rudyard Kipling*, Random House, New York, N.Y., 1978, p. 239.

15. Kipling to Charles Eliot Norton, Houghton Library, Harvard University, November 30, 1902.
16. SOM, p. 177.
17. Kipling to James Conland, December 17, 1897, LC.
18. Kipling to James Conland, June 13, 1902, LC.
19. Kipling to James Conland, January 27, 1903, LC.
20. "A Deal in Cotton," *Actions and Reactions*, Vol. 24, p. 187. Includes next sixteen quotations.
21. "Mrs. Bathurst," *Traffics and Discoveries*, Vol. 22, p. 394. Includes next seven quotations.
22. Crook, N. *Kipling's Myths of Love and Death*, St. Martin's Press, New York, 1989, pps. 61–86.
23. "Mrs. Bathurst," *Traffic and Discoveries*, Vol. 22, p. 378.
24. Bodelsen, C. A. *Aspects of Kipling's Art*, Manchester University, Manchester, 1964, p. 145n.
25. Gilbert, E. L. *The Good Kipling*, Manchester University, Manchester, 1972, p. 104.
26. Raine, C. Introduction to *A Choice of Kipling's Prose*, Fabert, London, 1987, pp. 14–18.
27. "Mrs. Bathurst, " *Traffics and Discoveries*, Vol. 22, p. 393.
28. SOM, p. 98.
29. Crook, p. 74–75.
30. "Mrs. Bathurst," *Traffics and Discoveries*, Vol. 22, p. 380. Includes next two quotations.
31. Crook, p. 85.
32. Lewis, Lisa A. F. "Technique and Experiment in 'Mrs. Bathurst,'" KJ, Dec. 1980, p. 37.
33. "They," *Traffics and Discoveries*, Vol. 22, p. 346. Includes next fourteen quotations.
34. Carrington, C. E. *The Life of Rudyard Kipling*, Doubleday and Co., N.Y., 1955, p. 289.
35. "They," *Traffics and Discoveries*, Vol. 22, p. 339. Includes next quotation.
36. "With the Night Mail," *Actions and Reactions*, Vol. 24, p. 158. Includes next five quotations.
37. Taylor, I. *Victorian Sisters*, Adler & Adler, Bethesda, Maryland, 1987, p. 161.
38. SOM, p. 181.
39. "Cold Iron," *Rewards and Fairies*, Vol. 25, p. 32.
40. "The Knife and the Naked Chalk," *Rewards and Fairies*, Vol. 25, p. 145. Includes next eleven quotations.
41. The *New York Times*, September 28, 1907, p. 1. Includes next quotation.
42. Kipling to Lord Milner, no date but 1908, as quoted in Carrington, p. 309.
43. SOM, p. 192.
44. The *New York Times*, September 28, 1907, p. 1. Includes next quotation.
45. The *New York Times*, October 11, 1907, p. 4. Includes next three quotations.
46. "As Easy as A.B.C.," *A Diversity of Creatures*, Vol. 26, p. 4. Includes next twelve quotations.
47. "Brother Square-Toes," *Rewards and Fairies*, Vol. 25, p. 186. Includes next two quotations.

REFERENCES

48. Tompkins, J.M.S. *The Art of Rudyard Kipling*, Methuen and Co., Ltd., London, England, 1959, p. 106.
49. "The Wish House," *Debits and Credits*, Vol. 31, p. 132.
50. "Their Lawful Occasions, Part II," *Traffics and Discoveries*, Vol. 22, p. 144.
51. "The Wrong Thing," *Rewards and Fairies*, Vol. 25, pp. 92–93.
52. "A Germ Destroyer," *Plain Tales from the Hills*, Vol. 1, p. 140.
53. "In the Pride of His Youth," *Plain Tales from the Hills*, Vol. 1, p. 235.
54. "Thrown Away," *Plain Tales from the Hills*, Vol. 1, p. 27.
55. "A Conference of the Powers," *Soldiers Three and Military Tales, Part II*, Vol. 3, p. 583. Includes next quotation.
56. "The Mark of the Beast," *The Phantom Rickshaw*, Vol. 5, p. 191.
57. "Judson and the Empire," *Soldiers Three and Military Tales, Part II*, Vol. 3, p. 552.
58. "My Son's Wife," *A Diversity of Creatures*, Vol. 26, p. 407. Includes next quotation.
59. "Their Lawful Occasions, Part II," *Traffics and Discoveries*, Vol. 22, p. 167.
60. "The Miracle of Saint Jubanus," *Limits and Renewals*, Vol. 33, p. 358.
61. SOM, p. 14.
62. As quoted in Carrington, pp. 298–300.
63. Manchester, W. *The Last Lion, Winston Spencer Churchill; Alone*, Little Brown & Co., Boston, 1988, p. 23.
64. Kipling papers, as quoted in Carrington, p. 302.
65. Baldwin, A. W. *The Macdonald Sisters*, Peter Davies, London, England, 1960, p. 125.
66. Baldwin, p. 134.
67. "An Habitation Enforced," *Actions and Reactions*, Vol. 24, p. 27. Includes next three quotations.
68. "My Son's Wife," *A Diversity of Creatures*, Vol. 26, p. 394.
69. "My Sunday at Home," *The Day's Work, Part II*, Vol. 14, p. 237.
70. "In Sight of Monadnock," *Letters of Travel*, Vol. 28, p. 6.
71. "Leaves from a Winter Note-book," *Letters of Travel*, Vol. 28, p. 133.
72. SOM, p. 39.
73. "The Female of the Species," *The Years between and Poems from History*, Vol. 27, p. 108.
74. Carrington, p. 322.
75. Ponton, D. *Rudyard Kipling at Home and at Work*, J. Looker, Ltd., Poole, England, (no date), p. 14.

XIV. THE WAR

1. Birkenhead, Lord. *Rudyard Kipling*, Random House, New York, N.Y., 1978, p. 258.
2. Carrington, C. E. *The Life of Rudyard Kipling*, Doubleday & Co., N.Y., 1955, p. 328.
3. "Sea Constables," *Debits and Credits*, Vol. 31, p. 54. Includes next four quotations.
4. "Mary Postgate," *A Diversity of Creatures*, Vol. 26, p. 489. Includes next two quotations.
5. "His Majesty the King," *Under the Deodars and Other Stories*, Vol. 6, p. 309.
6. "Mary Postgate," *A Diversity of Creatures*, Vol. 26, p. 496. Includes next eight quotations.

7. Wilson, E. *The Wound and the Bow*, Houghton Mifflin Co., The Riverside Press, Cambridge, Mass., 1941, p. 179.
8. Birkenhead, p. 267. Includes next quotation.
9. Carrington, pp. 338–339.
10. "The Gardener," *Debits and Credits*, Vol. 31, p. 440.
11. KJ, Vol. 49, June 1982, p. 15.
12. Carrington, p. 341.
13. "Gethsemane," *The Years Between and Poems from History*, Vol. 27, p. 71.
14. "1916: The Salient and the Somme," *The Irish Guards in the Great War, Part II*, Vol. 30, p. 126. Includes next quotation.
15. Introduction, *The Irish Guards in the Great War, Part II*, Vol. 30, p. xvi.
16. Birkenhead, p. 275. Includes next two quotations, p. 280, 284.

XV.   THE YEARS AFTER THE WAR

1. Ponton, D. *Rudyard Kipling at Home and at Work*, J. Looker, Ltd., Poole, England, (no date), p. 27.
2. Sheridan, C. *Naked Truth*, Harper & Brothers, New York, New York, 1928, p. 286. Includes next four quotations.
3. Cohen, M. *Rudyard Kipling to Rider Haggard*, Hutchinson & Co., London, England, 1965, p. 101.
4. Wells, C., personal communication.
5. "The Enemies to Each Other," *Debits and Credits*, Vol. 31, p. 3. Includes next five quotations.
6. "The Gardener," *Debits and Credits*, Vol. 31, p. 433. Includes next seven quotations.
7. "The Wish House," *Debits and Credits*, Vol. 31, p. 150. Includes next five quotations.
8. Carrington, C.E. *The Life of Rudyard Kipling*, Doubleday & Co., New York, 1955, p. 366.
9. Tompkins, J. M. S. *The Art of Rudyard Kipling*, Methuen and Co., Ltd., London, England, 1959, p. 208. Includes next quotation.
10. Bodelson, C. A. *Aspect of Kipling's Art*, Manchester University Press, 1964, p. 40n.
11. "The Wish House," *Debits and Credits*, Vol. 31, p. 145. Includes next five quotations.
12. Purefoy, A. E. B. KJ, Vol. 37, March 1971, p. 11.
13. Hart-Davis, R. *Hugh Walpole*, Harcourt, Brace and World, Inc., New York, New York, 1952, p. 274. Includes next two quotations.
14. "The Beginning of the Armadillos," *Just So Stories*, Vol. 20, p. 125.
15. *Brazilian Sketches*, Doubleday, Doran & Co., Inc., New York City, New York, 1940, p. 3. Includes next six quotations.
16. "The Woman in his Life," *Limits and Renewals*, Vol. 33, p. 43. Includes next six quotations.

XVI.   THE FINAL YEARS

1. The account of the Kiplings in London and Bermuda came from personal communications with Mrs. William Beebe.
2. Letter to Frank Doubleday, April 28, 1930. Firestone Library, Princeton University. The next five letters are there.

REFERENCES

3. Letter to Frank Doubleday, March 5, 1931.
4. Letter to Nelson Doubleday, October 31, 1931.
5. Letter to Frank Doubleday, December 24, 1931.
6. Letter to Frank Doubleday, March 18, 1932.
7. SOM, Vol. 36, p. 8. Includes next quotation, p. 127.
8. Letter to Nelson Doubleday, August 22, 1935.
9. Carrington, C. E. *The Life of Rudyard Kipling*, Doubleday & Co., New York, 1955, p. 391. Includes next quotation.
10. LC.

INDEX

Index

Index